The Archaeology of Early Egypt

In this fresh, authoritative and compelling survey of the archaeology of early Egypt, David Wengrow offers a new interpretation of the emergence of farming economies and the dynastic state, c.10,000 to 2650 BC. Exploring key themes such as the nature of state power, kingship and the inception of writing, Wengrow illuminates prehistoric social development along the Nile through comparison with neighbouring regions. Detailed analysis of the archaeological record reveals the interplay between large-scale processes of economic and political change and intimate material practices through which social identities were transformed, focusing upon ritual treatments of the dead. Employing rich empirical data and engaging critically with anthropological theory and the history of archaeological thought, Wengrow's work challenges the current theoretical isolation of Egyptian prehistory and breaches the methodological boundaries that separate prehistory from Egyptology. It is essential reading for anybody with an interest in ancient Egyptian civilisation or early state formation.

DAVID WENGROW is a Lecturer at the Institute of Archaeology, University College London, where he has established a new programme of study comparing ancient societies of the Middle East and Eastern Mediterranean.

Books in the series: Cambridge World Archaeology

CAMBRIDGE WORLD ARCHAEOLOGY

THE ARCHAEOLOGY OF EARLY EGYPT

SOCIAL TRANSFORMATIONS IN NORTH-EAST AFRICA, 10,000 TO 2650 BC

DAVID WENGROW

Institute of Archaeology
University College London

CAMBRIDGE
UNIVERSITY PRESS

CAMBRIDGE UNIVERSITY PRESS
Cambridge, New York, Melbourne, Madrid, Cape Town,
Singapore, São Paulo, Delhi, Mexico City

Cambridge University Press
The Edinburgh Building, Cambridge CB2 8RU, UK

Published in the United States of America by Cambridge University Press, New York

www.cambridge.org
Information on this title: www.cambridge.org/9780521543743

First published 2006
Reprinted 2009

A catalogue record for this publication is available from the British Library

ISBN 978-0-521-83586-2 Hardback
ISBN 978-0-521-54374-3 Paperback

For RINAT

CONTENTS

FIGURES

Abbreviations used in image credits, copyright and museum numbers which accompany the illustrations.

BM   Brooklyn Museum, Museum Collection Fund,
        New York
DAI   Deutsches Archäologisches Institut
EES   The Egypt Exploration Society, London
HE   The Hierakonpolis Expedition
IAA   The Israel Museum, Jerusalem; courtesy of the
        Israel Antiquities Authority
ML   Musée du Louvre, Département des antiquités
        égyptiennes
MMA   The Metropolitan Museum of Art, New York
Penn.   Pennsylvania-Yale-Institute of Fine Arts,
        New York University, Expedition to Abydos
Petrie The Petrie Museum of Egyptian Archaeology,
        University College London

TABLES

ACKNOWLEDGEMENTS

At the time of this book's conception I had been planning a quite different kind of study, more historiography than archaeology. When Norman Yoffee suggested writing something on Egypt for this series, I saw an opportunity to combine these two interests. The result is more archaeology than history of ideas, and I am grateful to him, and to the reviewers of my original proposal, for keeping my pretensions in check. I would also like to thank Norman and Simon Whitmore of CUP for their enthusiasm and guidance throughout the book's preparation.

The text was written during my time as a Junior Research Fellow at Christ Church, Oxford University, which provided an ideal working environment, stimulating company and freedom to pursue my research. I am also grateful to the Warburg Institute for my brief but rewarding stay there as Frankfort Fellow, which left a lasting impression. Completion of the manuscript took place at the Institute of Archaeology, University College London, whose staff and students I thank for making me welcome. I am indebted to the Institute for helping with the cost of illustrations, to Stuart Laidlaw for his patient assistance in preparing them for publication, and to all the excavators, museum staff and archivists who provided material. Full credits are given in the list of figure captions, and I would like to further acknowledge the generosity of Günter Dreyer, Renée Friedman, Stan Hendrickx, Donatella Usai, Baruch Brandl, Chris Naunton, Stephen Quirke, Christina Riggs and especially Helen Whitehouse. David O'Connor kindly made available as yet unpublished images and information relating to his work at Abydos.

Many of the ideas presented here took form during the completion of my doctoral thesis under the supervision of Roger Moorey. His unexpected death, and that of Jeremy Black in the same year, brings home to me how fortunate I was in my academic surroundings at Oxford University. Their presence, and that of Andrew and Sue Sherratt, provided as rich a set of influences and diverse a range of criticism as any student could have hoped for. My particular thanks are due to John Baines for his painstaking and invaluable comments on the manuscript of this book, which improved it enormously, and for his unflagging inspiration over the last few years.

I am grateful to the examiners of my doctoral thesis, Chris Gosden and Ian Hodder, for suggesting improvements and clarifications; Chris also provided numerous opportunities to present my work to a wider audience, from which I benefited greatly. The North-East Africa seminar in Oxford, run by Wendy James and Douglas Johnson, was another valued source of feedback and ideas. Individual discussions with Paul Treherne, Jeremy Coote, Lynn Meskell, Mukulika Banerjee, Maurice Bloch and Mike Rowlands sharpened my understanding of many issues. I have Dorian Fuller to thank for the opportunity to conduct fieldwork at the Fourth Cataract of the Nile, which informed several aspects of this study. No less essential were the resources of the Sackler, Balfour and Tylor libraries in Oxford, and the library of the Institute of Archaeology in London: my special gratitude to Diane Bergman, Mark Dickerson, Mike Morris and Robert Kirby for their expert assistance.

In writing this book I appreciated again Holly Pittman's kindness in inviting me, as a graduate student, to a conference on the origins of writing at the University of Pennsylvania. Peter Ucko, as well as being a constant source of motivation, gave me the opportunity to participate in the 'Encounters with Ancient Egypt' conference at UCL, which opened up new perspectives. Several of the following chapters draw upon my earlier research articles, including contributions to that conference, and chapter 5 is reworked from a paper co-written with John Baines (Wengrow and Baines 2004).

My final thanks go to my ever-growing family for their love and support.

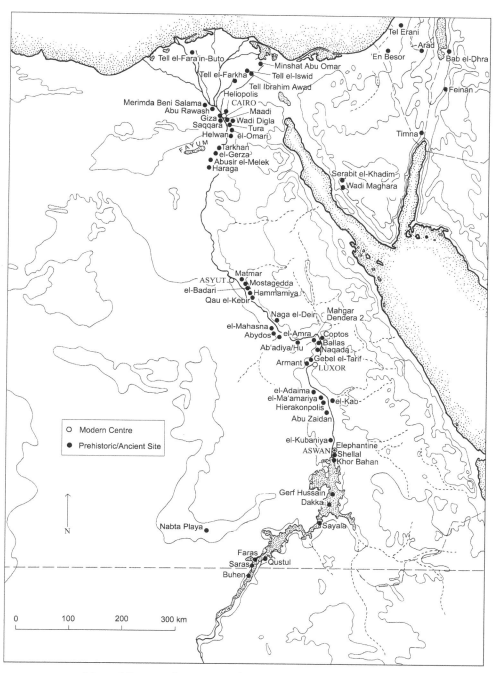

Map of Egypt, showing prehistoric and early dynastic sites

INTRODUCTION: THE IDEA OF PREHISTORY IN THE MIDDLE EAST AND NORTH-EAST AFRICA

Evidence is only evidence when someone contemplates it historically. Otherwise, it is merely perceived fact, historically dumb.

The Idea of History, R. G. Collingwood

Unlike Egyptologists, prehistorians of Egypt do not now and never have possessed a conscious unity of purpose.

Egypt before the Pharaohs, M. A. Hoffman

Echoing Gandhi's famous judgement on European civilisation, we might begin by observing that the prehistory of Egypt 'would be a good idea'. This may seem a very odd statement. The past century has seen virtually continuous field research into the cultures that preceded kingship in the valley and delta of the Nile. Syntheses have been written, site reports published, chronologies refined, museum collections established and expanded, analytical bibliographies compiled and websites created. In Michael Hoffman's (1991) *Egypt before the Pharaohs* we even have an engaging, if now slightly dated, history of research. So I will try to explain what I mean.

In western Europe a continuous development can be traced from the antiquarianism of the sixteenth to seventeenth centuries, often pursued within the field of jurisprudence, to the emergence of prehistoric archaeology. A direct line of thought and emotion links the literary resurrection of ancient Gaul and the 'republic of the Druids' to the reconstitution of prehistoric monuments as archives of national identity and social memory, and this recourse to a remote past echoes still earlier developments in Mediterranean humanism. By the eighteenth and nineteenth centuries, when archaeologists began to provide an independent account of their tribal origins, the vision of a time before kingship and written records—a time of freedom, equality and community—had already been woven into the political constitutions and historical imaginations of many European societies (Pocock 1957; Schnapp 1996).

By contrast, archaeological research was introduced to the Middle East and North-East Africa on the coat-tails of imperial conquest. At much the same time that the antiquaries of northern Europe were piecing together local evidence for the Three Age system of human prehistory (Stone, Bronze, Iron; Daniel 1950), the birth of Egyptology and Assyriology was heralded by the decipherment of royal proclamations such as the Rosetta Stone, found by French military engineers in 1799 and subsequently surrendered to the British (Pope 1975). Growing acceptance during the early and mid-nineteenth century of a long, secular chronology for human history initially made little impact upon the development of archaeology in these regions, fuelled as it was by an overriding sense that 'archaeologists were hunting for the very beginnings of human history, as perceived in the light of sacred writings' (Larsen 1996: xii). The primary concerns were to reveal, appropriate and study the cultural remnants of ancient and exotic forms of sacred kingship, and the civilisations where they first rose and fell, as described in biblical and Graeco-Roman sources. Nobody, in those early days of exploration, was looking for or thinking about a prehistory of the Middle East or North-East Africa.

When the visible, ancient remains of the Oriental landscape did inspire Europeans to contemplate the past on a broader philosophical canvas, it tended to be as a series of cycles rather than a linear development. Among the most influential and widely translated of these meditations was the Comte de Volney's *Les ruines, ou, Méditation sur les révolutions des empires* ('The Ruins, or, Meditation on the Revolutions of Empires'), published in 1791, in the wake of the French Revolution. The wreckage of the ancient Orient—its 'extravagant tombs, mausoleums, and pyramids', built 'for vain skeletons' under 'the cloak of religion'—appears there as an allegory for the fall of European monarchy. Less than a decade later, Napoleon Bonaparte, who had read and been inspired by Volney's works, stood triumphant before the people of Alexandria. In his victory speech he appealed, not to a pharaonic legacy, but to an idealised Islamic past of flourishing cities and trade, free from the yoke of Mameluke rule. And it was with French citizens, rather than the people of Egypt, in mind that Napoleon's *savants* were set to the task of documenting and removing the ancient monuments (Said 1995: 81–3; Bret 1999).

By the early twentieth century ancient Egypt served as a familiar *topos* (in Frances Yates's sense of a real or imaginary space in which memory can be anchored) where the discontents of Judeo-Christian, democratic, capitalist society could be explored. Then, as today, these discontents and contradictions extend far beyond the sphere of political experience. Among them we find the repressed desire to abdicate responsibility for life to a higher authority, which satisfies both spiritual and physical needs; the desire for material rather than simply spiritual continuity after death; and the closely related desire to root the life of living institutions in some form of direct commerce with the dead (cf. Baudrillard 1993). This modern need for ancient Egypt as symbol and metaphor has accorded it a privileged place in western cultural memory, but has hardly been conducive to seeing it as a product of historical development.

When significant quantities of prehistoric remains were eventually excavated in the Nile valley, at the close of the nineteenth century, it was more by accident than design, and at first the finds were not unanimously recognised as dating to a time before kingship. It was with a polite dismissal that W. M. F. Petrie, who subsequently went on to demonstrate almost single-handedly the existence of a 'predynastic' cultural sequence in Egypt, responded to the first volume of J. de Morgan's *Recherches sur les origines de l'Egypte*, published in 1896 (see Drower 1985: 225). It is a further irony that a number of Petrie's own early Egyptian discoveries, including the famous colossal statues found at Coptos (fig. 9.10), were subsequently rejected by the British Museum on grounds that they were 'unhistoric rather than prehistoric', a fit of pique for which Oxford's Ashmolean Museum and University College London—where Petrie, by way of retaliation, sent much of his predynastic material—have been grateful ever since (Petrie 1931: 153–7).

For some early twentieth-century scholars, notably the founding father of Sudanese anthropology C. G. Seligman, investigating ancient Egypt's prehistoric foundations was less a matter of excavating downwards than travelling southwards, beyond the perceived boundaries of the Oriental landscape. 'Africa', went the imperial slogan, 'begins at Malakal', in today's Southern Sudan. During the Anglo-Egyptian Condominium (1899–1956), Malakal also marked the point at which archaeological activity, focused upon the visible monuments of ancient kingdoms and empires to the north, came to an end, and ethnographic fieldwork—often oriented as much towards the past as the present—began in earnest (Wengrow 2003b). Seligman was particularly interested in the pastoral tribes of the Upper Nile Province, in whom he perceived a racially corrupted remnant of prehistoric Caucasian immigrants, whose arrival on the African continent—in his view, and that of some others—had precipitated the rise of dynastic civilisation in ancient Egypt (Seligman 1913; 1934).[1] By the late twentieth century such views had been rightly dismissed as malign fantasies (Sanders 1969). Nevertheless, the geographical division of labour between archaeology and anthropology that sustained them has persisted, and still delineates real boundaries and profound discrepancies in the depth of historical knowledge along the Nile. These boundaries have continued to influence the pattern of scholarship in North-East Africa to the present day. I discuss these issues further in chapters 3 and 5.

Prior to becoming a historical idea, Egypt 'before the pharaohs' therefore existed both as a largely unordered assemblage of prehistoric objects and unloved human remains excavated within Egypt itself, and in the ethnographic imagination of a wider African present. By 'a historical idea' I mean something more than just a subject of study for professional archaeologists or another gap filled along the chronological spectrum of human development. I mean something which, although rooted in the knowable past, resonates with the present, and is understood to have been a formative, or at least distinctly meaningful, episode in the making of the contemporary world.

---

[1] MacGaffey (1966) places Seligman's ideas within the wider setting of contemporary racial theory.

A recent survey of textbooks used to teach American college courses on Western Civilisation provides a useful indication of how far the prehistory of the Middle East and North-East Africa still is from becoming an idea, in that sense (Segal 2000). Daniel Segal, who conducted the survey, suggests that the 'Near East', including both ancient Iraq (Mesopotamia) and Egypt, still tends to be represented not so much as a place (or series of places), but as a stage of global history. Specifically, it is made to stand for 'early civilisation': a transitional phase between the simple life of Stone Age peoples and modern civilisation in its western, secular form. During that phase, so the story goes, human societies achieved some important technological advances (e.g. the invention of writing and monumental architecture), but at the expense of submission to exploitative, religiously motivated and economically dysfunctional regimes. The prehistories of Egypt and Iraq are not presented as histories of what happened to societies there before the appearance of kingship, cities and writing systems. Rather, they are absorbed into a generic prehistory of all humankind, during which 'people' achieved the transition from a hunter-gatherer lifestyle to early farming societies. The Neolithic, in particular, is conceived as a crucial episode of economic development, which of course it was, but like all human transformations it was many other things as well, and these tend to be excluded. In this established narrative, a change in *economic* conditions precipitates a change in *political* relations, such that the overall transformation of coherent life-worlds (always simultaneously economic, political and ideological) is obscured from view, and a genuine long-term history of social power in the Middle East and North-East Africa is rendered inconceivable.[2]

The conclusion seems, on the face of it, to be a depressing one. Instead of a prehistory rooted in temporal development, and encompassing multiple trajectories of social and cultural change, students and the public at large are still, for the most part, being offered a pastiche: a symbolic prehistory of humankind, which also acts as a repository—or rather graveyard—for aspects of the present deemed 'pre-modern'. In the present climate, with 'civilisation' firmly back on the political and intellectual agenda of the West, the retention of this topography of values has particularly strong implications for the regions concerned, which hardly need to be spelt out in detail. On a more positive note, accepting the reality of this status quo may provide archaeologists working in those regions with something approaching a 'conscious unity of purpose'; the purpose being to change or at least question it. The idea of prehistory in the Middle East and North-East Africa remains, in more senses than one, a subversive and 'disorienting' one.

---

[2] For a more wide-ranging critique of 'periodisation by stereotype' in archaeological and evolutionary thought, see Sherratt 1995.

Aims, scope and method of this book

Most scholars today would probably accept that hierarchy is a socially constructed, rather than a natural, feature of the Middle East's historical landscape
(although views to the contrary can still be found in some surprisingly prominent places). There is, however, a considerable difference between accepting a
viewpoint on political or philosophical grounds and demonstrating its validity
through the available evidence. In this book I will be aiming towards the latter
goal by providing a sustained interpretation of social and cultural change in
Egypt and neighbouring parts of Africa and Asia, spanning a period of more
than seven millennia between the onset of the Holocene and the early centuries of dynastic rule that preceded the Old Kingdom (c.10,000–2650 BC).

  In writing it I have repeatedly asked myself what contribution a 'world
archaeology' perspective should make to the study of early Egypt. World
archaeology of course means different things to different people. To me it
implies an approach that is comparative in scope, although not to the exclusion of inter-regional relationships and historical contingency. It also implies a
commitment to address questions of general anthropological significance,
including the variety of ways in which human groups and societies have
engaged with what Abner Cohen (1974: 60) termed 'perennial problems of
human existence', such as 'the meaning of life and death, fortune and mis-
fortune, good and evil, growth and decay'. In contrast to some other recent
studies (notably, Trigger 2003), I do not attempt an initial definition of ancient
Egypt as an example of some wider phenomenon, for instance: 'early civilisation', 'the archaic state' or 'complex society'. Categories of this kind impose
constraints and assumptions upon the analysis of social change that are un-
warranted in a study like the present one, where we have the luxury of 'thick
description'. Some of these conventions, and in particular the use of 'complexity' as a metaphor for processes of early state formation, will be unpacked and
questioned in the chapters that follow.

  What, then, of method? Here I define only some broad historical issues and
parameters of investigation, which are expanded upon in individual chapters.

  During the early twentieth century the archaeological record of early Egypt,
with its well-preserved cemeteries, was the envy of excavators working in other
parts of the Old World. Rich assemblages of objects recovered from burials were
well suited to the intellectual concerns of the day: seriation, typology, chronology, culture-groups, and the diffusion of peoples and traits (see Trigger 1989:
148–206). All was to change during the mid-twentieth century. While older
theories of social evolution, such as those of Lewis Henry Morgan (1877),
had placed considerable explanatory emphasis upon mobility and migration,
the work of V. Gordon Childe during the 1930s and 1940s recast the 'birth
of civilisation' in the mould of an 'urban revolution'—an epiphany of the
settled form of life, giving priority to those aspects of prehistoric development

associated with the establishment and growth of sedentary villages (e.g. Childe 1936). Robert Braidwood's expedition to the 'hilly flanks' of the Iraqi Zagros during the 1950s demonstrated the possibility of substantiating this account with empirical data derived from habitation zones, including animal and plant remains that shed light on the beginnings of Neolithic food production (Braidwood and Howe 1960). In Egypt, where agrarian life was mainly restricted to the Nile alluvium, much of the raw material for what had become a conventional study of social evolution (habitation sites, regional settlement patterns, faunal and plant assemblages) now suddenly appeared beyond reach, owing to the modern reuse of land and the build-up of fluvial silts over ancient living sites. As will become clear in the chapters that follow, and as has been apparent now for some time, this initial prognosis was over-pessimistic. It nevertheless remains the case that, for the periods covered in this book (and much of the dynastic period that follows), Egyptian cemeteries, rather than settlements, provide the bulk of information concerning material culture, patterns of trade, practices of production and consumption and, of course, the ritual structuring of the human lifecycle.

As Bruce Trigger (1979) has perceived, the prominence of sacred kingship in studies of early Egypt may have further contributed to its isolation from the social sciences during the late twentieth century. Once a cornerstone of social evolutionary thought, in the tradition developed by James Frazer (1911–15) and Arthur Hocart (1927), the institution of kingship was marginalized from much neo-evolutionary theory, which chose instead to ponder the transitions from 'tribe' to 'chiefdom' and from 'chiefdom' to 'archaic state'. Forms of status as diverse as 'warrior chief' and 'ritual leader' were subsumed within a single category; a common criticism of the 'chiefdom' has since been that it spans too broad a range of social variation and types of power (Yoffee 1993; Kristiansen 1998). At around the same time, the anthropology of sacred kingship took a semiological turn, inspired by Georges Dumézil's analyses of Indo-European mythology and the structural anthropology of Claude Lévi-Strauss (both ultimately grounded in comparative linguistics), and exemplified in Luc de Heusch's studies of Bantu myth and sacrifice, and Marshall Sahlins's work on perceptions of time and sacred power in Oceania.[3] There is no inherent reason why the study of ancient Egypt or Mesopotamia should have been excluded from this theoretical enterprise, and many of its central concerns were anticipated by Henri Frankfort (1948a), who attempted to discern consistent patterns of mythical thought and symbolic practice underlying the different forms of kingship in these two regions. More recent work (e.g. Hodder 1990; Rowlands 2003) suggests a belated, but nonetheless worthwhile engagement with aspects of structuralist thought in the archaeology of the Middle

---

[3] E.g. Dumézil 1968–73; Lévi-Strauss 1963; de Heusch 1982; Sahlins 1985.

East and North-East Africa; an engagement to which the present study also aspires.

One of the criticisms sometimes levelled at structuralism (although not all studies are equally culpable) has been that of logocentrism: an over-reliance on language as a model for understanding social organisation and cultural transmission. Many studies have emphasised the importance for human relations and their development of practices that are not language-like (e.g. Bourdieu 1977; Bloch 1998). Particular attention has been drawn to types of social knowledge that are pre-discursive, infiltrating the person directly via what Marcel Mauss (1979 [1935]) called *techniques du corps* and rarely, if ever, articulated as formal, linguistic propositions. As Alfred Gell (1993: 3) observed, the salience of Mauss's notion of 'body techniques' often 'stems from the fact that it is through the body, the way in which the body is deployed, displayed, and modified, that socially appropriate self-understandings are formed and reproduced'. Such knowledge may range from routines of comportment, personal presentation, work and consumption to prescribed modes of ritual and ceremonial activity. Practice-centred approaches to the analysis of social change enforce no rigid dichotomy between 'sacred' and 'profane' experience (or, for that matter, between 'art' and 'technology'), both of which are equally rooted in the socially educated bodies of individuals and their repertoires of behaviour and emotional response: part universal, part culturally learned. 'Gods', writes Dipesh Chakrabarty (2000: 78), 'are as real as ideology is—that is to say, they are embedded in practices.'

A notion of material practice as constituting and actively transforming the parameters of social experience is integral to the interpretative approach followed in this book. Archaeological data are studied, not through predetermined categories such as 'technology', 'art', 'administration' and 'cult', but as mutually constitutive elements within total, developing forms of social life. For early Egypt, as I have indicated, the most fertile ground for such an approach lies in funerary practices, which offer a continuous record of structured human activity, implicating both bodies and artefacts in the transformation of social experience. Instead of seeing this patterning of the record as a bias to be corrected or minimised, I intend to turn it to my advantage by placing activities surrounding death and the body at the core of my interpretation of long-term change. This does not mean treating funerary remains as if they were snapshots of mundane life, rather than the outcome of purposeful ritual transformations. Nor does it imply a denial of their distinctive qualities as formalised expressions of loss, or a reduction of sentient human beings to automata, playing out well-formulated ideological strategies in a fantasy world free of emotion and contingency.

What I *would* assert is that relationships between the living and the dead—sustained, negotiated and altered through ritual activity—were deeply interwoven, albeit in complex and indirect ways, with the material conditions of existence and production: sufficiently interwoven to provide meaningful insights into the political and economic developments covered in this book. Of these, two episodes of change stand out. They are, respectively, associated with the adoption of domesticated animals and plants during the fifth millennium BC and the establishment, a millennium and a half later, of a unified territorial state under the centralised rule of a sacred monarch. Over the long-term, as I seek to show, both episodes involved fundamental transformations in economy, ritual practice and the articulation of social power. I further argue, notably in chapters 1 and 7, that neither development can be adequately comprehended without considering Egypt's changing place within networks of communication and trade that spanned large areas of the western Old World, linking developments in North-East Africa to wider patterns of social and technological change in South-West Asia and the Eastern Mediterranean.

In its totality, a record of ritual practices formed over thousands of years constitutes a distinct kind of historical reality, which—however fragmentary and disturbed—offers particular challenges and possibilities for interpretation. It is a reality that cannot always be reduced to the conscious intentions of particular actors. Neither, however, can it be attributed to forces beyond their control, or consigned to a realm outside the strategic interests of predatory groups within society. Social life leaves a material trace of its own development that is not random, and yet can often be grasped only at a remove from the rhythms of ordinary existence and decision-making: a pattern created in time and space by the manifold, momentary actions of individual agents, which is only partly perceptible to them as they contribute to its making, but no less human, social or—with the benefit of distance—recognisable for that. As I hope to demonstrate, there may be particularly good empirical reasons for approaching the relationship between changes in ritual practice and in the politico-economic sphere on an archaeological time-scale: in the perspective of millennia and centuries, rather than decades and years. Here it is instructive to compare the methodological conclusions of Maurice Bloch's anthropological study of Merina circumcision rituals in Madagascar:

First, we have seen some change occur in the ritual, however slow it may be. This is change brought about by the functional changes the ritual has undergone. These are not to be understood as direct responses to circumstances; they often appear as ad hoc abbreviations or expansions. These changes are, moreover, not as insignificant as they might appear at first sight. They do alter what is done in a way that in the long run, must lead cumulatively to major changes. This, however, would be over a long time, a longer time than the two hundred years of this study.

(Bloch 1986: 193)

One of the principal arguments that will emerge from this study is that Neolithic social forms in North-East Africa and South-West Asia were more diverse, distinctive and robust than previously thought, and exerted a lasting influence upon the political development of those regions. There is a temporal continuity, an inertia, between Neolithic modes of engagement with the social and material worlds, and the modes of self-presentation adopted by dynastic elites. Such continuities, persisting within change, are not adequately accounted for either by evolutionary models which stress the progressive growth of technological and organisational complexity, or by evoking the internal structural and symbolic coherence of 'high cultures' and 'great traditions'. Despite the characteristic appeals of dynastic elites to what Bloch (1987: 272) describes as 'an order which transcends mere human experience', their establishment and survival depended, to a significant degree, upon successful co-option and transfiguration of clearly defined domains of knowledge, rooted in the everyday lives and habits of their Neolithic antecedents. That process of co-option was not simple, rapid or total. Rather, it involved a succession of cultural strategies for appropriating and restricting access to mobile resources, land and sacred power. The material residues of those strategies, and their analysis, constitute a guiding strand in the archaeology of early Egypt.

PART I

TRANSFORMATIONS IN PREHISTORY

EGYPT AND THE OUTSIDE WORLD I, c.10,000–3300 BC

Your head, O my lord, is adorned with the tress of a woman of Asia; . . .
your hair is bestrewn with lapis lazuli; the upper part of your
   face is as the shining of Re;
your visage is covered with gold and Horus has inlaid it with lapis lazuli . . .
   Extract from the *Book of the Dead* (fifteenth century BC); from the
   hieroglyphic papyrus of Nebseni,
   found at Memphis in northern Egypt
   (after Faulkner 1985: 171; 172.II)

I constructed the temple of the god Enlil . . . I erected in the rooms cedar doors
with silver and gold stars. (Under) the walls of the temple (I placed) silver, gold,
lapis lazuli (and) cornelian; cedar resin, best oil, honey and ghee I mixed in the
mortar.
   Extract from a commemorative inscription of
   Shamshi-Adad I (c.1813–1781 BC); one of nine
   on stone tablets found in the Temple of Ashur,
   at Qalat Shergat (Ashur) in northern Iraq (after Grayson 1972: 20; 39.1.II)

1.1 Opening considerations

In the second millennium BC, as from the time of their inception, the principal
dynastic powers of South-West Asia and North-East Africa were related
through material interests and exchanges, even as they remained culturally
and politically divided. The worlds evoked by their religious inscriptions are
not merely conceptual, but material ones, in which elite aspirations—whether
towards the divine body or the divine household—took sensuous form. The
demand for materials that encapsulated those desires, and the cross-cultural
etiquette of courtly exchange through which they were transmitted in times of
peace, are vividly attested in hundreds of cuneiform texts dating to the four-
teenth century BC, discovered at el-'Amarna, in central Egypt. This diplomatic
correspondence demonstrates that, like their modern counterparts, the ancient
elites of Egypt, Mesopotamia and surrounding regions had to operate within
multiple social worlds and domains of rationality in order to maintain their
status (Cohen and Westbrook 2000). Royal marriages, and the circulation of
precious metals and the products of palace workshops, provided an important

ingredient in the social cement that bound together the wider political and economic fortunes of Bronze Age states.

The common sensuous world, out of which the distinct life- (and death-) styles of dynastic elites in Egypt and Mesopotamia took form, was established long before the earliest known written documentation of long-distance exchange. Hetepheres I and Puabi, queens of the mid-third millennium BC, may not have been able to hold a conversation, but their respective funerary deposits at Giza and Ur were both saturated with objects crafted from gold, silver, cornelian and lapis lazuli.[1] Many of the material constituents of elite culture—notably metals, brightly coloured stones, certain tree crops and fine timber—were not native to the major alluvial plains of either region. Their sources lay, rather, along the outer frontiers of Mesopotamia and the Nile valley, arching across the highland ranges of the Fertile Crescent and the adjacent plateaux (copper, silver, iron, lead, coniferous forest, tree resins, vine, olive, obsidian, basalt and other stones), and passing south through the Sinai peninsula (turquoise, copper) along the desert margins of the Red Sea (gold, copper, tin,[2] granite, diorite, malachite, alabaster, jasper, cornelian and other stones in the eastern deserts of Egypt and Nubia; obsidian and aromatic tree resins along the southern margins of the Red Sea coast). Cornelian was imported to Mesopotamia from sources to the east, extending across the Iranian plateau to the outskirts of the Indus, while lapis lazuli was obtained exclusively from Badakhshan, in eastern Afghanistan (fig. 1.1).[3]

This shared contrast between lowland river basins, affording rich agricultural surpluses and paths of navigation, and adjacent peripheries endowed with ore and mineral deposits, was a major factor in the emergence of the world's earliest states, which took place almost simultaneously, though with markedly different results, in Egypt and Mesopotamia during the late fourth millennium BC. To posit geographical circumstances as the key that unlocked the emergence of a Bronze Age 'world system', however, is simply to restate, in another form, the old dichotomy between 'prehistoric savagery', embedded in timeless nature, and 'historical civilisation', conquering nature's gifts and turning them to its own devices.[4] Long before the emergence of palatial

---

[1] See Woolley 1934, pls. 128–31; Reisner 1955: 43–5, pls. 38–9; Malek 2003: 54.

[2] Tin bronze was produced in the Near East during the late fourth and third millennia BC, but only replaced arsenical copper as a staple alloy during the second millennium BC; see Potts 1993: 391.

[3] For general discussions of the prehistoric and ancient exploitation of raw materials in Mesopotamia, Egypt and adjacent regions, see Moorey 1994 (Mesopotamia); Lucas 1962; Nicholson and Shaw 2000 (Egypt).

[4] The application of world systems theory, derived from Immanuel Wallerstein's (1974) work on the global spread of capitalism since the fifteenth century AD, has been instrumental in highlighting the importance of inter-regional contacts and trade in the development of Bronze Age polities (e.g. Rowlands et al. 1987; Algaze 1993). Wallerstein's use of a blanket dichotomy between 'core' regions and their 'peripheries' to describe exploitative relations in the global market has, however, been criticised for ignoring the historical diversity of 'peripheral' societies and their responses to European expansion (e.g. Wolf 1982), a critique now widely echoed in the analysis of ancient world systems (e.g. Oates 1993; Stein 1999; Nissen 2001).

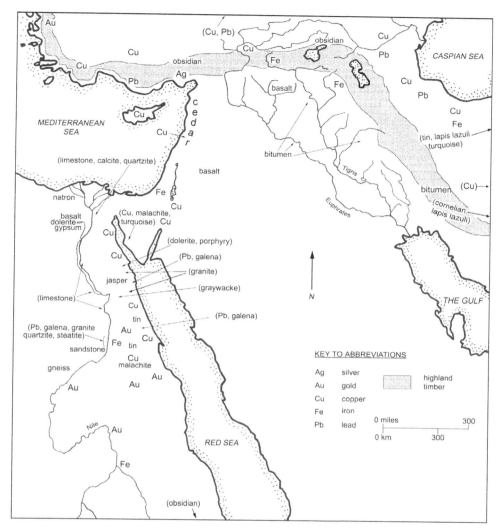

Figure 1.1 Map: Distribution of raw materials between the Nile valley and the Fertile Crescent

command economies and writing systems, manufactured objects and other commodities (including plant and animal products) circulated the length and breadth of South-West Asia and North-East Africa across social networks that mapped out shared arenas of communication, value and consumption (Runnels and Van Andel 1988). It was during these millennia of prehistoric interaction that many transformational properties of animals and plants, and also of clay, stone and metal, were first explored and incorporated into the formation of personal and collective identities. The resulting patterns of human activity, while often based upon shared technologies, differed markedly in form and distribution across the regions in question, constituting the cultural landscapes upon which early states sought to define the nature and extent of their own boundaries.

The aim of this chapter, and of a second in Part II, is to trace Egypt's changing structural position within these shifting patterns of interaction and innovation, from the waning of the last glacial to the formation of the Old Kingdom (c.10,000–2600 BC). Together with the accompanying maps, they are intended to serve as both a chronological overview and an interpretative framework for the detailed discussions of social change that follow, placing Egypt's development within the wider context of Old World prehistory. The present chapter covers a series of major transitions, including the introduction of domesticated animals and plants from South-West Asia, the development of new modes of transport by water and land, the emergence of large centres of population, and technological innovations in the use of metals, stone and a range of other materials. The story of Egypt's changing relations with the outside world is picked up again in chapter 7, which covers the period of rapid transformation during which the dynastic state was established.

In combination, these two chapters show how outside influences had a long-term, and by no means simple, part to play in the internal transformation of Egyptian society that cannot be accurately characterised by a piecemeal approach (e.g. by invoking periodic migrations or phases of contact). In order to understand such long-term processes it is necessary to treat the notion of 'Egypt' as a historical construct, rather than a timeless reality, and to venture far beyond the modern and ancient borders of that country. It is also necessary to adopt a flexible approach to the question of how social boundaries are constituted and maintained over time and space, taking into account the contingencies of historical development and interaction.

1.2 The ancient course of the Nile

The Early Holocene landscape of the Nile valley and adjacent regions was formed in relation to a distinct set of environmental conditions, arising from the influx of rains into North-East Africa.[5] From the south came tropical summer inundations, while a Mediterranean winter-rainfall regime advanced from the north. Over several millennia the combined effect brought lands to the east and west of the valley to life, dotting them with lakes and incising them with living wadis. The northward shift of rainfall patterns allowed savannah grasses to migrate into what are now hyper-arid areas, extending along the flanks of the Nile valley from central Sudan to southern Egypt. Through the middle of this increasingly hospitable environment surged the

---

[5] Haynes *et al.* 1989; Wendorf and Schild 1989: 771–3; Close 1996.

Nile, creating an ecologically diverse floodplain that supported a variety of terrestrial and aquatic fauna. Increased rainfall over its East African headwaters initially caused the river to flood catastrophically (the phase of 'wild Niles', c.12,500–12,000 BC), a pattern which gradually ameliorated as it cut down into the valley (Butzer 1980; 2000).

Prior to the major dam projects of the nineteenth and twentieth centuries AD, the influence of human agency over the flow of the Nile was restricted to the construction of irrigation canals and artificial catchment basins, which varied in extent from Pharaonic times to the British colonial period. The river is supplied from a number of sources that descend from the Ethiopian highlands where they are fed by summer rains. Today the principal sources are the Blue and White Niles, which converge at modern Khartoum, and the Atbara, which flows through the rain-fed steppe of the Butana grasslands in eastern Sudan. The prehistoric environment of this region is still poorly understood, but it seems certain that the configuration and volume of these rivers differed markedly from the present. Further to the west lie the channels of former watercourses such as the Wadi Milk and the Wadi Howar. The latter, through which the so-called Yellow Nile once flowed, descends from the mountains of eastern Chad and joins the Nile at the site of Old Dongola, near modern ad-Dabbah in central Sudan (Keding 1998).

The main Sudanese course of the Nile extends south from Egypt for approximately 2000 km, during which the height of the river drops less than 400 m as it passes through a valley cut into Nubian sandstone formations. At six points along this course, between Aswan and Khartoum, its flow is disrupted by cataracts formed by basal outcrops of igneous rock, which constitute serious obstacles to river transport (Shinnie 1996: 3–9). The longest stretches of rapids run from the Fifth Cataract, at the junction of the Nile and the Atbara, to the Fourth Cataract downstream of Abu Hamed, and between the Third and Second Cataracts in the Semna region. In these areas the river passes through narrow channels broken by small, inhospitable islands. Further downstream it crosses major granite outcrops near Wadi Halfa before entering Egypt at Aswan. From there it flows uninterrupted to the Mediterranean Sea, following a diversion into the Fayum depression near Bani Suwaif, and fanning out into a series of channels beyond Cairo to form one of the world's largest deltas.

Each year, during the autumn floods from August to October, the Nile deposited a thick layer of mineral-rich sediment along the length of its Egyptian course. Approximately a third of this alluvial sediment was distributed in a narrow band along the banks of the river-valley, the remainder accumulating in the delta. These seasonal deposits determined the rhythm of early Egyptian agriculture, which produced a single crop each year from Neolithic times down to the onset of the Graeco-Roman period. Crops were sown directly after the recession of the floodwaters, during October and November, and were harvested in the late winter or early spring. Multiple cropping was first achieved on a regular basis under the Ptolemies, with the introduction of mechanised water-lifting devices that made possible the expansion of canal systems beyond the floodplain.[6]

1.3 Early Holocene transformations, c.10,000–7000 BC

Prior to the introduction of cereal crops during the fifth millennium BC, the Nile valley may be best regarded as one of many aquatic environments exploited by human groups across the whole expanse of Saharan and Sahelian Africa, from the Atlantic coast to the Red Sea (Sutton 1977). Throughout the last phase of the Pleistocene, human groups maintained a close relationship with the river and its resources, collecting oysters and shallow-water fish (principally *Clarias* sp.) which spawned on the floodplain, and occasionally hunting hippo, waterfowl and a range of terrestrial mammals. Evidence for hunting and foraging practices derives primarily from Qadan sites in Lower Nubia (Shiner 1968a: 564–611) and Isnan sites in central Upper Egypt (the Makhadma-Qena region; Vermeersch *et al.* 1989). The Second Cataract remains a prime source of knowledge for the ninth and eighth millennia BC, accompanied by the el-Kab region of Upper Egypt, the Early Khartoum (or 'Khartoum Mesolithic') sites of central Sudan and the Qarunian sites of the Fayum depression (Table 3).[7] These cultural entities are loosely defined according to their distinct stone tool repertoires, which represent variations within a common microlithic tradition characterised by backed bladelets, burins, small scrapers, and geometric forms such as lunates, trapezes and triangles (Midant-Reynes 2000: 70–99).

There are uncertain indications that, during the ninth millennium BC, Early Holocene groups sought to manage herds of wild cattle around the northern boundary of savannah vegetation, in Egypt's south-western desert. As discussed in chapter 2, such practices, if attempted, did not lead to any significant alteration in the size or behaviour of these animals, let alone the production of milk surpluses for human consumption, which was a much later development.

By the seventh millennium BC, deep-water fish such as perch (*Lates*) were procured from the main channel of the Nile, probably with the aid of harpoons, nets and perhaps simple rafts (van Neer 1989: 52–5). This development appears to coincide broadly with the appearance of Epipalaeolithic (Arkinian and Shamarkian) stone tool industries in Lower Nubia, Upper Egypt and the

---

[6] For historical surveys of agricultural practices in Egypt, from ancient to modern times, see Butzer 1976 and the contributions in Bowman and Rogan 1999.

[7] Shiner 1968b (Lower Nubia; there seems increasingly little reason to see the so-called Khartoum Variant industry as anything other than Early Holocene/Mesolithic in date; Gatto 2002: 77); Vermeersch 1978; 1984 (el-Kab); Arkell 1949; Haaland 1992 (Khartoum region); Caton-Thompson and Gardner 1934; Brewer 1989b (the so-called Fayum B culture, wrongly identified as post-Neolithic by the excavators; Arkell and Ucko 1965: 146–7; Wendorf and Schild 1976: 155–226).

Fayum, and is roughly contemporaneous with the wider spread of sites along river and lake margins in central and eastern Africa, from Lake Chad to the East African Rift valley, and as far north as central Sudan.[8] Human groups also followed herds of hartebeest, aurochs and gazelle along the rejuvenated wadis, as far as the oases and seasonal playas of the Western Desert (McDonald 1999; Wendorf and Schild 2001). Movement into the Eastern Desert is attested by the presence of a Red Sea gastropod at an Early Holocene site in the Egyptian Nile valley, and Epipalaeolithic chipped-stone industries were discovered at the oasis of Laqeita, 35 km east of Qus (Vermeersch *et al.* 1989: 105; Debono 1950; 1951). Hunting of game may have been particularly important during the annual Nile floods, which restricted access to the alluvial plain for both people and animals (Wetterstrom 1993: 172). There is widespread evidence for the collection of roots and tubers, and sorghum grains (gathered rather than cultivated) are reported from Nabta Playa in Egypt's south-western desert (Wetterstrom 1993: 181, 189–90; Wasylikowa *et al.* 1993).

The accumulation of dense deposits at many Early Holocene sites, comprising hearths and large amounts of chipped stone and bone, suggests regular seasonal reoccupation and perhaps even perennial habitation at some locations (Wendorf 1968: 864–5; Vermeersch *et al.* 1989: 92, 97–9).[9] An abundance of grinding stones further supports the impression of a relatively sedentary existence, with movements confined to restricted locales where aquatic resources and wild plant foods were abundant.[10] In addition to processing plant foods, grinding stones were used in the preparation of red and yellow pigments.[11] Another common feature of Early Holocene sites in the Nile valley and Western Desert is the presence of coarse, tempered ceramic bowls covered with impressed or incised decoration. First noted by Arkell at Khartoum, vessels of this kind are attested over a vast area, extending east from the Middle Nile Basin into the central Sahara and south into the East African Rift valley (Close 1995). They bear a variety of surface designs made up of parallel rows of dots and wavy lines, perhaps imitating netting, created by combing the surface of the pot with a catfish spine or similar object (fig. 1.2; Arkell 1949: 81–3, pl. 59; Jesse 2002). While the manufacture of pottery is thought to have been a local affair, materials for stone implements such as agate and rhyolite were often acquired over tens or even hundreds of kilometres from their source areas.[12] The distribution of *Unio* sp. shells further testifies to the

---

[8] Schild *et al.* 1968; Midant-Reynes 2000: 77–80; cf. Sutton 1977; Haaland 1993; Muzzolini 1993: 232–4.
[9] Many sites along the Nile valley have suffered serious deflation, such that their original depths cannot be ascertained (Haaland 1993: 47, 52).
[10] Connor and Marks 1986: 191; cf. Haaland 1987: 200–1; Fuller 1998: 55.
[11] Arkell 1949: 52–4, pls. 26–33; Vermeersch 1984; Wendorf and Schild 1980: 154.
[12] Hays and Hassan 1974; Francaviglia and Palmieri 1983 (ceramic provenance); Wendorf and Schild 1980: 264; Clark 1984: 115; Close 1984 (stone provenance).

Figure 1.2 Rim sherd from a Mesolithic vessel, Khartoum

existence of exchange networks extending between the Western Desert and the Nile valley (Close 1984: 166).

Early Holocene hunter-fisher-gatherers used bone in the manufacture of tools and weapons such as harpoons (fig. 1.3; Haaland 1993: 79–80). Evidence for personal ornamentation is largely restricted to ostrich egg-shell beads, molluscs and simple bone pendants. Of these, ostrich egg-shell beads are by far the most ubiquitous, appearing in great numbers and at varying stages of manufacture throughout the eastern Sahara, Nile valley and Eastern Desert.[13] At Khartoum, Arkell excavated the burial of an individual wearing a necklace made up of hundreds of such beads, and the absence of semi-processed shell at the site led him to suggest their acquisition through trade.[14] Debono (1948, fig. 4) noted the presence of similar beads and *Dentalium* sp. shell ornaments in the Helwan region, near modern Cairo, and ostrich egg-shell fragments were also found along with Nilotic (*Aspatharia*) and Red Sea (cowrie) shells at Abu

[13] Arkell 1949: 37–40; Debono 1951: 66; Schild *et al.* 1968: 700–31, *passim*; Wendorf and Schild 1980: 103–65, 188; Vermeersch 1984; Hassan and Gross 1987; Klees 1989; Haaland 1993: 76; McDonald 1998: 131–2. Gautier (1980: 327) observes that ostrich remains are strikingly rare in contemporaneous faunal assemblages, speculating that 'this bird was not on the menu and may have been tabu'.

[14] Arkell 1949: 31, 38, pl. 9: 3–5. Human burials have also been excavated in small numbers at other Early Holocene sites in central Sudan, including el-Damer, where one may be associated with a gazelle skull; see Haaland 1993: 55, pl. 1.

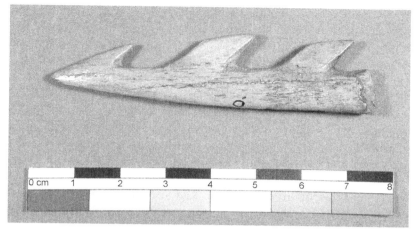

Figure 1.3 Bone harpoon, Khartoum, Mesolithic

Ballas in the Libyan Desert (Kuper 1993: 215–17). The latter site also marks the known northern extent of impressed pottery.

In terms of human habitation, the Nile delta remains the least understood part of Egypt's Early Holocene landscape, owing to millennia of sedimentation and constant reuse of arable land. Deep cores sunk into its coastal fringes reveal an increasingly complex history of land formation, guided by the interaction of the Nile with oscillations in the level of the Mediterranean Sea (Butzer 2002). Following the phase of 'wild Niles', the melting of sub-polar glaciers caused the coastline to advance almost 50 km inland, eroding the surface of the plain and forming sandy deposits along the delta-front. Throughout this period (c.9000–7500 BC) fluvial sedimentation continued further inland. As the sea level decreased, the flow of sediment cut new channels into the beaches at the head of the delta, and by the seventh millennium freshwater marshes and lagoons had formed along its Mediterranean profile. Further inland, Pleistocene sands projected above the active floodplain, forming areas of raised ground known as *geziras* or 'turtle backs'. In combination with the natural levees that built up along the Nile's distributaries, and the sandy outer margins of the delta, this provided ample opportunities for human habitation. These opportunities increased throughout the Early and Mid-Holocene, as Nile silts continued their gradual advance northwards (Butzer 1976: 22–5).

The Fertile Crescent

To the east, the deltaic alluvium gave way to the Sinai and Negev deserts, beyond which began the zone of Mediterranean coastal vegetation. Under the warmer and moister conditions of the Early Holocene, this zone expanded eastwards throughout much of the Fertile Crescent of South-West Asia, crossing the foothills of the Taurus and Zagros Mountains and invading adjacent parts of the steppe (Hillman 1996). During the Early Natufian period (c.12,500–11,000 BC), sedentary communities proliferated along its western arc, exploiting a wide range of newly available flora (Bar-Yosef and Belfer-Cohen 1989). Life in permanent villages also attracted a range of commensal animal species, including the house mouse and sparrow, and the dog, which was domesticated at this time (Tchernov 1984). Exchange networks extended between settled communities from the Middle Euphrates to the Negev, drawing in desired commodities from as far afield as central Turkey (obsidian; Cauvin and Chataigner 1998: 330–1) and the Mediterranean and Red Seas (shells; Bar-Yosef 1991). The discovery of three freshwater bivalves from the Nile valley at 'Ain Mallaha, in the Jordan valley, indicates the linkage of exchange systems across the Sinai peninsula (Mienis 1987).

It was in this latter region—modern-day Israel, Palestine, Jordan and Syria—that the earliest experiments in plant cultivation took place (Bar-Yosef and Meadow 1995). A relatively sudden and temporary reversion to Late Glacial climatic conditions after 11,000 BC (known as the Younger Dryas) prompted some human groups to pursue more specialised hunting practices in the semi-arid margins of the Levant, while others concentrated within sharply circumscribed habitats where plant foods remained a dependable resource, and continued to invest in sedentary life. Such habitats included perennial springs (e.g. 'Ain es-Sultan, near Jericho) and alluvial fans created by the recession of rivers and lakes (e.g. Lake Aateibé, in the Damascus Basin), which also attracted a wide range of mammals and waterfowl. The onset of the Holocene during the tenth millennium BC provided stable conditions for the expansion of these settlements along the 'Levantine Corridor', from the Jordan valley to the Middle Euphrates. By this time, domestic strains of wheat and barley are attested at a number of Pre-Pottery Neolithic A (PPNA) settlements in the Levant, reflecting the transfer of upland species to lowland habitats with fertile groundwater soils, where they were isolated from wild progenitors.[15]

Occupation of these restricted habitats also led to unprecedented experiments with the technological and communicative properties of clay, which was employed in the construction of mud-brick or *pisé* dwellings with interior furnishings such as storage bins and hearths, and in the manufacture of small vessels and figurines (Wengrow 1998). Repeated superimposition of mud-built houses over confined plots of land gave rise to habitation mounds (*tells*), forming living monuments to Neolithic occupation in the landscape. A concern with perpetuating occupational rights is also suggested by the burial of certain members of the community beneath or adjacent to domestic dwellings.

---

[15] Garrard *et al.* 1996; Sherratt 1997b; Moore *et al.* 2000: 376–93.

Such practices were further elaborated during the PPNB period (c.8500–7000 BC), when detached human skulls were revivified with plaster and paint, echoing the elaboration of house interiors with red paint, traces of which are preserved on the plaster surfaces of floors and walls.[16]

By the close of the eighth millennium, domestic forms of two-row barley, emmer and einkorn were disseminated throughout much of the Fertile Crescent. In south-eastern Turkey and along the Levantine Corridor, free-threshing wheat and naked six-row barley are also attested, as are domesticated pulses, rye and flax (Garrard 1999). These cultivars were transmitted across an ever-expanding web of social interaction, the extent of which is indicated by the presence of eastern Anatolian obsidian at sites from northern Israel to the highlands of western Iran (Cauvin and Chataigner 1998: 332–8). In addition to obsidian and marine shells, decorative body-rings, stone beads and fine bowls crafted in a variety of stones were disseminated across PPNB sites from the arid margins of the Jordan valley to the foothills of the Zagros Mountains (Moorey 1994: 38–9; Wright and Garrard 2003).

This growing field of interaction may be attributed in part to the domestication of animals during the ninth and eighth millennia BC: principally sheep and goat, followed by smaller numbers of cattle and pig (Legge 1996; Peters *et al.* 2000). As mobile wealth, domesticated herds would have transformed the scale and pace of human interaction, transgressing the temporal, spatial and social conventions that regulated the flow of objects between people. Their incorporation into existing regimes of value may be reflected in the spread of clay animal figurines and miniature geometric 'tokens', which appear across a similarly broad area, extending from the Levant to Khuzistan, during PPNB (Schmandt-Besserat 1992; cf. Wengrow 1998; 2003a). At a remarkably early stage in its development, towards the end of the ninth millennium BC (Early PPNB), the Neolithic animal economy was also transferred westwards over water to Cyprus, perhaps in response to rising sea levels along the Levantine coastal plain (Peltenburg *et al.* 2001).

1.4 The spread of primary farming, c.7000–5000 BC

The seventh and sixth millennia are among the most poorly documented in the archaeological record of the Nile valley. By the end of this period, domestic plants (emmer wheat and barley) and animals (sheep and goat), none of which had wild progenitors in Egypt, had been introduced from South-West Asia. These introductions formed part of a wider radiation of farming practices beyond the Fertile Crescent, a process most fully documented in Europe (fig. 1.4). There, Neolithic communities were established in the Balkans and the Aegean by the seventh millennium BC, and by the end of the sixth they had

---

[16] Kuijt 1996; 2000; Cauvin 2000: 44, 113–15; Akkermans and Schwartz 2003: 88–97.

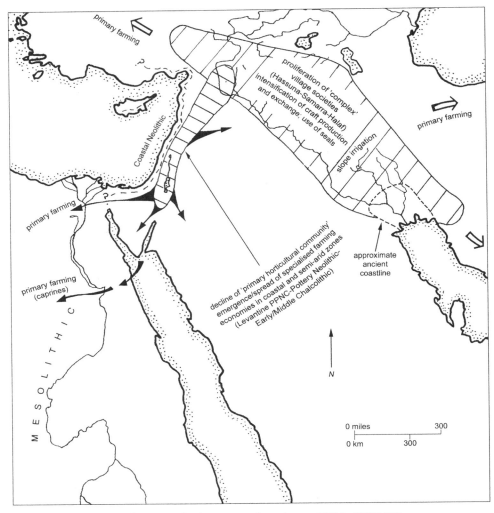

Figure 1.4 Map: The spread of primary farming, c.7000–5000 BC

begun to penetrate the Carpathian Basin, from whence primary farming spread into the loess-lands of central Europe and beyond (Whittle 1994). Following Andrew Sherratt (1981; 1997a: 6–30), the term 'primary farming' is taken to refer specifically to Early Neolithic forms of production which did not involve the regular extraction of milk and wool from domestic animals, nor their use as a source of power for transport or traction. These 'secondary products' developed as part of an extended process of social and technological innovation in South-West Asia, and were adopted to varying degrees and at different rates in adjacent parts of the Old World (chapters 7–8).

Just as the primary forms of Old World pastoralism were distinct from more recent patterns of animal use, so Neolithic cereal cultivation differed in important ways from observable modes of agriculture (Sherratt 1980). Almost all of the latter, including so-called 'traditional' farming practices, make use of fully domestic cultivars and employ some means of enhancing the productivity of soil, whether through irrigation, ploughing, hoeing, manure, flood control or land clearance. The earliest forms of cereal farming in the western Old World were simple by comparison, owing to their exploitation of alluvial soils on the edges of lakes, springs and rivers. In such environments the recession of annual floodwaters, which occurred at different times in different regions, exposed restricted niches of highly fertile and (in Egypt's case) naturally aerated soil. Provided that raised planting areas protected from the inundation were available, such as the naturally formed levees found in abundance along the Nile, seeds could simply be broadcast upon these soils and left to grow (Butzer 1976: 12–25, 89; 1995: 139–42).

The precise route through which domesticates were brought to Egypt has long been a subject of speculation, but can now be linked with increasing confidence to the expansion of Neolithic activity in the arid zones of the southern Levant, and along the northern and eastern flanks of the Sinai peninsula (Goring-Morris 1993). Their transmission may well have involved a maritime crossing via the Red Sea, passing via Aqaba to a point beyond Ras Muhammed, where caprid remains have been dated to the early sixth millennium at Sodmein Cave, c.35 km north-west of Quseir (Vermeersch *et al.* 1994). By the later sixth millennium, domestic sheep and goat may be attested at Nabta Playa, in Egypt's south-western desert, and are more firmly in evidence, together with emmer wheat and barley, in the Fayum depression, far to the north (Gautier 2001; von den Driesch 1986).

In the Levant itself, the seventh millennium has long been regarded as a period of decline resulting from the over-exploitation of particular niches of groundwater soil, and reflected in reduced settlement size and the abandonment of labour-intensive building in plaster and mud-brick (Rollefson and Köhler-Rollefson 1989). This decline was balanced by a shift of Neolithic activity to previously marginal areas. Domestic caprids are attested for the first time in the semi-arid steppe to the east of the Levantine Corridor, where they were integrated into a mixed economy of hunting and cereal cultivation (Martin 2000). Permanent settlements were also established along the Mediterranean coastal plain, combining herding and horticulture with the exploitation of marine resources, probably using nets and simple boats. Existing patterns of exchange may also have been transposed and adapted to the new setting, and by the sixth millennium BC this coastal form of Neolithic life was widely replicated around the shorelines of the Eastern Mediterranean, from Cilicia to the southern Levant (Galili *et al.* 2002). Whether this network of coastal communities already extended as far south as the Nile delta is as yet unknown.

Mesopotamia

Developments further to the east had no immediate effect upon Egypt at this time, but they involved innovations that were to transform the structure of social interaction in the Middle East over the long-term, and these should be briefly described.

In northern Mesopotamia, during the seventh millennium, small (Proto-Hassuna) farming and herding villages proliferated across the zone of reliable rainfall-fed farming between the Balikh and Tigris rivers (fig. 1.4; Akkermans 1993; Matthews 2000: 57–63). These lowland plains offered a premium environment for hunting and herding as well as privileged access to exchange networks spanning the Fertile Crescent. By the sixth millennium, domesticated plant crops are documented further south in the arid plains of central Iraq (e.g. at Tell es-Sawwan), implying the use of simple irrigation techniques to spread water from the distributaries of the Tigris (Oates 1973). Elaborately painted ceramics (Samarran and Halaf wares), closely replicating the appearance of woven vessels, were used throughout central and northern Mesopotamia during this period (Wengrow 2001b). Alongside the shared patterns of hospitality and consumption implied by such wares, a new technique of closure and restriction was also adopted, involving the use of stamp seals to impress identifying marks on to the clay sealings of vessels (Wickede 1990; Charvát 1994). The initial purpose of stamp seals may have been to sanction a separation between objects and persons that was temporary and reversible, affording seal-users greater strategic control over the dispensation of material resources. The social differentiation implied by this new form of property management is reflected in the internal layout of some Halaf villages (c.6500–5000 BC), which exhibit a formal demarcation of spaces for domestic production, the conduct of exchange and the transformation of exotic materials (Verhoeven 1999; Campbell 2000). The latter included small quantities of metal, and Halaf ceramics and architectural forms are found en route to the sources of copper, lead, gold and obsidian in eastern Turkey. Traffic in such materials is likely to have been mediated through seasonal movements of pastoralists out of their lowland villages and into the surrounding highlands (Wengrow 1998: 785–9; Akkermans and Schwartz 2003: 99–153).

1.5 The primary pastoral community in the Nile valley, c.5000–4000 BC

During the late sixth and fifth millennia, which encompass the Badarian period in Upper Egypt and the Khartoum Neolithic of central Sudan, herds of domestic cattle, sheep and goat were widely adopted throughout the Nile valley. By contrast with the earliest farming communities of the Fertile Crescent, which preceded them by some four millennia, those of Upper Egypt and Sudan show little sign of a village-based existence. Where occupation sites dating to the fifth and early fourth millennia have been found, they typically consist of a series of superimposed deposits containing quantities of ash, bone and cultural debris, sometimes associated with hearths and storage facilities, but with few traces of permanent architecture. Thick layers of animal droppings and remnants of ephemeral enclosures at many sites suggest that this pattern of deposition reflects the seasonal sojourns of mobile herding groups.

In terms of the richness and diversity of their material contents, Neolithic burial grounds present a marked contrast to contemporary habitation sites. Their known distribution is most dense in Middle Egypt and central Sudan, and has also been documented along the Dongola Reach and Fourth Cataract regions of northern Sudan (fig. 1.5). Throughout this entire region, funerary rites took on a strikingly similar form during the fifth millennium, suggesting a coherent body of beliefs and practices, widely disseminated from central Egypt to the region of modern Khartoum. The contents of these burials demonstrate a remarkable proliferation in the range of portable equipment available to individuals of both sexes and all ages. They further attest to a heightened circulation of materials deriving from beyond the Nile valley, and their incorporation into a new and elaborate repertoire of body display. Red Sea shells were attached to bracelets, necklaces and girdles, and beads were made from a wide variety of coloured stones including cornelian, jasper, alabaster, steatite, diorite, amazonite and serpentine, as well as small amounts of cold-worked copper.[17] This range of materials implies extensive prospection along the wadi routes leading to the Red Sea coast, where burials similar to those of the Nile valley have occasionally been discovered. Regular access to desert resources is also apparent in the cosmetic equipment used for decorating the body. Such equipment is virtually a standard component of Neolithic burial assemblages in the Nile valley, and included lightweight stone grinding palettes and coloured pigments such as malachite, galena and ochre. All of these developments are discussed in detail in chapters 2 and 3.

Given the shifting course of the Nile and the destructive effects of modern irrigation upon the archaeological record, it is highly unlikely that the range of surviving sites in the Nile valley represents the full spectrum of Neolithic habitation and economic life (Butzer 1976: 25, 33–6; cf. O'Connor 1990: 238–40). Nevertheless, a number of factors should be borne in mind before postulating the existence of permanent, but archaeologically unknown, villages along the prehistoric floodplain. Neolithic habitation sites have a similar, unstructured character from the el-Badari region of central Egypt to central

---

[17] For Egypt, see e.g. Brunton and Caton-Thompson 1928: 27–30, pls. 23, 24, 27, 49; Brunton 1937: 29, 51–3, pls. 22, 25, 39; 1948: 18–19, pls. 15–16; and also Lucas 1962, ch. 4; for Sudan, see e.g. Geus 1984b: 30; Lecointe 1987: 76–8, pl. 3: 2; Krzyżaniak 1984: 314; 1991: 518, 523, figs. 10–11.

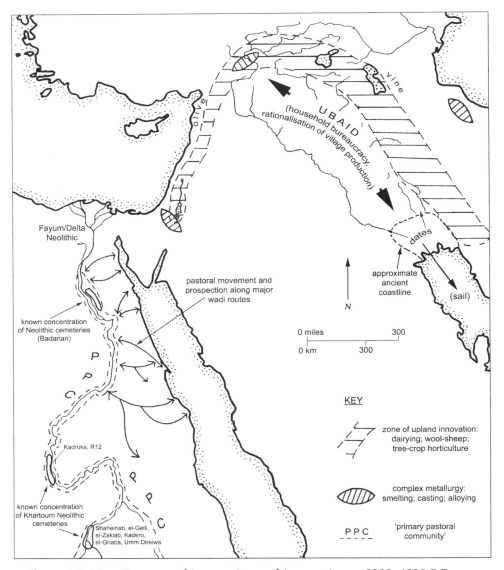

Figure 1.5 Map: Patterns of interaction and innovation, c.5000–4000 BC

Sudan. In the latter region, where the river was bordered by savannah and the alluvium more restricted than in Egypt, they are typically found at some distance from the ancient floodplain, prompting Isabella Caneva's (1991: 7) observation that:

Mesolithic [i.e. Early Holocene] gatherers and fishers were apparently more permanently attracted by riverine resources than Neolithic pastoralists who probably came to the river only seasonally . . . The complete transition to pastoralism seems to have led to the abandonment of permanent sites in favour of pastoral camps. The shift must have forced the inhabitants of the region to adopt a different life-style, consistent with the mobility required for stock breeding in arid climates.

It would be equally misleading, however, to characterise Neolithic communities in this region as nomadic or permanently on the move. Instead we should envisage a flexible pattern of existence, with possibilities of seasonal cultivation, foraging, fishing and hunting incorporated into a broad spectrum of activities, which centred upon the raising and movement of domestic herds, and—as I go on to discuss—did not lead to a heavy investment in sedentary life.

Lower Egypt

The record of contemporary developments in Lower Egypt during this period is confined to the Fayum depression, the Wadi Hof-Helwan region (south of Cairo), and a handful of sites on the outer margins of the Nile delta (Midant-Reynes 2000: 100–24). The available evidence indicates a pattern of Neolithic life distinct from that of the Nile valley. Among its distinguishing features was the use of large, basket-lined silos for the storage of emmer wheat and barley, which supplemented a rich variety of wild wetland and terrestrial species, the exploitation of which remained undiminished by the adoption of cultivated plants. Domestic animals, including cattle, sheep, goat and pig were also kept.[18] The material culture of sites in the Fayum depression, excavated by Gertrude Caton-Thompson during the early twentieth century around the former banks of Birket Qarun, is similarly diverse (Caton-Thompson and Gardner 1934; Arkell and Ucko 1965). Locally available stone was used in the production of bifacial sickle-blades, hafted on wooden handles, as well as concave-based arrowheads, adzes and stone celts made through a combination of grinding and flaking. Small quantities of amazonite, perhaps derived from the Tibesti Mountains of northern Chad and also found in Neolithic burials on the Middle Nile, demonstrate access to exchange networks extending south and west, and shells of Mediterranean and Red Sea origin were also found.[19] The associated pottery, which was hand-made and heavily tempered with crushed reeds, comprises a wide range of forms, including quite elaborate types such as footed cups and a dish resembling the inverted shell of a tortoise. Vessel surfaces were for the most part left plain, although a small proportion display red slip and burnish (Friedman 1994: 893–4).

---

[18] Caton-Thompson and Gardner 1934: 43–56; Brewer 1989a (Fayum A: Kom K); Hayes 1965: 117–19; Debono and Mortensen 1990 (el-Omari); Junker 1929–40; Wetterstrom 1993: 210–13 (Merimda Beni Salama).

[19] A more local source for amazonite cannot be excluded: Lucas 1962: 393–4; cf. Midant-Reynes 2000: 102.

Like their neighbours to the south, the Neolithic inhabitants of the Fayum and Helwan regions do not appear to have invested in long-lived settlements or permanent architecture, greater evidence for which may lie deep beneath the delta alluvium to the north (Hassan 1988: 146–54). This is suggested by the stratified sequence of occupations at Merimda Beni Salama, on the western edge of the delta, the later phases of which (c.4600–4100 BC) comprised semi-subterranean oval houses with mud foundations and internal hearths, their thresholds sometimes marked by hippopotamus tibia (Junker 1929–40/1932: 43–51; Eiwanger 1982).[20] Neolithic communities in Lower Egypt were also distinct from those of the Nile valley in their funerary customs. Numerous burials were discovered within the settlement at Merimda, although they appear not to have been directly associated with particular dwellings. The majority belonged to infants, interred without any grave goods (Junker 1929–40/1929; Kemp 1968a).

A comparison: South-East Europe

In considering the emergence of a more mobile and display-oriented lifestyle in the Nile valley, it is instructive to compare contemporary developments in Neolithic South-East Europe. The initial adoption of farming in Europe was characterised by the establishment of permanent villages, reflected in the formation of *tell* sites in Greece, Bulgaria and Serbia. Other features of domestic life, such as the manufacture of painted pottery and clay figurines, and the burial of the dead within houses, were transmitted from South-West Asia as part of this same cultural package (Whittle 1994: 136–49). During the later fifth millennium, however, this pattern of Neolithic life—which Sherratt has termed the 'primary horticultural community'—was altered, as South-East Europe entered the Copper Age (Sherratt 1997a: 359).

The European Copper Age witnessed the penetration of human settlement into mineral-rich zones beyond the core areas of early farming, and a resulting infusion of new materials, notably coloured stones and small quantities of metal, into existing exchange networks. By contrast with Mesopotamia, however, these developments were associated with a decreased emphasis on village life, and with the establishment of large communal cemeteries. The influx of new materials and techniques is reflected in the elaborate contents of burials, which contrast with the increasingly plain character of domestic architecture and equipment. As in the Nile valley, items of personal care and portable objects in metal and highland stone indicate a more mobile pattern of social display, centred upon the body, rather than the house. It has been suggested that the regular flow of resources between upland and lowland zones was linked, both practically and symbolically, to an increasing investment in livestock

---

[20] For the chronological range of Merimda Beni Salama, see also Hassan 1985: 104–5; 1988: 150–1.

as a form of mobile wealth, reflected in the depiction of cattle on sheet-gold ornaments found in the cemetery at Varna, on the shores of the Black Sea (Sherratt 1982; 1994; cf. Hodder 1990: 71–99).

It is this latter, Copper Age cultural pattern to which the Neolithic of the Nile valley bears closest comparison. By contrast with South-East Europe, however, the key elements of the pattern—an emphasis on herding and mobile wealth, the elaboration of portable material culture, and investment in personal and funerary display—were primary characteristics of Neolithic life in Upper Egypt and Sudan, and do not appear to have been superimposed upon an earlier, village-based farming economy. In describing the Neolithic of the Nile valley, the term 'primary pastoral community' (Wengrow 2003b) serves to convey this contrast, while also emphasising the as yet limited importance of domestic animals in providing secondary products such as milk and physical power.

1.6 The reconfiguration of village life in South-West Asia, c.5000–4000 BC

Throughout the fourth millennium both Lower and Upper Egyptian societies continued to be influenced, albeit in different ways, by developments further to the east. This period of rapid change witnessed the cultural and political unification of Egypt and its progressive differentiation from neighbouring societies in North-East Africa. In order to grasp the role played by external factors in these changes, it is necessary to consider a series of earlier social and economic transformations that occurred in South-West Asia during the preceding, fifth millennium, as farming communities were first being established along the Nile valley (fig. 1.5).

Among the most important of these innovations was the cultivation of tree-crops, the wild ancestors of which were distributed around the outer rim of the Fertile Crescent. Olive, fig and almond were concentrated in the Mediterranean highlands, grape in the uplands of eastern Turkey and dates in the palm-groves of the Persian Gulf.[21] From an early stage in their cultivation, tree-crops were subject to secondary techniques of transformation that enhanced their desirability as consumable products. They included the extraction of olive oil and the fermentation of grapes and dates to produce wine, as well as the addition of aromatic flavourings and preservatives (McGovern *et al.* 1997). As Sherratt (1997a: 9–10) has pointed out, it is likely to have been experimentation with the properties of sugar-rich fruits that unlocked the potential for subsequent transformations in the processing of cereals to produce leavened bread and beer, with major consequences for both Mesopotamian and Egyptian society during the fourth millennium (chapter 4).

---

[21] Stager 1985; Esse 1991: 119–25; Lipschitz *et al.* 1991; Zohary 1995; Sherratt 1999.

Regular opportunities for exchange are likely to have been crucial to the development of horticultural products, which required long-term investment in orchards and vineyards, as well as the added labour of processing and packaging. It is therefore no coincidence that, throughout much of the Fertile Crescent, tree-crop horticulture emerged alongside other specialised farming pursuits, notably the raising of wool-sheep and the use of goats for dairying.[22] These developments, which may first have taken place in the upland valleys of western Iran, were rapidly disseminated, with both wool textile and ceramic churns attested in the southern Levant by the beginning of the fourth millennium (Bar-Adon 1980: 143, 153, 229–31). The outcome was a new system of farming, distinguished from its Neolithic precursors by a more diverse use of the landscape, and a higher degree of regional integration between specialised forms of production. They comprised lowland cereal farming, making increasing use of irrigation and the cattle-drawn plough, highland horticulture (olive trees and grape vines) and pastoralism (wool-sheep and milk-goat) in less well-watered upland or steppe zones.

In the Fertile Crescent, the fifth millennium also witnessed the development of complex metallurgical techniques around the sources of native copper in highland Anatolia, in the arid margins of the southern Levant, and at a series of sites extending from the Qazvin Plain (near the southern shores of the Caspian Sea) on to the Iranian plateau (Majidzadeh 1979; Matthews and Fazeli 2004). At Değirmentepe, in south-eastern Turkey, there is evidence for smelting, casting and experimental alloying (Yener 2000). In the southern Levant, copper sources were distributed in a broad arc extending from Wadi Feinan, c.80 km south of the Dead Sea, to southern Sinai. During the Chalcolithic period (c.4500–3500 BC), Feinan ores were transported to village sites established along the major wadi systems of the Beersheba valley, where they were used to cast tools in open moulds. The exotic composition of ceremonial copper objects (containing arsenic and antimony) found at Nahal Mishmar, near the Dead Sea, indicates that metals also circulated on a larger scale along the Mediterranean littoral between Anatolia and the southern Levant.[23]

In the eastern arc of the Fertile Crescent, the distribution of stamp seals bearing increasingly complex figural designs demonstrates the articulation of upland and lowland zones along the hilly flanks of the Zagros Mountains, from Khuzistan to the Tigris piedmont (Pittman 2001: 411–14). Early forms of village bureaucracy allowed domestic products to be removed from everyday routines of consumption and exchange, and mobilised in the acquisition of commodities (e.g. metals, precious stones) that could not be locally produced, and may only occasionally have been available. Within this increasingly fluid arena of interaction, older and less flexible media of display such as ceramics

---

[22] Davis 1984; Philip 2001: 183–9.
[23] Hauptmann 1991; Levy 1995b; Philip and Rehren 1996.

underwent marked simplification and standardisation. Pottery decorated with simple linear designs (Late 'Ubaid ware) is now found over an unprecedented area, reaching from the modern Gulf States and south-western Iran, via Meso-potamia, to the northern Levant and eastern Turkey (Roaf 1990: 51–6). Its production is symptomatic of the intensification of village industries through-out northern and central Mesopotamia, where the reconfiguration of domestic life is apparent in the spread of rectangular houses constructed to a standard tripartite plan (Roaf 1984; 1989). By the close of the fifth millennium, build-ings of this kind had appeared as far north as Değirmentepe, en route to the copper and silver sources of Anatolia, and on the southern Mesopotamian alluvium, where they took on a monumental aspect unknown in their prob-able area of origin (Wengrow 1998: 790–2). The growing scale of inter-regional trade is demonstrated by the transmission of lapis lazuli from north-eastern Afghanistan to villages such as Tepe Gawra, in northern Iraq, while the expansion of sail-powered travel in the Arabian Gulf may be reflected in the design of a model boat found at Eridu in southern Iraq.[24]

1.7 The acceleration of change in Egypt and Lower Nubia, c.4000–3650 BC

During the early centuries of the fourth millennium BC (Naqada I – Naqada IIA–B), the cultural uniformity of the Nile valley came to an end. This growing disparity followed related developments in water transport and cereal cultiva-tion, which gave new salience to the topographical diversity of the valley. South of Aswan, cataracts limited the impact of paddled boats, which now appear among the painted designs on Upper Egyptian pottery (Landström 1970: 11–15; Wengrow 2001a: 97, 100, n.9). Such vessels gradually transformed the pace of life on the Egyptian Nile, where they could travel relatively unhindered from Elephantine to the Mediterranean coast.[25] In consequence, human activ-ity gravitated towards nodal points along the floodplain (cf. Trigger 1983: 27–40). It may be at this juncture (roughly the Naqada I–II transition) that cereal farming began to play a decisive role in Egypt's development, providing oppor-tunities for long-term occupation at key points of contact between the Nile valley and its resource-rich hinterlands. Cultivated cereal grains are found in abundance at early fourth-millennium sites in the Naqada and Armant re-gions, and further south at Hierakonpolis.[26] Increased sedentism is also appar-ent in the adoption of mud-brick, and of plaster derived from mud or animal

---

[24] Rothman 2001b: 391–9; Safar *et al.* 1981: 230–1, fig. 111; cf. Crawford 1998.
[25] Angus Graham (2005) offers an outline of localised, surmountable difficulties encountered by more recent travellers on the Egyptian Nile, the navigability of which has, he points out, occasionally been exaggerated.
[26] el-Hadidi 1982 (Hierakonpolis); Midant-Reynes and Buchez 2002: 485–99 (el-Adaima); Litynska 1994 (Armant-Gurna region); Wetterstrom 1993: 222–4 (Naqada-Khattara region); Rosen 1996 (Hu-Semaina region).

dung, to reinforce post-built structures, although these techniques may not yet have been widespread. Larger and more permanent areas of habitation appear to have developed through the opportunistic clustering of smaller units, rather than as pre-planned or integrated settlements. Evidence of barnyard-like enclosures, a trough containing barley spikelets, and herding stations at Hierakonpolis suggests a desire to combine the maintenance of herds with increased sedentism.

Within these changing patterns of productive life and interaction, further discussed in chapter 4, the development of material culture in Upper Egypt proceeded along lines established in the previous millennium. This is particularly clear in evolving codes of self-presentation, including the addition of figural decoration to a range of cosmetic implements and an increasingly diverse suite of ceramic vessels (chapter 5). Diversification is also apparent in other industries (fig. 1.6) such as the production of stone tools, which now included large blades made on tabular flint and bifacially retouched.[27] Cast copper implements such as chisels, awls, hooks and harpoons were added to the existing range of cold-worked, decorative objects, but there is no direct evidence of metallurgical knowledge within Egypt until the late fourth millennium BC.[28] Most striking, perhaps, is the emergence during Naqada I–II of a stone vessel industry employing a variety of hard and soft materials (e.g. limestone, basalt, diorite) from outcrops in the Nile valley, the Fayum depression and the Eastern Desert. The interiors and handles of these vases were formed using a rotary drilling technique, and copper chisels may have been used to carve smaller features such as lips and handles.[29] Many of these developments in material culture are attested in Lower Nubia (Early A-Group), despite the obstacle to river-borne transport posed by the First Cataract and the more limited extent of arable land there.[30] As demand for imported goods increased within Egypt, this latter region took on new significance in mediating the northward flow of resources such as gold and ebony from the Nubian Desert and sub-Saharan Africa, linking its own social and economic development firmly to that of groups to the north (Smith 1991; Trigger 1976: 38–9).

The early fourth millennium also saw an intensification of cross-cultural interaction along the Mediterranean littoral. Its impact was felt from southeastern Turkey to Lower Egypt, encompassing the Late Chalcolithic and Early Bronze (EB) IA societies of the Levant (Philip 2002; de Miroschedji 2002: 39–41). The circulation of sheet metal throughout this region is indicated by skeuomorphic imitations of carinated serving-bowls and fenestrated vessel-stands. They appear as grey burnished pottery in the northern Levant, with

---

[27] Baumgartel 1960: 26–43; Holmes 1989; Payne 1993: 153–97.
[28] Baumgartel 1960: 2–3, 16–20; Needler 1984: 264, 290–2, cat. 155, 156, 200, 201, 202; Payne 1993: 148, cat. 1231–3.
[29] el-Khouli 1978; Aston 1994; Aston et al. 2000: 64–5.
[30] e.g. Reisner 1910: 132, pls. 62b–c, 63a–b, 64a–b, 66a: 14–18, 66b: 1–13, 68b; Firth 1915, pl. 28c, e.

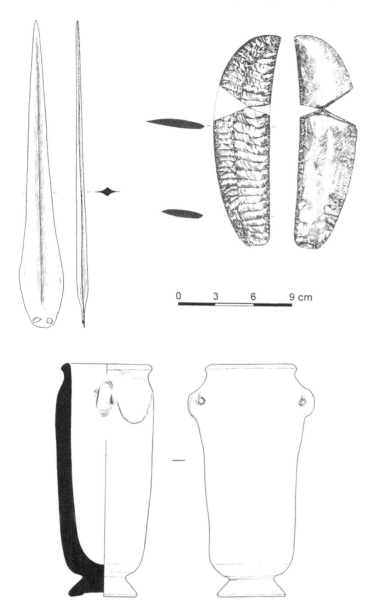

Figure 1.6 Naqada II industries: copper dagger-blade, pressure-flaked flint knife, ground limestone vessel

basalt equivalents traded southwards from the Upper Jordan valley towards the Mediterranean coast (Philip and Williams-Thorpe 1993; Philip and Rehren 1996). The influence of Levantine vessel forms upon ceramic production is evident at the Lower Egyptian site of Maadi, near modern Cairo, and local production of wheel-made bowls and churns at Buto (Stratum I), in the north-western part of the Nile delta, suggests the fluid movement of people, knowledge and consumption practices between these regions.[31] Little of this interaction is reflected in Lower Egyptian cemeteries. Burials at Maadi, Wadi Digla and Heliopolis comprise mostly single inhumations in small pits, with few grave goods and little ornamentation of the body, presenting a clear contrast with the increasingly elaborate burials of Upper Egypt and Lower Nubia.[32] A binary opposition between the cultures of Lower Egypt and the Nile valley is not, however, borne out by ceramic and lithic assemblages from habitation sites. As discussed in chapter 4, these suggest a more complex mosaic of regional traditions throughout Egypt, rooted in the preceding Neolithic period.

Short-haul maritime contacts along the Mediterranean coast may already have been well established by this time, but few traces of them have been identified in the archaeological record (Marcus 2002: 406–7; Sharvit et al. 2002). An impetus towards new modes of overland transport is reflected in figurines from southern Israel, depicting herd animals bearing large vessels (fig. 1.7). By the late fourth millennium this led to the domestication of the donkey and its conversion into a specialised pack animal, with major consequences for interaction between Egypt and the southern Levant (Ovadia 1992; Sherratt 1997a: 209–11).[33] Until that time, the bulk of traffic between these regions appears to have moved from north to south, reflecting the structural position of the Levant in relation to an increasingly urbanised core area, located in south-eastern Turkey and northern Syria.

1.8 Early urbanisation in South-West Asia, c.4000–3300 BC

During the early–mid fourth millennium BC, settlements on the Upper Euphrates and in the piedmont to the east underwent a series of further structural transformations, which were to have repercussions far beyond Mesopotamia. At a number of sites, administrative practices—involving the use of seals to manage and record the flow of people and goods—were concentrated within a small number of buildings, distinguished by their monumental size and public functions, but retaining vernacular traditions of house construction in their layout. At Hacinebi, on the Upper Euphrates, these developments are associated with the smelting and casting of copper on a scale far beyond the

---

[31] Rizkana and Seeher 1987: 73–7; 1989: 78–80; Kantor 1992: 13–14; Faltings 1998a; 2002: 165–7; Faltings et al. 2000: 135–6. Interrelationships have also been discerned between the stone tool assemblages of Maadi and those of sites in the southern Levant (Rizkana and Seeher 1985); vessels of Levantine origin are present among the basalt containers found there (Porat and Seeher 1988).

[32] Rizkana and Seeher 1990 (Maadi and Wadi Digla; also Seeher 1990 for the chronological range of these cemeteries); Debono and Mortensen 1988 (Heliopolis).

[33] For early remains of domesticated donkey (Equus asinus) at Maadi and Tell el-Iswid, in the Nile delta, see Rizkana and Seeher 1989: 75; Boessneck et al. 1989: 90–2; van den Brink et al. 1989.

Figure 1.7 Figurine of a laden donkey, Azor, S. Israel, Early Bronze Age

capacity of any individual household. The location of this site, some two hundred kilometres south of the nearest sources of copper in the Ergani region, indicates the pace at which such materials now moved within the Fertile Crescent (Stein 2002). Other settlements, such as Arslantepe on the Malatya Plain (Frangipane 1997) and Tepe Gawra (Rothman 1994), appear to have developed into regional administrative nodes, each serving a rural hinterland, without becoming large centres of population. At both sites, the growth of centralised institutions precipitated a reduction of residential activity in their immediate vicinities. An exception to this pattern was Tell Brak, in the Khabur region of northern Syria. By the mid-fourth millennium, this site had expanded to a hundred hectares in size, and presents evidence for the centralised management of resources using elaborate pot-marks, tokens, and perhaps also numerical and pictographic notation (Oates 2002). The appearance of the cylinder seal at this time is documented from the Middle Euphrates to Khuzistan, in south-western Iran, where comparable processes of urbanisation and administrative centralisation had been underway since the late fifth millennium BC (Pittman 2001: 419–35; Wright and Johnson 1975).

1.9 Cultural movements and converging networks, c.3650–3300 BC

During Naqada IIC–D (Table 2), display-oriented funerary rituals—and their associated repertoire of cosmetic articles, decorative vessels and personal ornaments—spread northwards from the Nile valley into Lower Egypt. This development created an area of broadly uniform material culture, extending from Upper Egypt to the mouth of the Nile delta. It also had a clear impact upon Lower Nubia (chapter 8), where Middle A-Group burials contain large numbers of Egyptian imports, alongside an increasingly well-defined range of local object-types such as ripple-burnished and heavily incised pottery. A further shift of human habitation towards the Nile alluvium at this time renders many key occupation sites in Egypt inaccessible to modern investigation. Increasing use of mud-brick in both living and funerary contexts can be detected at Hierakonpolis and Naqada in Upper Egypt. Much architecture, however, remained in perishable media such as reed matting. These changing patterns of settlement, discussed in chapter 4, are echoed in the proliferation and expansion of cemeteries, particularly in Upper Egypt along the Qena bend (from Abydos to Armant) and further south to Kom Ombo.

At Hierakonpolis, the concentration of activity along the floodplain is associated with the earliest evidence for specialised manufacturing areas, including a bounded ceremonial complex (HK29A) that yielded vast quantities of stone debitage (chapter 4.3).[34] The co-ordination and refinement of craft production is evident throughout Egypt and Lower Nubia at this time in the increasingly sophisticated objects that were deposited as grave goods. These now included composite items such as pressure-flaked flint knives, hafted to wooden or ivory handles with delicately carved surface ornament (fig. 9.5).[35] Such handles were sometimes embossed with sheet gold, and both gold and silver foil were used to ornament stone vessels, now fashioned from an increasingly wide range of patterned materials such as porphyry and serpentine.[36] A new form of painted pottery (known as D-Ware) was also developed, using marl clays of limited distribution, rather than the abundant Nile silt from which earlier fine wares were made (fig. 4.6). In their form and, occasionally, their surface decoration, these vessels replicated the appearance of contemporary stone vases.

The volume of copper objects in Egyptian and Lower Nubian burials increased markedly during Naqada IIC–D, as did the scale and sophistication of

---

[34] Numbers in parentheses refer to particular sections within chapters.
[35] Needler 1984: 265–8, cat. 160–4; Payne 1993: 166–79, cat. 1385–1477, figs. 65–8.
[36] Baumgartel 1960: 3–10; Payne 1993: 139, 141, 168, cat. 1155, 1180, 1390.

individual pieces. They now included implements such as axes, adzes and ribbed knife-blades, of which a single example in silver is attested from a burial at el-Amra.[37] Both the form and technological properties of these items point towards close relationships with contemporary (early EB IB) metallurgical industries in the southern Levant.[38] The latter underwent significant restructuring during this period, which set a pattern for Levantine metalwork that lasted throughout the Early Bronze Age (EB I–III; c.3600–2300 BC; Shalev 1994). Copper was extracted at the mining source, and manufacturing processes, now separated in time and space from smelting operations, became increasingly standardised. Hammering and annealing of sheet metal was adopted as the basic technique for producing a wide range of objects, from ornaments and vessels to tools and weaponry. Metal also began to circulate in semi-processed form, either as ingots cast in shallow moulds, or as standardised pieces of sheet (Rehren *et al.* 1997; Golden 2002). An Early Bronze Age hoard of copper objects from Kfar Monash, in Israel's central coastal plain, contained some eight hundred such pieces, packaged in groups of between eight and ten (Tadmor 2002: 240).

The scale of interaction between Egypt and the Levant was transformed during the mid-fourth millennium by the establishment of a pack-donkey route, crossing from the Nile delta to southern Israel across northern Sinai, where a network of small sites sprang up (Oren 1989). It is during this period that small quantities of Egyptian material, including D-Ware and cosmetic palettes, as well as remains of imported fish and molluscs (transported in ceramic jars), begin to appear at sites along the southern coastal plain of the Levant (Oren and Yekutieli 1992; de Miroschedji 2002: 40–4). Cultivated grape vines had by now been transferred to the central highlands of Palestine from their native habitat to the north, and the appearance of imported ledge-handled jars in Egypt during Naqada IIC–D may represent the beginnings of a southward trade in processed liquid commodities such as wine, resin and olive oil (van den Brink and Braun 2002: 168, n.3; Hendrickx and Bavay 2002: 67). At roughly the same time, local variants of coarse pottery were replaced throughout Egypt with a relatively standard suite of straw-tempered bowls, necked jars and basins. It seems likely that their adoption was linked to the use of cereals in the production of leavened bread and beer, echoing earlier developments in the alluvial lowlands of Mesopotamia (chapter 4.4, 4.5). It is also from this point onwards that large numbers of coarse vessels, and their contents, began to be regularly included in Egyptian burial assemblages, augmenting a trend that commenced at the start of the Naqada II period.

---

[37] Baumgartel 1960: 10–16; Needler 1984: 280–2, cat. 180–3; Payne 1993: 146–7, cat. 1215–20; Randall-MacIver and Mace 1902: 23, pl. 6: 1–2.
[38] Hestrin and Tadmor 1963; Ben-Tor 1971 (with alternative chronology); Tadmor 2002.

The growing momentum of material transfers across the whole of South-West Asia is reflected at this time in the presence of small, but consistent, quantities of lapis lazuli in Upper Egyptian graves (Hendrickx and Bavay 2002: 61–6). Finished items of Mesopotamian or Iranian derivation, of which cylinder and stamp seals—supremely portable and durable—are the main surviving examples, also entered Naqada IIC–D Egypt through established lines of contact extending along the Mediterranean littoral.[39] At their northern extremities, on the Upper Euphrates, these channels of supply converged with larger networks encompassing the Tigris and Euphrates basins, now closely articulated with the urban centres of southern Mesopotamia and Khuzistan (fig. 7.1; cf. Nissen 2001). Within Egypt, the procurement of such objects, and the images they carried, coincided with (and was in part motivated by) a phase of unprecedented innovation in funerary practices, which by Naqada II were rapidly becoming a primary forum for competitive social transactions and ceremonial display (chapter 5).

The overview provided in this chapter no doubt excludes information that some consider essential, and may give an impression of finality to what often remain unresolved issues of interpretation. It is best thought of as a skeletal account of times, places and large-scale transformations, to which the flesh of local meanings and the skin of social change will now be added.

[39] Moorey 1987; cf. Joffe 2000; Philip 2002.

NEOLITHIC ECONOMY AND SOCIETY

2.1 To begin at the end

The Narmer Palette (figs. 2.1, 2.2) is one of the best-known artefacts of the ancient world. It was discovered over a century ago at the site of Hierakonpolis in Upper Egypt (Quibell 1898). Over 60 cm in height, the palette is one of a series of elaborately carved, portable objects dating to the formative period of dynastic culture in Egypt, around the turn of the third millennium BC. Other well-known examples include the Narmer Mace-head (fig. 2.3), which depicts the presentation of cattle, goats and human captives to a seated ruler (Millet 1990); the famous flint knife reportedly acquired near Gebel el-Araq (fig. 2.4), its decorated ivory handle showing a scene of combat (Sievertsen 1992); and a slightly later ivory comb bearing the name of a king of the First Dynasty (fig. 2.5). As Frankfort (1951: 79) observed, the material and shape of the Narmer Palette 'proclaim it a specimen of a common type of toilet article'. On its obverse, a small circular depression is left between the intertwined necks of two mythical creatures for the grinding and containment of pigments, thereafter mixed into a coloured paste and applied to a human body, or perhaps that of a statue (cf. O'Connor 2002: 9–10).

Interpretations of the Narmer Palette have traditionally focused upon its significance as a marker of discontinuity, signifying the emergence of a new social and political order, with its attendant modes of communication and display.[1] Its decorative scenes constitute an early and definitive manifestation of what was by then a standard mode of representation relating to dynastic rulers in Egypt. The king smiting his enemies remained an important motif throughout the Old, Middle and New Kingdoms and into Roman times, when it was reproduced in monumental scale on the outer walls of temples (Hall 1986). By contrast, the cosmetic function of the palette (or, if it was never actually used, the function to which its form refers) has rarely been considered as a core aspect of its meaning. Any such consideration must be oriented towards continuities with the prehistoric past, rather than the discontinuities associated with the process of state formation. For while ceremonial objects of this kind ceased to be made during the early part of the First Dynasty, their less

---

[1] e.g. Asselberghs 1961: 291; Kaiser 1964; 1990; cf. Köhler 2002.

Figure 2.1 The Narmer Palette, reverse side, from the Main Deposit,
          Hierakonpolis

ornate precursors, and the techniques of personal care and display they embody, had a history of social use extending back some two thousand years
(Wengrow 2001a). The ceremonial maces, knives and combs of this period are
also large and elaborate versions of common artefact types that first became

Figure 2.2 The Narmer Palette, obverse side

widespread in the Nile valley, along with cosmetic palettes, during the fifth and early fourth millennia. These objects conveyed meaning at the level of close interpersonal conduct and performance, drawing from and transforming an archive of cultural practices and knowledge that became established at the onset of the Neolithic period. To examine the Neolithic of the Nile valley is

Figure 2.3 The Narmer Mace-head, from the Main Deposit, Hierakonpolis

therefore to consider, not only the material foundations of the early Egyptian state, laid down through the domestication of animals and plants, but also its social foundations.

2.2 The inception of Neolithic economy and society

In the Nile valley, the adoption of domestic animals is attested prior to that of cereal farming, and gave rise to a pattern of Neolithic cultural development readily distinguishable from those of South-West Asia and Europe. In its essentials this pattern, which I described earlier as the 'primary pastoral community',

Figure 2.4 The Gebel el-Araq Knife

remained common to the Nile valley, from the Khartoum region of central Sudan to the Asyut/el-Badari region of Middle Egypt, throughout the fifth millennium. It can also be traced in the neighbouring deserts to the east and west, but appears not to have taken root in Lower Egypt, where a distinct form of Neolithic life developed. In terms of social and cultural development, a broad regional distinction between the Nile valley and Lower Egypt is therefore more salient than that between Egypt and Sudan for the period in question. An outline of this development has been presented in chapter 1. Here I document transformations in material culture and social life that accompanied the adoption of domesticates, and in the next chapter I explore how these various fields of innovation were interrelated during the fifth

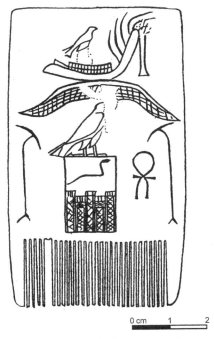

Figure 2.5 Ivory comb, inscribed with the name of Djet, Abydos, First Dynasty

millennium. The first aim is most simply achieved through a somewhat artificial division of the evidence along conventional lines of economy, habitation, craft and ritual. In moving beyond this division, the second aim will require us to range more widely in the archaeological and anthropological literature, and to critically examine a series of general preconceptions about mobile communities, past and present, and about processes of innovation in Neolithic societies.

Evidence for herding, hunting and plant cultivation

By the beginning of the fifth millennium BC domestic herds, including sheep, goats and cattle, had been adopted throughout much of Egypt and Sudan (Gautier 1987; Chenal-Velardé 1997). At some sites, such as Kadero and Umm Direiwa in central Sudan, they make up the bulk of the faunal assemblage (Gautier 1984; Tigani el-Mahi 1988: 53–62). At others in the same region, such as Shaheinab, aquatic resources predominate (Peters 1986). Neolithic sites along the Egyptian Nile valley, where this period is termed the Badarian after the modern town of el-Badari (c.30 km south-east of Asyut), were excavated during the early twentieth century, when little reliable information was recorded concerning the associated economy.[2] The presence there of domesticated animals has been widely assumed on the basis of dung deposits at habitation sites (Wetterstrom 1993: 214–16; Midant-Reynes 2000: 160), and recent excavations at Mahgar Dendera 2 in Upper Egypt support this interpretation (Hendrickx *et al.* 2001: 91–102). Small numbers of wild mammal bones, including hippopotamus, antelope and gazelle, are present in Neolithic faunal assemblages from both Egypt and Sudan, and the continued importance of hunting is evident in contemporary stone tool assemblages. In Egypt these assemblages feature a significant component of projectile points (Tangri 1992), while in central Sudan it is microliths (most commonly lunates), rather than arrowheads, that constitute the main evidence of hunting technology (e.g. Haaland 1987: 74; Caneva 1988, fig. 21). This disparity may to some extent reflect the different potential of local raw materials. Many Sudanese tools were made on small quartz pebbles, while those of Upper Egypt were flaked from the large flint cores available there in abundance. In Badarian Egypt, flint also formed the raw material for a range of new scraping, cutting and piercing implements, replacing the microlithic industries of the Early Holocene (Holmes 1989: 101–7, 176–88; Hendrickx *et al.* 2001: 29–58).

Evidence for plant use in Sudan during the Neolithic derives largely from grain impressions preserved on pot-sherds, which offer evidence of sorghum exploitation but do not indicate whether this grain was cultivated (Stemler 1990). The fruits of the hackberry tree and dom palm were also collected in the Khartoum region. Plant remains from Badarian sites in Middle Egypt have never been systematically studied, but crops of South-West Asian derivation (emmer wheat, six-row hulled barley and flax) were identified during the original excavations (Wetterstrom 1993: 216, with references). More extensive studies have been undertaken of plant remains from Neolithic (Fayum A) sites distributed around the former shores of Birket Qarun (Lake Moeris) in the Fayum depression. One particular location, known as Kom K, produced abundant evidence for the storage of emmer wheat and six-row barley in pits lined with baskets and matting. In the Fayum, the raising of these cultivars, as well as flax and a range of animal domesticates, appears to have been integrated into a much broader seasonal pattern of hunting, fishing and foraging practices (Wetterstrom 1993: 204–11).

The case for independent cattle domestication in Egypt

On the basis of excavations in the eastern Sahara, Fred Wendorf and Romuald Schild have argued that cattle were independently domesticated during the

---

[2] Brunton and Caton-Thompson 1928; Brunton 1937; 1948. The chronological range of known Badarian sites covers the latter half of the fifth millennium, such that the early part of the Nile valley Neolithic is currently better represented in central and northern Sudan.

Early Holocene in the semi-arid margins of Egypt's Western Desert (e.g. Wendorf and Schild 1980: 277–8; 2001: 653–8). The principal area concerned is Nabta Playa, a large, internally drained basin lying approximately 100 km west of Abu Simbel, near what is today Egypt's southern border. The postulated episode of cattle domestication is dated to the ninth millennium BC, and a regional chronology has been proposed in which the Neolithic of Nabta Playa commences some four thousand years before that of the Nile valley (see also Wendorf and Schild 1998). No firm evidence of cattle domestication in North-East Africa is available between the eighth and sixth millennia, so it is not clear what is supposed to have become of these early cattle-keepers during the intervening period, which is represented by only a single site (E-75–8) at Nabta Playa itself (Close 2001). The material culture of Nabta Playa during the el-Adam phase (c.8750–7700 BC) is not markedly different from that of other Early Holocene sites in the eastern Sahara and Nile valley (Wendorf and Schild 2001: 653–4), and hence the case for independent cattle domestication rests, in its own proponents' terms, upon 'ecological arguments, and less firmly on metrical evidence' (Wendorf and Schild 2002: 14).

The metrical evidence for cattle domestication draws upon a very small and equivocal assemblage of bone and tooth. One recent re-examination of the sizes of Early Holocene *Bos* bones from Nabta Playa and nearby Bir Kiseiba does 'not support the notion that these cattle were domestic' (Grigson 2000: 47–9, fig. 4.7). The earliest clear evidence for a reduction in the size of cattle bones dates to the sixth and fifth millennia, but it is unclear whether this is due to the introduction of domestic herds from further east or a gradual, local process of herd management (Gautier 2001: 625–9, fig. 23.2). A combination of the two processes is also possible, with local cattle domestication set in motion by the arrival of domesticated sheep and goats.

The argument that cattle domestication began independently at Nabta Playa during the Early Holocene is based on the assertion that wild cattle could not otherwise have survived in this region, due to its aridity. However, botanical remains demonstrate that this locale was situated close to the northern frontier of savannah vegetation, and such semi-arid environments are known to have supported wild mammals throughout much of post-Pleistocene Africa.[3] The implications for this debate of mitochondrial DNA evidence for the ancient divergence of Old World *Bos* species remain equally equivocal (Bradley and Loftus 2000: 249; *contra* Wendorf and Schild 1998: 101). Finally, it seems highly unlikely that Early Holocene cattle could have served as 'walking larders' in the manner suggested by the excavators of Nabta Playa. The earliest phases of domestication would have involved the removal of small numbers of animals from wild populations and minor alterations in their behaviour, rather

---

[3] Wasylikowa 2001: 581–6; cf. Smith 1986; Muzzolini 1989; MacDonald 2000: 4–6.

than any systematic attempt at manipulating reproductive patterns in favour of enhanced milk yields (Higgs and Jarman 1972: 5–7; Uerpmann 1979: 126).[4] That such sustained manipulation could have occurred among relatively small communities already engaged in a wide range of other subsistence pursuits seems still less plausible. While earlier attempts at animal management cannot be entirely excluded, the first secure evidence for cattle domestication in the eastern Sahara therefore corresponds chronologically to the wider regional pattern outlined above.

Habitation sites and cemeteries

Badarian habitation sites have been identified along the desert margins of the floodplain in central Egypt, with concentrations at Matmar, Mostagedda, el-Badari and Hammamiya (Holmes and Friedman 1994; above, n.2). Each occupation is composed of a series of superimposed deposits containing quantities of ash, charcoal and cultural debris. These middens often reached considerable heights and were sometimes associated with hearths and storage pits, but no traces of permanent residential architecture were recorded.[5] Many comprised thick layers of animal dung, as well as remnants of ephemeral enclosures.[6] Located c.150 km south of el-Badari, and dating to the very end of the fifth millennium, Mahgar Dendera 2 is the only Badarian site in the Egyptian Nile valley to have been excavated on a significant scale since the early twentieth century (Hendrickx *et al.* 2001). It is similarly located above the floodplain, on the low fringes of the Western Desert. A lack of stratified deposits indicates that the site was produced through a single and relatively brief episode of use, during which numerous hearths were established. Postholes and pits, some of which contained storage jars, constitute the only other evidence of occupation. The predominance of fish and livestock within the faunal assemblage suggests that this site was inhabited as part of a seasonal round of habitation, rather than as a permanent settlement.

Over the last two decades, numerous contemporary (Khartoum Neolithic) sites and cemeteries have been excavated in central Sudan, between the confluence of the White and Blue Niles and the Sixth Cataract.[7] Building upon the pioneering work of Arkell (1953) at Shaheinab, this fieldwork, which includes

---

[4] For some of the adaptive complexities involved in the regular extraction by humans of milk yields from prehistoric herds (at first almost certainly ovicaprids rather than cattle), and their archaeological recognition, see Sherratt 1997a: 174–82, 205–8; McCormick 1992.

[5] Caton-Thompson reported 2 m of midden deposit at Hammamiya (North Spur; Brunton and Caton-Thompson 1928: 69, 72–4); see also Brunton 1937: 7–25, pl. 21b; 1948: 4–7; Holmes and Friedman 1994: 118.

[6] Brunton and Caton-Thompson 1928: 94, 106 (Areas A1, E); Brunton 1937: 14, 21; 1948: 5; and cf. Krzyżaniak 1977: 70; Hassan 1988: 154.

[7] Mohammed-Ali 1982; Haaland 1987; Caneva 1988; Krzyżaniak 1991; for chronology, see also Hassan 1986.

regional surveys, reveals for the first time the overall character of Neolithic society along the southern extent of the Nile valley. As already noted, the most striking point to emerge has been the continuity of practices in habitation, exchange, material culture and mortuary customs between this region and the Egyptian Nile valley, far to the north.[8] To date, there has been only limited investigation of Neolithic sites between these two distant areas, and many are rendered permanently inaccessible by major dam construction. Nevertheless, fieldwork in the vicinity of the Fourth Cataract and along the Dongola Reach (e.g. at Umm Melyekta in the Amri-Kirbekan region, and at Kadruka and Site R12 in the Seleim Basin) has produced vital evidence, in the form of Neolithic cemeteries, linking the northern and southern extremities of the Nile valley (fig. 1.5).[9]

Habitation sites of the Khartoum Neolithic are located either on raised levees along the edges of the alluvium (e.g. el-Geili, Shaheinab), or some kilometres into the adjacent plains, often atop natural promontories (e.g. el-Zakiab, Umm Direiwa, Kadero). As in Middle and Upper Egypt, they comprise unstratified midden deposits, largely devoid of surviving architectural features. A concentration of hearths found at Shaheinab constitutes the only clear evidence of fixed, permanent installations presently known.[10] Throughout the Egyptian and Sudanese Nile valley, this apparent poverty of domestic remains contrasts with the rich material culture associated with contemporary burial grounds. Along a 35 km stretch of the Middle Egyptian Nile, from Etmaniya to Matmar, over 750 Badarian graves were excavated in the low desert abutting the floodplain during the early twentieth century.[11] They may now be compared with contemporary cemeteries in central Sudan, such as those of Kadero (Krzyżaniak 1984; 1991) and el-Ghaba (Geus 1986; Lecointe 1987), and in northern Sudan, such as R12 (Salvatori and Usai 2001; 2002) and the extensive burial grounds of Kadruka (Reinold 1991; 1994; 2001). Unlike those of the Egyptian Nile valley, cemeteries of the Khartoum Neolithic were often established on raised mounds, which in some cases appear to have been formed through human activity (Reinold 2001: 9).

Burial rites and a new system of objects

Throughout much of the area described, from Middle Egypt to modern Khartoum, funerary rites took on a strikingly similar form during the fifth millennium BC. Cemeteries usually contained a cross-section of the living population, including adults of both sexes and children. Most comprise between

---

[8] See also Wengrow 2001a; 2003b; Edwards 2003: 150; O'Connor and Reid 2003b: 18.
[9] Welsby 2003: 569–72; Fuller 2004; Reinold 1994; 2001; Salvatori and Usai 2001; 2002.
[10] Arkell 1953: 79–81; cf. Haaland 1987: 39–47; Caneva 1988: 26.
[11] Brunton and Caton-Thompson 1928, pls. 2, 5–8; Brunton 1937, pls. 1–4, 7–10; 1948: pls. 1–3; Anderson 1992: 54; Holmes and Friedman 1994: 100.

50 and 300 graves, suggesting the division of commemorative space between numerous, relatively small social units, although much larger Neolithic cemeteries, perhaps containing over 1000 graves, are documented at Kadruka in northern Sudan. While the contents of particular interments differed, all appear to represent variations within a common, loosely structured form of funerary practice, applied equally to adults and infants. Its material characteristics may be broadly outlined.

The individual was laid within an oval pit in a flexed position, knees contracted and hands often cupping the face. The body was wrapped in animal skins or reed mats and decorated with ornaments made of coloured stone beads, pierced shells, worked bone, tooth and ivory: remnant vocabulary from a lost language of display, which must have expressed occasions in the human lifecycle other than death alone. Many ornaments have been found *in situ*, indicating that they were worn over a wide range of body parts including the wrist, ankle, arm, leg, head, neck and around the waist. Nose and lip studs are also common.[12] Around the decorated body were placed salient artefacts of the social world (fig. 2.8). These typically included small pottery vessels and simple cosmetic palettes accompanied by grinding pebbles and pigments (sometimes found within leather pouches or other small containers), as well as implements made of bone or ivory. While Badarian cosmetic palettes are usually made from siltstone (previously termed 'slate' or 'schist') and grooved for suspension (Baumgartel 1960: 55–7), those of the Khartoum Neolithic are sandstone or porphyry, and most are not grooved (Geus 1984b: 30; Krzyżaniak 1991: 523). Malachite, obtained from deposits in the Eastern Desert, is the most frequently reported pigment in Badarian graves, and produced a green stain. Galena, derived from lead ores located close to the Red Sea coast, was discovered in a burial at Mostagedda. Red and yellow ochre were also used in Egypt, but appear to have been more common in burials of the Khartoum Neolithic.[13]

Animal bone and ivory were also put to new decorative and practical uses during the fifth millennium BC, including the manufacture of bands for the arms and legs, often worn in considerable numbers. Combs make their first appearance in Badarian graves, as do spatulas, probably used with small ivory vessels and hollowed tusks for mixing and manipulating fluids (fig. 2.6).[14] Similar articles have been recovered from burials at Kadruka, but more humid conditions further south have caused organic material to decompose, a factor that must be taken into account in considering their apparent absence (as well

---

[12] For the disposition of body ornaments, see e.g. Brunton and Caton-Thompson 1928: 27–8; Brunton 1937: 29, 52, 85–6; 1948: pl. 70; Geus 1984b: 21, 30, figs. 48, 67; Lecointe 1987: 76, 86–7, pls. 2: 1–2, 3: 1; Krzyżaniak 1991: 522–3, 528, fig. 10.

[13] Lucas 1962: 80, 243; Aston *et al.* 2000: 43–4 (Egypt); Lecointe 1987: 76; Geus 1991: 58; Krzyżaniak 1991: 520, 524–5, fig. 3, table 2 (Sudan).

[14] Brunton and Caton-Thompson 1928: 30–1, pls. 22–7; Brunton 1937: 30, 53–4, 57, pls. 13, 22–4.

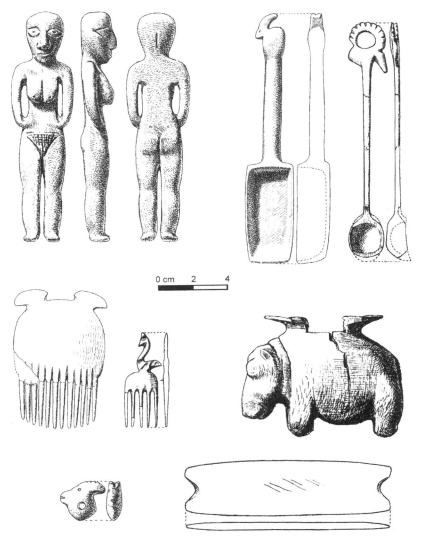

Figure 2.6 Neolithic objects from burials in the el-Badari region, Middle Egypt

as that of leather and woven items) in the Khartoum region.[15] It is in this latter region that ground and polished stone mace-heads, which were to become a common feature of Egyptian material culture during the fourth millennium

---

[15] Reinold 2000: 78–9; Salvatori and Usai 2001: 15, fig. 12; and see Geus 1984b: 23, fig. 55; Lecointe 1987: 73.

Figure 2.7 Badarian ceramic vessel

BC (Naqada I–II; fig. 5.4), make their first appearance as grave goods in Neolithic burials (Lecointe 1987, figs. 5, 7; Krzyżaniak 1991: 523, fig. 11: 4).

The fifth millennium also saw the introduction of polished ceramics in the Nile valley, and these too are known primarily from funerary deposits. Most take the form of small hemispherical or globular bowls, the outer surfaces of which were coated with a red ochre wash and burnished. On Egyptian (Badarian) wares, the burnishing overlies an earlier stage of decoration, in which the thin vessel wall was combed to create a rippled texture. In the course of firing these vessels acquired a distinct black band around the area of the mouth (fig. 2.7; below, chapter 4.5). In terms of its final appearance, and perhaps in aspects of its manufacture, this type of Badarian ware appears to emulate leather prototypes (Baumgartel 1955: 17; cf. Van Driel-Murray 2000: 302–8). This impression is reinforced by the punctuated incisions with which some vessels are marked, mimicking the seams that bound their leather counterparts together. The arid setting of Neolithic cemeteries in Middle Egypt has also preserved actual leather objects, including bags, headrests, ornaments and clothing, as well as examples of matting and coiled basketry.[16]

---

[16] Brunton and Caton-Thompson 1928, graves 5739, 5773, 5802, 5803, 5805, 5806; Brunton 1937, graves 303, 408, 438, 497, 2224, 2229, 2853, 3538, 5213.

Polished bowls with round bases and red-coated surfaces are also typical of Neolithic pottery in the Khartoum region, and some vessels exhibit blackened rims. Like Badarian pottery they were made from Nile silt, but unlike the former they retained Early Holocene forms of stamped or impressed surface decoration.[17]

Neolithic networks in the Eastern and Western Deserts

As noted in chapter 1, the contents of Neolithic burials in the Nile valley clearly demonstrate the extraction and circulation of mineral and metal resources from the Eastern Desert. There has occasionally been a tendency to project a much later contrast between 'desert' and 'sown' on to this early phase of development, leading some scholars to envisage distinct 'valley' and 'desert' cultures or even populations, or to postulate large-scale migrations from one area to another. As Majer (1992) observes, however, the sheer quantity of desert resources in valley cemeteries suggests the existence of regular networks of procurement and exchange throughout the fifth millennium (cf. Tutundzic 1989). It is plausible that some part of the rich corpus of rock art documented from the Eastern and Western Deserts was created at this time, but attempts to isolate Neolithic imagery from other carvings have to date been speculative (chapter 5.2).

Neolithic habitation sites are reported from the Western Desert at Nabta Playa (Mohamed 2001) and Dakhla Oasis (Bashendi B phase; McDonald 1998; 1999), where they are characterised by dense agglomerations of stone-filled hearths. An increase in exotic materials such as coloured stones and marine shells is reported in the latter area, reflecting its location at the terminus of a major wadi system entering the Nile valley via Kharga Oasis to the east. The clearest evidence for contacts between the valley and the adjacent deserts derives from occasional discoveries of burials, rather than occupation sites. Isolated graves containing typical Badarian artefacts (rectangular and oval palettes, pigments, coloured beads, marine shell, etc.) have been found in the heart of Egypt's Eastern Desert, along the Wadi Hammamat (Debono 1950; 1951) and the Wadi Atulla (Friedman and Hobbs 2002), and near the Red Sea coast at Ras Samadi (Murray and Derry 1923; Resch 1963b). A number of tumulus burials, one of which contained a gold-wire bracelet, have also been dated to this period along the Wadi Elei in the eastern desert of Lower Nubia (Sadr 1997).

A group of Neolithic burials, furnished with the usual range of body ornaments and cosmetic equipment, has also been discovered at Gebel Ramlah, approximately 25 km north-west of Gebel Nabta in Egypt's south-western desert (Schild et al. 2002). Among the grave goods found there were examples

---

[17] Arkell 1953: 75–6; Chłodnicki 1984; Krzyżaniak 1991: 520–2.

of a distinctive type of tulip-shaped ('caliciform') beaker, decorated with incised and stippled patterns and pierced for suspension. Similar vessels are documented from Wadi Atulla and from Early Neolithic cemeteries in the Dongola Reach (e.g. Reinold 2000: 61; Salvatori and Usai 2002: 5, fig. 5), but are almost completely unknown from the Badarian cemeteries of Middle Egypt.[18] Given the relatively late chronological range of the latter (c.4500–4000 BC), this pattern of finds may point towards an Early Neolithic phase, dating to the early–mid fifth millennium BC, which is not yet fully attested in the Egyptian Nile valley, but may have existed there as well.[19]

Earliest images

The Neolithic period has produced the earliest clearly dated examples of representational art in the Nile valley, comprising a handful of figurines and ornamented objects, some of which are represented in figure 2.6. The earliest documented appearance of clay animal figurines in Egypt in fact derives, not from the valley, but from the village site of Merimda Beni Salama on the western edge of the Nile delta (chapter 1.5). Fourteen examples were published from excavated levels spanning the entire occupation, which may cover a considerable portion of the fifth millennium. Aside from the layer in which they were discovered, little is known of their archaeological contexts. All are identified in the site report as representations of domestic cattle, and some commentators have contrasted this apparent predominance with the diverse nature of the faunal assemblage at the site, suggesting a special role for cattle in local systems of belief and symbolic behaviour.[20] Most of the figurines are, however, much too fragmentary to be identified with any particular species, and the more complete examples vary substantially in size and form, making it difficult to accept the proposal that they represent any single species.

Four Badarian graves in Middle Egypt each contained a single human figurine in clay; a highly schematic animal figurine is also reported from this region.[21] Animal forms are more widely documented among the carved implements and ornaments deposited as grave goods at el-Badari and Mostagedda. They include two bone pendants, one found in an adult's grave with a string of

---

[18] A comparable, but not identical vessel was found in a burial in the el-Badari region, together with a loop-handled, globular jar, the closest parallels for which are in the southern Levant; see Kantor 1992: 12; Friedman 1999a.

[19] Renée Friedman (Friedman and Hobbs 2002) associates this phase with Guy Brunton's (1937) problematic identification of a 'Tasian' culture, represented by c.50 burials in Middle Egypt, which he dated earlier than neighbouring Badarian cemeteries on typological grounds that have been widely questioned (Kaiser 1985a; Friedman 1999a; Midant-Reynes 2000: 165–6).

[20] Eiwanger 1984: 114; 1988: 96–7; 1992: 59–60, 127, n.299; Midant-Reynes 2000: 117.

[21] Brunton and Caton-Thompson 1928, pl. 24: 1, 3; Brunton 1937, pl. 24: 31–2; and see Ucko 1968: 69–71, cat. 1–3.

bone beads, and the other in an infant's grave together with beads and Red
Sea shells (Brunton and Caton-Thompson 1928, pls. 6, 8, 24: 14–15, 27: 1).
Among the ivory spoons found in burials at these two sites, six had handles
extending into animal forms, providing both ornamentation and a means of
gripping and suspension. Some handles take the form of horned animals, and
one terminates in what appear to be human hands. A wide-toothed comb
with a handle fashioned into an avian form was found in a burial at
Mostagedda, deposited together with an ivory spoon and tusk, both bearing
traces of green pigment (Brunton 1937: 34, pls. 24: 21–2, vii). Finally, a detailed
carving of a hippopotamus, hollowed out to serve as a container, was discovered within a rare multiple burial containing the remains of three individuals at the same site (Brunton 1937: 53, pl. 24: 33). Various miniature
objects from Early Neolithic burials in Sudan have been tentatively identified
as human or animal figurines; all, however, are highly schematic (e.g. Reinold
2000: 67).

Ritual treatments of human and animal bodies

Among the most intriguing features of Neolithic life in the Nile valley is the
interment of animals, whole or partial, within human cemeteries and burials.
The practice was common to Egypt and Sudan, but with regional variations in
the selection, treatment and positioning of body parts.[22] A review of these
practices provides the opportunity for fuller description of particular human
burials, best exemplified from the Khartoum Neolithic. Such 'thick description' is necessary in order to convey the complexity and variability of activities
performed around the human body in death, the wider implications of which
are considered in the following chapter.

At el-Badari (Cemetery 5300–5400), animal burials formed a discrete concentration adjacent to two larger groups of human burials. They lay in individual oval pits and included a large bovid 'covered in matting in exactly the
same way as the human burials' (Brunton and Caton-Thompson 1928: 12). The
body had been disturbed and was missing its skull. Another bovid burial was
complete but for a single horn core, the remaining horn curving downwards
over the skull; this may indicate that horns were sometimes deliberately
'trained' into particular shapes, a widespread practice among more recent
pastoralists. Directly to the north lay the graves of two caprids, both disturbed
and one containing traces of matting. The mixed burial of an infant together
with the partial remains of a calf was noted within a nearby cluster of human
graves. Fish spines were included among the grave goods in two heavily disturbed burials in Cemetery 5100, which also contained the discrete burial of a

---

[22] The Egyptian data are described by Flores 2003: 13–14, 67–8, 81–2, but their value is limited by
the lack of reliable species-identification in early twentieth-century excavation reports.

canid, covered with matting (Brunton and Caton-Thompson 1928: 6–7, 10–12, 18, pl. 10: 6). At Mostagedda, various body parts of small ruminants were found within the graves of adults and infants, widely distributed among the other burials. The complete skeletons of animals tentatively identified as gazelle were found within two adult burials, in one case accompanied by the remains of a felid. Feathers were placed above the heads of three undisturbed human burials, including that of an infant, and lay across the body of a fourth, a practice also documented from an infant burial at el-Badari (Brunton 1937: 5–7, 34, 42, 57, pl. 6: 8).

Several stone-built tumuli containing both articulated and disarticulated remains of cattle are reported from a late sixth–fifth millennium site at Nabta Playa. They line the edge of a wadi leading to the remnants of a former seasonal lake. The excavators have proposed that these burials form part of a complex of 'megalithic' sculpture and architecture, incorporating a solar calendar made up of small sandstone slabs (Wendorf and Schild 2001: 463–520). The *in situ* evidence for these structures is weak, however, as is their dating, which rests upon three widely varying radiocarbon determinations and a small number of loosely associated artefacts.

Along the Dongola Reach, in the central Sudanese Nile valley, the placing of cattle horns within both adult and infant burials appears to have become a common practice during the Neolithic. At Site R12, a cemetery containing an estimated 250–300 burials, bucrania were typically found lying close to or upon the head (fig. 2.8). An example is the grave of an adult male interred with numerous cosmetic palettes and bone spatulae carrying traces of ochre, fragments of which (including yellow, white and red chunks) were also placed within the grave. Among the other grave goods were five stone axes of various materials, a necklace made up of cornelian, agate, amazonite and shell beads, and a large shell containing a group of unfinished bead-blanks in agate and quartz, awaiting perforation. Remains of goat kids were also found in two human burials at this site (Salvatori and Usai 2002: 4–5, fig. 2, pls. 2–4).

Ritual treatments of animal bodies at Kadruka are exemplified by a well-preserved burial from Cemetery KDK 1 (Reinold 1987: 50). The grave was cut into sandy soil and its extent indicated by a fugitive colouring around the body; perhaps the remains of an animal skin. The interred was an adult female, loosely contracted on her right side. She was buried with a number of personal ornaments, including a bracelet of droplet-shaped beads on the wrist and two pendants beneath the forearm. A bucranium was placed over her knees, the skull having been reduced to a bony stump holding the horns in place. Burials at KDK 1 exhibit unusually clear spatial patterning over time. They were arranged concentrically across a raised mound, with the most elaborate burial—that of a mature male—located near the summit. His body was loosely flexed and covered with cattle hides tinted with yellow pigment. Six ivory bracelets adorned the lower part of his right arm and another the elbow of his

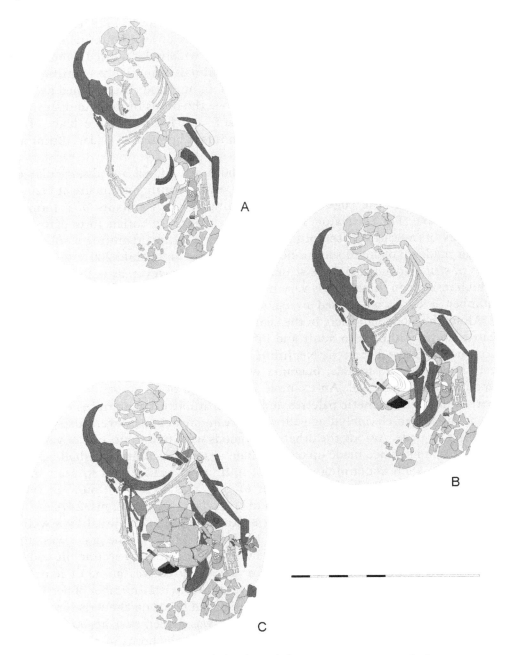

Figure 2.8 Formation of a Neolithic burial deposit, Site R12, N. Sudan

left arm. Two bucrania, coated in a white substance, were placed over the skeleton, as well as a grinding stone and two stone mace-heads. Other objects were placed in discrete concentrations around the edge of the grave, including two further groups of mace-heads, ceramic vessels, an ivory jar, *Aspatharia* shells, and various bone items. Two cosmetic palettes and ivory combs were located at the feet, together with a block of yellow pigment and a worked stone (Reinold 1994: 97).

Comparable practices are documented further south, at el-Ghaba in central Sudan. In one case, two superimposed bucrania were placed between the head of the deceased and the side of the burial pit. Objects positioned around the corpse included three vessels, placed face down, a stone mace-head, a necklace of twelve agate beads and a fragment of malachite. The teeth and facial bones of the skeleton were stained green, and areas of white pigment were detected beneath the head and feet. Double and single bucrania were found in several other graves, again with only the horns and upper cranium present (Lecointe 1987: 74, 77–8).

2.3 Religion, capitalism and the origins of farming: a critical excursus

These practices demand some further comment. In terms of spatial and temporal distribution, they appear integral to the spectrum of social and technological transformations that accompanied the beginnings of farming. But what was their relationship to this process? Were they in some way fundamental to the adoption and spread of domesticates, or merely the ritual gloss on a self-sustaining process of economic innovation and diffusion?

Questions of this nature are far from new, and it is instructive to situate them within a wider perspective on the beginnings of farming and its long-term consequences for human social development. Two broadly distinct and opposing paradigms have co-existed—among various others—from the nineteenth century to the present day, and at the risk of caricature their basic tenets may be briefly summarised.

The first paradigm is enshrined in the work of Gordon Childe (1936), but has a deeper genealogy in Marxist thought and Victorian evolutionism.[23] From this perspective, domestication forms a critical point of departure for the story of humanity's emancipation, through technological progress, from a primordial and essentially unchanging condition of 'nature'. Among other things, the new capacity to control a captive food supply is thought to have provided unprecedented opportunities for further technological innovations and the expansion of human populations, in turn leading to a growth in social inequality, based upon the uneven distribution of property and an increasingly hierarchical structuring of the forces governing production. Thus, as Barbara

---

[23] For more extensive discussion of the intellectual context and legacy of Childe's work, see Sherratt 1989.

Bender (1989: 84) has perspicaciously observed, technology (farming) becomes 'the tail that wags the social dog (complexity)'. By representing them as rooted in 'the exigencies of subsistence', relations of power and control are abstracted from the realm of social relations and are themselves 'naturalised'. She identifies a source for this narrative in the modern experience of industrial capitalism, an observation that might be extended from the economic to the moral sphere. An important aspect of modern European development, as Norbert Elias (1994 [1939]) demonstrated, was the ascendance of a social class that associated civilised values with the rational conquering and control of 'natural' forces and inclinations. Civilisation and domination were inextricably bound up in its modes of bodily comportment, its approach to the environment, its engagement with non-European peoples and its perspective on human evolution. The logical underpinnings of this world-view were elegantly satirised, in a Marxian vein, by Franz Steiner in his 1944 essay, *On the Process of Civilization* (reproduced in Adler and Fardon 1999: 125):

We have dropped the idea of measuring our powers with nature, as this is simply an allegory with the help of which predatory elites transfigure the beliefs appropriate to their own technology. There is no such thing as the powers of nature on the one hand, those of 'the human being' on the other, an ensuing struggle, a growth of human powers, and finally a defeat of nature. That is simply the trite myth of capitalism.

The late nineteenth century also bequeathed a second, very different vision of the origins of farming and its role in the development of human societies; one that has recently enjoyed something of a revival, albeit in more or less modified forms. For a number of scholars whose work was to influence the development of archaeological thought, the domestication of plants and animals was of interest primarily in defining the earliest forms of human religious experience. Frazer (1887: 95; 1910: 20–1, n.1) was among the first to propose that the impetus for domestication derived from totemic relationships between prehistoric societies and species that symbolised the life of the clan.[24] William Robertson Smith (1889: 294–311) discussed at length the fundamental changes wrought by animal domestication upon the relationship between Semitic peoples and their gods, devoting a section of his famous *Lectures on the Religion of the Semites* to the 'ancient holiness of cattle' in the Near East and Eastern Mediterranean. Among the early studies of animal domestication to be influenced by theories of religious evolution was Hahn's *Die Haustiere und ihre Beziehungen zur Wirtschaft des Menschen* (1896), which asserts that cattle were tamed as sacrificial animals for a supreme goddess, to whom prehistoric societies were in thrall.[25] Glyn Daniel (1962: 9–30) termed such

---

[24] For the concept of totemism in early anthropological thought, see Kuper 1988.
[25] Echoes of this theory may be detected throughout the twentieth-century literature on animal domestication; e.g. Reed 1960; Isaac 1971; Gautier 1990.

studies the 'pre-archaeological prehistory of man', their primary sources being Graeco-Roman and ancient Near Eastern texts, and what were viewed as survivals of prehistoric beliefs and practices among 'contemporary savages'. The special status often ascribed to cattle derived from the prominent role of this species in classical and biblical mythology (e.g. Robertson Smith 1889: 294–311).

In these accounts the origins of agriculture came to represent, not the dawn of technological progress, but a mystical engagement with the non-human world, in opposition to which Victorian scholars tended to define the dominant rationality of their own time.[26] As Godfrey Lienhardt (1966: 116) observed, 'primitive religion and magic were erroneous means towards a knowledge and control of human circumstance, and particularly of the physical world which in their day men of science had begun to achieve by rational methods'. The modern development of rational control over the non-human world was also an important theme in the historical sociology of capitalism:

If the point of departure for the religious history of humanity is a world peopled with the sacred, the point of arrival in our time is what Weber calls *Entzauberung der Welt*: the disenchantment of the world. The sacred, the exceptional quality which was attached to the things and creatures surrounding us at the dawn of the human adventure, has been banished. The capitalist's world—that is, the world we all live in . . . is composed of forces and creatures which offer themselves to us to be used, transformed, and consumed, but which no longer carry the charm of charisma. (Aron 1967: 229)

During the twentieth century the notion of domestication as symbolic transformation was periodically revived as an alternative to the overall predominance of models centred upon changes in diet and ecology (Cauvin 1972; 2000). The special significance of cattle in prehistoric societies was also given fresh consideration in light of discoveries such as the decorated houses of Çatalhöyük in central Turkey (Mellaart 1967), the bucranium-adorned Halaf pottery of northern Mesopotamia (Goff 1963) and model terracotta 'sanctuaries' from tombs of the Cypriot Early Bronze Age, such as that from Vounous, which contains a ritual scene involving a figure with mixed human and bovine attributes (Karageorghis 1991). In spite of their importance, however, forms and images relating to cattle have often remained subject to cliché and generalisation in archaeological interpretation. There has been a tendency to accord them a qualitatively different status from other, contemporaneous forms of animal art—a legacy of earlier writings, Jungian psychoanalysis and traditional western imaginings of the ancient world.

---

[26] Childe's later work combines elements of both views—the Near Eastern Neolithic as simultaneously 'technological self' and 'social other'—the tension between them forming part of a dialectical relationship between Oriental and Occidental societies in prehistory; see Wengrow 1999: 610–13.

Jacques Cauvin, whose work has been particularly influential, saw the complex development of cattle-related imagery and ritual practices in the Near East from Neolithic to Bronze Age times as expressing a *'pensée mythique d'Orient et de Méditerranée'*, based around the interplay of primordial symbols: 'Woman' and 'Bull'. His postulated *'religion de taureau'* stems from primeval and, he asserted, universal associations between the bull and *'une force brute, instinctive et violente'* (Cauvin 1994: 44–52, 163–6). Similar assumptions also seem to underpin the seductive view that the incorporation of cattle skulls into houses or burials represents a symbolic domestication or control of 'the wild' within cultural categories, occurring parallel to the process of biological domestication in plants and animals (Hodder 1990).

As I will attempt to show, recourse to generalising metaphors such as 'socialising', 'domesticating' or 'humanising' does not appear to provide an adequate framework for grasping the complexities of change in Neolithic societies and their relationships with the non-human world. They demand that human perceptions and uses of plants and animals should either resolve themselves into a dichotomy between 'controlled' or 'uncontrolled', or align themselves upon a continuum between these or similar values. Animals, as a category, are made to stand either for that which is unclassified, formless, wild and threatening, or as abstract matter 'waiting to be given shape and content by the mind of man' (Sahlins 1976: 209–10). As Tim Ingold and others have observed, such a view seems fundamentally alien to known societies where people interact with animals and plants in their everyday lives:

I have suggested that the negative stereotype of the hunter's relation to his prey, marked by the absence of control, be replaced by a more positive characterisation as a certain mode of engagement . . . the emergence of pastoralism does not depend, as orthodox definitions of domestication imply, upon humans achieving a state of being that takes them above and beyond the world in which other creatures live. Thus the transition from trust to domination is not to be understood as a movement from engagement to disengagement, from a situation where humans and animals are co-participants in the same world to one in which they hive off into their own separate worlds of society and nature. Quite to the contrary, the transition involves a *change in the terms of engagement.*

(Ingold 2000: 75, original emphasis)

In the following chapter I discuss how the new 'terms of engagement' between humans and the non-human world, formulated during the adoption and spread of farming, differed markedly in adjacent parts of the western Old World. The emergence of early farming societies will be treated, not in terms of a universal transition between fixed values (wild/domestic, nature/culture, trust/domination), but as the unfolding of regionally distinct, and historically interrelated, transformations.

DOMESTICATION AND EMBODIMENT IN THE NILE VALLEY

A nomad power is something inconceivable [for the ancient Greeks]; if it is power, it cannot be nomad.

The Mirror of Herodotus, F. Hartog

3.1 Complexity without villages?

In Egypt, the only clear evidence for permanent village life during the Neolithic period derives from Merimda Beni Salama, on the fringes of the Nile delta. As I have already noted, the material culture of that site, and the burials found there, exhibit little sign of the technological innovations, circulation of exotic materials and elaborate forms of personal display that characterised contemporary cemeteries of the Nile valley. Despite their original designation as 'villages', the occupation middens associated with Badarian cemeteries in Middle Egypt exhibit no such evidence of a permanent constructed environment. The most carefully excavated, at Hammamiya, was in fact interpreted by Gertrude Caton-Thompson as a 'temporary camping ground' (Brunton and Caton-Thompson 1928: 74).

More recently, Karl Butzer (1976: 14) has related the distribution of Badarian sites along the outskirts of the Nile valley to pastoral activity, and Béatrix Midant-Reynes (2000: 160) sees them as 'mainly . . . the result of pastoralism' and a 'relatively mobile existence'. Despite the lack of evidence for permanent dwellings or organised sedentary life, however, many other commentators continue to describe Neolithic habitation sites in the Nile valley as 'villages', 'settlements', 'homesteads' or even 'hamlets'.[1] It is often suggested that more substantial settlements were established close to the floodplain, where horticulture was possible, and have therefore been destroyed or buried by the changing course of the river, or through the recent spread of irrigation.[2] There remains, however, little evidence that cereal cultivation became an important economic pursuit in Egypt prior to the fourth millennium (i.e. from

---

[1] e.g. Krzyżaniak 1977: 81–2; Bard 1987: 86; 1994b: 24; Hassan 1988: 154; Hendrickx and Vermeersch 2000: 40–2.
[2] e.g. Trigger 1983: 10; Hendrickx and Vermeersch 2000: 42–3; Midant-Reynes 2000: 160.

Naqada I onwards). It cannot, therefore, be assumed on ecological grounds that Neolithic occupation of the landscape gravitated towards permanent settlement on the floodplain.

Curiously, there have been no such efforts to explain away the lack of villages in Neolithic Sudan. The adoption there of domesticated animals is in fact associated with a marked decline in the number of occupation sites adjacent to the floodplain, and is widely viewed as precipitating a relatively mobile existence oriented around the keeping of livestock (e.g. Caneva 1991: 7). Similarities in patterns of site formation, material culture, exchange and mortuary practices, described in the previous chapter, suggest that this view might be applied with equal validity to the Egyptian Nile valley. Resistance to such an interpretation can be accounted for only by the assumption that emergent cultural complexity, as documented in Neolithic burials, is 'inconsistent with the small, poor camp sites and with the pastoral economy that seems to have been the sole support for these communities' (Caneva 1991: 7–8).

Constructions of prehistoric pastoralism

The view that mobile, pastoral societies have poor material cultures and were marginal to the mainstream of cultural development in the prehistoric and ancient worlds has been pervasive in late twentieth-century archaeology.[3] While the economic foundations of early states are conventionally sought in the development of agrarian production, the archaeology of pastoral societies has concentrated upon 'inhospitable hinterlands' (Sadr 1991: 73; cf. A. B. Smith 1992: 17). The pastoralist, as Israel Finkelstein (1995) puts it, is to be sought 'living on the fringe', rather than at the hub of social change.

Ethnoarchaeological studies of modern pastoralists in Africa and the Middle East have contributed heavily to this image of pastoralism as an inherently marginal pursuit. Frank Hole (1978: 131), for instance, proposed that in order 'to gain some perspectives on pastoralism in prehistory', we must ignore those pastoral groups 'whose exceptional exploits have affected history and become the elaborate stuff of myth and legend', and turn instead to 'the tribes of the Zagros slopes, who missed most of the glorious episodes of the past just as they stand outside the course of history today'. Roger Cribb's extensive study of pastoralism in modern Turkey leads him to a similar conclusion: 'I am confident that nomadic campsites will continue to emerge as a minor component of the archaeological record of the Near East . . . The significant finding which emerged from this research is that nomadic campsites are structured in a distinctive way that bears the imprint of an inherently unstable mode of subsistence' (1991: 228). Andrew Smith, drawing upon descriptions of the

---

[3] e.g. Zeuner 1954: 353, 374; Gifford 1978; Chang and Koster 1986; Cribb 1991; Sadr 1991; A. B. Smith 1992.

Tuareg, Nuer, Fulani and Khoikhoi, proposes that 'pastoralism is a strategy of residential mobility designed to obtain minimum resources, such as pasture and water for domestic herds, as well as access to markets where commodities not readily available can be produced by exchange' (1992: 11).

It seems a curious strategy, however, to systematically pursue the minimum rewards, and there are surely echoes here of a puritanical view of pastoralism, rooted in the Old Testament narrative of pious Israelites pitted against the 'dark moral exemplar' of urban Canaan and Babylon (cf. McIntosh 1999: 58).[4] Since the 1970s, social anthropologists have increasingly argued that the widespread occurrence of poverty, instability and marginality among modern pastoralists relates to the impact of colonialism, urbanisation and the hostile expansion of agro-industrial nation states during the past two centuries.[5] The fact that these characteristics are widely present among pastoral populations says more about their resistance to today's dominant political and economic interests than it does about the inherent ability of pastoralists to alter the course of historical—or prehistorical—events (Wengrow 2003b: 131–2). This does not imply that archaeologists have nothing to learn from the study of modern pastoralists, rather, that the lesson has nothing to do with the potential of a given form of economy. Just as the lifeways of modern pastoralists are most clearly understood in terms of their relationships with today's 'outside world' (Khazanov 1984), so that of prehistoric pastoralists needs to be understood in terms of the outside world of prehistory.

3.2 The Neolithic paradox

The preceding discussions have attempted to clear the way for an integrated interpretation of social and economic transformations in the Neolithic Nile valley. In this region, as elsewhere, the range of these transformations defies explanation in terms of either a narrow materialist or an idealist account. In addition to new modes of food production and consumption, they encompassed patterns of movement and habitation, the extraction of new materials from the landscape, the production of a new repertoire of everyday objects and images together with their associated meanings and uses, and the ritual practices surrounding death. The 'total' character of this social transformation raises the wider issue that Claude Lévi-Strauss (1966: 13–16), observing the broad and to us strangely diffuse spectrum of innovations that took place during later human prehistory, called the 'Neolithic paradox'. It is our

---

[4] The pastoral societies of North-East Africa were, in fact, regularly compared to the biblical Israelites by late nineteenth- and early twentieth-century ethnographers, interested in the origins of 'primitive monotheism'; see the historiographical essays by W. S. F. Pickering and W. James, in James and Allen 1998.

[5] e.g. Asad 1973; 1979; Carr 1977; Comaroff and Comaroff 1992; Galaty and Salzman 1981; Spencer 1998.

culturally supplied institutions and habits of thought, he argued, that tend to assign special causal status to technological change, decoupling it and setting it apart from other realms of experience. New empirical knowledge may be generated or assimilated through the performance of a whole range of social activities that we might be tempted to classify as 'symbolic' or 'ritual'. Such activities, while not utilitarian in the narrow sense, serve to generate and transmit concrete understandings of the material world and its properties of movement and change. Equally, prehistoric innovations which served obvious utilitarian ends—such as the firing of clay to produce ceramic containers, or the cultivation of a new source of food—often also demanded engagement with what Mircea Eliade (1978: 34–5) termed new 'modalities of matter' and 'worlds of work', fuelling the imagination as well as the motor skills. As Bryan Pfaffenberger has put it, any technology should therefore be seen 'as a system, not just of tools, but also of related social behaviours and techniques' (1988: 241).

These rather abstract notions require some concrete exemplification from the archaeological record. Among the most widely discussed and documented transitions from hunter-gatherer to early farming society is that which began in the Levant during the Natufian period (c.13,000–10,000 BC), leading to the earliest domestication of plants and animals and, ultimately, to their dissemination beyond the Fertile Crescent (chapter 1.3, 1.4). A brief excursus on these processes provides a source of comparisons and contrasts, bringing the character of subsequent Neolithic transformations in the Nile valley into clearer focus.

Animals, death and the house in Natufian society

In addition to witnessing the earliest known steps towards plant domestication and sedentary life, the Natufian period in the Levant is associated with a spectrum of other transformations in the archaeological record, including new burial practices and a proliferation of mobile figural art (Noy 1991; Byrd and Monahan 1995). The wider social context for these developments was the establishment of increasingly permanent households and villages. This process is attested through a range of material practices such as the construction of semi-subterranean dwellings with postholes, stone linings, paved or plastered floors and interior hearths, and the use of increasing numbers of heavy ground-stone tools for processing plants (Valla 1995; Wright 1994: 251–4). Growing investment in sedentary life went hand-in-hand with the expansion of social networks between settlements, and a broadened exploitation of plant and animal species within their surrounding habitats (Lieberman 1993).

It is particularly instructive to consider how changes in human relations with the animal world are manifested archaeologically during the Natufian period. Such changes are brought into focus through the diverse uses to which the bodies of gazelle were put (fig. 3.1, upper). Gazelle were the most

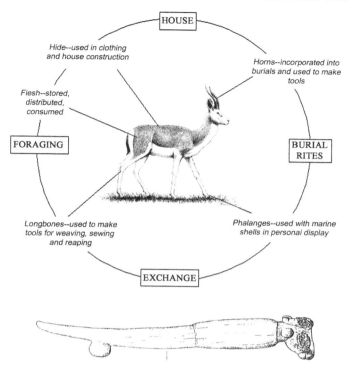

Figure 3.1 The gazelle as a social resource in the Natufian Levant; ornamented sickle from Kebara, N. Israel

frequently hunted mammals at this time and may have been subject to a degree of human management (Legge 1972; cf. Dayan and Simberloff 1995). Following consumption of the animal's flesh, its phalanges were retained and incorporated into personal ornaments alongside marine shells obtained through exchange with groups outside the immediate community. Longbones and horn cores provided a common raw material for manufacturing awls, barbed and plain points, spatulas and sickle-hafts. One of the best-known artefacts of this period is a bone sickle-haft from Kebara, ornamented with a detailed carving of a ruminant head (fig. 3.1, lower).[6] Bone tools were sometimes incised with designs thought to imitate weaving patterns and, in the absence of pottery, woven vessels may have been important in the collection and transport of plant foods (Campana 1989). It has been pointed out that the use of flint sickles, long recognised as a key technological component in the domestication of cereals, may initially have been motivated by the desire to harvest the long-stemmed plants used in weaving (Sherratt 1997b: 274).

[6] Garrod and Bate 1937: 36–41; Bar-Yosef and Tchernov 1970; Stordeur 1988.

A similar interpenetration of materials and technologies can be traced from the points and awls that were made of gazelle bones to their respective functions in the predation of other animals and the preparation of hides for use as clothing, or in the construction and renovation of houses (cf. Valla 1995: 175, fig. 5; Moore et al. 2000: 119).

From this surviving repertoire of objects, it may be inferred that the seasonal acquisition of gazelle in large numbers would have set in motion a phase of domestic renewal and craft production in Natufian communities, as well as creating opportunities for the redefinition of social arrangements within and beyond the local group. Such activities would probably have extended over some months following the actual slaughter of the animals, which is likely to have lasted only a few weeks (Moore et al. 2000: 484–92). This cycle of activities provides the context in which a further use of gazelle bodies may be considered: their incorporation into funerary practices within the settlement. At Mallaha, gazelle horns are associated with human remains derived from secondary burials, which took precedence over primary (and heavily ornamented) interments during the later Natufian period (Belfer-Cohen 1988; Byrd and Monahan 1995: 279). In separating the timing of burial from that of biological death, secondary burial would have allowed the scheduling of these funerary events at times of communal significance. Collective labour in a public spectacle is further suggested by a multiple interment at Hayonim Terrace, containing remains of humans, gazelle horns and domestic dogs (perhaps used in hunting), interspersed with heavy stone blocks and layers of soil (Valla et al. 1991).

By dramatically assimilating human death to the culling of herds, funerary rites may have represented it as part of a repetitive, cyclical order of destruction and rejuvenation, upon which domestic and social regeneration also depended. At Mallaha, patterned deposits of gazelle and other animal remains also mark the closing of a house and the foundation of a new one above it (Boyd 1995). Both symbolically and as materials of construction, animals appear to have been associated with the birth, maturation and death of houses, and of the people they contained (cf. Carsten and Hugh-Jones 1995). Ritualised activity within and around dwellings appears not to have expressed opposition to outside forces, so much as the role of the settled community as an epicentre from which experience of the outside world was configured and infused into the rhythms and practices of social life. Similarly the ornamented bone sickle-haft from Kebara brings together the different 'worlds of work' occupied by the forager and the hunter, reversing the process through which the body of the animal was deconstructed and filtered into a spectrum of distinct, but related, activities. A single element is made to evoke the whole by the extension of its form into a miniature replica, enabling the image to be diverted into a new chain of signification. The movement of the forager's arm during work merges with the motivations encapsulated in the image of the predated animal, which also forms a nexus of social relations past, present and future.

3.3 'Domestication' and 'embodiment' in the Nile valley

Archaeologists are accustomed to treating settlement sites as the starting point for a reconstruction of past social forms, and in many instances, such as that just described, this is a fertile method. As John Burton (1980: 273) has pointed out, there exists a broader tendency to assume that the village is 'the primordial fully social arrangement and that the physical existence of clustered habitation sites imbues social relationships with a measure of permanence'. However, in approaching the Neolithic of the Nile valley it seems necessary, as Jacques Reinold (2001) argues, to suspend these expectations. It is the domain of funerary, rather than domestic, activity that provides a window not only on to rituals that structured the human lifecycle, but also on to the wider range of social practices through which Neolithic communities established their stability in space and their continuity in time. The focus of these practices was not, I suggest, the house, but the bodies of people and animals, which themselves provided primary generative frameworks for configuring social experience.

This distinction between the social morphologies of the Neolithic Fertile Crescent and Nile valley cannot be satisfactorily attributed to different conditions of archaeological preservation.[7] Ritual treatments of animal and human bodies in Neolithic South-West Asia focus on reproducing relationships between people via the house, as is widely exemplified through the placing of body parts beneath domestic floors and within walls or furnishings, and in the decoration of human skulls with plaster and paint during Pre-Pottery Neolithic B (c.8500–7000 BC; chapter 1.3). The latter practice extended the techniques used in house construction to the symbolic reversal of human mutability. Mediating between structure and event, practices such as these would have given shape and continuity to social life.

The funerary record of the Neolithic Nile valley testifies to a very different set of procedures for absorbing the contingencies of death into the reproduction of wider social structures. At the time of burial, individuals, parted from the living group, were accompanied to the grave by those objects through which they had observed its self-imposed rules of consumption and presentation (chapter 2.2). As demonstrated by the contents of Neolithic cemeteries, these codes of expression encompassed biological differences of age and sex, articulating the process of personal growth from infancy to adulthood. Rather than constituting a vehicle for ostentatious display or the temporary assertion of status,[8] I would argue that the elaboration of the body constituted the main objective framework for experience of self and commemoration of social identity. Nearly all of the items interred with the dead were designed to be easily

---

[7] For more on the concept of 'social morphology', see Mauss and Beuchat 1979.
[8] e.g. Hoffman 1991: 143, 181–9; Anderson 1992; Spencer 1993; Wilkinson 1999: 29.

carried by, or attached to, the individual person, many relating directly to the alteration of the body through cosmetic treatments or the ingestion of (as yet unidentified) substances (Wengrow 2001a).

Cosmetic implements such as palettes and combs further suggest the particular importance of skin and hair as symbolic media, which could be extended by wrapping the body in hides or fabrics, and through its decoration with ornaments and selected elements of animal bodies. In combination, these objects formed a complex material repertoire from which a distinct funerary image of the deceased could be formed on the body. This body-centred *habitus* was also compatible with the everyday demands of a mobile, pastoral lifestyle, perhaps accounting for the apparent lack of long-term investment in static, bounded environments for dwelling and socialisation.[9] Pigments, as well as many of the coloured stones used in personal ornamentation, derived from deposits located along wadi routes extending east of the Nile valley towards the Red Sea, reflecting the sustained mobility afforded by herding (chapter 1.5). The diverse suite of body ornamentation available to most individuals, in life as well as death, therefore implied movement and exchange as basic conditions of social existence through its constituent materials, as well as its inherently portable character.

Concomitantly, Neolithic habitation sites in the Nile valley did not constitute immovable centres of domestic space, but temporary loci of social activity. They seem best thought of as marking out arenas for movement and periodic aggregation, rather than a series of bounded settlements and hiatuses in a static social landscape. Only in funerary rites was the flux of geographical and social space suspended, and the body of the individual, together with objects which formed the nexus of relationships with other persons, withdrawn from circulation and laid to rest in a fixed, communal location.

The integration of animal bodies and images into these rituals highlights the fact that, as in other parts of the world, the inception of a Neolithic economy in the Nile valley was experienced simultaneously through objective and subjective processes of transformation. Burial rites formed part of a wider configuration of relationships with the landscape and its non-human inhabitants, which extended beyond the animate field of living relations to the time and space of death. They also testify to an investment of human values and concerns in animals more wide-ranging and pervasive than is implied by the usual discussions of 'cattle cults', and which seems likely to have been woven into the political and economic, as well as spiritual, aspects of social life.

The significance of these practices is thrown into relief by comparison with processes of cultural change that accompanied the adoption of domesticates in

---

[9] For the notion of *habitus*, see Bourdieu 1977: 78. As W. James (2003: 215) observes, this term 'has found wide currency, as it captures in its sense of pattern both environmental constraints and human agency, without allowing a collapse into cosy images of tradition and harmony'.

South-West Asia and many parts of Europe. There, as Ian Hodder (1990; 1992) has observed and as illustrated by the Natufian case, houses provided a central symbolic locus through which economic transformations became encoded and objectified within networks of social meaning. The term 'domestication', etymologically linked to the house, serves to convey both the cultural and biological aspects of this process. In the Nile valley, however, there is as yet little indication that domestic practices played a formative role in restructuring human conceptions of the world during the crucial period of the fifth millennium BC. Rather, the adoption of a herding lifestyle was associated over the long-term with the spread of new ritual practices and schemes of social classification, visible to us only as they pertained to death, and the primary vehicle for their articulation was not the house, but the bodies of people and animals. Hence 'domestication' is an inappropriate metaphor in this case. The cultural idiom of Neolithic transformation in the Nile valley seems better understood in terms of 'incorporation' or 'embodiment'.

THE URBANISATION OF THE DEAD:
NAQADA I–II

'Did you ever happen to see a city resembling this one?' Kublai asked Marco Polo.

Invisible Cities, I. Calvino

4.1 Predynastic Egypt: reappraising the record

The conventional term 'predynastic', applied to the Naqada I–II periods, emphasises the weight of evolutionary expectation that bears upon a consideration of the early–mid fourth millennium BC in Egypt. The temptation in many studies of this period has been to posit some a priori notion of 'the State', and trace the emergence of its constituent elements as a story of gradual, linear change. Older accounts may now be accused of historical naivety in treating dynastic representations of political unification through conquest as faithful accounts of the prehistoric past. They did, however, have the advantage of remaining faithful to the archaeological record, and generated much concrete evidence for the expansion of Upper Egyptian burial customs and material culture into Lower Egypt during the Naqada II period (c.3650–3300 BC).[1] More recent models have stressed the importance of urbanisation, positing the emergence of 'proto-kingdoms' centred upon distinct city-states in Upper Egypt.[2] Such accounts remain highly abstract and have yet to offer a convincing definition of Egyptian urbanisation that marries up with the archaeological evidence for this period. Claims that such an attempt is doomed from the outset, owing to the inaccessibility of prehistoric settlement sites beneath the modern cultivation, carry decreasing weight as careful excavation strategies in both the Nile valley and particularly the delta reveal a body of empirical information for the study of habitation practices.

Other recent research has explored the use of statistics to gauge the emergence of hierarchy from the changing contents of burial deposits, which continue to furnish the bulk of material for a study of this period.[3] The main forms of mortuary evidence currently cited for the emergence of elites at particular locations are the spatial clustering of graves, the energy expended in their

---

[1] The fundamental studies are those of Kaiser: 1956; 1957; 1959; 1960; 1961; 1964; 1985a; 1990; critiqued by Köhler 1995, with a rebuttal by Kaiser 1995.

[2] Hassan 1988: 161–3; Kemp 1989: 31–46, fig. 7; Wilkinson 1999: 323–8.

[3] Castillos 1982; Griswold 1992; Bard 1994b; Wilkinson 1996; Savage 1997.

construction and the presence within them of large numbers of artefacts. The latter include those defined by various analysts as 'badges of status' or 'symbols of authority' owing to their exotic origins, skilled craftsmanship or similarity to later dynastic forms. A recurrent difficulty with such approaches has been their tendency to assume that all categories of grave good act to signify individuation and wealth in the same way, such that every kind of material deposit, from a lapis lazuli necklace to a sacrificed animal, can be arranged on a single scale of value and used to index the status of the deceased. Despite their well-known unreliability, age and sex determinations for skeletons given in late nineteenth- and early twentieth-century reports have often been used as further indicators of social differentiation (see also, e.g., Savage 2000).[4]

By contrast, more concrete forms of evidence, such as changes in the treatment of the corpse or in the qualitative attributes and disposition of objects within graves, including the development of extensive systems of figural art, have been left largely out of account in interpretations of social change. I argue in this chapter, and more directly in the following, that such developments are far from trivial in seeking to understand long-term processes of social and political transformation. In particular, they suggest a much more complex and dynamic relationship between networks of material exchange, the individual person and the role of commemorative ritual than is allowed for in many existing studies. As I go on to discuss in chapters 8–10, a number of the forms taken by this relationship during the predynastic period were to exert a direct and lasting influence upon the ideology of Egyptian kingship.

4.2 Prestige goods: an economic context for the rise of Upper Egypt

The site of Hierakonpolis lies on the west bank of the Nile, 113 km north of Aswan in southern Egypt (fig. 4.1). Its Greek name, meaning 'City of the Hawk', refers to the ancient walled town of Nekhen, the remains of which are now bounded on all sides by the modern cultivation. A temple dedicated to the god Horus stood there in dynastic times. Archaeological soundings beneath the ancient town have revealed a sequence of occupations extending back from Old Kingdom times into the predynastic period, as well as sherds of Neolithic (possibly Badarian) pottery (Hoffman *et al.* 1986: 181; Adams 1995: 26–31). A few hundred metres to the south, the modern cultivation begins to give way to the low desert. It is here that a series of expeditions, beginning in the late nineteenth century and continuing to the present day (with a hiatus

---

[4] For the unreliability of such determinations, see Mann 1989. An inventory of human remains identified by trained specialists is only now beginning to accumulate through projects such as those underway at Hierakonpolis and el-Adaima, and should eventually provide clearer insight into how biological difference was implicated (or diguised) in the patterning of predynastic funerary activities and deposits.

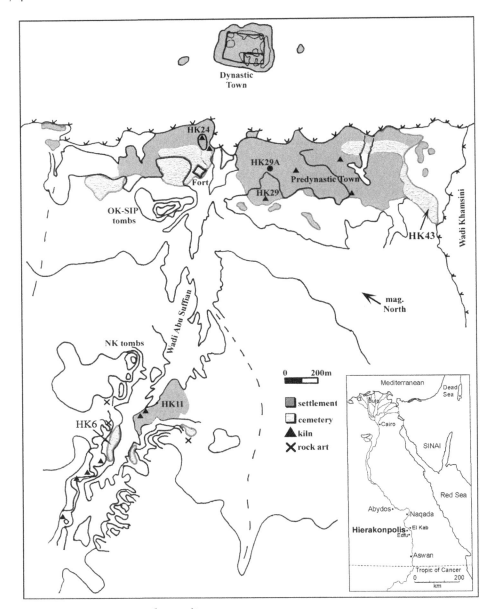

Figure 4.1 Map: Hierakonpolis

in the early twentieth century), have uncovered the largest known expanse
of habitation and cemetery sites dating to the Naqada I and II periods (c.4000–
3300 BC).[5] The total horizontal distribution of remains dating to these periods

[5] Quibell and Green 1902: 19–22; Lansing 1935; Kaiser 1958; Fairservis *et al.* 1971–2; Hoffman
et al. 1982; 1986; Adams 1987; Friedman *et al.* 1999.

exceeds 30 ha in size, and unusually for sites of this period it extends some 3.5 km into the adjacent desert, following the terraces of a large drainage system called the Wadi Abu Suffian (Hoffman *et al.* 1982: 2–3, 123). A smaller drainage course, the Wadi Khamsini, demarcates the approximate extent of known predynastic remains to the east.

The total number of individuals buried at Hierakonpolis during Naqada I and II can only be broadly estimated in the thousands, owing to the extensive plundering of graves which has been the fate of this, and most other, predynastic cemeteries. Hierakonpolis is one of a series of locales extending throughout Upper Egypt, from north of the Qena bend to the vicinity of Kom Ombo, which saw the development of extensive burial grounds at this time. One of the largest concentrations was at Naqada, the site that furnished Petrie with much of the material for his relative chronology of the predynastic period. There a cluster of three cemeteries contained over two thousand graves, and a further thousand or so are known from nearby Ballas (Petrie and Quibell 1896; Baumgartel 1970). Smaller predynastic cemeteries in Upper Egypt held between one and two hundred burials (e.g. Armant, Abu Zaidan, el-Masa'id, el-Ma'amariya), while the majority are thought to have comprised between six hundred and a little over a thousand interments (e.g. Ab'adiya, Hu, el-Amra, el-Mahasna, Naga el-Deir). Naqada I–II cemeteries of between one and two hundred graves existed at el-Badari, Matmar and Mostagedda in Middle Egypt, but did not attain the sizes reached by many new funerary centres in Upper Egypt.[6] Small cemeteries containing around a hundred burials each are also documented further to the south in Lower Nubia (e.g. at Shellal, el-Kubaniya South, Khor Bahan, Gerf Hussain and Dakka).[7] According to Nubian regional chronology they make up a unit called the Early A-Group (Table 2), but their constituent burials are almost indistinguishable in form and general content from those of cemeteries to the north (Nordström 1972: 28–9; Smith 1991).

The concentration of activity in Upper Egypt during this period cannot be understood without reference to wider regional and inter-regional patterns of interaction. Grave goods deposited in Upper Egyptian burials during Naqada I–II included an increasingly wide repertoire of items obtained through long-distance trade (chapter 1.9). For reasons that are more fully explored in the following chapter, such objects seem best understood as forming the basis of a prestige-goods economy. The social mechanisms of a prestige-goods system, as defined by Michael Rowlands and Susan Frankenstein (1998: 337), are 'dominated by the political advantage gained through exercising control over access to resources that can only be obtained through external trade'. The

---

[6] Detailed estimates of cemetery sizes are provided by Castillos 1982 and Bard 1987; 1994b: 7–23; and see also Adams and Hoffman 1987.

[7] Reisner 1910: 16–52, 114–41; Firth 1912: 110–51; 1915: 41–104; Junker 1919.

availability of such resources in Egypt increased during Naqada II, owing to the establishment of a pack-donkey route crossing the Sinai desert, and the contemporaneous expansion of urban trading systems in Mesopotamia (chapter 1.7–1.9). River transport along the Nile was essential in providing access to these external trade networks. Only in Upper Egypt, however, could the expansion of river-borne trade (unfettered by major natural obstacles) be combined with access to the major wadi routes through which metal and mineral resources were procured from the Eastern Desert. As well as forming material constituents for a changing pattern of social life, these resources were also necessary for participation in long-distance trade.

The combination of circumstances outlined above provided unique opportunities for groups in Upper Egypt to exercise control over wider networks of exchange. This could be achieved by adding value to local resources through sophisticated manufacturing processes, and by developing and disseminating new forms of ritual practice and sumptuary codes. I argue that a cycle of development was set in motion, whereby the acquisition of exotic trade goods stimulated local processes of technological innovation and social change, which in turn reinforced control over regional networks of circulation. By the end of Naqada II (c.3300 BC), groups in Upper Egypt were able to mobilise small but regular quantities of exotic materials and manufactured goods for deployment as funerary gifts.

The interplay of local and supra-local systems in this process can be most clearly observed at Hierakonpolis, providing a focal point from which to view wider patterns of development during Naqada I–II. The emphasis of discussion in this chapter is upon relationships between cemetery and habitation sites, in order to elucidate how ritual commerce between the living and the dead structured the wider organisation of labour and consumption over time. Then follows more detailed consideration of developments in material culture, focusing in chapter 5 upon the significance of painted pottery and other decorated objects. At the end of that chapter, I seek to tie together these various strands of argument by considering how funerary rites—as a distinct domain of social creativity, and a powerful locus of memory and emotion—gave new meaning to human bodies through their relations with a changing world of objects and images.

4.3 Towns on the move: the character of early urbanisation in Upper Egypt

Urbanisation has been defined in myriad ways.[8] Of the possible elements that go to make up a town or city, the most frequently cited are the existence of a class or classes of individuals not directly involved in agrarian production,

---

[8] See, e.g., Wheatley 1972; Braudel 1985, ch. 8; Hansen 2000.

a high density of permanent residents, access to ports and trade routes, centralised bureaucracy, a concentration of knowledge and specialised crafts, political and/or economic control over a rural hinterland and the existence of institutions that embody civic identity. There are also more basic, and perhaps less frequently articulated, assumptions about the physical form of the city: its bounded nature, its permanence and its monumentality.

It has long been recognised that a remarkable plurality of urban forms existed in the remote past, many of which are only partially covered by these expectations. Trigger (1985: 348), for instance, has suggested that the urban centres of Old Kingdom Egypt, like those of Shang China and Inca Peru, had relatively small populations, and 'functioned mainly as elite residential, administrative, and cult centres', combining these functions with a monopoly on sophisticated craft production and restricted cultural knowledge. Some might argue that to retain the term urbanisation in such cases is simply a matter of anthropological dogma and threatens to elide the specific characteristics that distinguish each particular social form and trajectory. On the other hand, an overly narrow definition of urbanisation may inhibit comparison among large-scale social organisations in the ancient world, while also masking alternative trajectories from past to present and future modes of urbanisation. The latter, in particular, may force us to rethink many basic assumptions about the materiality of city life, as its parameters are broadened and questioned by the possibilities of electronic mass communication and high-speed travel (cf. Wolff 1998).

The case of early Egypt offers a significant and distinctive contribution to these debates. Craft specialisation and the expansion of trade networks are amply attested from funerary contexts, as is a degree of political centralisation. These features appear to have emerged in the absence of specialised administrative technologies, such as developed in Mesopotamia from the seventh millennium onwards. I have argued in earlier chapters that, relative to the latter region, the Nile valley did not possess a long tradition of sedentary village life prior to the period of state formation. The question at hand is whether a distinct trajectory towards urbanisation can now be discerned, building upon the characteristic features of Neolithic society in Egypt. In addressing this question, it is necessary to review the archaeological evidence for changing patterns of habitation in Naqada I–II in some detail. The picture is extremely fragmentary, and much fieldwork remains at a preliminary stage of publication. Consistent features may nevertheless be identified, and these bring the issues outlined above into clearer focus.

Naqada I–IIB, c.4000–3650 BC

A figure of 30 ha was given above for the predynastic site of Hierakonpolis. That figure does not correspond to an integrated or contiguous settlement, but rather to a spread of occupational debris and burial grounds extending beyond the modern alluvium. The predynastic 'site' comprises many distinct localities, represented by unstructured surface scatters of lithic and ceramic material, fire installations, low middens and cemeteries, which range widely in size and length of use (Hoffman *et al.* 1982: 123–9, table 6.1). Stratified architectural sequences are difficult to discern, and evidence of permanent structures has proved hard to recover. These characteristics are replicated with striking regularity at other predynastic sites throughout Egypt. It is precisely this consistency that prompts us to seek out positive explanations for the poor definition of settlement remains, arising from the patterning of past human activities rather than just defective site preservation.

Excavation at HK29, part of an extensive zone of Naqada I habitation sprawling along the edge of the modern floodplain at Hierakonpolis, has revealed evidence for a system of 'barnyard-like enclosures', demarcated by narrow trenches and posthole alignments. A conflagration in the same area preserved what is still the most fully documented example of a permanent domestic dwelling from predynastic Egypt, dating to Naqada IB–C (c.3700 BC; Hoffman *et al.* 1982: 10–13, 138, fig. 6.4; Hoffman 1980). Its surviving features included a rectangular subterranean depression (c.4 x 3.5 m) with traces of mud-brick preserved near the entrance. An internal oven and storage pot were embedded in the floor surface, and a series of wooden posts provides the only indication of a superstructure. Another large zone of Naqada I–IIB activity at Hierakonpolis expanded along the eastern terraces of the Wadi Abu Suffian, some 1.5 km from the edge of the modern cultivation (HK11C). Initial excavations revealed 'myriad trash lenses of ash, charcoal and organic remains representing either the leavings of individual activities or the refuse of individual hearths' (Hoffman *et al.* 1982: 25). Structural remains included a semi-circular arrangement of wooden posts (c.8 m in diameter) and a mud-brick installation comprising a large basin and two troughs, one of which was found to contain barley spikelets. These features, and an adjoining row of postholes, were interpreted by the excavators as seasonally used facilities for keeping livestock, while a circular arrangement of huts (HK3) lying still further from the alluvium was identified as a herding station (Hoffman *et al.* 1982: 16–25, 130, 143, fig. 6.2). More recent work has uncovered a stratified sequence of floors, refuse pits and linear enclosures marked by mud-coated reed fencing suspended on wooden posts, still visible in their original locations. Associated with them were a stone-lined hearth, grinding stones and mud-lined pits that served as pot emplacements. Animal dung was stored as a source of fuel (Watrall 2001a; 2001b).

The habitation remains at Hierakonpolis bear comparison with those of other Naqada I sites in Middle and Upper Egypt. At Hammamiya, in the el-Badari region, Caton-Thompson excavated a series of circular mud-brick installations ranging from one to two metres in diameter. One was completely filled with animal dung, while the surviving contents of others were described as 'dark midden material'. Of the nine structures investigated, only one produced possible evidence of habitation in the form of a concave depression, identified as a hearth. Small pits, remnants of a mud wall and a row of twelve wooden post-stubs were also dated to this period (Brunton and Caton-Thompson 1928: 82–8, pl. 66). In more recent fieldwork, Diane Holmes and Renée Friedman (1994: 119–20, 123, figs. 12, 13, 15) uncovered another round structure and associated deposits of animal dung at the same location. Over twenty further habitation sites have been identified in the Mostagedda area, where Guy Brunton excavated mud-huts and an alignment of wooden stakes associated with a large ash deposit. They range from shallow artefact scatters to middens exceeding a metre in height (Brunton 1937: 75–82, pl. 71b: 1; cf. Holmes and Friedman 1994: 111–16, table 1).

Excavations near the modern village of el-Khattara, close to Naqada, have revealed a series of Naqada I habitation sites.[9] Small postholes constituted the only clear evidence of structural features, while remains of pastoral activity in the form of midden deposits were, by contrast, abundant. Fekri Hassan (1988: 155) observed that:

Animal enclosures (*zeriba*), indicated by sheep/goat droppings, are ubiquitous. Some sites are very thin, but a few had deposits as much as a metre thick. Very thick layers of sheep/goat droppings also suggest prolonged occupation over several generations. Microstratigraphy revealed sets of up to five overlapping occupations with lateral shifts suggesting a pattern of abandonment and reoccupation. The sites are almost regularly spaced about 2 km apart.[10]

A shallow expanse of habitation remains of the late Naqada I to mid-Naqada II periods extends along the edges of the modern cultivation at el-Adaima, in proximity to a contemporaneous cemetery (Midant-Reynes and Buchez 2002). As at Hierakonpolis, which lies c.15 km to the south, recent excavations have produced little evidence of permanent houses, the most common features being pits lined with alluvial mud, hearths, postholes, and narrow trenches marking the outline of animal enclosures. Consistent spatial relations proved hard to discern among these various features, and in only one case could a clear plan be made out among the postholes, demarcating an elongated oval space devoid of domestic installations (Midant-Reynes and Buchez 2002: 37). The

---

[9] Initially dated erroneously to the Badarian period by Hays (1976); see comments in Hassan (1984: 107–8).

[10] In terms of site formation processes, this pattern (as first pointed out to me by Andrew Sherratt) can be compared with the Neolithic ash-mounds of the Deccan plain in India (Allchin 1963; Paddaya 1973). Dotted throughout the central part of this region are immense mounds formed by superimposed strata of ash, shown by chemical analysis to be the product of burned cow dung, interspersed with layers of packed soil containing cultural remains. Excavated mounds have yielded evidence of livestock enclosures in the form of posthole settings, as well as frequent finds of cattle bones. The largest, at Kudatini, reached a diameter of 30–50 m and a height of 8–13 m. For pastoralists, such mounds may take on an ancestral significance analogous to that of the mud-brick *tells* formed by repeated superimposition of houses in traditionally constructed Middle Eastern settlements (see Kramer 1982; and cf. Burton 1980: 275).

excavators' summarising remarks may serve as a general commentary upon the character of Naqada I–II habitation in Upper Egypt, which suggests nothing more clearly than a reconciliation between the habits of a relatively mobile lifestyle and a growing tendency towards the nucleation of social activity in particular locales:

One must take into account the fact that we are not dealing with a single phase of occupation, a snapshot in time, but on the contrary with multiple phases of the same period, phases during which constructions were erected, demolished, and refurbished, with all the greater ease for their flimsiness.[11]

Naqada IIC–D, c.3650–3300 BC

At Hierakonpolis, remains of occupation and cemeteries dating to Naqada IIC–D extend only about three hundred metres beyond the edge of the modern cultivation. They are also known to continue beneath it at least as far as the location of the Old Kingdom town at Nekhen (Hoffman *et al.* 1982: 130–2). This shift of activity towards the floodplain was associated with the establishment of specialised craft zones within the wider spread of habitation. These zones included an enigmatic oval enclosure (c.32 x 13 m) with a series of mud-plaster floors (HK29A), associated with vast amounts of debitage from the manufacture of flint bladelets and crescent-shaped drills (fig. 4.2; R. F. Friedman 1996; 2003). The latter were used to make beads and vessels in a variety of coloured stones procured from the Eastern Desert (e.g. cornelian, diorite) or through long-distance trade networks (e.g. obsidian), residues of which were found within the complex. A lack of finished objects suggests that much of what was produced left the site shortly after manufacture, and associated ceramic finds indicate access to trading networks extending as far north as the Levant, and southwards into Lower Nubia (Holmes 1992: 39–44).

Fragments from bifacial knives were also recovered in large numbers from the oval complex at HK29A, as were remains from an unusual assemblage of aquatic fauna, including turtle, crocodile and exceptionally large perch (Linseele and van Neer 2003). A preponderance of young livestock was noted within the assemblage of terrestrial fauna, and it has been suggested that butchery, perhaps of a sacrificial nature, took place there (R. F. Friedman 1996: 24; cf. Whitehouse 2002: 439). Initially bounded by a large trench supporting an enclosure of wooden posts and lattice work, the complex was later encircled by a more robust perimeter wall of mud-brick and stone, incorporating a gateway flanked by four wooden columns and a row of ancillary structures. The columns would have framed the monumental façade of a building about 13 m in width, the appearance of which may have resembled that of later (royal)

---

[11] Midant-Reynes and Buchez 2002: 38; author's translation, with the assistance of Anne Haour.

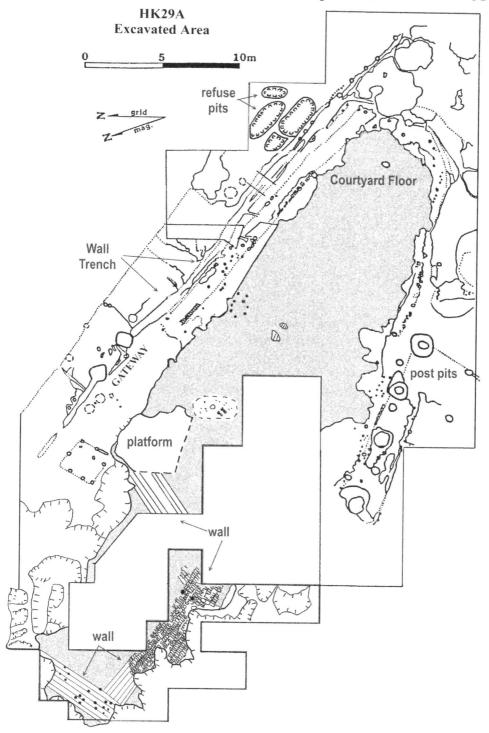

HK29A
Excavated Area

0   5   10m

N — grid
N — mag.

refuse pits

Courtyard Floor

Wall Trench

GATEWAY

post pits

platform

wall

wall

Figure 4.2 Ceremonial enclosure HK29A, Naqada II, Hierakonpolis

monuments in stone, which in turn evoke prototypes in perishable materials.[12] The postholes in which they were set measured over 1.5 m in depth
and almost the same in diameter, and one contained remnants of what has
been tentatively identified as cedar imported from the Levant (R. F. Friedman
1996: 24).

Surface survey at Naqada, Abydos and el-Adaima suggests that a shift of
activity away from the desert and towards the alluvium occurred throughout
Upper Egypt during Naqada IIC–D.[13] At Naqada itself, remnants of a large
rectangular complex with mud-brick walls were excavated by Petrie (who
named them the 'South Town') during the late nineteenth century, and are
now generally dated to the late Naqada II period.[14] The functions and wider
context of these remains are unknown, although the excavators reported large
amounts of painted and coarse pottery, as well as stone tools and objects
identified as spindle-whorls. More recent soundings in the same area revealed
postholes and ditches, but no further information relating to these buildings,
which have not been relocated (Barocas et al. 1989: 300–1). A second area of
occupation at Naqada, misleadingly termed the 'North Town', was devoid of
architecture, and comprised a thin layer of ashes and sherds cut by small pits
containing grinding stones and spindle-whorls (Petrie and Quibell 1896: 2–3).
Traces of Naqada II habitation have also been recorded c.45 km north-west of
Naqada in proximity to the large predynastic cemeteries at Semaina (Site SH)
and Ab'adiya (Site HG). The sites comprised artefact scatters, including an
extensive zone in which stone tools were manufactured, but no surviving
structures (Bard 1989; 1994a: 273–4).

The urbanisation of the dead

Does this accumulated evidence support the view that a process of urbanisation was underway in Upper Egypt, prior to the emergence of a politically
unified state in the Naqada III period? The answer, I suggest, is 'yes', so long as
we agree what is, and is not, implied by the term urbanisation in this context.
Here a contrast with broadly contemporary developments in Mesopotamia is
again instructive. In the latter region, trajectories towards urban life correspond to many of our conventional expectations, both through their association with the development of administrative techniques for controlling labour
and resources, and in their physical manifestations on the ground (see van de

---

[12] R. F. Friedman (1996: 33–4) draws a specific parallel with the colonnaded façade of the 'House of
     the South', located within the Third Dynasty Step Pyramid complex of Djoser at Saqqara; see
     Lauer 1936: 154–77.
[13] Hassan and Matson 1989; Patch 1991; cf. Midant-Reynes 2000: 199.
[14] Petrie and Quibell 1896: 50, 54, pl. 85; cf. Kemp 1977: 198; 1989: 36, fig. 9. The dating of the
     complex is based upon surface finds and the absence of later ceramics, as well as four radio-
     carbon dates obtained from the vicinity; see Hassan 1984: 109; Hassan and Matson 1989: 309.

Mieroop 1997). Oriented around its elevated complexes of mud-brick and stone, the layout of the early Mesopotamian city embodies the permanence, self-confidence and heterogeneity that we tend to associate with urban life.

In the early centres of the Nile valley, by contrast, the arrangement of domestic life remained fluid, just as the materials of construction were for the most part light and ephemeral. The largest concentrations of human activity are defined by lateral spreading of cultural material along a horizontal axis, rather than the vertical *tell*-urbanisation of Mesopotamian towns. We might therefore consider whether the more permanent aspect of the settlement lay not on the surface, but below the ground. In attaching growing numbers of people to particular places, and in reproducing those attachments over generations, the urbanisation of the dead may have been more important than the urbanisation of the living, the density of social memory more vital than the massing of permanent dwellings. Equally, as I discuss below, the expansion of influence among the living appears to have flowed, not from bureaucratic control over economic resources, but from the control exercised over new forms of ritual commerce with the dead. First, however, I reconsider what has long been regarded as the defining 'event' of the predynastic period: the 'cultural unification' of Upper and Lower Egypt during the Naqada II period.

4.4 The transformation of Lower Egypt

For a variety of reasons, the archaeology of Lower Egypt has traditionally played the role of poor relative to that of the Nile valley. An expansive and ever-rising water table, land reclamation and the growth of modern urban settlement have conspired to discourage fieldwork and endanger the survival of known sites. Extensive excavation of predynastic remains was undertaken during the early and mid-twentieth century on the outskirts of Cairo, at Maadi, Wadi Digla and Heliopolis, but owing to the outbreak of the Second World War many of the results have only been fully published in recent decades (Debono and Mortensen 1988; Rizkana and Seeher 1990; above, chapter 1.7). All revealed cemeteries dating to the early–mid fourth millennium, a period now termed the Maadi-Buto phase to reflect the distinct cultural trajectories of Lower and Upper Egypt at this time. They were immediately distinguished from contemporaneous (Naqada I–IIB) cemeteries in the Nile valley, largely on the grounds of what was absent from the burials, that is, large numbers of ceramic vessels, decorative objects, imported goods and elaborate treatments of the body. By contrast, cemeteries previously excavated in the Fayum—at Haraga (Engelbach 1923), Abusir el-Melek (Scharff 1926) and el-Gerza (Petrie *et al.* 1912)—contained rich burial assemblages indistinguishable from those of Upper Egypt, and dating to a later phase of the Naqada II period. This suggested a sequence of development in which Lower Egyptian funerary customs were supplanted by more display-oriented practices from the south; a sequence confirmed by the earliest phase of burials at Minshat Abu Omar in the north-eastern delta; the latter date to Naqada IIC–D (c.3650–3300 BC) and are Upper Egyptian in character and contents (Kroeper and Wildung 1985; 1994).

During the early fourth millennium, regional differences in funerary practices stand in contrast to the overall similarity of subsistence patterns in Lower and Upper Egypt. Botanical assemblages from both regions contain a large proportion of cultivated cereals (emmer wheat and six-row barley) as well as flax, lentil and pea, and a similar range of wild root-foods, figs and berries (chapter 1.7).[15] Animal remains demonstrate the pursuit of a mixed herding economy throughout the Nile valley and delta—centred around cattle, sheep and goats, often supplemented by pigs—and the predation of aquatic fauna on a limited, opportunistic scale.

At Maadi, large areas of habitation remains dating to the early fourth millennium were investigated between 1930 and 1948, but no coherent chronological sequence was defined among them (Rizkana and Seeher 1989). They lie at the convergence of two wadis, extending 1.5 km in a narrow band along a terrace overlooking the floodplain, and covering a total area of 18 ha, of which around four were exposed. Since the mid-1980s, further excavations have taken place in the western part of the site, in response to its progressive destruction by modern settlement. A local predecessor for Maadi was excavated at el-Omari, at the mouth of the Wadi Hof near Helwan (Debono and Mortensen 1990). Dating to the late fifth or early fourth millennium, it comprised numerous storage pits lined with mud or reed matting, interspersed with postholes. Over forty burials of uncertain date were also excavated, some of them placed within storage pits.

In general accounts, Maadi has sometimes been reconstructed as a burgeoning Lower Egyptian town, acting as a staging post for the movement of commodities (notably copper) between the Levant and the Nile valley (e.g. Hoffman 1991: 201–9). Following eventual publication of the site reports on earlier twentieth-century work, as well as subsequent investigations, these claims now appear somewhat overblown. The habitation zone is described as 'a rather arbitrarily divided area loosely settled with simple small huts made of several posts supporting walls primarily of wattle and matting' (Rizkana and Seeher 1989: 75–80). Although cultural deposits in some areas reached a depth of 2 m, this is thought to result from later displacements of material (daub, animal dung and hearth remains) rather than settlement accumulation. Three cast copper ingots and a few pieces of copper ore were recovered from the site,

---

[15] For Middle and Lower Egypt, see Wetterstrom 1993: 218–19 (el-Badari, Mostagedda, Matmar); Barakat 1990 (el-Omari); Kroll 1989 (Maadi); van den Brink et al. 1989: 103–8 (Tell el-Iswid); Thanheiser 1996 (Tell el-Fara'in-Buto, Tell Ibrahim Awad).

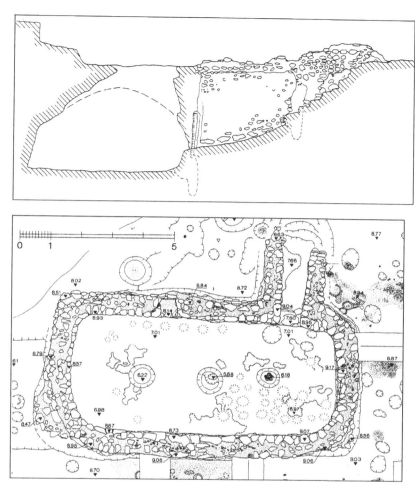

Figure 4.3 Stone-built architecture at Maadi, N. Egypt

but no evidence of metallurgy was found (Rizkana and Seeher 1989: 13–18, 38–9; cf. Ogden 2000: 149).

The overall character of the occupation at Maadi appears comparable to that of predynastic centres in Upper Egypt, with few clearly defined areas for dwelling, food processing or other kinds of activity. It is distinguished, however, by a series of highly distinctive stone-built structures, of which six examples are currently known, four in the east and two in the western part of the site (fig. 4.3). All were built either partially or entirely below ground (roofing is not preserved), had stepped entrances and were surrounded by storage pits of varying size, some of which housed large ceramic jars. The eastern group is remarkable both for the depth of the structures (between 1.5 and 3 m), and for the use of mud-brick and rough limestone blocks in their construction (Rizkana and Seeher 1989: 49–56, figs. 15, 18). They appear similar in plan to one of the more westerly structures, which comprised a stairway (c.2 m long) descending into a corridor (c.3 m) built of stone blocks, with carefully applied mud-plaster facing. This corridor led in turn to a dome-shaped room cut down almost 2.5 m into bedrock. Two areas of dense ash were detected in this room, yielding evidence of everyday activity in the form of five limestone spindle-whorls, worked animal bone and a rhomboid knife of a type familiar from Upper Egyptian burials. Postholes at either end of the adjacent corridor indicate substantial roofing, which appears to have collapsed in a conflagration, following which the remains of the structure were given over to storage (Hartung et al. 2003: 157–60, fig. 4). Approximately 50 m to the south-west was found a second subterranean building, which differed markedly in plan from those just described (Badawi 2003; Hartung et al. 2003: 155–7, fig. 3). Its thick, stone-built walls enclosed a roughly oval space of 8.5 x 4 m, which was sunk around 2 m into the ground and entered via a stepped passageway in the north wall, where a small niche was also present. Remnants of a wooden post were found within one of three large pits aligned across the centre of the room, confirming the former existence of a well-supported roof, while smaller depressions distributed around the floor area served as placements for ceramic vessels. Fragments of pottery recovered from the building include a small number of lug-handled jars imported from the Levant. Sherds from similar vessels were also found among a large assemblage of locally made wares within the corridor-and-dome structure described above (Badawi 2003: 7, fig. 3: g, h; Hartung et al. 2003: 179, fig. 14: b–d).

Given the apparent absence of substantial stone architecture elsewhere in Egypt, comparisons for the Maadi structures have often been sought to the east, in southern Israel and further north along the Levantine littoral. Subterranean rooms with circular plans are widely reported from Chalcolithic sites such as Bir es-Safadi and Abu Matar in the Beersheba valley, where—by contrast with the situation at Maadi—they form extensive complexes linked by tunnels. The purpose of these complexes has been widely debated, 'with interpretations ranging from special architectural adaptations to a hot desert environment, storage facilities associated with open-air villages, and defense and storage systems' (Levy 1995b: 229; see also Perrot 1984). As Ulrich Hartung observes, the single oval-shaped structure at Maadi has affinities with what Eliot Braun (1989) describes as the 'apsidal' tradition of domestic architecture, which achieved a wide distribution across the central and northern Levant during the EBI period (Hartung et al. 2003: 165–7). Braun's survey of thirty sites with curvilinear architecture, located between central Israel and the northern coast of Lebanon, encompasses a wide variety of types, none of which were built below ground or furnished with a wall-niche. Moreover, only at En Shadud in the Jezreel valley is there evidence for substantial roof supports within these buildings, and they appear to have been raised upon stone slabs (interpreted by another excavator as work-surfaces) rather than placed within postholes (Braun 1985: 68–72, figs. 28: b–31; cf. Ben-Tor 1973: 94). Some exchange of architectural concepts and practices between the Levant and Lower Egypt at this time would not be surprising, and fits well into an overall picture of intensified movement, trade and cultural interchange along the Mediterranean coastline, as demonstrated by the forms and distribution of mobile goods such as pottery (chapter 1.7). By contrast, widely evoked images of 'Asiatic traders' settled within an 'Egyptian' settlement at Maadi (e.g. Wilkinson 2002: 516) appear anachronistic, owing more to the later, dynastic ideology of territorial-cum-ethnic exclusivity than to the archaeological record of the early–mid fourth millennium BC.

Pump-assisted excavation, supplemented by core drillings, has made possible the limited exposure of a number of fourth-millennium sites in the northern and eastern parts of the Nile delta. Most were established on sandy promontories (*geziras*) rising above the ancient floodplain (van den Brink *et al.* 1989: 78, table 1). The most extensively investigated—Tell el-Iswid, Tell Ibrahim Awad, Tell el-Farkha and Tell el-Fara'in-Buto (Levels I–II)—have revealed a similar range of habitation features to those observed at Maadi. They include hearths, refuse middens and mud- or basket-lined pits, as well as numerous postholes mapping out the former distribution of reed structures.[16] At Buto, a continuous ceramic sequence now extends from predynastic to Old Kingdom times, and is partially corroborated by assemblages from other Lower Egyptian sites (Table 2; Köhler 1998a). A marked characteristic of this sequence seems to be the shift, around the middle of the fourth millennium, from a repertoire of everyday ceramic forms including types closely comparable to those of the southern Levant to a new range of heavily tempered coarse wares for the preparation and consumption of food. The latter include small, oval jars with rounded bases, flat-bottomed dishes, and bowls with flaring sides and everted rims. These forms find parallels at sites in the eastern delta (Tell el-Iswid, Tell Ibrahim Awad, Tell el-Farkha) and in the Nile valley, where they date to Naqada IIC–D (fig. 4.4, upper; Friedman 1994: 917–19).[17] As I go on to discuss, their widespread adoption in Egypt at this time may be linked to

---

[16] van den Brink *et al.* 1989; van den Brink 1992a; Chłodnicki *et al.* 1992; von der Way 1997: 61, 64–7, 80–1.

[17] This ceramic horizon corresponds to Phase A at Tell el-Iswid (van den Brink *et al.* 1989: 59–64), Phase II at Buto (Köhler 1992; 1998a), Phases 2–3 at Tell el-Farkha (Chłodnicki and Ciałowicz 2002: 104–6) and Phase 7 at Tell Ibrahim Awad (van den Brink 1992a: 53–5), and is further characterised by the occasional use of a rocker-stamp technique to impress linear decoration on to vessel surfaces, echoing much earlier practices of the Early Holocene; see Caneva 1992; van den Brink 1992a: 54, fig. 10; Faltings 2002: 167.

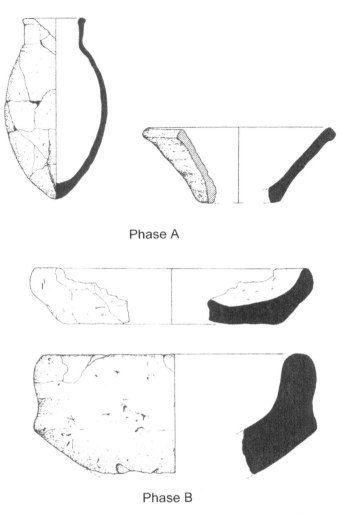

Phase A

Phase B

Figure 4.4 Coarse wares from late fourth- and early third-millennium strata at Tell el-Iswid, Nile delta

important dietary changes, following the introduction of fermented cereal products.

The appearance of Upper Egyptian funerary customs and their associated material culture in Lower Egypt during Naqada IIC–D has sometimes been thought to reflect the northward migration of significant numbers of people, and even entire communities. It is equally possible that internal factors led existing Lower Egyptian communities to adopt practices from the Nile valley at this time. Some combination of the two processes seems most likely. Relatively large-scale movements of people from the valley into the delta should not be ruled out, and find parallels both in Uruk-period Mesopotamia (e.g. at Habuba Kabira) and in a subsequent phase of Egyptian expansion into the coastal plain of the southern Levant (chapter 7.1, 7.2). They are further suggested by a marked overall increase in the number of sites in Lower Egypt during the succeeding Naqada III period (Krzyżaniak 1989).[18] Given the absence of mechanisms for sustained political and economic control over long distances, such movements may have been crucial in consolidating access to trade routes, the configuration of which was periodically altered by technological innovations such as the use of pack-donkeys.

The characterisation of this process as a 'cultural unification' of Upper and Lower Egypt is heavily influenced by the later ideology of kingship, in which the unification of the 'Two Lands' forms a core principle of royal action (chapter 9). Insofar as this phrase assumes an earlier binary opposition between the societies of Upper and Lower Egypt, it must be abandoned (Wildung 1984; Köhler 1995). As I go on to discuss, the picture during Naqada I–IIB was more complex, with a number of distinct cultural patterns co-existing within the Nile valley. What differentiated societies in the valley at that time, both from those of Lower Egypt and Sudan south of the Second Cataract, were constantly evolving conceptions of the land, the body and its treatment in death, which fuelled an expanding cycle of demand for particular display items (chapter 5). It was, among other things, this set of ideas that spread northwards into the Nile delta, following the opening up of trade routes along the Mediterranean littoral during the mid-fourth millennium. The role of newly established communities such as Minshat Abu Omar in this process was not that of passive conduits for long-distance trade. Rather, each would have generated its own competing demands for prestige goods and other forms of social display. No less significant was the widespread adoption of a common set of dietary practices at this time: over the long-term, Upper and Lower Egypt came to be unified as much by the consumption of leavened bread and beer as by the often-hypothesised activities of chiefs and kings.

4.5 Pots for the living, pots for the dead

At Hierakonpolis, predynastic burial zones form a boundary around areas of habitation, occupying the up- and downstream terraces of the Wadi Abu Suffian and demarcating the desert margins of human occupation (fig. 4.1; Adams and Hoffman 1987: 191). In these marginal areas, the spatial frontier between the living and the dead was not inviolable, and burial grounds sometimes expanded over the site of earlier habitations. This is the case with two Naqada IIC–D cemeteries, HK33 and HK27, the so-called 'Fort Cemetery'. Like other predynastic burials, these were not marked by permanent superstructures,

---

[18] van Wetering and Tassie (2003) provide an extensive list and distribution map of pre-Early Dynastic sites in the eastern delta, the majority as yet identified only through field survey.

although modest piles of stones and (more rarely) perishable enclosures were sometimes built upon or around them. As sites of ritual performance, consumers of material wealth and loci of social memory, cemeteries would nevertheless have exerted a strong influence over the conduct of the living. For an initial discussion of this relationship between the dead and the living, the most informative type of object in the archaeological record is pottery.

Rough and smooth: the social roles of containers in Naqada I

The distinction between tempered and untempered wares provides a starting point. The former were coarse, everyday products, made rapidly by hand and used predominantly for the preparation of food. The quantity of cereal remains (emmer wheat and barley) at sites of this period suggests that such products as porridge, grits and flat bread were common comestibles, supplementing a wide range of fruits (e.g. dates and *nabk* berries) and vegetables (e.g. lentils, peas, legumes). In an authoritative study, Renée Friedman (1994) has discerned three distinct regional traditions for the manufacture of coarse wares, based primarily on the temper habitually chosen to improve their thermal properties. The first extends along a 35 km stretch of the Nile in the el-Badari region; the second was centred upon the bend of the Nile near modern Qena, where Naqada is located; the third encompasses the areas around Hierakonpolis. A complementary study by Diane Holmes (1989) demonstrates a similar configuration of regional traditions in the manufacture of flint tools, which comprised a wide range of scrapers, burins, notches and blades. In combination, these studies argue for the existence of three well-defined interaction spheres along the Egyptian Nile valley, operating at the level of everyday contacts and habits of work. As Friedman (1994: 879–81) points out, the objects circulating within them were rarely incorporated into funerary assemblages during Naqada I.

Untempered ceramics are immediately distinguishable from coarse wares by their smooth and highly polished surfaces, and by their shapes, comprising a distinct range of beakers, jars and rounded or carinated bowls (fig. 4.5). They were labour-intensive products, created from finely sorted alluvial clay and carefully baked (probably in a stack formation) within an open fire to produce a plum-red surface colour. Due to variations in temperature and oxidising levels during firing (closed kilns with uniform firing temperatures were a later innovation), vessels heated at the bottom of the stack acquired a distinctive black rim during firing, which also made them less porous.[19] Vessels without

---

[19] This conclusion, based on experimental work by Hendrickx, Friedman and Loyens (2000), seems more economical than the earlier view that polished red pots were subject to a secondary firing process aimed specifically at producing the blackened mouth (Lucas 1932). By implication, the ubiquity of blackened mouths on earlier (Badarian) fine ware would reflect a lower overall output of untempered vessels, which were not then fired in multiple layers. The practice of stacking vessels during firing might also account for the greater number of flat-based forms during Naqada I, by contrast with the predominance of hemispherical bowls in Badarian times.

Figure 4.5 Naqada I fine ware: black-topped ('B-Ware')

black mouths were sometimes decorated with a range of designs in white paint, derived from calcareous clay (chapter 5.1; figs. 5.2, 5.5). In classifying the corpus of predynastic pottery, Petrie (1921) used the term C-Ware as convenient shorthand for this type of painted vessel. 'B-Ware' referred in turn to pots with a black mouth, and 'P-Ware' to polished red containers that exhibit neither of these features.[20]

Although not exclusively used as funerary objects, fine polished wares were regularly deposited as grave goods in the Egyptian Nile valley and Lower Nubia. Throughout this region they exhibit substantial commonalities of form, firing technique and surface treatment, suggesting the transmission of knowledge and finished goods across social networks that transcended the more localised arenas of everyday production, and were sustained by a desire for objects appropriate to the grave (cf. Friedman 1994: 879–81). Direct evidence for the centralised manufacture of polished wares derives from a series of production sites at Hierakonpolis (Geller 1984). The sites (HK39, 40, 59 and 59A) are aligned along a secluded terrace deep within the Wadi Abu Suffian, over 2.5 km from the edge of the modern cultivation. They comprise dense scatters of sherds from untempered plum-red pottery, including large quantities of wasters created during the firing process. These production sites were established directly adjacent to a series of heavily plundered Naqada I–IIB cemeteries (HK6, 12 and 13), beyond which the large habitation zone known as HK11C extends in the direction of the alluvium. The HK6 cemetery contained a number of graves of exceptional size, the contents of which included remains of exotic animals such as a juvenile elephant and desert baboons (Adams 1996a; 2000). At least one very large burial pit was demarcated by a rectangular enclosure of reed matting, supported on acacia posts (Adams 2001). Elaborate burial rites, fine pottery production and general habitation all appear to have ended at roughly the same date in this locale, as activity shifted towards the floodplain during Naqada IIC–D.

Leavened bread and beer: a dietary revolution in Naqada II?

The transition from Naqada I to Naqada II has long been recognised by a marked change in the nature of decorated pottery: the replacement of C-Ware by a new range of painted vessels known collectively as D- (Decorated) Ware (fig. 4.6). D-Ware used pale marl clay, of much more limited distribution than the Nile silt from which C-Ware was made, to fashion a ceramic product of entirely new appearance (Nordström and Bourriau 1993: 160; Payne 1993: 97–101). Bowls, which had been prominent in the repertory of C-Ware, hardly occur among D-Ware forms, which comprise mostly closed, globular containers sometimes furnished with perforated lug-handles allowing, or perhaps alluding to, transport. Their size varies from tiny vessels that could be held in the palm to very bulky forms on which the scale of painted decoration expands to fill the enlarged surface area. The marl clay of D-Ware is the earliest ceramic widely distributed in Egypt that offered a pale ground for painting,

---

[20] C-Ware = White Cross-Lined, B-Ware = Black-Topped, P-Ware = Polished Red.

Figure 4.6 Naqada II decorated marl ware ('D-Ware')

which was executed in a dull red, ochre-derived pigment, by contrast with the white-on-dark painting of C-Ware. It also fired to considerably higher temperatures than Nile silt and would probably have required the construction of closed up-draught kilns, although no such facility has yet been discovered (Bourriau *et al.* 2000: 124–5, 131, 137; Hendrickx *et al.* 2000: 185). This postulated change in firing technology may be related to the decline of black-topped pottery, which accompanied the spread of marl wares during Naqada IIC–D.

Similarities in the form and decorative style of vessels found throughout Egypt and Lower Nubia suggest that the making of D-Ware was, like that of C-Ware, a specialised affair (cf. Smith 1993). Paint was applied before firing and so was integral to this product, which was probably distributed from a small number of points of manufacture. Its primary use seems to have been as a grave good, although small numbers of sherds are reported from habitation sites (Brunton and Caton-Thompson 1928: 77–8; Mond and Myers 1937: 166–81). The most complete examples derive from burials of Naqada IIC–D (c.3650–3300 BC). By contrast with its relatively limited currency, the spatial distribution of D-Ware was wide, extending from Lower Nubia in the south as far north as the Nile delta, with isolated sherds also reported from the southern Levantine coast.[21] The decoration of C-Ware and D-Ware, and their

---

[21] Some hundreds of D-Ware vessels are known from publications and museum collections. Of these, something in the order of 350 were painted with recognisably figural motifs, and out of these, approximately 200 have a known archaeological provenance (Graff 2002). For more specific inventories, see Adams 2002: 5; Hendrickx 2000; 2002a; 2002b.

relationship to other media of display, is considered in the next chapter. Marl clay was also used at this time for a variety of undecorated vessel forms. They include a range of distinctive jars with wavy ledge handles (W-Ware), which played a central role in Petrie's (1901b: 4–12) elucidation of the predynastic chronological sequence (see Table 1). W-Ware was inspired by Early Bronze I prototypes imported from the central hill country of the southern Levant, which are likely to have carried a liquid commodity, perhaps wine or olive oil. Like D-Ware, locally made W-Ware has rarely been documented from habitation sites and appears to have been valued primarily for use in funerary contexts.[22]

The alteration of ceramic techniques during Naqada II was not restricted to fine wares. As Friedman has demonstrated, the production of coarse, undecorated pottery also underwent a major transformation. Throughout the Egyptian Nile valley regional traditions of manufacture were replaced by a single, uniform technique, which used straw in preference to local varieties of temper such as shale and grog (crushed pot-sherds), respectively employed in the Hierakonpolis and Naqada areas during Naqada I–IIB. This process of replacement is associated with a marked increase in the overall output of coarse vessels, typical forms of which included mould-made bowls, bottles (fig. 4.4, upper), high-shouldered jars with modelled rims and rounded bases, and large basins with thick walls (Friedman 1994: 9–10, 900–6; Adams and Friedman 1992: 325–7). Unlike their Naqada I predecessors, these coarse vessels were deposited in graves alongside fine wares. By Naqada IIC–D they often constituted more than half the ceramic repertoire in any given burial (Kaiser 1957; Friedman 1994: 26–8, 900, table 1.2). While this figure may be influenced by looters' preference for decorative wares, it holds good for many undisturbed contexts.

How should this widespread change in attitude towards coarse containers be interpreted? Since the vessels themselves are unlikely display items, their significance would presumably have resided in their contents. In Mesopotamia, a comparable spread of mass-produced chaff-tempered bowls (with distinctive bevelled rims) during the fourth millennium BC (Uruk period) has been convincingly associated with the centralised production of leavened bread, for which they are thought to have served as baking moulds. This latter process may have been closely related, both practically and socially, to the earliest production of beer, for which fermenting techniques were similarly essential (Schmidt 1982; Millard 1988).[23] Correspondences between the earliest written symbols for bread and beer in Egypt and Mesopotamia have been

[22] Amiran 1970: 35–40; Payne 1993: 97, 130–3; Hendrickx and Bavay 2002: 67.
[23] The following discussion owes much to an unpublished manuscript by Andrew Sherratt ('Bread, butter and beer: dietary change and urbanisation in early Mesopotamia and surrounding areas') and discussions with its author.

widely noted, and the parallel development of bread moulds in these regions during the fourth and third millennia has been discussed by Michael Chazan and Mark Lehner (1990), providing a long-term perspective on the matter at hand.

During the Old Kingdom the standard Egyptian bread mould, known as the *bedja*, was a large, thick-walled bowl produced from Nile silt and tempered with straw and sand (Jacquet-Gordon 1981). Remains of vast quantities of these vessels have been found at sites from the First to the Sixth Dynasties, ranging from habitation areas and royal pyramid complexes to the contents of elite tombs. Pictorial decoration in tombs of the late Old Kingdom (Faltings 1998b) depicts the processes of bread and beer manufacture in considerable detail (fig. 4.7). Unlike the smaller Mesopotamian bread moulds, which were stacked inside the oven with their contents, *bedja* bowls were preheated to receive the dough, acting, in Chazan and Lehner's (1990: 29) terms, as 'portable ovens'. Leavened bread in turn provided the basic ingredient for beer, which was brewed from a mixture of crumbled, part-baked loaves and water, presumably mixed with other flavourings that may also have borne additional yeasts and sugars to aid fermentation. The resulting mixture was strained into ceramic jars, produced in bulk and sealed with mud stoppers (Samuel 2000).

The evolution of *bedja* bowls from predynastic coarse wares, which has been widely hypothesised, is plausibly supported by the identification of brewing installations at Naqada II–III sites in the Nile valley and delta. The most clearly documented is HK24A at Hierakonpolis, dating to the mid-Naqada II period (Geller 1992; Samuel 2000: 539–41). It comprises parallel rows of large ceramic vats supported by bar-shaped bricks, built into brick-lined channels. Cereal residues from these vessels, and the presence of an adjacent area for pottery production, strongly suggest a role in brewing. In light of this discovery, comparable installations have been identified in older site reports from Abydos, el-Mahasna and perhaps Ballas (Geller 1989: 43–6). Their scale implies the centralised manufacture of what would, by comparison with earlier cereal-based foods, have been a labour- and fuel-intensive product (cf. Friedman 1994: 862, 911–12).

Ceramic sequences from numerous sites suggest that these developments were paralleled in the Nile delta (chapter 4.4), and a malting installation has been tentatively identified in a Naqada IIIA context at Buto (von der Way 1992: 6–7). As in the Nile valley, thick-walled bread moulds make up a significant proportion of the pottery assemblage at Naqada III sites in Lower Egypt, where their appearance coincides with the widespread use of mud-brick. In both regions, however, the Naqada II predecessors for these vessels were smaller and more comparable in form to the ubiquitous bevelled-rim bowls of Uruk-period Mesopotamia. Given the limited, but well-documented passage of objects and images between these regions during Naqada IIC–D, the adoption of fermented cereal products in Egypt might be viewed as a further appropriation

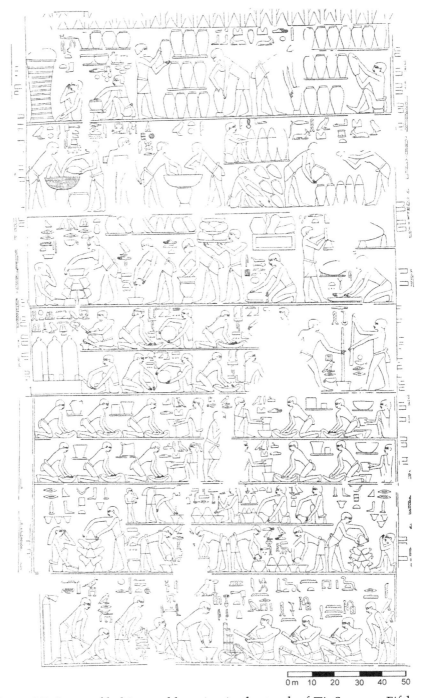

Figure 4.7 Scene of baking and brewing in the tomb of Ti, Saqqara, Fifth
    Dynasty

of prestige technologies from the outside. This implies a more direct form of contact between Egypt and Mesopotamia than would be necessary for the procurement of items such as seals or lapis lazuli, limited quantities of which could easily have entered long-established trade networks along the Levantine littoral. Significantly, however, evidence for bevelled-rim bowls is lacking in the latter region, as are many other material signatures of contact with urban centres in southern Mesopotamia, such as are found further inland on the Euphrates and to the east (Philip 2002).

One such signature is a distinctive form of mosaic wall-decoration typically applied to public buildings in Mesopotamia, using coloured pegs inserted by the thousand into the plaster sealing of mud-brick walls (e.g. Frankfort 1996: 24–5, figs. 8–9). This type of decoration is documented at Uruk and at sites on the Upper Euphrates, where it is found in association with bevelled-rim bowls, complex accounting systems and forms of architecture related to those of the southern alluvium (Moorey 1990). A small number of objects resembling these wall-pegs have also been discovered in the lower levels at Buto, leading some commentators to suggest the presence of immigrants from Mesopotamia in the Nile delta during the mid-fourth millennium (e.g. von der Way 1987: 247–9, fig. 3). Others have since pointed out the lack of evidence for mud-brick architecture in the levels concerned, and that the isolated discovery of these objects in small numbers is inconsistent with the proposed usage (Friedman 2000).[24] It is therefore unclear whether these finds have any real bearing upon the nature of contacts between Mesopotamia and Egypt, and hence upon the adoption of brewing and baking techniques in the latter region. Less direct forms of external stimulus might also be considered, notably the transfer of fermentation techniques from the Levant, where they were applied in the manufacture of wine and dairy products (chapter 1.6, 1.9). What remains clear is that, as with other cultural features introduced from outside, any such influence was subject to local redefinition, reflected in the development of a distinctively Egyptian method of bread-preparation by the Naqada III period.

It may be more rewarding to dwell upon the consequences rather than the genesis of this process. As Andrew Sherratt (2002: 69–70) observes:

In the ultimate analysis it was not so much the individual technologies of food-preparation themselves which were distinctive as the fact that they involved a concentration of relatively expensive elements and implied lengthened production-chains and additional labour costs, so that they were not necessarily equally available to society as a whole . . . Along with new foods would have been a change in the nature of feasting, from simply the provision of abundant food to the concentration of resources in order to prepare more complex items (and especially, but not exclusively, intoxicating beverages), implying control of wider social

---

[24] See also Wilde and Behnert 2002, with an alternative interpretation of the pegs as implements used in the production of salt.

networks to procure supplies of relatively rare or expensive resources. In this respect the provision of food parallels other items of material culture such as metalwork or clothing, which might also be described in similar terms.

As I go on to discuss, this formulation corresponds well to the heightened patterns of trade, consumption and competitive display attested in the funerary record of Naqada II Egypt. The association of coarse ceramics with burial practices further suggests that, by contrast with Mesopotamia, rituals surrounding the dead provided an important forum for the creation of new needs and the legitimation of new sumptuary practices. If the emerging picture of ceramic production and use in predynastic Egypt is broadly correct—and further detailed studies are desirable—then by the end of Naqada II leavened bread and beer had become socially necessary for the proper commemoration of the dead in Egypt (cf. Joffe 1998). This implies a significant loss of autonomy for individuals without direct access to the means of their production, as well as a fundamental change in the social setting and emotional context of funerary rites, not least through the consumption of alcohol. The full nature of this transformation can be appreciated only by taking into account a range of other innovations in the material culture of commemoration.

IMAGE, RITUAL AND THE CONSTRUCTION OF IDENTITY IN LATE PREHISTORY

Designs are social forms external to the individual that yet are in contact with the body . . . elements that traverse the boundaries of the individual body [are detached from it] and yet are constantly being bound back into bodily experience.

Walbiri Iconography, N. Munn

5.1 Between body and land: predynastic art as a cultural landscape

The most striking of the innovations referred to at the end of the last chapter was an expansion in the range of decorated objects available to most individuals, in life as well as death. Not only were images of humans, animals and plants painted on the surface of pots during Naqada I–II. They were also carved out of the ivory and bone bodies of cosmetic implements (fig. 5.1), chipped from stone and formed in clay on an unprecedented scale. If settlement practices remained for the most part ephemeral and weakly structured, attributes of the landscape were nevertheless 'extracted from nature and transferred to culture', as Lévi-Strauss (1966: 107) puts it, through conversion into portable forms and pictures. Applied to cosmetic implements, personal ornaments, vessels and other objects, these images were incorporated into established techniques of interaction and personal display. Although mobile and diffuse, they may legitimately be considered from the perspective of recent theoretical work on the construction of cultural landscapes. Susanne Küchler (1993: 85) points out that we are used to thinking of landscape as 'a record of, or stage for, significant human actions . . . an inscribed surface which can be measured, described or depicted', and upon which memories are captured 'in the form of architectural or other visual landmarks'. In contexts where the built environment is weakly emphasised as a structure for social action and learning, the experience of landscape—as mediated by mobile objects and observable differences within the domains of vegetation, animal life and in the form of the land itself—nevertheless continues to provide a source of generative frameworks for processes of cultural transmission. As Andrew Jones (1998: 301–2) puts it, the 'fluid nature of place' may be studied through daily or ritual activities that 'embody landscape in a number of very specific ways, especially by presencing and articulating memory associated with particular places and people'.

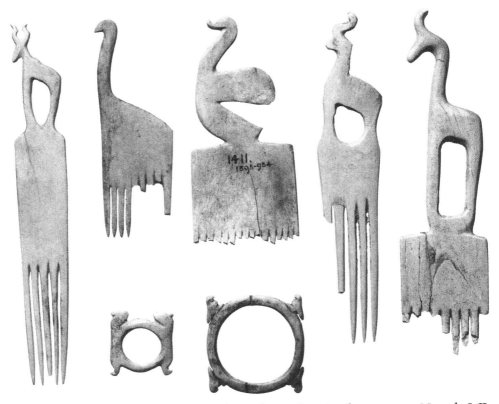

Figure 5.1 Bone and ivory personal articles with animal ornament, Naqada I–II

Reconsidering Capart: predynastic art as 'Primitive Art'

For western audiences, attuned to a particular vision of ancient Egypt, predynastic art objects have always held a capacity to shock. They differ markedly in scale and appearance from the often monumental works of painting and sculpture that have long been the familiar constituents of ancient Egyptian art. The majority were excavated from burials or purchased on the burgeoning Egyptian antiquities market of the late nineteenth and early twentieth centuries. Their overtly functional attributes meant that, with the exception of painted pots and figurines (which quickly caught the eye of dealers), they— like much so-called Primitive Art—could not easily be accommodated to a notion of the art object as passively viewed, rather than actively used.[1] Nor does their visual style arouse the impression of timeless familiarity felt by many modern observers when standing before a dynastic relief or sculpted figure.

---

[1] For questions of authenticity with regard to figurines and painted vessels, see Brunton 1934; Ucko and Hodges 1963; Lupton 1992.

The definition of predynastic art as generic Primitive Art can be attributed in large measure to Jean Capart, Keeper of Egyptian Antiquities at the Royal Museum of Brussels, at the turn of the twentieth century. In *Les débuts de l'art en Egypte* (1904; *Primitive Art in Egypt*, 1905) Capart attempted the first interpretative synthesis of this material, much of which had already been published by Petrie.[2] Petrie's tendency, understandable given his burden of fieldwork and range of interests, was to describe prehistoric objects economically in terms of their probable functions. Remarkably few of his original judgements have since been subject to revision. A pertinent example is his now widely accepted suggestion that cosmetic palettes, among the most common decorated objects found in predynastic burials, were used to produce eye paint. Like their Neolithic precursors, predynastic palettes were certainly used for grinding paint, as indicated by surface stains and wear, and their common association with pigment in burials. Petrie's specific interpretation, however, appears to have been formulated largely on the basis of a single ethnographic analogy, which offered a pragmatic justification for the use of body paint: 'coating the skin around the eye' would serve to 'stop out the glare of the desert, as the Eskimo blackens the skin to save the eye from the glare of the snow' (Petrie 1901b: 21). Elise Baumgartel (1960: 82) later drew attention to the use of green eye paint on Old Kingdom statuary and painted mummy wrappings, and its mention in mortuary inscriptions such as offering lists and the Pyramid Texts of the Fifth Dynasty (cf. Ciałowicz 1991: 40; Kroeper 1996: 72). To this day, however, no evidence exists from the relevant period to support Petrie's suggestion that the application of body paint was restricted to the area around the eyes in predynastic times.

Capart, unlike Petrie, appears to have been struck more by the possible differences between predynastic and dynastic treatments of the body, rather than any potential continuity. For Capart, inspired by a reading of Pacific ethnography, the extensive ornamentation and marking of the skin was a definitive function of predynastic art, distinguishing predynastic bodies from the austere appearance of Egyptians in dynastic painting and sculpture. The small decorative objects that formed his main subject matter—palettes, combs, pins, tags, spoons, amulets, flint tools, ceramic and stone vessels, and figurines—still constitute the known repertoire of predynastic art. In the event, however, Capart devoted remarkably little attention to the study of their functional and stylistic attributes. Instead he dwelt upon the use of techniques for altering the body directly, such as coiffure, scarification and

---

[2] In the preface to *Primitive Art*, Capart (1905: vii) anticipated that an English readership might be 'most prepared both to receive and to criticise' his work, perhaps implying that the French edition had received a lukewarm reception. The reason he gave is that, in his own words, 'The works of English ethnologists, more especially of Lubbock, Tylor, Lang, Haddon, Frazer, Spencer and Gillen, were the first to draw attention to a whole series of problems of the greatest importance for a study of the origin of Art.'

tattooing. Despite favourable conditions of preservation, such practices could rarely be investigated from surviving corpses. To reconstruct Polynesia in prehistoric Egypt, Capart was therefore forced to rely upon indirect evidence from the markings on figurines, comparisons with the ethnographic record and depictions of non-Egyptians in dynastic art, where they are stereotypically portrayed with extravagantly ornamented bodies (see, e.g., Shaw 2000b). In spite of its shortcomings, Capart's work drew valuable attention to the close connection between predynastic art and social practices relating to the modification of the body. With hindsight, this theme seems best addressed through the objects themselves; that is, through their attributes of image, form and function, and their contextual relationships to bodies within the grave.

The escaping image: considerations of form, place and function

In considering these attributes it is useful to begin by comparing the two main styles of painted pottery, C-Ware and the chronologically later D-Ware (see also chapter 4.5). One of the most striking features of painting on D-Ware is the absence of regularity in spatial composition (fig. 4.6; cf. Tefnin 1993). By contrast with the decorated pottery of prehistoric Mesopotamia or Iran, motif form and placement are only weakly integrated with the morphology of the pot. The presence of symmetrically arranged handles—which may be tubular, triangular or wavy—may have influenced the basic division of the decorative field, as with the numerous jars on which boats are depicted. With other motifs, however, the painted designs often simply extend over the handles. As on earlier C-Ware beakers (but not bowls), these motifs vary in content and arrangement around the surface, in such a way that the relationships between them can never be viewed in their entirety (except in modern publications, which transfer the decoration from its three-dimensional support to the surface of the page). Rotation of the vessel, and hence some form of memory-work, are therefore essential to any reading of their content: a point not addressed by interpreters who treat the decoration as a momentary scene or tableau (e.g. Dreyer *et al.* 1998: 111–12; cf. Garfinkel 2001).

   In short, there is little sense of a particular pattern to D-Ware decoration that might either relate to the technology of ceramic production or indicate formal derivation from more rigidly structured media such as basketry (cf. Wengrow 2001b). Here it is tempting to draw a contrast with the painting of C-Ware, in which geometrical stylisation and cross-hatching are quite commonly employed. Early commentators such as Petrie (1920: 14) and Frankfort (1924: 94) related the use of linear decoration on C-Ware to basketry techniques, but acknowledged that this hypothesis cannot be extended to the form or deployment of figural elements, with which linear designs are often closely interwoven (e.g. fig. 5.2). Helene Kantor (1953: 76) pertinently observed how in

Figure 5.2 White Cross-Lined ('C-Ware') bowl with model hippopotami, el-Mahasna, Naqada I

such cases 'the pot surfaces are merely a medium, a place for the representation, not a formative factor in the composition . . . vessels on which representation designs have been subordinated to decorative schemes are exceedingly rare'. Even in such cases, found only on bowl interiors, the symmetry of animal figures on C-Ware is not exact, and the central motif lies some way off the geometrical centre of the vessel.

More pronounced contrasts between the painting of C-Ware and D-Ware are found in the relationship between figural and non-figural decoration. C-Ware vessels are typically ornamented with linear, geometrical shapes, often made up of radiating lines that are also used to fill the outlined bodies of adjacent animal figures such as hippopotami, horned quadrupeds, reptiles and dogs. Figural and non-figural images interpenetrate, differentiating C-Ware from D-Ware, where there is little overlap of this kind and both animal and human figures are often filled with solid colour. Solid figures do, however, appear on a minority of C-Ware vessels, such as a widely discussed series of tall beakers with anthropomorphic decoration (Hendrickx 1998; Dreyer *et al.* 1998, pl. 6: d–f). Many commentators have sought to identify the non-figural patterns on both wares as particular features of the landscape, such as mountains, water or plants (e.g. Finkenstaedt 1981; Fairservis 1983). While a generic association with landscape seems likely, such specific readings should be treated with caution. Franz Boas (1955 [1927]: 88–143) long ago demonstrated that associations between visual patterns and natural features are not universally recognised, but mediated through culturally acquired knowledge of the non-human world. Thus, in Shoshone art of the North American Plains a straight red line was used to represent the river, while triangles could signify mountains, tents or sand. More recently, Howard Morphy (1989: 155) observed that in Yolngu carvings and paintings in Arnhem Land (northern Australia) white cross-hatching may stand for smoke, dots for ash, and diamond patterns for water. Moreover, for Yolngu, knowledge of these visual meanings, which serve as memory cues for stories about the making of the world, is closely regulated through linkage to group identity and ancestral status (Morphy 1991).

A further point of difference between C-Ware and D-Ware resides in the relationship between two- and three-dimensional decoration. The deployment of animal images on C-Ware sometimes escapes the bounds of the vessel, extending from the surface into plastic ornamentation along the rim (fig. 5.2). These three-dimensional figures are burnished, painted and fired to harmonise with the container that fails altogether to contain them. They appear, then, to be materialisations of images that were painted on vessel surfaces, such as hippopotami, crocodiles, elephants and cattle.[3] Fluidity between surface decoration and plastic modelling is further exemplified by a beaker discovered in Cemetery U at Abydos. From its rim extend modelled anthropomorphic figures with breasts and beak-like heads, closely comparable to a well-known series of individual figurines found at el-Ma'amariya and Hierakonpolis (Kom el-Ahmar), far to the south (fig. 5.3).[4] Anthropomorphic figures with raised arm postures, such as are found on some of these figurines, also feature among the painted decoration on C-Ware bowls and beakers, and become more frequent on D-Ware, where they are often accompanied by smaller figures with penis sheaths.[5] Penis sheaths also appear on some figurines, and actual leather examples have been found in burials at Naga el-Deir and perhaps also at Hierakonpolis (Ucko 1967: 350–2; Friedman *et al.* 1999: 7).

A similar propensity for decorative forms to move between images, three-dimensional objects and use on the body can be documented in relation to D-Ware, but is differently expressed. In the few known examples, the entire vessel takes on the shape of a boat or animal, to which painted motifs are applied in the usual fashion (Payne 1993: 24, 113, figs. 17, 50, cat. 88, 927). One

---

[3] Quibell 1905, pl. 24, cat. 11570; von Bissing 1913: 23–4, cat. 18804; Scharff 1926, pl. 1: 1; 1928, pl. 27: 2; Brunton 1948, pl. 12: 7; Baumgartel 1960, pl. 5.6; Page-Gasser and Wiese 1997: 24–5.
[4] Dreyer *et al.* 1998: 114, fig. 12: 4; pl. 6: c; cf. Ucko 1968: 44–8, 53, 99–100, 105, cat. 69–73, 83; Ucko and Hodges 1963: 207; Needler 1984: 336–43, cat. 267–73.
[5] Petrie 1920, pl. 18: 74; Payne 1993: 58, fig. 27, cat. 389; Hendrickx 1998, figs. 5–6; 2002a.

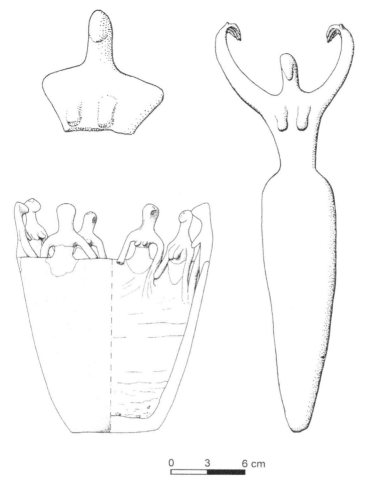

Figure 5.3 Clay figurines from el-Ma'amariya and ornamented vessel from Abydos, Naqada I

such vessel, from a burial at Hierakonpolis, has the shape of a fish, the animal form most commonly used for cosmetic palettes of the period (fig. 5.4, lower right; Payne 1993: 113, fig. 50, cat. 929; cf. Ciałowicz 1991: 21–4). A clay figurine from a burial at Ab'adiya has the same form; this was found together with three anthropomorphic figurines, an anthropomorphic vase, a mud model wall surmounted by two human figures, and a number of other animal figurines.[6] The last group included a well-preserved turtle figurine: an animal form which, like the fish, was frequently used for cosmetic palettes (Payne 1993: 22, fig. 15, cat. 68; Ciałowicz 1991: 35–7). In the world of three-dimensional objects, typical forms of animal ornament such as horns and bird-heads move

---

[6] Petrie 1901b: 32, pl. 6; Payne 1993: 22, fig. 16, cat. 69; see also Williams 1994.

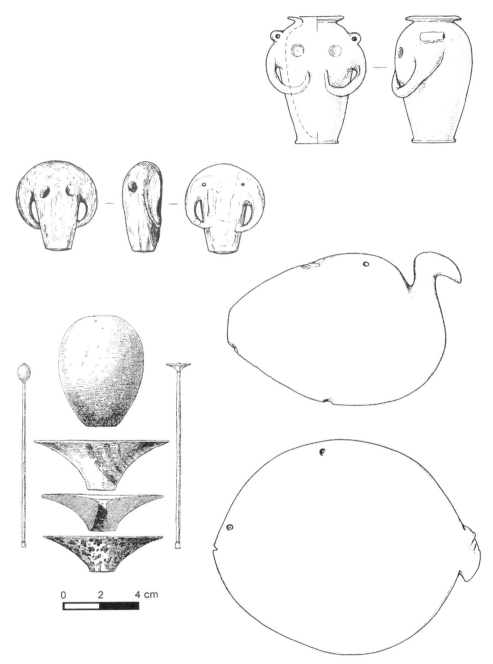

Figure 5.4 Serpentine vessel, ivory pendant, stone maces and figured palettes, Naqada II

seamlessly between bone or ivory combs, pendants, pins and cosmetic palettes (cf. Baumgartel 1960: 48–57, 84–7; Hendrickx 2002b). Another widely diffused image, variously identified as the head of a bull or elephant, is also not confined to a single class of object; most commonly distributed as a pendant, it occurs on the surface of a mace-head and as the body of a stone vessel (fig. 5.4, upper).[7] Just as an image might be transferred from a pendant to the surface of a functional container, so the form of an implement could be replicated in miniature for use as an ornament. Such is the case with the centrepiece of a necklace from a burial at Abusir el-Melek, which takes the form of a lozenge with opposing birds' heads, imitating the shape of a well-known type of cosmetic palette (Scharff 1926, pl. 36: 312/392; cf. Ciałowicz 1991: 30–2).

These interrelationships of decorative form across media point towards a more general feature of predynastic art that has not perhaps been sufficiently recognised. It is highlighted with striking clarity by two C-Ware bowls, on which the painted images appear to depict, not living beings, but manufactured objects of a kind familiar from the archaeological record (Kantor 1953). One vessel, from a burial at el-Masaid, is decorated with images of combs adorned with horned animals. The second, which is unprovenanced, shows a dog attacking a picture of a similar object (fig. 5.5). For predynastic art as a whole, such objects may be the exceptions that prove the rule. Relationships between them transcend any rigid distinction between decorative form, medium and function. Functional objects are containers for images, but may themselves become objects of containment. If anything, it is the autonomous connections between images, rather than their incorporation into discrete categories of artefact, that appear to give unity to an otherwise disparate world of things.

The function of decorated objects, most of which are either portable or provided with some means of binding to the body, may have resided as much in their potential to keep these images close to the person as in their complementary roles in personal grooming, paint preparation and consumption (Midant-Reynes 1992: 172; 2000: 80; Wengrow 2001a).[8] In addition to moving between media, they were images in motion, introducing elements from a coherent vision of the landscape into the intimate spaces of human circulation, and—through their mobilisation as gifts (funerary or otherwise)

---

[7] Scharff 1929–31: 80–1, fig. 21, pl. 8, cat. 152; Payne 1993: 144, fig. 57, cat. 1201; see also van Lepp 1999; Hendrickx 2002b: 284–7.

[8] Much animal ornament on cosmetic articles and tags centres upon the interplay of beaks and horns (Baumgartel 1960: 85–6; Hendrickx 2002b). In addition to their desired visual qualities, these forms provided another effective means of fixing the object to the body (cf. Baumgartel 1960: 45). Other common decorative items, such as cosmetic palettes in the shape of fish, were usually perforated, and leather bindings have been discovered still attached to various kinds of personal ornaments in a number of graves (e.g. Reisner 1910: 122, fig. 75, pl. 63: b5). The fluidity between decorative form and function is vividly illustrated by a well-preserved burial at Ab'adiya, the remains of which are now in the Ashmolean Museum, Oxford. Projecting from the deceased's hair were two pins ornamented with birds, and the functional ends of an undecorated spoon and comb (Petrie 1901b: 34, pl. 6, grave B378).

Figure 5.5 White Cross-Lined ('C-Ware') bowl, Naqada I

and practical objects—into the flow of social memory. The nexus of all these relationships in life and death was the human body.

5.2 Pictorial composition: the wider context

Enough has been said above to indicate that, for a study of predynastic material culture in structured contexts, the remains of the dead provide a more fertile ground than those of the living. While the values ascribed to grave goods almost certainly differed from those borne by the same objects in everyday life, funerary rituals were a significant framework within which they acquired meanings in relation to the deceased and to the group conducting the burial. Such rituals constitute a continuous perspective on the transformation of social behaviour over time. I now look in greater detail at the nature of relationships between objects and persons created through ritual, and how they compare with earlier practices, starting with the fragmentary evidence for media of display that have barely survived in the archaeological record, but which should be incorporated—if only as spaces of the imagination—into any model of social change.

Painted surfaces

Pottery is simply the most durable medium to which paint was applied in predynastic times. It is beyond doubt that pictorial images were also distributed over a range of perishable materials. This is most clearly exemplified by fragments of painted linen found during the early twentieth century in a burial at Gebelein (Scamuzzi 1965, pls. 1–5; Donadoni Roveri 1990: 23–5). The linen is usually dated to Naqada I or early Naqada II, and its decoration includes images of boats and human figures with raised arms, executed in a somewhat different manner to those that became widespread on D-Ware. A unique assortment of painted objects fashioned in stucco plaster has been recovered from a Naqada IIA burial at el-Adaima (Crubézy *et al.* 2002: 72–82, 468–71). They include replicas of a knife, three maces (with ceramic heads), a hollow cylindrical quiver or sheath, and two imitation sandals with the leather soles painted in red, the straps and stitching indicated in white. In addition to their importance in highlighting an otherwise missing medium of display, these finds add a further dimension to the explicit interplay between object and sign discussed earlier.

The most extensive pictorial composition to survive from predynastic Egypt is the painted wall decoration of tomb 100 (the 'Painted Tomb') at Hierakonpolis, discovered by Quibell and Green at the turn of the twentieth century, and still without parallel (fig. 5.6).[9] A date of Naqada IIC is now generally accepted for the tomb, the contents of which had been heavily plundered (Kaiser and Dreyer 1982: 242). The painting in tomb 100, like that on the Gebelein linen, is polychrome—principally red and black with some white—differentiating it from the monochrome decoration of painted pottery. For reasons that will become apparent, its decoration—comprising images of boats, animals, and humans in combat—has long been pivotal to discussions of social and political change in predynastic Egypt (e.g. Kantor 1944: 111–19; Baines 1995: 97).

The Painted Tomb was one of a number of exceptionally large, rectangular funerary structures discovered in the midst of about 150 smaller burials lying west of the Wadi Khamsini. Regrettably, these large burials have not been relocated by more recent expeditions to the site. All were subterranean, with no recorded traces of a superstructure. Mud-brick was extensively used in constructing the walls of tomb 100, which were 4.5 m long and descended to a depth of 1.5 m. A partition wall divided the burial chamber, and its interior surfaces were coated with plaster to which the paint was applied. In terms of

---

[9] Quibell and Green 1902: 20–3, pls. 75–9; Case and Payne 1962; Kemp 1973.

0   10   20 cm

Figure 5.6 Selected human figures and section of wall painting from tomb
100, Hierakonpolis, Naqada IIC

layout and construction, the tomb finds its closest parallels among the Naqada
II graves of Cemetery T at Naqada, a discrete cluster of burials excavated by
Petrie to the south of the main predynastic cemetery.[10] For the period in
question, the larger tombs at these two locations are unparalleled in scale

---

[10] Petrie and Quibell 1896: 18–20; Kemp 1973: 38–43; 1989: 35–7, fig. 9; Kaiser and Dreyer 1982:
243–4; Davis 1983.

and architectural sophistication, although two burials of comparable size (but without constructed surfaces) are known from early excavations in Cemetery B at Ab'adiya (Petrie 1901b: 33; cf. Kaiser and Dreyer 1982: 243–4).

Before considering the wider significance of the Painted Tomb it is necessary to engage with one of the most difficult, but potentially important, aspects of Egypt's archaeological record. Ever since the expeditions of Arthur Weigall and Hans Winkler in the first half of the twentieth century, the rock art of Egypt's Eastern and Western Deserts has influenced both scholarly and unscholarly understandings of the predynastic period. Another early expedition, involving Count Laszlo Almásy, was immortalised in Anthony Minghella's film, *The English Patient* (1996).[11] For many Egyptologists, the study of rock art is most infamously associated with the once-popular (but now discredited) hypothesis that Egypt was subject to a major invasion by foreign peoples directly prior to the establishment of dynastic culture (e.g. Petrie 1920: 49; Emery 1961: 38). Regrettably, this variant on the colonial fantasy of a 'dynastic race', coming from outside to civilise a savage Africa, has still not been totally expunged from popular and pseudo-scholarly writing on early Egypt. Professional archaeology must bear some of the responsibility for this. By comparison with the better analyses of rock art in South Africa, western Europe and Australia, its investigation in Egypt and Sudan has too often been unsystematic in method and over-speculative in interpretation (cf. Wilkinson *et al.* 2004).[12] Caution is therefore necessary.

Rock art of Egypt and Nubia: prehistory or wishful thinking?

The majority of known rock carvings in Egypt are distributed across the western part of the Eastern Desert, notably along the sandstone formations of the Wadi Hammamat and its tributaries. These form a relatively short (c.130 km) and well-watered route from the Nile valley (Qena-Qift region) to the Red Sea at Quseir.[13] Carved and pecked images are documented further south in Upper Egypt (e.g. near Hierakonpolis; Berger 1982; 1992; Huyge 1998a; 2002), and in particularly large numbers on igneous and sandstone formations in the Wadi Halfa region of Lower Nubia.[14] The identification of predynastic images among this corpus presents serious problems of dating which, contrary to some recent (as well as much older) claims,[15] cannot be resolved by typological means alone. An increasing number of claims to the contrary risks creating an

---

[11] For an evaluation of Almásy's work, in the light of new research in the eastern Sahara, see Kuper 2002, with references.

[12] For exemplary studies in other parts of the world, see, e.g., Ucko and Rosenfeld 1967; Vinnicombe 1976; Lewis-Williams 1983; Layton 1992.

[13] Weigall 1909; Winkler 1937; 1938; 1939; Resch 1963a; Červíček 1974; 1986; Redford and Redford 1989; Alfano 1992.

[14] Dunbar 1941; Bietak and Engelmayer 1963; Engelmayer 1965; Resch 1967; Almagro Basch and Almagro Gorbea 1968; Hellström 1970; Otto and Buschendorf-Otto 1993.

[15] e.g. Červíček 1986; Wilkinson 2000a; Huyge 2002.

atmosphere of indifference to, or even fostering, the ongoing destruction of Egyptian rock art through quarrying and road construction, by implying that it has been fully studied and that the groundwork for its dating has been achieved.[16] It has not.

In the regions mentioned, the chronological range of rock carvings probably extends from prehistoric to modern times. To date, the only examples associated with stratified deposits containing datable artefacts are at Abka, in the Second Cataract region (Myers 1949; 1958; 1960). The related deposits appear to have been poorly excavated, and are generally thought to antedate the predynastic period by some millennia. The almost complete restriction of Egyptian and Sudanese rock art to hammered, pecked and incised images means that methods of chemical analysis, which have been used (not without controversy) to date painted images in other parts of the world, cannot be applied. Scholars have sometimes attempted to use rock patina as an independent chronological guide, but this method is discredited by studies in other regions.[17] Super-positioning of images, which provides a relative indication of their age, has been documented in isolated cases, but no systematic regional analysis of its occurrence has yet been undertaken. In consequence, formal comparisons between figural decoration on pottery (C- and D-Ware) and petroglyphs have played a key role in dating the latter, an approach which posits some meaningful relationship between these two media.

The idea of such a relationship is appealing. Movement through the alien topography of the Eastern Desert, an important repository of socially valued materials, may have been accomplished and regulated through familiar modes of display deriving from the Nile valley. In seeking out such connections, analysts have focused upon a limited number of visual parallels: boats, hunting scenes and human figures with raised arms (often combined with boats in both D-Ware and rock art).[18] The correspondences are, however, far from precise, and the discrepancies cannot easily be accounted for by technological factors. It is difficult, for instance, to imagine any practical obstacle to carving linear animal designs comparable to those on C-Ware into the rock, where they would have stood out as pale outlines against the darker stone. Despite this, only a handful of images out of the many hundreds of published animal carvings correspond closely to the manner in which animals are depicted on C-Ware. One frequently cited example is located along the Wadi Menih, roughly midway between Tod, south of Luxor, and the Red Sea coast, and shows a hippopotamus-like figure in outline, filled with pecked dots, from which extends a line terminating in concentric circles (fig. 5.7, centre).[19]

---

[16] For the current threat to Egyptian rock art, see, e.g., Huyge 1998b.
[17] e.g. Dunbar 1941: 26–33; cf. Lewis-Williams 1983: 29; Layton 1992: 221. For a more recent, inconclusive attempt at the scientific dating of natural deposits on petroglyphs at el-Hosh in Upper Egypt, see Huyge 1998a.
[18] e.g. Resch 1967: 48–56; Červíček 1986; 1994; Fuchs 1989; Midant-Reynes 1994.
[19] Winkler 1937: 8–9, fig. 8; cf. Resch 1967: 51, figs. 7–8; Payne 1993: 58, 61, figs. 27, 29, cat. 389, 411.

0   4   8 cm

Figure 5.7 White Cross-Lined ('C-Ware') bowl from Abydos, and rock carvings in Wadi Menih and Wadi Abu Wasil

Carved images of human figures with raised arms standing on boats are widely attested in the Eastern Desert (fig. 5.7, lower), where they are commonly dated to the predynastic period on the basis of comparisons with D-Ware.[20] Only a single example was documented by Reinhold Engelmayer in his extensive study of boat carvings in the Sayala region of Lower Nubia (1965, pl. 3: 8), and no further examples have been brought to light during numerous expeditions between the First and Second Cataracts. The most southerly part of the Eastern Desert where such images have been found lies

---

[20] e.g. Winkler 1938, pls. 33–40; Redford and Redford 1989, figs. 63–4; Berger 1992, figs. 5–10; for dating, see Fuchs 1989; Červíček 1994.

along the Wadi Barramiya, east of el-Kab, where Gerald Fuchs (1989) has recorded a continuous series stretching along the wadi east of el-Kanayis. The boats in question, however, exhibit features not paralleled on D-Ware. The parallel lines departing from the hull, usually interpreted as paddles, extend either upwards or up and down, while on all known cases of D-Ware they extend only downwards. Many of the carved boats have elaborate prows, which often resemble horned animal heads (Berger 1992). The only parallel for this on pottery derives, not from D-Ware, but from a painted C-Ware box found in a burial at el-Amra (Randall-MacIver and Mace 1902, pl. 12: 11; Payne 1993: 79, fig. 32, cat. 600). Later examples appear as miniature carvings on the Gebel el-Araq knife-handle (opposite side to that shown in fig. 2.4), and on ivory tags from elite burials at Abydos and Naqada (fig. 6.1, lower; Bénédite 1916; Landström 1970, figs. 18, 76). Only a single carving of a boat with a central standard has been reported from the entire corpus of published rock art,[21] while such standards are present on most D-Ware boats. Finally, as Midant-Reynes (1994: 230) points out, many decorative images and conventions typical of painted pottery, including various floral and non-figural motifs, have no parallel in the known corpus of rock art.

It may be misleading to expect direct correspondences between painted designs on pottery and the often much larger images incised on rock. However, the alternative method of asserting relationships purely on the basis of shared subject matter or general resemblance presents considerable pitfalls. These are highlighted by recent work at Hierakonpolis (HK64), where carvings of ostriches—which feature widely on D-Ware—were found superimposed upon a cartouche of Amenhotep I (Friedman *et al.* 1999: 23; Friedman 1999b).

Image, memory and ritual economy: the Painted Tomb revisited

In view of these difficulties, the primary pictorial source for chronologically reliable comparisons with painted pottery remains the wall decoration of tomb 100 at Hierakonpolis. Numerous features of this mural have long been recognised as pointing to a relationship with D-Ware, notably the arrangement of boats in a central band (e.g. Kantor 1944). They have cabins and anchors/rudders similar to those on D-Ware; paddles, however, are absent. There is a further thematic correspondence in the depiction of human figures with raised arms, but in the tomb these have angular outlines different from the softer forms on painted vessels. They also diverge in other details such as the painted eyes and garments. Two rarely discussed human figures with sticks and penis sheaths (one sheath is lost), painted on the interior cross-wall of tomb 100, correspond more closely in detail to the smaller male figures on D-Ware

---

[21] Along the Wadi el-Arab in Lower Nubia; the standard is crescent-shaped (Dunbar 1941, pl. 11: 47).

(fig. 5.6, upper right; Quibell and Green 1902: 21, pl. 79). Other groups have no parallels on pottery, notably the more violent images of human combat towards the bottom of the composition.[22]

As noted above, the symbolic content of the images in tomb 100, particularly their relationship to the later iconography of kingship (note the miniature smiting scene), has been widely discussed. Less attention, however, has been given to the particular context of the painting and the process of its execution. While the Gebelein linen, like many other portable objects used as grave goods, may have circulated prior to its deposition in a burial, the visibility of the tomb 100 painting, and the time available for its creation, were almost certainly circumscribed by the funerary ritual itself. The painting of images would have formed part of that ritual, and hence of a collective performance, perhaps presenting the status or biography of the deceased.

The diversity of motifs in the wall painting is striking. They include a variety of approaches to the depiction of human and animal forms, and are distributed between spatially discrete groups that do not conform to any single scale, orientation or mode of composition. Two of the more tightly composed groups are arranged on base-lines (among the earliest known examples of what would become an important convention in dynastic art), while others form confronting pairs or, in one case, a circular arrangement sometimes thought to represent an animal trap. Yet other figures are more loosely distributed or appear in relative isolation. It has generally been assumed that tomb 100 was decorated by a single hand, but for these various reasons of formal content and social context, this should not be taken for granted. The sources of the motifs, and their relative values, could have been equally diverse. One very distinctive group, the so-called 'master of animals' (fig. 5.6, centre top), has long been thought to derive from a South-West Asian prototype, and reappears rather later in unmistakably foreign style on the handle of the Gebel el-Araq knife (fig. 2.4; Bénédite 1916; cf. Schmandt-Besserat 1993). Such elements presuppose the transmission of motifs, and their restricted circulation among emergent elites, in media that are largely lost.

The Painted Tomb also exemplifies a more general feature of predynastic funerary practice: the creation of an image below ground, incorporating some notion of place, which burial rendered absent or invisible in a deliberate and orchestrated manner. Whether the image was formed through the deposition of mobile objects or through the creation of a static image within the tomb is secondary to this basic intention. In such contexts the deployment of images, or rather their withdrawal from circulation, seems best thought of as forming part of a wider ritual economy, in which something of the donor's distinct social history was attached to the memory of the deceased.

---

[22] Some commentators, however, find possible precursors on C-Ware; see Williams 1988a: 46–51; Dreyer *et al.* 1998: 112; for an alternative reading of the combat scenes in tomb 100, see Hendrickx 1998: 223–4.

5.3 Dismembered bodies and the beginnings of mummification

I will now attempt to bring together the diverse strands of evidence explored in this chapter, by exploring their common relationships to treatments of the human body in death. Two intact burials from Cemetery A at el-Amra, in Upper Egypt, provide a point of departure (fig. 5.8). Both were excavated by David Randall-MacIver and Arthur Mace between 1899 and 1901, and published in 1902. Such contexts might be considered too dated or inaccurate for reinterpretation, and clearly the age and sex determinations given for human skeletons, as well as identifications of animal species, must be treated with extreme caution. The detailed descriptions and illustrations of these undisturbed graves nevertheless offer possibilities for examining the disposition of objects in relation to bodies that are rarely matched by more recent descriptions of looted or poorly preserved burials.

The first burial comprised an unroofed pit containing a single body lying in the flexed pose that had been the standard burial position in the Nile valley since Neolithic times (Randall-MacIver and Mace 1902: 17–18, pl. 5: 2). A small limestone vase was placed between the hands, almost touching the jaw. Adjacent to it, one on either side of the upper arms, lay two fish-shaped cosmetic palettes. Beneath one of them, lying over the elbow, were three 'mud sticks', described by the excavators as 'perhaps ill-made dolls'. Directly to the left of the skeleton were arrayed five pots, including a 'mud saucer', a coarse jar with a pointed base and three globular D-Ware jars of varying sizes. The body of the uppermost vessel, placed parallel with the head, was painted with wavy lines, and that of the adjacent, smaller jar with spirals. The largest D-Ware vessel lay behind the pelvis, separated from the other two by coarse pots. Its painted decoration was also non-figural, of a type that imitates stone vases of the period. On a raised ledge behind these pots were aligned five large vessels, three coarse, one polished red and another black-topped. These contents suggest a Naqada IIC date (S. Hendrickx, pers. com.).

The second grave (Randall-MacIver and Mace 1902: 19, pl. 5: 6) may be similarly dated. The excavators noted that the body 'had been dismembered before interment', and the arrangement of bones and objects within the grave confirms this. The leg bones were separated from the upper part of the skeleton and carefully aligned with a row of fish-tail-shaped flint knives (a lithic form that became widespread at this time), among which lay a diorite mace-head. Above them, framed by the human remains, were placed a breccia celt, two more mace-heads, a breccia peg lying on a fish-shaped cosmetic palette, and an ivory pin on a double-bird palette. The leg bone of a small animal and a number of stones lay behind the body, while a range of ceramic containers was distributed above the head. They comprised various coarse vessels interspersed with burnished, black-topped and painted pots, including a D-Ware jar painted with spirals and an unusual D-Ware beaker with a flared rim and mottled decoration.

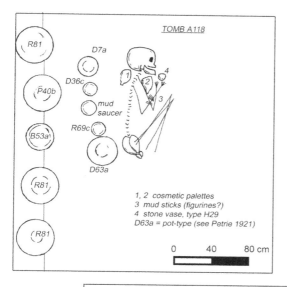

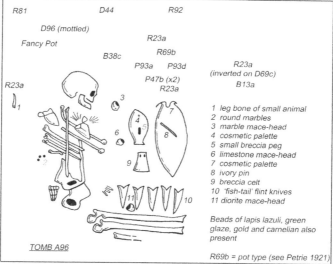

Figure 5.8 Naqada II burials from el-Amra, Upper Egypt

In each of these cases, a wide range of object types was integrated with the patterned deposition of human remains to form an overall image of the deceased within the grave. In combination the selection of objects, their spatial distribution in relation to one another and to the body, and the treatment of the body itself constituted broad parameters for a unique funerary realisation of the deceased individual. The co-ordinated grouping of objects and body parts is particularly clear in the second case, but both of these intact contexts confirm that forming a burial assemblage was a controlled, presumably collective, procedure. They also convey something of the enormous variability of pre-dynastic burials, which implies that this procedure was not a formulaic enactment of some prescribed ritual or set of beliefs. Rather it was a creative process that generated an authoritative image of the person as a relational being, which was in theory—but not in actuality—rendered immune from further manipulation through burial beneath the ground. Seen against the backdrop of Neolithic funerary rites, in which the body nearly always remained intact, it is the practice of dismemberment that stands out as a distinctive social innovation, in need of further elucidation.

Dividing the body

Petrie and Quibell (1896: 30) first recorded cases of pre-burial dismemberment in their excavations at Naqada, before they became aware of the relative antiquity of the burials concerned. Further evidence of this practice was subsequently presented in a number of other early reports, notably those of Peet (1914: 14) at Abydos (Cemetery U) and of Petrie, Wainwright and MacKay (1912: 8) at el-Gerza in the Fayum region. Their desire to identify and record these contexts in detail appears to have arisen through an interest in the origins of the Osiris myth, in which the dismemberment and reintegration of the body plays a central role (Petrie et al. 1912: 8–15). Conscious of the complications caused by grave plundering, they were at pains to describe a number of burials in which the in situ evidence for these practices appeared incontrovertible (Petrie 1896: 30). Such evidence derived from undisturbed contexts or from assemblages in which the distribution of human remains and objects militated against any explanation in terms of random destruction or looting. The widest range of dismemberment practices was documented from burials at Naqada, most of which may now be dated within Naqada II, although a minority can be assigned to Naqada IC.[23]

They included three graves in which one or more complete vessels took the place of the skull, and another where this role was filled by an ostrich-egg incised with animal figures. In other cases the skull was discovered mounted on a pile of stones or mud-bricks, rotated above an intact body, placed carefully between the legs or feet, or in the corner of the grave together with the lower arms. Double human burials had skulls lying apart at opposite ends of the grave or together at the side. Two adjacent burials each contained only a skull, one of which was surrounded with clay pendants. In five cases, only the lower arms and hands of the skeleton were absent and had been replaced by ceramic jars. In others they were simply absent or displaced, and in one instance only the wrists and hands had been removed and the fingers placed beneath the skull. A further grave is reported as containing a body 'buried without skull or

---

[23] The following descriptions are distilled from Petrie and Quibell 1896: 30–3, pls. 82–3.

lower arms, with its truncated neck resting on a mat, on which older bones are arranged parallel' (Petrie and Quibell 1896: 31). The complete dismemberment and rearrangement of the bones into a pattern was observed in two cases. The first comprised leg bones from four different bodies lying parallel, with the pelvic bones scattered about. The second, in Cemetery T, contained discrete piles of pelvic bones, with the leg bones distributed to opposite corners of the burial pit, the ribs between them encircled by vertebrae, and the arm bones in the centre of the grave.

Many of these practices were combined in a multiple burial of Naqada IIC date, also in Cemetery T, which 'had every appearance of never having been opened' (Petrie and Quibell 1896: 32).[24] Five polished stone vases and approximately forty-two ceramic vessels, some containing remnants of ash, fat or liquid, stood in the centre and along the sides of the rectangular pit, where stone beads and a double-bird palette were also placed. The pottery included numerous coarse and wavy-handled forms, but apparently no black-topped or painted wares. Six skulls were distributed across the floor. One was associated with an assemblage of malachite and beads made from cornelian, steatite, garnet, lapis lazuli and gold foil. Concentrated near the centre was a large pile of disjointed bones, while others lay around the sides, many bearing tooth-marks. Petrie reported that in some cases their ends were broken and the marrow removed, which he took as evidence of anthropophagy. Whitney Davis (1983) has suggested, more plausibly, that damage to the bones—whether by humans or animals—occurred during their exposure prior to interment (cf. Hoffman 1991: 116).

Having been somewhat neglected, the practice of dismemberment is now receiving renewed attention in the light of current excavations at el-Adaima (Crubézy *et al.* 2002). Pre-burial skull removal has been documented in undisturbed Naqada II graves, and from a single contemporaneous burial found within the habitation zone of the site.[25] Comparable finds have also come to light during the recent fieldwork at Hierakonpolis.[26] For various reasons, in particular the widespread plundering of burials, the frequency of these practices cannot be accurately evaluated in relation to the thousands of known predynastic graves. It is clear that dismemberment was used only for a minority of burials, but probably a higher proportion than any raw statistics would suggest.

Wrapping the body

Recent excavations also point to the development of preservative treatments for the body in predynastic times, forming a previously unsuspected precursor

---

[24] For further details of contents, see Baumgartel 1970: lxvii; for dating, see Kaiser and Dreyer 1982: 243.
[25] Midant-Reynes *et al.* 1996: 96; Crubézy 1998; cf. Janin 1992.
[26] Friedman *et al.* 1999: 13; Maish and Friedman 1999; Friedman 2002b: 10.

to the practice of mummification (Jones 2002a; 2002b). They are most strikingly illustrated within a newly discovered cemetery near the banks of the Wadi Khamsini at Hierakonpolis (Friedman *et al.* 1999: 3–11; Friedman 1998; 2002b). The cemetery, known as HK43, was in use throughout Naqada II, and is situated within a much larger expanse of contemporary habitation remains and burial grounds that must have included the site of the Painted Tomb. Many burials were arranged in circular groups that may have surrounded some form of monument; they incorporated individuals of all ages and both sexes. Most contained traces of reed matting, often several layers thick, and in some cases the body appears to have been entirely covered by a linen shroud or confined within a leather sack. The exceptional level of organic preservation at HK43 has also produced evidence for the binding of body parts—notably the head and hands—with multiple layers of linen that had been soaked in resin. Several examples of this practice have been documented, all of which derive from female burials dated no later than Naqada IIB. In a number of cases, resin-soaked linen was also used to pad out certain areas of the body before the final wrappings were applied.[27] By Naqada II these preservative techniques were applied not only to humans, but also to some species of animal, including cattle, highlighting the ongoing importance of the latter as carriers of human agency (Hoffman *et al.* 1982: 55–6, 59; Warman 2000). Their emergence alongside new practices of body dismemberment would appear to represent conflicting, rather than complementary, innovations. The two techniques seem best understood as distinct processes developing within a phase of unprecedented experimentation in ritual practice, a point to which I return below.

5.4 Some conclusions on death and power before kingship

L'espace est une société de lieux dits, comme les personnes sont des points de repère au sein du groupe.   *La pensée sauvage*, C. Lévi-Strauss[28]

The anthropology of death

Death may be understood as constituting not merely an end to physical movement, but also the stilling of an accumulated flow of social relations (Hertz 1960 [1909]). Funerary rites across cultures negotiate between the organic unity of the physical body and the dispersed relations that make up the social person (Bloch

---

[27] As Friedman (1998: 5) points out, these discoveries cast doubt upon a long-standing (but never very satisfactory) utilitarian theory for the origins of mummification, according to which it was a practical solution to the unforeseen consequences of burying bodies in constructed tombs for their protection, rather than in the desert sands, which had acted as a natural preservative but left them vulnerable to disturbance.

[28] 'Space is a society of particular places as people are landmarks within the group'; Lévi-Strauss 1966: 168.

and Parry 1982). Mortuary traditions may be ranged on a spectrum from those in which the physical body is totally obliterated to those in which the corpse—or some tangible extension of it—constitutes a focus towards which the living may direct material acts of relatedness (cf. Vernant 1991). No universal associations can be assumed, however, between the material traces left by mortuary ritual, and beliefs regarding the extent of influence that the dead continue to exercise over the living (see, e.g., Küchler 1997).

The funerary culture of dynastic Egypt has generally been considered emblematic of the latter end of this spectrum, in which the future status of the living is bound up with maintaining a sensory existence for the deceased. Predynastic burial practices, which involved the deposition of objects but provided no means of lasting access to the body, have usually been interpreted simply as provision for the afterlife, or as material reflections of the individual's status during life. The growth documented above in the range of burial forms, body treatments and grave goods during Naqada I–II does not sit easily within this limited interpretative frame. Quite apart from glossing over the very limited material provision implied by most grave assemblages, it seems to underestimate grossly the creative role of ritual in establishing a positive image of the deceased in social memory. Already in Neolithic times, the body was transformed in burial from a force of outward signification into the focus of a confined space, upon which others imprinted tangible signs of relatedness. In a society where the animated body provided the primary medium for constructing identity, the direction of social acts towards the deceased may be understood as a symbolic inversion of processes through which influence was expanded among the living. By considering the new ways in which predynastic burial rites gave form to absence, we may yet hope to understand something of their role in processes of social and political transformation.

Distributed persons and the nature of pre-royal power

As a clear departure from earlier forms of commemoration, the practice of body dismemberment, documented from at least Naqada IC onwards, provides a useful starting point. One effect of this practice would have been to make possible the distribution of remains from particular individuals between multiple locations, and hence between multiple arenas of commemoration. Burials that contained only skulls, juxtaposed with others where an object takes up the place of the skull, point strongly towards such a possibility. In such cases, grave goods served the new function of completing the body in its dismembered form—of remaking it as a totality and recalling its unique extension in the social world. I argue that images provided a map of memory through which this extension could be expressed in a shared idiom of place, encompassing both the living and the dead. Those images which evoked movement and circulation, either figuratively or through their exotic origins, may have had a particular salience. Like the prestige goods acquired through trade networks, they gave tangible expression to the person's mobility within, and command over, social space via the material landscapes it encompassed.

In considering the relation of such performances to forms of social power, it is useful to think of them as actively and competitively creating a new realisation of the deceased subject. An interpretation of ritual processes on the Melanesian island of Sabarl by Debbora Battaglia (1990: 195) serves to illustrate the political dimensions of this process, in terms that seem particularly resonant:

> *Commemorating others is a process of commemorating self.* But conversely, as relational persons delineate an image of the dead, performing for the last time the summarizing signs of social activity and social growth, they effect the constriction of their own social domains, becoming agents of the loss of a bit of their own history—'officially' forgetting it.
> . . . This awareness of an absence of an aspect of self is also the precondition of new acts of social extension, and new stories of life (new exchange partnerships, new kin relations, the manufacture or acquisition of wealth, the production of children, and so forth). [original emphasis]

Predynastic funerary rites may be similarly understood as a process of constituting 'positively valued negative spaces' (Battaglia 1990: 196) to be filled by the living. One aspect of this process was a new manner of presenting the person as transcending the physical boundaries of the skin, allowing relations of equivalence between internal objects (bones), objects worn on the body-surface (combs, ornaments, etc.), and objects that mediated the passage of substances between the body and other kinds of container (ceramic, woven and stone vessels).

Since dismemberment required protracted exposure of the corpse prior to interment, its practice expanded the scope of funerary rituals in time as well as space. In this regard it may be compared with a range of other burial techniques that became common during Naqada II, such as the manufacture of rectangular wooden frames and roofing for the grave, the wrapping of bodies and artefacts in multiple layers of matting, an overall increase in grave size and the use of mud-brick linings for some tombs. Many of these developments are documented in the recent excavations at Abydos (Cemetery U) and el-Adaima, and are paralleled at sites southward into Lower Nubia.[29] As social events, burial rites would have been further extended in duration through the preparation and deposition of increasingly sophisticated material goods. A study of ceramic vessels deposited in graves at el-Adaima (Buchez 1998) revealed traces of animal remains and remnants of bread and beer. Similar residues were found

---

[29] Dreyer *et al.* 1998; 2000 (Abydos); Lythgoe and Dunham 1965; Ucko 1967: 351 (Naga el-Deir); Crubézy 1998: 45, 51 (el-Adaima); Hoffman *et al.* 1982: 38–53; Adams 1996a; 2000 (Hierakonpolis); Reisner 1910: 115–16, 125–7 (Khor Bahan).

in jars from Cemetery HK43 at Hierakonpolis, and were widely reported from other predynastic cemeteries investigated during the late nineteenth and early twentieth centuries (Buchez 1998; Friedman *et al.* 1999: 15–18). Earlier excavators also noted the presence in Naqada I–II burials of conical storage jars filled to the brim with ash, perhaps derived from nearby hearths used during the preparation of the burial and its contents.[30] The value and significance of such grave goods should be considered, not merely in terms of their materials of manufacture or perceived aesthetic properties, but also their possible functions in the context of the ritual. Activities such as food preparation, over which new forms of control were also exercised during Naqada II, would not only have extended its scope as a social transaction, but may also have been basic expressions of participation, intimacy and care between the deceased and those attending.

Against the background of these developments, the practice of dismemberment takes on a particular significance in understanding the forms of social power that preceded the political unification of Egypt and the establishment of kingship. It suggests that the static, articulated body had become an inadequate framework for making a funerary image commensurate with the social ties amassed by some individuals during life. Elaborate post-mortem treatments of the body, presumably accompanied by appropriate rituals, would have provided ever-larger spatial and temporal arenas for the construction of social memory. Contemporaneous practices, including the ritual killing of animals and more isolated cases of human sacrifice (Crubézy and Midant-Reynes 2000; Friedman *et al.* 1999: 13, fig. 13), demonstrate that the taking of life—as well as its ritual conservation and redistribution—formed an integral part of this political economy of memory.

It was not the practice of dismemberment, but those of mummification and preservation which prevailed as the standard mortuary treatment for elite bodies through the dynastic period and into Graeco-Roman times. Insofar as the technical process of mummification aims to keep the body intact, it is virtually the polar opposite of dismemberment. Yet by transforming the body into an image—an explicit feature in many later styles of mummification—it made possible its replication and extension into wider chains of signification, which eventually came to include both human and divine subjects. In their ritual and social functions, then, these two practices have paradoxically similar potential and attributes. The adoption of mummification among the elite meant that a particular choice was made among possible ways of extending the period between death and burial, and treating the body as image and sign.

[30] Petrie and Quibell 1896: 19; Friedman 1994, table 6.2; Buchez 1998: 90, 96, fig. 1: a–c.

PART II

THE MAKING OF KINGSHIP

OPENING CONSIDERATIONS: *LA MÉMOIRE MONARCHIQUE*

Royal symbolism is, I believe, constructed out of non-royal symbolism, both logically and probably also historically.

Bloch 1987

6.1 Kingship and time

How, we might ask in response to Bloch, could it be otherwise? To do so, however, is perhaps to miss the point that constructions of the past that dynastic elites provide, and which may come to be accepted as incontrovertible by their subjects, invariably run counter to the reality of royal origins. As John Pocock (1957: 19) reminds us, Machiavelli and his contemporaries still saw the institution of monarchy in Europe as the creation of a single royal originator, much as some nineteenth- and twentieth-century scholars, following Manetho, viewed ancient Egyptian kingship as the founding act of a legendary ruler called Menes.[1] And a kingship made by kingship, whether under the auspices of an earthly or a divine sovereign, is beyond the power of ordinary human beings to alter or annul, except 'by some extraordinary and excessive force' (Machiavelli 1993 [1513]: 11).

In many parts of Europe, the prising apart of these two phenomena—kingship and the collective experience of time—was important, not just in formulating alternatives to monarchy as the only conceivable system of social government, but also in the emergence of a new consciousness of the past. During the sixteenth and seventeenth centuries, as part of the constitutional struggle waged by jurist-antiquarians against royal absolutism, new priority was given to the recognition of 'gradual process, imperceptible change, the origin and slow growth of institutions in usage, tacit consent, prescription and adaptation' (Pocock 1957: 19). The notion of historical change through shifts in the configuration of customary practice, rather than dictates from some higher agency, later became integral to the development both of European prehistory and of the social sciences more generally. By contrast, the archaeology of early Egypt, with its occasionally obsessive interest in the chronology and succession of named rulers, still bears the stamp of an earlier historiography, which Michel Baud

---

[1] For the historiography of Menes, see Allen 1992.

(1999) has aptly termed *la mémoire monarchique*. In order to clarify the *kind* of history of the early Egyptian state that is explored in the following chapters, a brief consideration of the relationship between kingship, knowledge and time is therefore appropriate.

6.2 The dynastic continuum

Prior to the late nineteenth century, sources for a study of kingship's origins in Egypt were virtually restricted to lists of royal names, titles and activities. These included ancient Egyptian texts dating mostly to the Eighteenth and Nineteenth Dynasties of the New Kingdom (mid–late second millennium BC), and still later interpretations of these and other sources by scholars of late antiquity. The most important are the three books of *Aegyptiaca*, composed in the time of Ptolemy II (third century BC) by Manetho—a priest of the temple at Heliopolis and native of the Nile delta—as a presentation of Egypt's past to the Greeks (Waddell 1940; Verbrugghe and Wickersham 1996). Fragments of this text preserved in the later writings of Josephus, Africanus, Eusebius and others form the basis for all subsequent dynastic divisions of Egypt's ancient history. Manetho includes a framework for Egypt's earliest dynasties that has now been rendered untenable by primary archaeological evidence from the period in question, and from that which precedes it. For better or worse, this framework is nevertheless widely retained, such that the First Dynasty now corresponds to a period post-dating the earliest named rulers. The latter, whose authority may not have extended throughout all of Egypt, are in turn consigned to a new chronological unit known as Dynasty 0, corresponding to the archaeological period Naqada IIIA–C1 (c.3300–3100 BC; Table 5).

In Egypt, modes of signification that conflated the experience of kingship and time can be traced back to the origins of that institution at the end of the fourth millennium (Wildung 1969a; Redford 1986: 86). By the beginning of the First Dynasty (c.3100 BC), pictorial and written signs were combined in the presentation of 'year-names': formal demarcations of time divided according to the actions of particular, named kings (fig. 6.1). Archetypal royal actions that marked the passage of a year included a census of all the country's cattle wealth, festive appearances and processions, the construction of ceremonial boats, the conquest of foreign enemies, and the fashioning and dedication of statues or other furnishings for temples of the divine cult. As Jan Assmann (2002: 37) observes, the subjects recalled by year-names should not be considered historical 'events' in our normal sense of something marked out from the ordinary scheme of things. Rather, the events they record are precisely those performances 'that actually constitute the "scheme of things"', presenting a set of ideal outcomes, a form proper to governance, and a standard against which the realities of royal power might be judged.

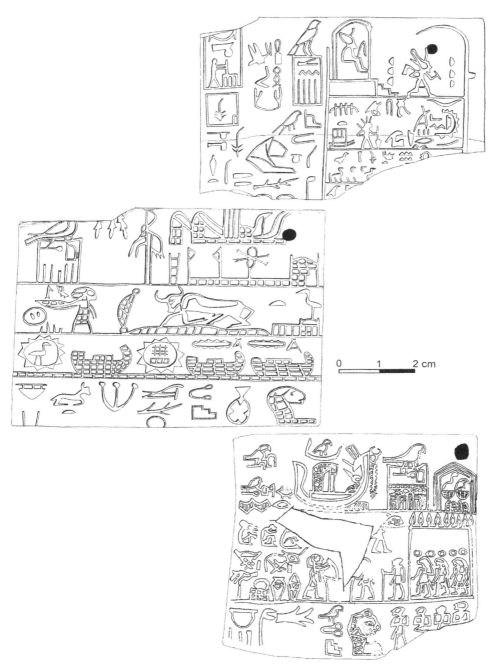

Figure 6.1 Year-labels of the First Dynasty

Figure 6.2 Section of wall relief showing Seti I and Prince Rameses before the 'Table of Kings', Gallery of Lists, West Wall, Temple of Seti I, Abydos, Nineteenth Dynasty

Year-names were compiled into extensive series, the earliest surviving evidence of which dates to the Fifth Dynasty. Such series may, however, have been transmitted in the context of oral recitation long before they were committed to writing, and long after. A link between oral performance and the encoding of royal genealogies is alluded to in much later groupings of royal names, such as that carved within a gallery of the New Kingdom temple of Seti I at Abydos (fig. 6.2; Redford 1986: 18–20; cf. Kemp 1989: 21–2). There the list forms part of a complex presentation of the son's role in perpetuating his father's name by providing him with offerings. The scene encompasses relationships between the king and his heir Rameses, depicted in the act of recitation, and between the king and his royal ancestors, whose names—beginning with Meni (Menes)—are listed in two continuous registers. At the foot of each column the titles of Seti I are repeated. A further inscription above these registers contextualises the entire sequence of offerings as an enactment of duties performed by the god Horus for his father Osiris, and incorporates the gods as recipients of royal food offerings.

The historical accuracy of this and other known king-lists is conventionally assessed in relation to the so-called Turin Canon, which contains the most complete and detailed listing of royal succession from the origins of kingship to the Nineteenth Dynasty (Gardiner 1959). By contrast with genealogies incorporated into the decoration of temples and tombs, the Turin Canon was written in hieratic on the reverse side of a papyrus, now badly fragmented, which had previously been used to keep tax records. Accordingly, its content may not have been subject to the restrictions and cultic functions associated with temple ritual. The latter, as discussed above, centred upon the presentation of offerings from the king to deities. This in turn sustained a ritual 'food chain' extending down from the gods to the king and his dependants, including both the royal and non-royal dead in their mortuary temples and tombs (Assmann 2001: 3–5; cf. Baines and Lacovara 2002: 11–12). In principle, the efficacy of ritual gifts to the dead at all levels of society was attributed to the successful maintenance of this higher register of exchange between kingship and the gods. Accordingly the selection of royal names for inclusion in such lists may have been more closely dictated by their efficacy in the present, as recipients and channels of cultic offerings, than by any desire to present an objective history of royal succession. This is further implied by other New Kingdom offering scenes, found in both temples and tombs, where the sequence of named royal ancestors receiving cult is more fully depicted as a series of seated statues, the ritually sanctioned recipients of offerings.[2]

Among the earliest known objects on which a sequence of royal names can be traced are a handful of clay sealings recovered from Umm el-Qaab, the royal cemetery of Abydos during the First Dynasty (fig. 6.3; Dreyer 1987; Dreyer *et al.* 1996: 71–3). The form of the sealings suggests that they were originally applied to both vessels and portals, no doubt used in royal funerary rites. The impressions they bear are from cylinder seals, one of which carried a sequence of eight royal names from Narmer to Merneith, the latter being the only queen in the group. The other extends the sequence of male rulers to the reign of Qa'a. The location of the sealings within an early royal cemetery, and the inclusion of the god Khentiamentiu—signified by a canine form—within the sequence of royal names, suggest comparisons with the later king-lists in tombs and temples, rather than with the less restricted context of the Turin Canon (cf. Kaiser 1986). The use of cylinder seals for the transmission of royal genealogies further suggests that, from its early stages of development, kingship was a quality to be replicated and distributed among material objects, particularly those associated with the dead.

Intermediate in time between these early king-lists and the much later New Kingdom examples are the royal annals of the late Old Kingdom: tabular presentations of the succession of reigns and the individual year-names

---

[2] Lepsius 1849–56: III, 2 a, d; Wildung 1969b: 214–17; Kemp 1989: 21–2, fig. 4.

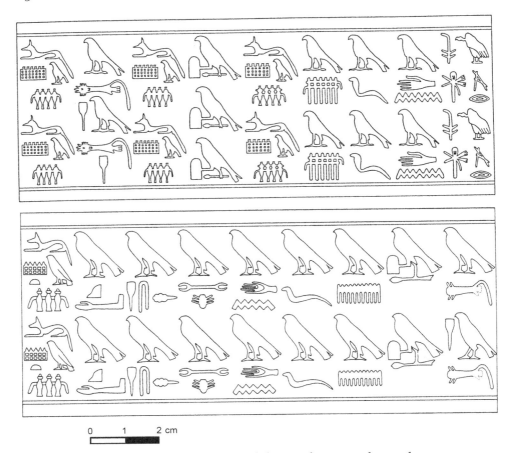

0   1   2 cm

Figure 6.3 Reconstructed cylinder-seal designs listing early royal names,
Abydos, Umm el-Qaab

they comprised. The annals are preserved as inscriptions on the Fifth Dynasty
Palermo Stone and its associated fragments, and on the lid of a stone sarco-
phagus found in the pyramid complex of Pepi II at Saqqara.[3] Each regnal year is
commemorated by ceremonial appearances and ritual acts of the king, which
these monuments link both to taxation and to the annual height of the Nile
inundation, upon which all agricultural productivity depended.[4] Although the
precise content of these ceremonies remains enigmatic, their names—such as
the 'appearance of the King of Upper and Lower Egypt' and the 'following

---

[3] Schäfer 1902; Gauthier 1914; Baud and Dobrev 1995; 1997. Wilkinson's (2000b) treatment of the
Palermo Stone and associated fragments suffers from serious omissions and problems of interpretation; see Baud 2003.

[4] At the beginning of the Fourth Dynasty a numerical system was introduced for the recording of
regnal years, and the composition of year-names became more extensive and elaborate in consequence; see Baines 1997a: 134; Baud 1999.

of Horus'—often suggest a markedly public and visible character, making manifest the king's presence throughout the land. Accordingly, the ordered cycle of royal ceremony and the temporal cycle of change in the non-human world would have occupied the same space of social memory, reinforcing the encompassment of life and its generative forces within the lifecycle of the king. The annals also serve as a reminder that mortuary monuments, the permanence of which has become almost synonymous with ancient Egyptian culture, are only the most durable aspect of an aesthetic apparatus, through which the dynastic state constructed the political consciousness of time and space among its subjects.

6.3 Traditional authority and the making of kingship

The top register of the Palermo Stone gives a line of succession extending back beyond rulers with year-names to a series of seated figures, each of which wears the Red Crown. Both in content and manner of writing, the names given for these earliest rulers differ from the royal names documented on excavated artefacts of Dynasty 0, the period they purport to commemorate. The continuation of this register is partially preserved on a fragment of the same monument, now in Cairo, where these primordial kings have exchanged the Red Crown for the combined crown of Upper and Lower Egypt. In the much later Turin Canon, kingship is traced back more explicitly beyond its human embodiments, via an enigmatic group termed 'followers of Horus', to a series of divine rulers. Their reigns are precisely numbered in lengths that vastly exceed the normal extent of human life. As John Baines (1989b: 134) puts it, prehistory 'as a mythical time, and a golden time', was thereby 'integrated into the official chronology of rule'.

Written sources from ancient Mesopotamia similarly identify the emergence of kingship as a primordial occurrence. In the Sumerian king-list the arrival of kingship on earth is characterised as a descent from heaven into cities at the beginning of time (Jacobsen 1939; Michalowski 1983). The notion that cities, and in particular their temple-households, *make* the relationship between humans and gods is restated in a wider range of other commemorative and mythological sources.[5] It is when building houses for the gods that Mesopotamian kings are most clearly and consistently cast as their physical, moral and intellectual representatives on earth. In Egypt the legitimate transfer of kingship, both between gods and between a succession of human manifestations, tended to be envisaged rather as a sequence of embodiments. Embodiment was variously presented as an act of sexual procreation, or as the violent dismemberment and distribution of royal body parts across the

---

[5] See, e.g., Winter 1996; Edzard 1997; Suter 2000; Wengrow 2004.

land, followed by their reconstitution into a unified, living whole. This latter set of relationships (or 'mytheme', to use Lévi-Strauss's term; 1963: 206–31) forms the core content of a cycle of myths, centred upon the death of Osiris and the ascendance of his son Horus, elements of which were incorporated into the mortuary texts of kings from Old Kingdom times onwards (Frankfort 1948a; Allen 1988).

These broad contrasts, which could be further explored in a variety of directions (e.g. Frankfort 1948a; 1951; Baines and Yoffee 1998), serve to highlight continuities between the core content of dynastic symbolism and the equally distinct social forms that preceded the emergence of kingship in Mesopotamia and Egypt. There need be nothing surprising in this, and yet such appeals to what Max Weber (1978 [1921]: 215–16, and *passim*) termed 'traditional authority' have rarely been considered as a factor in the emergence of early states. In charting a course through the archaeological record of Egypt's earliest dynasties, I therefore attempt to give due consideration to this interplay of continuity and change, and to the underlying frameworks of experience and power out of which formal hierarchies were constructed. In particular, I seek to show how 'monarchic memory' in early Egypt was not an arbitrary ideological fiction, but drew many of its conventional forms and practices from what Wendy James (2003: 101) has called 'the unspoken archive of social memory'.

It is a precondition of such a perspective that the archaeology of Egypt before kingship, which forms the point of departure for this book, should be understood in something other than generic terms, that is, as something more than a series of procrustean movements from 'hunting and gathering' to 'settled life' and 'food production', followed by 'progressive stratification', and so on. Nor should we any longer make do with an amorphous and teleological prehistory of half-legible symbols, waiting to be given definition by the stamp of written sources. I therefore attempted, in the preceding chapters, to trace an outline of dynamic but rule-bound prehistoric communities, with clearly defined and distinctive ideas about how individuals should be constituted as social beings, and an equally clear logic of power and its principles of extension.

EGYPT AND THE OUTSIDE WORLD II, c.3300–2500 BC

7.1 The 'Uruk expansion', c.3300–3000 BC

Within a relatively short time-span, around the middle of the fourth millennium BC, the southern alluvium of Mesopotamia was occupied on a scale that was both unprecedented and without parallel anywhere in the Old World. Rural populations converged upon particular centres, the best known of which is the site of Warka (Uruk) in southern Iraq. By c.3300 BC, this settlement had expanded to around 250 hectares. While very little can be said about typical living conditions in the city, its central precinct is known to have contained an extensive complex of monumental buildings, some of which replicated the tripartite layout of earlier village house-forms (Nissen 1988: 65–127; 2002).

The invention of the proto-cuneiform script, impressed with a reed stylus on to tablets of damp clay, responded to the scale of managerial functions carried out by these institutions during the late fourth millennium BC (Uruk/Eanna IVA; Nissen et al. 1993). Administrative records, which make up the vast bulk of these early documents, demonstrate (among many other things) the centralised manufacture of textiles and milk-based products, implying the availability of wool and dairy herds. On the southern alluvium, these large-scale industries were supported by unrivalled agricultural yields, enhanced by the use of irrigation and the cattle-drawn plough. Cereals had probably been used to produce leavened bread and beer in lowland Mesopotamia since the early fourth millennium BC, as indicated by the spread of related ceramic containers (chapter 4.5). In the context of urban expansion, the production and distribution of these foods was organised on a massive scale, and is likely to have been central to the recruitment and maintenance of a centralised population and workforce (Joffe 1998).

The growth of cities during the mid–late fourth millennium BC was linked to the northward expansion of southern Mesopotamian influence along the Middle and Upper Euphrates (fig. 7.1). Initially, small settlements were established in sparsely populated areas such as the Tabqa region; enclaves of southern culture were also founded within existing urban settlements in northern Syria and south-eastern Turkey. Subsequently, major fortified centres with close links to the southern alluvium were established at Habuba Kabira and Jebel Aruda on the Middle Euphrates, representing a more direct attempt to

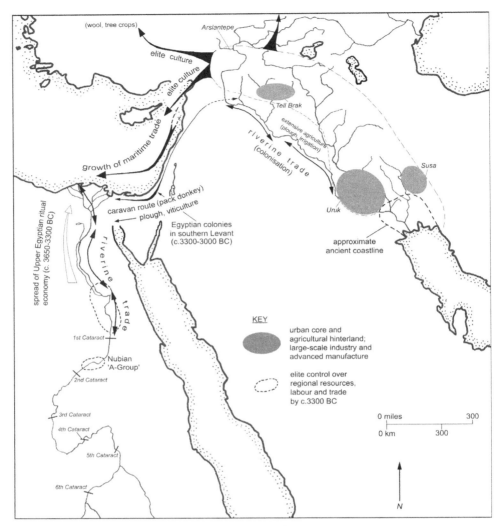

Figure 7.1 Map: Economic and social reconfiguration, c.4000–3000 BC

control the flow of trade across the northern steppe.[1] Administrative tools
such as numerical tablets and sealings, as well as building plans and ceramic
assemblages from these latter sites, are virtually indistinguishable from those
of the southern alluvium. By contrast, systematic use of proto-cuneiform
writing is currently attested only in the south, notably at Uruk itself, and
also in smaller quantities at Jemdet Nasr.[2] In the absence of mechanisms of

---

[1] Algaze 1993; cf. Oates 1993; Nissen 2001.
[2] The tablets from Jemdet Nasr correspond to Uruk/Eanna III, around the start of the third
millennium BC, rather than to the earliest phase of writing at Uruk; see Englund and Grégoire
1991; Matthews 2002.

long-distance political and economic control, such movements of the productive population (using wheeled carts as well as river-going boats) appear to have been necessary in order to alter the flow of commodities. There is now a degree of consensus that their main incentive was the acquisition of valued resources that were lacking or scarce in the southern metropolis—notably metals, timber and precious stones—but they would also have had unforeseen consequences, for example, in the transmission and hybridisation of dietary practices and modes of consumption.[3]

The expansion of settlement and trade along the Euphrates added a new frontier to exchange routes in the Fertile Crescent, creating a zone of heightened interaction oriented increasingly towards the large manufacturing centres on the southern Mesopotamian alluvium. The margins of this zone were defined to the north and east by the Taurus and Zagros mountain ranges, and to the west by the Syrian and Jordanian deserts. Isolated components of urban culture and technology nevertheless escaped these natural boundaries across established networks of procurement, and were incorporated into new frameworks of meaning and use by recipient groups. During the late fourth millennium BC, cross-cultural transfers of this kind influenced a range of societies around the fringes of the Fertile Crescent, from the Iranian plateau to Egypt.

7.2 Egypt and the Levant, c.3300–3000 BC

The closing centuries of the fourth millennium BC witnessed the emergence of a politically unified state in Egypt. At its apex stood the institution of kingship and an inner circle of elite dependants with access to restricted modes of communication and display, including the newly invented writing system. Throughout the initial period of state formation (Naqada IIIA–C1) Egypt maintained and expanded terrestrial and maritime relations with the southern Levant. By c.3300 BC, Levantine products—notably highland commodities such as wine, oil, resin and timber—played an important role in local patterns of consumption and display. This is illustrated by the contents of tomb U-j, the largest of a series of mud-brick funerary structures established at Abydos in Upper Egypt, adjacent to the site of later royal burials dating to the First and Second Dynasties (fig. 9.11). In addition to a cedar box, an obsidian vessel and hundreds of ceramic wine bottles, its surviving contents include evidence for the local use of cylinder seals and an early form of hieroglyphic writing (fig. 9.12). The combination of elements in this ritual deposit illustrates the fusion of exotic tastes with a local repertoire of elite cultural practices, and highlights the evolving relationship between new forms of consumption and visual communication.

---

[3] A. G. Sherratt, pers. com. and unpublished manuscript: 'Bread, butter and beer: dietary change and urbanisation in early Mesopotamia and surrounding areas'.

The changing relationship between Egypt and the Levant during the mid–late fourth millennium BC parallels the contemporary articulation of lowland (Late Uruk) Mesopotamia with the northern margins of the Fertile Crescent (fig. 7.1). In both cases major river systems provided the crucial link between an expanding alluvial core, rich in cereal surpluses and human resources, and neighbouring economies engaged in tree-crop horticulture and metalworking. In terms of social organisation, however, the southern Levant had more in common with the small-scale communities of the Iranian highlands (e.g. Godin Tepe V) than the large, bureaucratically organised centres of the Upper Euphrates (Weiss and Young 1975). Craft production was organised at the household level, and centralised areas for manufacture and administration appear not to have existed, even at larger sites in the Jezreel and Jordan valleys (Philip 2001: 176–8; Joffe 2001). The mobilisation of resources above the household level was mediated by periodic ritual practices rooted in Chalcolithic traditions, such as the founding of supra-local shrines (e.g. Megiddo XIX) and collective burial spaces located beyond settlements (e.g. Bab el-Dhra; see Ben-Tor 1992). These communal practices increased in scale during the third millennium (EB II–III), when central storage areas and fortifications were established at many sites, forming what Graham Philip (2001) has described as a network of 'corporate villages' across the southern Levant (cf. Joffe 1993).

During the late fourth millennium (mid–late EB IB/Naqada IIIA–C1), the imbalance between Egyptian demand for highland products and the capacity (and/or desire) of local communities to organise their supply prompted a direct expansion of Egyptian groups into the southern coastal plain of the Levant.[4] Interaction between incoming and local populations was concentrated along river systems extending between the central hill country and the Mediterranean littoral, from the Yarkon River in the north to the Besor in the south, providing access (via the Arad Basin) to the copper resources of the Arava (Ilan 2002: 316–18). The southern piedmont of the Levant also offered ample opportunities for cereal farming. Dietary habits based on the consumption of leavened bread and beer were transferred to this region from the Nile alluvium, along with associated ceramic forms (made in local fabrics) and simple techniques of administration, using cylinder seals and pot-marks. The latter included abbreviated renderings of royal names, that of Narmer being the most widely attested.[5]

A resulting increase in traffic across the southern Levant is reflected in the appearance of specialised containers for liquid products. On the Levantine side, these included squat, flat-based storage jars with wavy-ledged or looped handles, burnished to reduce porosity, and painted juglets with narrow necks and spouts.[6] Examples of both wares were found in tomb U-j at Abydos, where the

---

[4] See Ben-Tor 1991; Ward 1991; and the contributions in van den Brink and Levy 2002.
[5] See, e.g., Weinstein 1984; Kempinski 1992 (Tel Erani); Gophna and Gazit 1985; Porat 1992 ('En Besor); Levy et al. 2001; Kansa and Levy 2002 (Nahal Tillah).
[6] Amiran 1970: 49–53; Stager 1992: 28–39; Marcus 2002: 410.

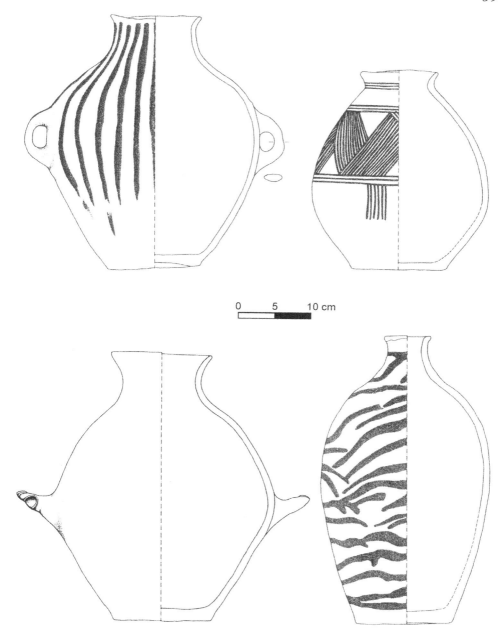

Figure 7.2 Liquid containers from tomb U-j, Abydos, c.3300 BC

vertical stacking of storage jars and flasks indicates their suitability for bulk transport, presumably by boat (fig. 7.2; Hartung 2002; cf. Braun and van den Brink 1998). As in earlier periods, however, Levantine vessel forms were also imitated in local Egyptian fabrics, and such imitations were traded—together with actual imports—as far south as Lower Nubia, where they were deposited in the elaborate (Late A-Group) burials of an emerging local elite (Williams 1986: 78–9, 104; Gophna and van den Brink 2002). By the end of the fourth millennium, cultivated vines had been adopted around the fringes of the Nile delta, prompting the development of a new form of transport vessel, distinguished from its Levantine counterparts by a narrow, ovoid body, pointed base and lack of handles (fig. 9.15, left). This form of liquid container, which foreshadows the wheel-made 'Canaanite jars' of the Middle Bronze Age, may initially have been developed for river transport along the Nile rather than maritime trade, and examples outside Egypt are largely confined to the period of direct Egyptian involvement in the southern Levant.[7]

7.3 The formation of elite cultures, c.3300–3000 BC

While sea-borne and terrestrial routes converged upon the southern Levant, direct maritime links were also being consolidated between the northern Levant and the Nile delta. Owing to a lack of offshore winds, and a consequent danger of becoming land-locked, southbound boats on this route may have avoided the coastal stretch from the southern Levant to the eastern delta, following the prevailing currents to a more westerly point such as Buto (Stratum III), where pottery from the Amuq region of coastal Syria has been found (Marcus 2002: 403–4; Köhler 1998a: 37–9). Via this route, groups within Egypt (presumably with access to local commodities such as gold) maintained access to small quantities of crafted goods and exotic materials deriving from lowland Mesopotamia/Iran and the Fertile Crescent.

The reception of such goods in Egypt must be seen in the context of existing local trends towards new techniques of display among a restricted elite, further explored in chapters 8 and 9. These are evident across a range of durable media—such as stone and metal vessels, ivory and wooden furniture—and were no doubt paralleled in more perishable materials such as linen textiles. Among the most prestigious artefacts to have survived from this period (Naqada IIIA–C1) are elaborately carved, ceremonial versions of familiar portable objects such as knife-handles, cosmetic palettes and mace-heads. Less elaborate versions of these artefact types now ceased to be widely available and by the beginning of the First Dynasty their production had stopped altogether, as relief carving shifted increasingly to the static and monumental surfaces of temples and tombs. The restriction of access to established forms of representation and personal display is echoed in the virtual disappearance of

---

[7] van den Brink 1992c: 267–70; 1996, pls. 24–32; James 1995: 198–202; Dreyer *et al.* 1996: 51–4; McGovern *et al.* 1997: 5–9; Levy and van den Brink 2002: 20, and n. 40; van den Brink and Braun 2002. For early evidence of domesticated grape in the Nile delta, see Thanheiser 1990; 1992; more generally, Murray *et al.* 2000.

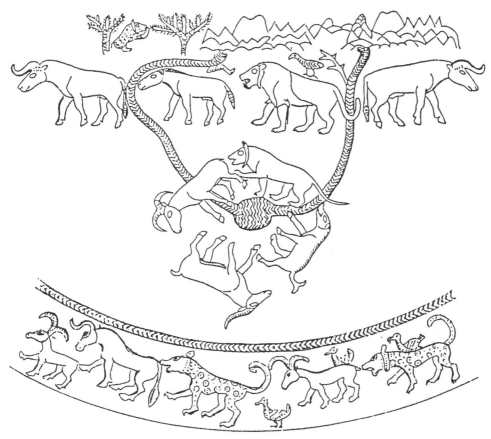

Figure 7.3 Scenes from figured silver vessels, Maikop (Caucasus), Early
Bronze Age

elaborately painted pottery throughout Egypt after Naqada II, the implications
of which are discussed in chapter 8.

The decoration of ceremonial objects during Naqada III includes artistic
motifs that derive from sources outside Egypt. Several find their closest parallels in the glyptic art of Mesopotamia and south-west Iran (figs. 2.4, 9.2, 9.8).
At this time the latter region was emerging as the centre of a new network of
polities extending eastwards on to the Iranian plateau, and using a system of
writing on clay (Proto-Elamite) related to that of southern Mesopotamia (Potts
1999: 43–84).[8] Long singled out as a special case, the transmission of these
motifs to Egypt may now be understood as part of a much wider phenomenon,

---

[8] For comparison of long-term economic and political change in the southern Levant and south-
west Iran during the fourth and third millennia, see de Miroschedji 2002.

taking place around the periphery of the Late Uruk expansion. Within this broad zone of influence, Egypt was one of a number of societies in which long-distance contacts augmented the emergence of local hierarchies. What these societies had in common was access to regional hinterlands, providing metal and mineral deposits for exchange, as well as local traditions of craft speciali-sation, allowing exotic forms to be acquired and absorbed into vernacular idioms of expression.[9] In addition to Egypt they are exemplified by the osten-tatious tombs of Maikop, in the Caucasus (fig. 7.3), and by the temple/palace complex of Arslantepe VIA on the Malatya Plain of south-eastern Turkey (Frangipane 1997; Sherratt 1997a: 457–70).

7.4 The constitution of dynastic Egypt, c.3000–2500 BC

By the end of the fourth millennium BC, the proto-literate polities of Egypt and Elam demarcated the western and eastern extremes of a koine of elite cultures, extending across the northern arc of the Fertile Crescent. At much the same time the city-states of southern Mesopotamia began to expand their maritime interests in the Persian Gulf (notably towards the copper and mineral sources of Oman), opening up a new trading frontier that subsequently expanded to the mouth of the Indus valley (Potts 1993). It was against this wider backdrop that elites within Egypt consolidated their control over nearby metal and mineral resources, and engaged in a major restructuring of the rural economy, based upon capital-intensive production techniques introduced from South-West Asia. The outcome of these developments was an increasingly polarised so-ciety, in which the vast majority of primary producers were isolated from large-scale networks of communication and trade, and in which movement over long distances was increasingly confined to a framework of formalised political action, centred upon the royal court (fig. 7.4).

Internal colonisation and the making of a peasantry

In order to appreciate the transformation of productive life that accompanied the process of state formation in Egypt, it is instructive to look ahead to the rich pictorial record of the Old Kingdom (c.2580–2150 BC), and in parti-cular to the extensive scenes of everyday life that decorate the walls of private tombs belonging to the inner elite of the Fifth and Sixth Dynasties (c.2465–2150 BC; fig. 7.5; Harpur 1987; Faltings 1998b). They depict a world of rural estates, planted with vineyards and orchards, and farmed with the aid of cattle-drawn ploughs. Agricultural work is organised hierarchically, as is

---

[9] In the later Bronze Age, the movement of craft specialists played a significant role in transfers of this kind, but their importance during the period under discussion cannot easily be assessed; see Moorey 2001.

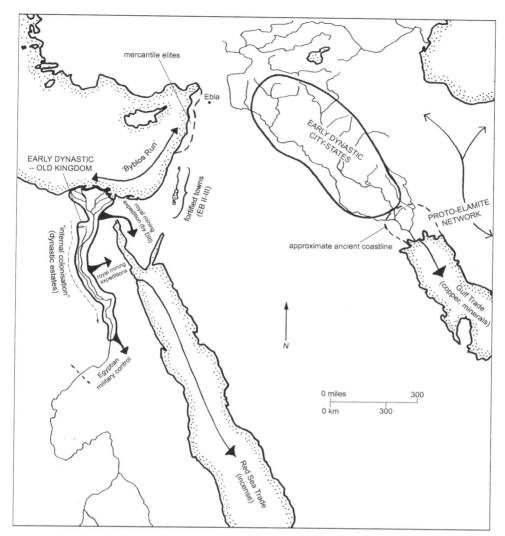

Figure 7.4 Map: The inter-regional context of state formation, c.3000–2500 BC

the use of centralised facilities for manufacturing bread, beer and wine (fig. 4.7). Scenes of hunting and herding are common, and there are occasional depictions of dairying. Artisans working in metal, wood, clay and stone are also carefully rendered, as are the scribes and inspectors who regulate these activities.[10]

---

[10] For coverage of textual sources relating to the economic organisation of the Old Kingdom, see, e.g., Eyre 1987; 1994.

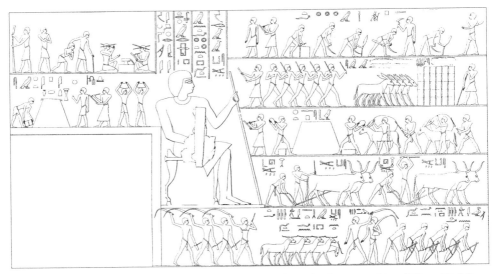

Figure 7.5 Agricultural scenes in the tomb chapel of Imeri, Giza (West Field), Fifth Dynasty

Such scenes must of course be understood in terms of iconographic conventions and their particular roles within the tomb (e.g. Groenewegen-Frankfort 1951: 30–6; Kanawati 1981). Nevertheless there seems little reason to see their basic subject matter as divorced from contemporary material realities. To the contrary, they present a coherent image of the Old Kingdom estate as a complex social unit; a hierarchically organised 'factory in the field', created through a concentration of capital and knowledge far beyond the means of most individuals or kin-groups. Its products were not directly consumed, but filtered through an internal system of redistribution that provided staple foods for the main workforce, as well as a surplus to support secondary manufacturing processes. The latter furnished estate-owners with a range of high-value finished commodities—such as wine, dairy products, furniture and jewellery—that were not locally redistributed, but used to gain entry to a more restricted sumptuary world, defined by the activities of the royal court.

During the third millennium, as in many later periods, the foundation of rural estates was a centrally directed affair, under royal or temple patronage, through which elite control of the country and its resources was expanded and consolidated.[11] This process is likely to have commenced no later than the Naqada IIIB period, when cultivated vines were transferred from the Levant to the well-drained soils around the margins of the Nile delta. Use of

[11] Jacquet-Gordon 1962; Seidlmayer 1996a; 1996b; Baines and Yoffee 1998: 222–4; Moreno García 1999.

Figure 7.6 Bowl with model figures of yoked oxen, Tel el-Farah (North), N. Israel, Early Bronze Age

the cattle-drawn plough is firmly attested in the southern Levant during the late fourth millennium BC (fig. 7.6; Grigson 1995) and the period of direct Egyptian involvement in this region from Naqada IIIA–C1 seems a likely context for its adoption on the Nile alluvium, together, perhaps, with small numbers of dairy herds (fig. 7.1). The manufacture of fermented cereal products may already have been established in Egypt by late Naqada II (chapter 4.5), and now played a central role in the deployment of labour for new plantations, and for periodic construction of royal monuments. In South-West Asia the growth of urban economies was fuelled at this time by a massive expansion in wool production, notably around the dry-farming zone of the Syrian steppe. Wool textiles had begun their westward spread into Europe by c.3000 BC, but—like wheeled transport—they were resisted in Egypt, where linen woven from flax remained the primary material for cloth manufacture (McCorriston 1997).

Through a relatively rapid process of 'internal colonisation', the early Egyptian state brought about major structural changes in the organisation of rural production, which in South-West Asia were typically achieved through the growth of city-states (Kees 1961; Eyre 1999). In both regions, primary producers were increasingly bound into local institutional frameworks, where labour and its products were experienced in terms of vertical (i.e. hierarchical) relations, rather than as an outward proliferation of horizontal social networks such as those that characterised earlier, Neolithic economies. Hierarchy was defined and experienced in cosmological terms, and made manifest through centrally organised ceremony and ritual. In Old Kingdom Egypt these activities appealed to a set of core values and images, which had been formulated in their essentials by no later than c.3000 BC, and remained a feature of dynastic culture until Roman times. The prevailing image projected by royal ritual and display was that of a bounded world, differentiated from its neighbours by the presence within it of kingship and the gods. Internally, this world was represented as a duality—the Two Lands of Upper and Lower Egypt—bound to each other, and to a unified vision of the cosmos, by royal agency. Outside this web of relations lay a domain of disorder, identified with particular territories beyond the Nile alluvium, the fate of which in royal iconography was to be forcibly subdued or rendered subservient to the centre. They included regions with which Upper and Lower Egypt had formerly shared close cultural affinities and social ties (respectively Lower Nubia and the Levant), as well as the deserts to the east and west of the Nile valley, all of which were now represented as 'foreign' (Shaw 2000b).

This self-contained, idealised vision was directed principally towards an inner elite and sought to redefine engagements with the outside world in terms of a moral economy of movement and interaction, managed by the court for the benefit of subordinates. Its formulation coincided with a major reconfiguration of relations between the Nile alluvium and neighbouring regions, which took place directly prior to and during the First Dynasty, and can be independently traced in the archaeological record (fig. 7.4). This reconfiguration had numerous dimensions, and involved a range of centrally directed strategies. In the short term they included the circumscription of non-royal access to territories immediately surrounding Egypt, combined with a heightened exploitation of their natural resources by the centre; the destruction of a rival polity in Lower Nubia; and the abandonment of regular overland contacts with the southern Levant, in favour of maritime relations with coastal polities further to the north. The common, long-term effect of these changes was to replace fluid relations of movement and exchange across Egypt's frontiers with new modes of interaction, defined and executed by the court: the mining expedition, the punitive raid, and the conduct of official diplomacy and commerce with foreign elites.

7.5 Regimes of movement

Egypt's southern border at Elephantine was fortified during the First Dynasty, shortly after its establishment (Ziermann 1993; Seidlmayer 1996b). By no later than the beginning of the Old Kingdom, a permanent garrison was established overlooking the Nile at Buhen, deep within Lower Nubia (Emery

1963). The cessation of Egyptian trade with this region after Naqada IIIB had withdrawn a vital source of legitimation from local elites, whose modes of commemoration and display—attested at the Late/Final A-Group cemetery of Qustul—closely echoed those of Egypt's first rulers (chapter 8.6). Punitive raids, commemorated in rock carvings near the Second Cataract, served to further erode local power structures during the late fourth millennium BC.[12] The outcome was the creation of what Baines (2003: 37) has termed a 'vastly extended frontier zone' to the south of Egypt, providing Egyptian rulers with unmediated access to the gold and mineral deposits of the Nubian Desert. Commemorative objects suggest that a similar process may have occurred, or was at least envisioned, to the west of the Nile valley, in the area that Egyptian sources term Tjehenu and Tjemhu ('Libya'; perhaps located as far west as Cyrenaica), but direct archaeological information is lacking (Baines 2003: 29–34).

In the Eastern Desert, pottery dating to the early dynasties and Old Kingdom is reported from quarries near the Gebel Zeit massif, where there is evidence for on-site smelting of copper and the extraction of gold and iron (Castel *et al.* 1992; Abdel Tawab *et al.* 1990). Early royal names, including those of Narmer and Djet, mark rock surfaces along major routes between the Nile valley and the Red Sea, such as the Wadi Qash (a tributary of the Wadi Hammamat) and the Wadi Abbad.[13] Old Kingdom sources document expeditions along the Red Sea coast to the land of Punt in search of the aromatic plant resin 'ntyw, which may refer to both frankincense and myrrh. The location of Punt, like that of Tjehenu, is uncertain, but probably lay between modern Port Sudan and northern Eritrea (O'Connor and Quirke 2003b; cf. Meeks 2003). Obsidian from Ethiopia or southern Arabia is documented in Egyptian burials as early as Naqada II (Zarins 1989), and Egyptian rulers maintained privileged trading contacts with this region until the late second millennium BC, when an alternative route was established between Yemen and the Levant using dromedary camels to pass along the western margins of the Arabian peninsula (Artzy 1994).

By the Third Dynasty (c.2650–2580 BC), when the earliest step pyramid complexes were built at Saqqara, the Egyptian court had asserted direct control over the copper and turquoise mines of south-western Sinai (Stager 1992: 35).[14] This development was preceded by the abandonment of the trans-Sinaitic caravan route during the First Dynasty, bringing close relations between Egypt and the southern Levant to an end.[15] The isolation of this latter region during the EB II–III periods was compounded by a decisive shift of Egyptian maritime activity to the northern Levant, which took place no later than the Second

---

[12] The most important of these carvings, formerly located at Gebel Sheikh Suleiman, is now on display at the Sudan National Museum in Khartoum; Murnane 1987.

[13] Winkler 1938: 10, pl. 11: 1; Legrain 1903: 221, fig. 7; Porter and Moss 1937: 207.

[14] For royal inscriptions of Netjerikhet (Djoser), Sekhemkhet and Sanakht at Wadi Maghara, see Gardiner and Peet 1952; Gardiner *et al.* 1955; Giveon 1974.

[15] Ben-Tor 1991: 5; Stager 1992: 40–1; but see also de Miroschedji's (2002: 45–7) reservations.

Dynasty. The long-term significance of this shift resided in a combination of factors—social, material and historical—that are best exemplified by Egypt's relations with Byblos, on the Lebanese coast.

7.6 The impact of maritime trade

During the first half of the third millennium BC, the port of Byblos occupied a nodal position between Egypt and a growing network of powerful city-states on the Syrian steppe, with diplomatic links extending to palatial centres beyond the Euphrates. As documented in the palace archives of Ebla, these latter polities mobilised a considerable workforce in the manufacture of wool textiles, and conducted large-scale transactions in precious metals, equivalent to tons of silver and hundreds of kilos of gold (Pettinato 1981; Sherratt and Sherratt 1991). In addition to an extensive agricultural hinterland, the traders of Byblos also had access to abundant sources of high-quality timber, a raw material that was lacking in Egypt. This unprecedented combination of circumstances generated what Leon Marfoe (1987: 27) has described as a 'spiralling interdependence between timber procurement, ship construction and carrying capacity', which progressively expanded the scope of maritime trade in the Eastern Mediterranean during this period.

Along the northern Levantine littoral, access to this burgeoning maritime trade stimulated the production of organic commodities on an increasingly large scale. Oil, wine and resin were packaged and transported in purpose-made ceramic containers (principally a range of highly fired storage jars, jugs and flasks), produced in large quantities at centres in the vicinity of Mount Hermon, and near Lake Kinneret to the south.[16] During the Egyptian early dynastic period, such vessels and their contents were traded to elites (who represented them internally as tributary gifts), and certain forms remained a consistent feature of royal funerary assemblages throughout the Old Kingdom (fig. 7.7).[17] At Byblos, the restructuring of the regional economy took place under the aegis of urban elites, giving rise to a local form of kingship that bolstered its legitimacy through the absorption of Egyptian cultural values and material symbols (Marfoe 1987).

---

[16] Adams and Porat 1996; Greenberg and Porat 1996; Stager 1992: 37–41; Marcus 2002: 410–11.

[17] Kantor 1992: 19–20. Ceramic jugs and flasks of the so-called 'Abydos ware' (in fact documented, not just from Abydos, but also cemeteries in the Memphite region and eastern Nile delta) appear to have a more restricted chronological distribution in Egypt, extending from the reign of Djer to the end of the First Dynasty (Hennessey 1967). A petrographic study of vessels incised with schematic pot-marks indicates that such signs may have denoted particular regions of origin within the Levant, which corresponded to the distinct organic commodities carried (Adams and Porat 1996; for the Levantine origin of these wares, see Hennessey and Millett 1963). An analysis of organic residues adhering to imported Levantine jars from the tomb associated with king Djer at Abydos provides direct evidence for trade in coniferous resins (Serpico and White 1996).

Figure 7.7 Copper vessels and Levantine imports from elite burials at Saqqara, First Dynasty

In Egypt itself, the 'Byblos run' provided a foundation for the regular use of fine woods as sculptural and architectural media, and for the development of river-going barges capable of carrying large quantities of stone, which greatly increased the potential for monumental construction during the Old Kingdom (Kantor 1992: 19).[18] Sophisticated boats also transformed the character of elite ceremonial practices, and their incorporation into royal funerary rites—famously exemplified by the enormous cedar barque discovered adjacent to the pyramid of Khufu at Giza—can be traced back to the First Dynasty (figs. 10.12, 10.13). The scale of maritime trade at this time is indicated by an entry on the Palermo Stone, commemorating the arrival of a fleet of forty ships carrying cedar to Egypt during the reign of Sneferu, first king of the Fourth Dynasty (Marcus 2002: 408, with references). Maritime concerns are also prominent in Old Kingdom royal reliefs, such as those of the Fifth Dynasty pyramid temple of Sahure at Abusir, which depict large sailing vessels manned

---

[18] For the development of ship design and carrying capacity, see Landström 1970; Ward 2000.

by foreign crews and bearing a cargo including Levantine flasks and tethered bears (Smith 1965, figs. 6–7; Wachsmann 1998: 12–15).[19]

These various sources serve to highlight, not just the scale of maritime activity between Egypt and the Levant, but also its elite character. Long-distance trade was increasingly conducted, not through the dense social networks of village exchange—as in Neolithic times—or large-scale movements of population—as in the fourth millennium—but through direct contact between restricted groups, who were able to mobilise the local production of commodities on a far larger scale. The nature of these contacts is further indicated by surviving Egyptian imports at Byblos and Ebla, comprising stone vessels inscribed with royal names, which retained some form of currency within and outside Egypt long after the reign of the king whose name they bore (Bevan 2003; Sparks 2003). Such objects are hardly informative by comparison with the extensive royal correspondence of the Amarna Age, but they do preserve a trace of the earlier cosmopolitan networks upon which that later correspondence was founded.

---

[19] For relationships between nautical terminology and male initiation in elite systems of social organisation during the early dynasties and Old Kingdom, see Roth 1991.

THE EVOLUTION OF SIMPLICITY:
NAQADA III

I have found the following law and present it to mankind; the evolution of civilization is tantamount to the removal of ornament from objects of use.
Ornament and Crime, A. Loos (translation, E. Gombrich)

8.1 An approach to state formation

Conventional accounts of early state formation have taken the explanation of
innovation and complexity as their central problem. This places the focus
squarely upon what a society, or rather some part of it, gains by such a process
in terms of technology and other cultural accretions, as well as more widespread changes in patterns of social organisation. Only recently have analysts
begun to pay attention to parallel processes, characterised—at least in the
domain of material culture—by an opposite trend towards simplification and
subtraction.[1] With this latter approach goes a greater awareness of what, in a
society's repertoire of behaviours and forms of experience, may be lost or
forgotten during the formation of states. It also brings into clearer focus an
intermediate set of transformations, whereby something of a society's cultural
heritage is retained, but under altered conditions that favour the interests of
new power groups by representing those interests as a seamless continuity
from the past.

In both Egypt and Mesopotamia, the simplification of everyday practices
is most clearly evident in the production of widely disseminated media such
as pottery. In the latter region a long-term trend can be followed from the
highly decorated and individualised serving vessels of Late Neolithic times to
increasingly standardised and plain containers, culminating in the crude,
mass-produced bevelled-rim bowls of the Uruk period. From these and other
forms of early urban pottery it may be deduced that, for the majority of people,
those daily acts of consumption which structured the socially charged life
of the household became increasingly impersonal, ephemeral and routine
during the process of state formation. The wider implications of this and
similar processes are succinctly expressed in Susan Kus's (1989) call for an

---

[1] Wengrow 2001b; Yoffee 2002; Smith 2003: 277–8.

'archaeology of bread and circuses', which takes into account the dualistic nature of social change in the transition from 'simple' to 'complex' societies. It becomes necessary to understand, not merely how certain aspects of life were subject to complexification (the circus-like features which appear in every archaeological check-list of state formation) but also how others, notably everyday activities such as eating, were divested of symbolic significance and subjected to routinisation and simplification.[2] Only then can the links between these two aspects of social change come into focus to form a rounded picture of state formation as a series of meaningful interventions in the flow of life, rather than the inexorable unfolding of abstract structures.

To take just one example, the simplification and standardisation of material culture in Mesopotamia may be linked to the emergence of the proto-cuneiform writing system towards the end of the fourth millennium BC (Nissen et al. 1993). Such a system could serve the administrative functions for which it was designed only so long as the real objects to which it referred conformed in some measure to the ordered categories and classificatory schemes into which it divided and organised the material world. A basic requisite was that they should be qualitatively similar and interchangeable: one beer jar essentially the same as any other, and so on. Only when the production and exchange of objects had been disentangled from social processes that invested them with particular life histories could they begin to be effectively treated as information in this way. In the form of bureaucracy, the early Mesopotamian city-state compensated for the erosion of established social procedures for the dispensation of goods and services. In the form of periodic ceremonies, such as those surrounding the construction of temples as divine households, it offered vicarious gratification and the spectacular celebration or safeguarding of 'traditional' values as a surrogate for the customary rituals of village life.

In the case of Egypt, the theoretical concerns outlined above have been most clearly articulated by John Baines. In a number of studies he draws attention to how the emergence of the dynastic state was accompanied by the specialisation and circumscription of artistic production within elite circles *and* the 'aesthetic deprivation of the non-elite' (1994: 71; 1989a: 476–7). The restriction of access to visual display is evident, not just in pottery, but across the whole range of personal ornaments and implements that had previously constituted customary signs of extension in the social world. Just as the material culture of bodily appearance was simplified, so too were treatments of the body in death, which for the majority of the population became increasingly formulaic. These widespread developments were juxtaposed to

---

[2] Because of its probable function in baking, the bevelled-rim bowl is the ideal symbol for an approach that problematises the evolution of the 'bread' as well as the 'circus'.

a much more restricted process of innovation that was confined to emergent elites—linked to one another from the Nile delta to Lower Nubia through a web of exchanges—and spanned a range of material crafts, modes of communication and the funerary arts (fig. 8.8).

Ornament and stratification

The approach I develop here owes much to a study by Alfred Gell (1993) of the relationship between body tattooing and political change in Polynesia during the nineteenth and twentieth centuries AD. It is from that study that I take the preposterous statement by Adolf Loos, critic and pioneer of architectural modernism, which opens this chapter. The full citation from his *Ornament und Verbrechen* ('Ornament and Crime'; Loos 1998 [1908]) reads as follows:

The child is amoral. The Papuans are equally so for us. The Papuans slaughter their enemies and eat them. They are not criminals. If, however, a man of this century slaughters and eats someone, he is a criminal and degenerate. The Papuans tattoo their skins, their boats, their oars, in short, everything within reach. But a man of this century who tattoos himself is a criminal and a degenerate . . . I have found the following law and present it to mankind; the evolution of civilization is tantamount to the removal of ornament from objects of use.

(Loos 1908, as cited in Gell 1993: 15)

It is tempting to dismiss this anachronistic piece of cultural chauvinism as precisely that but, as Gell was at pains to show, to do so is to close off a potentially important field of analysis in the interests of political correctness. In comparing various Polynesian societies he observed correlations between the extent of body art and the extent of political stratification that cannot simply be explained away as a figment of the European imagination. Put briefly:

There seemed, on first inspection, to be some kind of 'elective affinity' between societies with elaborate tattooing and an Open (competitive) status hierarchy and conversely, there seemed to be a disaffinity between Closed (stratified) societies and the existence of a culturally stressed tradition of body art.   (Gell 1993: 2)

In interrogating these patterns Gell evoked a theoretical notion of the body, derived from Foucault, which seems useful in the present context. The body 'is directly involved in the political field; power relations have an immediate hold over it; they invest, mark it, train it, torture it, force it to carry out tasks, to perform ceremonies, to emit signs' (Foucault 1979: 25). Power 'exercised over and through the body' constrains the lives of both ruler and ruled, albeit in different ways, and is contested through differential access to those particular material resources, forms of knowledge and modes of self-presentation and consumption that signify the attainment of a full and worthy life (cf. Gell 1993: 3–4). It is in pursuing access to these sources of social power that individuals become bound, emotionally and psychologically, into institutional lifestyles that offer rewards in return for surrendering some aspect of the self.

Such considerations impinge upon the processes usually referred to by archaeologists as 'state formation' or 'the evolution of complex societies'. They point towards the particular forms and histories of social power that underlie these processes, and the manner in which they are expressed through engagements with the material world. Accordingly, they allow us to pursue the lines of investigation established earlier in this book into a new phase of social transformations, highlighting aspects of continuity and change along the way.

8.2 The constriction of social and material worlds

Extensive and elaborate traditions of personal display, whether in the late nineteenth-century Marquesas or Naqada II Egypt, express the tendency of social interaction towards a certain spatial resolution. That resolution may be defined somewhere between the extremes of personal familiarity and alienation respectively associated with close kin and cultural aliens, for whom such regular acts of display have little salience. As Gell (1993: 298) put it, they are directed towards 'a collective social other whose gaze must be met and whose sensibilities must be captured and entranced' on a frequent basis. In order to perform this function, the objects through which such extensive traditions of display are transmitted—personal ornaments, ceramic containers, or whatever—must fulfil two conditions. First, their manufacture should involve the use of skills that are socially learned but allow for the expression of individual identity and prowess. Second, both the objects themselves, and the materials and equipment used in their production, should be widely available as part of the milieu of everyday social action (cf. Wengrow 2001b). Documenting the absence of something is inherently difficult, but by looking in detail at a fairly typical group of burials and their contents we may get a sense of how these established patterns of production and display were disrupted and altered during the Naqada III period.

A view from el-Kab

The Naqada III cemetery of el-Kab lies on the east bank of the Nile in southern Upper Egypt, near the mouth of the Wadi Helal and just north of the important west bank site of Hierakonpolis. Owing to the location of an Old Kingdom necropolis over the same site, its original extent is unknown. Almost fifty surviving graves dating to Naqada IIIA (c.3300–3200 BC) have been excavated there, as well as a smaller number of Naqada IIIB–D burials (c.3200–2900 BC; Hendrickx 1994). On conventional criteria of grave structure and contents, their overall character would be described as 'low status' by comparison with the more elaborate cemeteries of this period, such as those of Abydos to the north.[3] Single inhumations were most common, although double-burials—about half of which contained the bodies of an adult and child—were also found. There is no evidence from el-Kab of pre-burial dismemberment or preservative treatments of the body, although extensive disturbance of the graves precludes any final statement on this matter (van Rossum 1994).

Grave forms at el-Kab were for the most part more clearly defined than typical burials of earlier periods, with vertical walls and level floors. Further elaboration of the burial space was restricted to the placing of unworked stone slabs along the interior walls, over the burial, or between the burial and grave goods. In a few cases a special recess was created within the grave for the placement of objects (Hendrickx 1994: 149–204). For present purposes, the interest of these burials resides in the sparseness of their material contents, which provides a point of entry to wider changes in material culture that followed the end of the Naqada II period. Few of the objects found within them are decorated in any way and various forms of personal adornment that had formerly been widespread are no longer in evidence. An explanation in terms of looting can be excluded, both through comparisons with contemporaneous cemeteries elsewhere, and through a closer inspection of the surviving range of objects from el-Kab itself.

The latter suggest a continuation of earlier practices and concerns relating to the body, but make use of a much restricted and impoverished material culture that is replicated in non-elite cemeteries throughout Egypt at this time (see Adams and Ciałowicz 1997: 24–35). The twenty cosmetic palettes recovered from various burials at el-Kab are mostly plain (Hendrickx 1994: 129–34, pls. 26–7). They include a number of unworked pieces of stone bearing traces of pigment, more comparable to the crude grinders of the Early Holocene than to their elaborate Naqada II predecessors. With the occasional exception of fish-shaped palettes, the decorative extension of the palette form is no longer practised, and simple geometrical shapes such as rectangles and ovals are now the norm. A new, if very limited, emphasis on surface ornament is, however, apparent in the incision of parallel lines around the circumference of the palette. Only a single, fragmentary mace-head was recovered and the number of bone and ivory items is also diminished by comparison with earlier burials. Surviving examples include unornamented hairpins, spoons and bracelets, concentrated within a handful of graves, of which a number also contained stone vessels (Hendrickx 1994: 135–9, 142, pl. 28; and for stone vessels, 109–28, pls. 24–5). The latter, which typically exhibit no figural ornament, retained a relatively wide circulation during the Naqada III period, and were by no means restricted to elite cemeteries (see el-Khouli 1978; Krzyżaniak 1989).

---

[3] See, e.g., Castillos 1982; Griswold 1992; Wilkinson 1996.

Pronounced changes are also evident in the ceramic repertoire at el-Kab, and again these are paralleled throughout Egypt.[4] Gone entirely is the figural painting of the predynastic period, and pottery assemblages as a whole exhibit a much greater degree of homogeneity and repetition of form (fig. 8.1). Simple linear ornament, usually forming a loose net pattern, was sometimes applied to cylindrical jars in a dull red paint. Vessels of this latter type, made in the same marl clay as the earlier D-Ware, became widespread in Egypt during Naqada III, and are sometimes also decorated with a thin, undulating ridge pinched out around the neck (Bourriau 1981: 133; Dreyer *et al.* 1996: 54–6). The latter ornament may derive from the more pronounced type of 'wavy-handle' decoration, which continued to be applied to storage jars after Naqada II.[5] Closer parallels may perhaps be drawn with a kind of relief decoration found on contemporary stone vessels, sometimes elaborated to resemble a thin rope tied around the neck of the jar (e.g. Klasens 1958b: 42, fig. 15; Hendrickx 1994: 118, pl. 25). By Naqada IIIC1 (c.3100 BC) even these limited forms of ornament had been abandoned, and plain cylindrical vessels predominate (e.g. Petrie 1953, pl. 9; Bourriau 1981: 133, cat. 260). Marl clay was also used to make ovoid liquid containers of varying sizes, which are among the most ubiquitous ceramic forms interred with the dead at el-Kab and other Naqada III cemeteries (fig. 8.1, top right). Other new forms in this fabric include simple bowls with flat bases, on which decoration is restricted to the application of a red or white slip. All these vessel types were coil-built, either in a single piece or starting from a separately modelled base (Vandier 1952: 327–8; Hendrickx 1994: 79).

Coarse, chaff-tempered ceramics made from Nile silt continued to be in-cluded within burial assemblages. To the existing repertoire of thick-walled baking dishes, jars with rolled rims and flat-based bowls with flaring sides was added a new form of tall jar that tapers to a pointed base (fig. 8.1, bottom left; Hendrickx 1994: 78–9, 93, pls. 21–2). Throughout Egypt the scale of coarse-ware production increased markedly at this time, as is most clearly attested at settlement sites in the Nile delta such as Buto and Tell el-Farkha, discussed below. In the el-Kab assemblage the intensification of ceramic production is reflected in the presence of coarse bowls finished on a slow-wheel, which

---

[4] Various classificatory schemes have been proposed for Naqada III pottery since Petrie's original corpora were assembled (Petrie 1921, pls. 45–51: 'Late Ware'; 1953). These are discussed in some detail by Hendrickx (1994: 15–17), who develops the typology of Nordström (1972). Extensive presentations of Naqada III ceramic types and stone vessels can be found in excavation reports from the cemeteries of Abu Rawash, on the fringes of the Western Desert, c.16 km north of Cairo; see Klasens 1957; 1958a; 1958b; 1959; 1960; 1961; also discussion by Vandier 1952: 318–27.

[5] The form of these jars, to which the wavy handles were usually attached as separately modelled pieces, became progressively narrower and more cylindrical during the Naqada III period, departing from the squat and globular forms of the Naqada II period. This trend has provided a cornerstone of relative chronology from Petrie to the present (Petrie 1901b: 5; Kaiser 1957; Hendrickx 1996; 1999).

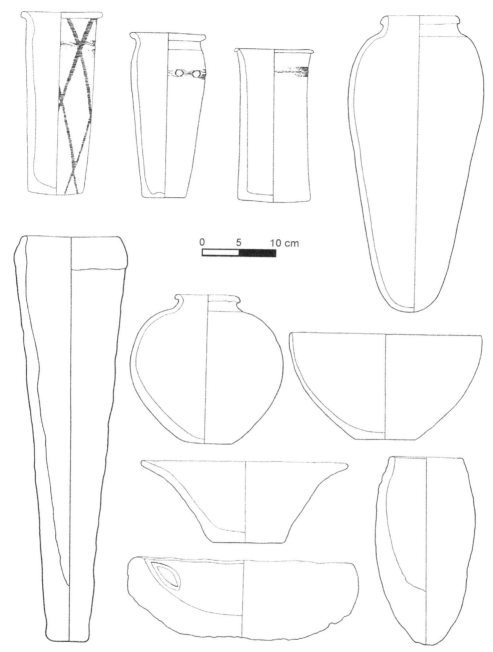

Figure 8.1 Naqada III ceramic types, el-Kab, Upper Egypt

exhibit string-cut bases like those found on contemporary mass-produced bowls in Mesopotamia (Hendrickx 1994: 78–9, pl. 71; cf. Frangipane 2001: 330).

8.3 Production, consumption and hierarchy

The range of ceramic vessel types attested at el-Kab is broadly representative for Egypt from Naqada IIIA to Naqada IIIC1 (Dynasty 0); hence, an understanding of their respective functions is of general significance for interpreting social developments during this period. Here the combined circumstances of increased conservatism in ceramic production and the availability of a rich pictorial record from the Old Kingdom offer unique opportunities that have been explored by Stan Hendrickx (1994: 80–93) and Dina Faltings (1998b). Of the coarse vessels found at el-Kab, thick-walled dishes are virtually identical in form and fabric to later bread moulds, the early development of which was discussed in chapter 4. Hendrickx suggests that the smaller type of porous, coarse-ware bowl with flaring sides was used to produce the lightly baked bread used in beer production, a possibility that is consistent with current views on the introduction of fermented cereal products to the Nile valley. A similarly ubiquitous form with a lentoid body corresponds closely to the idealised depiction of a beer jar that features, alongside bread, as a standard component of the offering lists that appear in Old Kingdom tombs (fig. 8.1, bottom right).

Purely on the basis of form and fabric, large ovoid jars and small bowls made in the finer marl clay (fig. 8.1, centre) seem likely to have served complementary functions in the storage and serving of liquids. The morphology of cylindrical vessels is less immediately suggestive, but as Hendrickx notes this form is associated in Old Kingdom sources with cosmetic oils and scented ornaments. These substances could have been produced from a range of raw materials such as vegetable oils, animal fat, plant extracts and seeds. Many of these ingredients were widely available, but, like beer and wine, the properties of oils and ointments could potentially be enhanced by using more exotic substances and complex methods of manufacture. Their consumption and application might therefore express a far greater range of social values than earlier comestibles or simple cosmetic paints derived from ochre and malachite. This development no doubt played an important role in constituting and reinforcing new relations of hierarchy during Naqada III. It therefore seems significant that cylindrical containers were themselves produced both in a relatively restricted ceramic fabric and in a range of coloured stones, many of which had to be procured from areas beyond the alluvium (Petrie 1921: 34–36; Krzyżaniak 1989, figs. 6, 7, 9, 11). This may point towards the establishment of a hierarchical scale of value within a common range of vessel forms and contents. Other materials, notably metals, that are hardly preserved in the archaeological record would have occupied the upper end of this scale.

A small cylindrical vessel made in sheet gold from a Naqada III burial at Kafr Hassan Dawud, on the eastern margins of the delta, provides only the faintest indication of what might have existed (el-Hangary 1992: 215).

These changes in material culture and patterns of consumption are broadly consistent with the wider transformations outlined in chapter 7, where the restructuring of Egypt's economy during Naqada III was modelled along similarly hierarchical principles. New, capital-intensive modes of farming, introduced to Egypt during a phase of particularly close interaction with the southern Levant, played an important role, setting in motion a process of internal colonisation that elites were in a position to control and define to their own advantage. It must be emphasised, however, that new productive technologies did not in themselves cause social transformations to follow a hierarchical trajectory in Egypt, as is highlighted by the case of their source area, the Early Bronze Age Levant. There, as Graham Philip (2001) has argued, capital- and labour-intensive farming—making use of animal traction, irrigation and tree-crops—was established through a fluid pattern of segmentary alliance among village groups, rather than political stratification. In Egypt, by contrast, these technologies were harnessed (quite literally in the case of animal traction) to the needs of social groups already set on a distinct path of internal differentiation and competitive expansion. The economic underpinnings of this process had once to be hypothesised from Old Kingdom sources and a limited corpus of earlier inscriptions extending back beyond the First Dynasty, that refer to the existence of royal vineyards and estates (chapter 10.6). Fieldwork in Lower Egypt, however, has now begun to provide archaeological insights into the transformation of Egypt's productive economy in the late fourth millennium.

8.4 New foundations in the Nile delta: the expansion of agrarian production

The Naqada III period saw a marked expansion of settlement in the Nile delta, which has now been documented through excavation and regional survey (see the contributions in van den Brink 1988b; 1992b). Excavated settlement mounds, which rise between three and five metres above the modern floodplain, include the eastern delta sites of Kufur Nigm (Bakr 1988; 1994; 2000), Tell el-Iswid (van den Brink 1989), Tell el-Farkha (Chłodnicki *et al.* 1992; Chłodnicki and Ciałowicz 2002) and Tell Ibrahim Awad (van den Brink 1988a; 1992a), and the site of Buto (Tell el-Fara'in), which is located in the north-western delta along a bourgeoning axis of maritime trade.[6] Many have yielded stratified deposits that extend from the earlier Maadi-Buto phase into Old Kingdom times (Table 2). Cemeteries of the same period—for instance at Minshat Abu Omar (Kroeper 1988; 1992; Kroeper and Wildung 1985; 1994;

---

[6] von der Way 1997; Faltings and Köhler 1996; Faltings *et al.* 2000.

2000) and Kafr Hassan Dawud (Bakr *et al.* 1996; Hassan 2000a)—which may have been accompanied by settlements, are known to extend to the eastern fringes of the delta. There they were established along important overland routes extending between Egypt and the Levant—traversed with the aid of pack-donkeys—along which passed a regular flow of people and commodities (chapter 7.2, 7.3).

Although the scale of horizontal excavation in this region is severely restricted, limited exposures at settlement sites in the delta have revealed a remarkably uniform set of cultural transformations at the onset of Naqada III.[7] They are most clearly signalled by the appearance of well-made mud-brick architecture with compacted silt floors, which either replaces or supplements more ephemeral modes of construction. What is striking at all the sites in question is the scale of mud-brick architecture at the point of its introduction (fig. 8.2). On current, limited evidence there appears to be little evolution from small domestic units to large complexes. The earliest mud-brick walls at all of these sites typically extend beyond the margins of the excavated areas to lengths exceeding ten metres. Most are rectilinear in form, while circular features include grain silos, ovens and a large brewing installation found at Tell el-Farkha. In terms of size and layout, and the suddenness of their appearance, these buildings point towards the foundation of large corporate entities of an entirely new kind. This interpretation is further borne out by their associated material culture. Ceramic assemblages at all of these sites reflect a relatively sudden increase in the scale of production, with thick-walled bread moulds appearing in consistently large quantities (fig. 4.4, lower), along with a new range of storage and serving vessels in both marl and alluvial fabrics.[8] Most of the latter have close parallels in the Nile valley, and may indicate the establishment of similar productive units there as well (cf. Köhler 1998a: 75–8).

Stone tool repertoires in Lower Egypt also underwent a marked transformation at this time, with the appearance in unprecedented numbers of rectangular sickle elements. These would have been set in groups into wooden or bone handles, and have direct parallels at southern Levantine sites such as Tel Erani and 'En Besor (fig. 8.3).[9] Many exhibit denticular retouch along the cutting edge, which has a surface sheen acquired during the reaping of grasses. Although smaller and more gracile, they closely resemble a lithic type, misleadingly termed the 'Canaanean blade', that became widespread

[7] The strata are: Tell el-Fara'in/Buto IIIb–f, Tell el-Iswid Phase B (Stratum 7), Tell el-Farkha (West Mound, Phases 3–4) and Tell Ibrahim Awad Phase 6.
[8] Köhler 1998a; van den Brink 1989: 71–7; 1992a: 52–3; Chłodnicki and Ciałowicz 2002: 100–7; Jucha 2003.
[9] Chłodnicki and Ciałowicz 2002: 107–10; Kabacinski 2003; Schmidt (in van den Brink 1989: 91–4); 1992: 34–5. A number of intact sickles were recovered from the First Dynasty tomb of Hemaka at Saqqara, their blades still bonded to the wooden handles (Emery 1938: 33, pl. 15; further discussion by Hikade 1999: 52–3).

Figure 8.2 Mud-brick architecture at Tell el-Farkha, Nile delta

throughout much of northern Mesopotamia and the Levant during the fourth millennium.[10] These symmetrical tools were struck from a pre-prepared single platform core, producing an elongated blade that could be snapped into

[10] Rosen 1983; 1988: 109–11; see also Edens 1999; Philip 2001: 211; Oates 2002. Small numbers of Canaanean blades are present in the earlier lithic assemblage from Maadi, perhaps arriving there as trade items; Rizkana and Seeher 1988: 35–6.

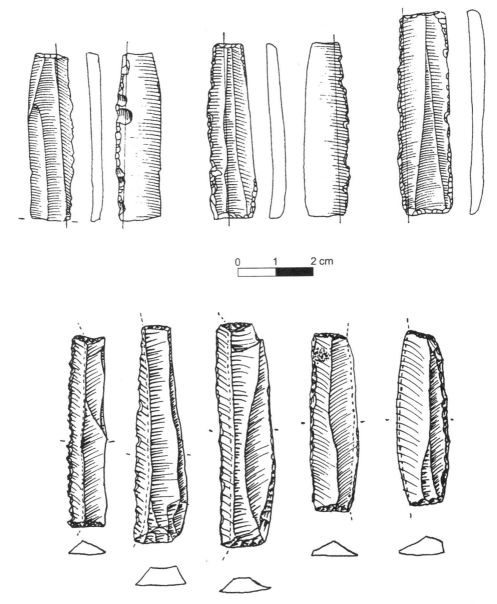

0   1   2 cm

Figure 8.3 Flint sickle-blades from Tell el-Farkha, Nile delta (above) and Tel Erani, S. Israel (below)

shorter segments. In the southern Levant their adoption is associated with early evidence for the use of draught animals, both in plough agriculture and conceivably in threshing operations using a specially designed sledge, which, as Patricia Anderson suggests, may have been fitted with similar blades

(Anderson and Inizan 1994; Anderson 1999: 139–44).[11] It therefore formed part of a new complex of planting and harvesting techniques that would have greatly increased the scale of cereal production and processing. The identification of both long- and shorthorn cattle in the faunal assemblage at Tell el-Farkha (Chłodnicki and Ciałowicz 2002: 113) is significant in this context, and perhaps suggests that other aspects of this complex, including animal traction and dairying, were also introduced into Lower Egypt during the late fourth millennium (chapter 7.4). At Tell el-Farkha it was noted that over two-thirds of the lithic assemblage comprised finished tools, with only one heavily exploited core recovered from the entire excavated zone (Chłodnicki and Ciałowicz 2002: 110). It is therefore likely that considerable quantities of blades were brought in semi-processed or finished forms to the site. Here, as elsewhere in the Nile delta, their appearance coincides with a marked increase in the use of stone querns, grinders and pestles.

Changes in ground- and chipped-stone industry, as well as ceramics, combine to suggest a strong emphasis upon the centrally organised processing of grain, now widely used in the manufacture of leavened bread and beer, which was also conducted in centralised facilities. This is borne out by the discovery of malting and brewing installations, respectively at Buto (chapter 4.5) and Tell el-Farkha. The latter comprised an arrangement of mud-brick channels supporting the remains of large ceramic vats, and encircled by a further series of circular mud-brick walls, around which were situated postholes to support some kind of roofing (Chłodnicki and Ciałowicz 2002: 92). At the majority of sites the appearance of mud-brick complexes is associated with these wider changes in material culture and forms of production, suggesting a co-ordinated restructuring of the local economy. Only at Buto is a more gradual and staggered sequence of changes attested, with the appearance of mud-brick buildings in Stratum IIIb (roughly equivalent to Naqada IID–IIIA1) preceding a marked transformation in ceramic production in Strata IIId–f (Naqada IIIA2–C1).[12] From this point onwards, the range and frequency of vessel types at Buto is largely consistent with that of other delta sites. Christiana Köhler's detailed analysis of these wares confirms that they were the products of specialised workshops, oriented increasingly towards large-scale production and utility of form (1998a: 63–72).

---

[11] Anderson's conclusions rely heavily upon ethnographic analogies, and have yet to be clearly substantiated. For possible evidence of threshing operations in the Uvda valley of southern Israel, see Avner 1990, but also Rosen's (1997: 100) reservations. For plough agriculture, see Grigson 1995: 267–8; Philip 2001: 186–7. I am grateful to Steve Rosen for discussions on these topics.

[12] Another unusual feature of the ceramic assemblage at Buto is the appearance of large, ovoid storage jars in Strata IIId–f; elsewhere in Egypt, except at Minshat Abu Omar, this form is hardly attested before Naqada IIIC1–2, perhaps suggesting its dissemination from north to south; cf. Köhler 1998a: 49, fig. 24.

Figure 8.4 Seal impressions showing scenes of ceremonial threshing, from Arslantepe, S. E. Turkey (above) and Uruk, S. Iraq (below), late fourth millennium BC

The need to view these various developments in more than simply economic terms is highlighted by scenes of ceremonial threshing, identified by M. A. Littauer and J. H. Crouwel (1990) on carved objects of the late fourth millennium from Iraq and south-east Turkey (fig. 8.4). They show an individual of high status seated within an elaborate litter, which is mounted upon a threshing sledge drawn by an ox. On a cylinder-seal impression from Arslantepe, figures carrying winnowing shovels follow behind this composite vehicle. As Littauer and Crouwel observe, the carrying litters depicted on these objects closely resemble that which contains the figure facing the king on the ceremonial mace-head of Narmer from Hierakonpolis, dating to the close of the fourth millennium (fig. 2.3). Scenes of animal traction, however, are notably absent from early royal imagery in Egypt, suggesting that—like many other aspects of elite culture—prestigious modes of transport and their associated equipment, adopted from outside, acquired new meanings within a locally defined context of ceremonial display.

8.5 The absorption of social power

We are now in a position to consider more closely the unifying factor behind the various developments discussed so far in this chapter. What was the role of those groups in society that benefited most from them, and translated them into a new currency of power with its own, restricted logic of extension and reproduction? In the next chapter I discuss the ideological underpinnings of this process, arguing that the co-option and transformation of established modes of ritual action and display, rooted in the predynastic past, had a fundamental part to play. First, however, it is important to understand something of the scale and distribution of these transformations in time and space, and in particular the changing interplay of local and supra-local forces in the formalisation of social hierarchies. The archaeological sources for such an understanding derive, once again, from funerary contexts. As a prelude to the developments of the Naqada III period, I therefore briefly revisit the conclusions of chapters 4 and 5 concerning the relationship between ritual and political centralisation in predynastic Egypt.

Setting the scene: the body as a container and the staging of death

I argued that, by Naqada II times, a complex relationship had already been established between the organisation of commemorative performances and the expansion of social power. The relationship between ritual and political centralisation was mediated by the enactment of specific activities relating to the body, and by the deployment of certain kinds of widely circulated objects and images. Changes in modes of signification and ritual practice could be quite rapid, taking place within a few generations across large geographical areas, mapped out by the flow of knowledge and material goods across extensive social networks. The increasing scope of funerary rites during Naqada II was also contingent upon mobilising labour to create, in each case, an appropriate setting for the material transactions that followed between the living and the dead. It was in this context that brick architecture was first used as a space for burial, exemplified by the Painted Tomb at Hierakonpolis and comparable structures at Naqada. Elaborate treatments of the body after death—including dismemberment and preservative techniques—were also explored, and pictorial images that conveyed culturally received notions of landscape and place were widely circulated.

The overall effect of predynastic burial practices might be best characterised as the transformation of the body into an idealised vessel for the containment of social relations. During the ritual process, such relations were given material form through images and through a diverse symbolism of containers that constituted a part of all burial rites. A dense vocabulary of vessel forms and fabrics—coarse beer jars and bread moulds, painted or plain fine wares, stone vases of various sorts, baskets, and so on—was available for framing the spatial boundaries of the burial around the body. The number of containers (what we might call the 'social capacity' of the grave) often correlates to the presence of other desired objects such as trade goods and extensive body ornamentation. The body itself was contained within a series of more or less durable wrappings—such as layers of ornamentation, woven matting, animal skins, and occasionally linen bindings or large ceramic jars—while, in cases of dismemberment, body parts and manufactured objects or images were sometimes interchangeable. By the end of the Naqada II period the expression of status through ritual transformation was also intertwined with the growth of social networks that cut across ties of locality and descent, providing access to exotic goods that acted as material signs of social mobility.

The total burial space might then be usefully thought of as a kind of extended skin, emanating from the body via its dressings and accoutrements to the surrounding structure. The purpose of this skin was to attract material tokens of relationship from the surrounding social environment, so that status—in the temporary, objectified form that it acquired during funerary rites—might be transmitted to the living as a social void in need of substance. This understanding provides a point of departure from which to consider the further role of funerary practices in the transition from an 'open (competitive) status hierarchy' to an increasingly 'closed (stratified) society' during Naqada III. I begin this consideration, not in Egypt, but in Lower Nubia.

8.6 Regional dynamics of centralisation: a view from Nubia

During the late fourth millennium, Egyptian and Nubian societies drew from a common reservoir of ideas concerning the construction of social identities that derived from a shared Neolithic heritage, which also extended further south in the Middle Nile region, and perhaps beyond (see chapters 2 and 3). From Naqada II onwards, however, groups in Lower Nubia (between the First and Second Cataracts) began to develop a distinct repertoire of objects for the preparation of food and cosmetic substances, as well as vernacular techniques for decorating vessels and the body (Williams 1986: 12–13). These differed more or less markedly from contemporary Egyptian practices. In cemeteries of the Middle to Late A-Group (Naqada IID–IIIB; c.3400–3100 BC), locally produced markers of personal identity may be clearly distinguished from imported Egyptian goods. The flow of imported goods southwards into Lower Nubia increased progressively, fuelling the emergence of centralised societies (cf. O'Connor 1993: 14–23). It becomes possible to gain access to regional dynamics of interaction that are often obscured in the archaeological record of Egypt itself, where objects tend to present themselves to us either as 'Egyptian' or 'foreign'. The role of inter-regional (horizontal/reciprocal) exchanges between aspiring elites, as well as their impact upon more localised (vertical/hierarchical) patterns of consumption and display, are therefore more clearly visible in Lower Nubia than in Egypt itself.

Such smaller-scale processes, defined at the regional level, are most evident at a high-status cemetery excavated near Qustul, known as Cemetery L (Williams 1986). It lies within a much broader zone of Late or Final A-Group burial grounds, extending north of the Second Cataract in the region now submerged beneath Lake Nasser (Nordström 1972; Williams 1989: 14–120). The precise dating of Cemetery L has been a matter of some debate, but certainly falls within the Naqada IIIA–B range (Table 2). Many of these burials were plundered prior to excavation, and detailed information on human remains is often lacking. Discussions of Cemetery L have been heavily influenced by the discovery there of a series of stone bowls, generally considered to have been used as incense burners, which bear carved images that clearly relate to the development of royal iconography, as manifested in Egypt during this and subsequent periods (fig. 8.5, middle; Williams 1986: 108–11, 138–47, pls. 26–38). While the significance of these objects has been widely debated, rather less attention has been given to other evidence within the cemetery that relates to the definition of social hierarchies.[13] Three principal categories may be identified for discussion: the concentration of local markers of personal identity in vast numbers within particular tombs; their direct association with large numbers of imported objects, including sophisticated items such as stone vessels and metalwork; and the presentation of all these objects through impressive styles of burial. The latter included the enlargement of tomb structures and the use of new kinds of equipment that heightened the movement of the body towards the grave as a social spectacle.

The first of these categories is best exemplified by the density of local pottery distributed among the tombs at Cemetery L. By contrast with Egypt, communities in Lower Nubia continued to produce highly decorated ceramics during the late fourth millennium. Most striking is a type of deep bowl with very thin walls (sometimes called 'eggshell ware'), the surfaces of which were painted with linear bands of geometrical ornament and then heavily burnished to create a shimmering effect (fig. 8.5, lower; Nordström 1972: 87–8, pls. 175–7). The final product was highly individualised, and identical painted vessels are difficult to find among the extensive assemblage from Qustul, which numbers around a thousand such pieces (Williams 1986: 27–61, 198–388). This greatly exceeds the quantities of this ware reported from other Late A-Group cemeteries and suggests a gathering in of local forms of wealth towards a particular focus of ritual activity. The absorption of local markers of

---

[13] Arguments made by Bruce Williams (1980; 1986) for the Nubian origins of ancient Egyptian kingship, based upon his analysis of the Qustul material, have not been widely accepted (e.g. O'Connor 1993: 21; Baines 1995: 104–5), and are difficult to reconcile with growing evidence for the emergence of local elites within Egypt during the early Naqada III period.

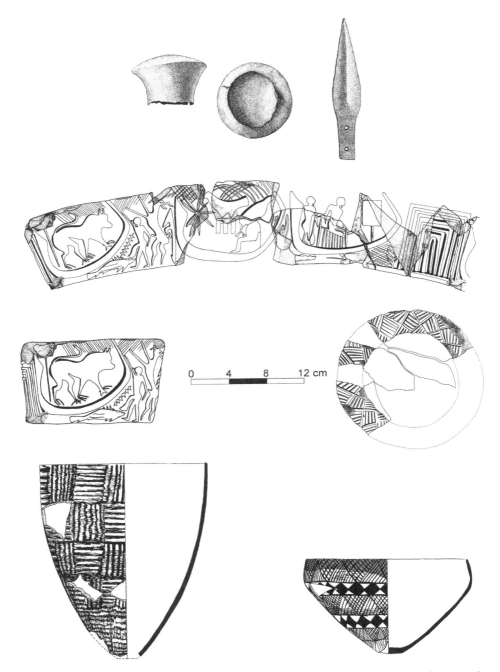

Figure 8.5 Copper finial and spearhead, decorated incense burner and painted
pottery from Qustul, Cemetery L, Lower Nubia, Late/Final A-Group

identity is further exemplified by a remarkable concentration, in one burial, of 4,700 items of personal adornment including armlets, studs, beads and hooks (Williams 1986: 306–13, grave L17, pl. 50).[14] Most were made in shell, but small numbers of beads in gold and various coloured stones were also present.

Imported objects at Cemetery L included unusually large quantities of Egyptian marl vessels, such as serving bowls, bottles, cylindrical jars and large, ovoid storage jars. In addition, over a hundred Egyptian stone vessels, mostly cylindrical forms, were found within the tombs (Williams 1986: 65–78, 123–37). These latter objects are rarely documented at other Nubian cemeteries. External influence on patterns of consumption and ritual display was not confined to vessels and their contents. More isolated finds indicate that the groups whose activities are represented at Cemetery L had access to new kinds of equipment for presenting the body that also appear in high-status Egyptian burials during the early Naqada III period. Notable among them are items of sheet copper, including a tanged spearhead and a hollow fitting shaped to resemble the flower of a papyrus plant (fig. 8.5; Williams 1986: 359, grave L24, pls. 64: a–b, 65: b–c). The latter object would have been one of four attached to the wooden beams of a carrying bed or litter. These items can be paralleled in graves at Minshat Abu Omar (Grave Group IIIB), far to the north in the eastern Nile delta, where they form part of a larger assemblage of copper vessels, ornaments, tools and personal weaponry.[15] Papyrus-shaped fittings in copper, some still containing decomposed wood, were found in two burials there. In one case they were positioned at opposite corners of the rectangular burial pit, framing the flexed body and its accoutrements as they would have during its passage to the grave. Wooden and reed elements from carrying beds were recovered in good states of preservation during Petrie's excavations at Tarkhan, in the northern Nile valley, and display a sophisticated mortise-and-tenon construction. In one case the legs of the bed-frame terminate in delicately carved bull's hooves, a feature paralleled on a similar piece from a Naqada IIIA2 tomb at Hierakonpolis, and on numerous items of furniture found and depicted within high-status Egyptian tombs from the First Dynasty onwards (figs. 7.5, 10.1, 10.6; Petrie *et al.* 1913: 23–4, pls. 8–9). The early Naqada III assemblage at Tarkhan also included copper tools and spearheads comparable to those from Minshat Abu Omar and Qustul (Petrie *et al.* 1913: 24, pls. 4–6). The elite character of these items is highlighted by a cache of copper objects and associated finds from a multiple burial at Sayala (Cemetery 137), which lies c.20 km south of the entrance to the Wadi el-Allaqi in Lower Nubia. In addition to copper adzes, ingots, chisels and a harpoon, the burial—which dates to the Middle to Late A-Group (Naqada

---

[14] As Williams (1986: 117) notes, shell hooks 'have been found in Egypt, at Mostagedda, actually on the burials, placed across the bridge of the nose as though worn on the forehead'.
[15] Kroeper 1988: 15, pls. 8, 9: a–c; and cf. Tadmor 2002: 247; Gophna and van den Brink 2002.

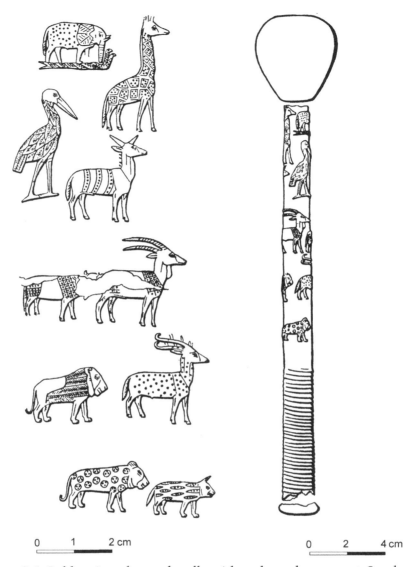

0   1   2 cm   0   2   4 cm

Figure 8.6 Gold casing of mace-handle with embossed ornament, Sayala,
Lower Nubia, Middle–Late A-Group

IID–IIIA1)—contained the sheet-gold casings of two mace-handles (stolen from
the Egyptian Museum in Cairo in 1920), one of which was decorated with an
embossed animal frieze (fig. 8.6; Firth 1927: 201–8, grave 1, pl. 18: a–c, fig. 8).

The wide distribution of these distinctive display items suggests emulation
and exchange among local elites at the beginning of the Naqada III period. The
spatial arena encompassed by such high-status interactions extended from

Lower Nubia to the Nile delta and beyond, as further demonstrated by the discovery of small quantities of Nubian pottery at Minshat Abu Omar and by the presence of Levantine liquid containers with high loop-handles at Qustul (Williams 1986: 78–80, fig. 48, pl. 25; Kroeper 1988: 15, figs. 113–14). Aside from Qustul, the known find-spots of these distinctive loop-handled jugs—so far documented only in small numbers—extend northwards to Hierakonpolis, Minshat Abu Omar, and thence to two sites on the southern coastal plain of the Levant (Gophna and van den Brink 2002). At Azor, south of Tel Aviv, vessels of this type were found in cave burials, together with a copper spear-head (fitted with rivet holes in the same manner as the Qustul spearhead) and a ripple-flaked knife of Egyptian manufacture (Ben-Tor 1975). This assemblage hardly seems fortuitous. Rather it suggests that elements of a new culture of violence and prestige may have circulated, not as isolated objects, but as meaningful groups or sets, through which coherent social routines of action and display were disseminated among elites.

8.7 The tomb as a site of elaboration in early Naqada III
Egypt and Lower Nubia

As in contemporary Egypt, the overall setting of elite funerary rites at Qustul was further extended and dramatised by the preparation of exceptionally large burial pits. Many of the most imposing tombs have a bipartite form, comprising a trench up to ten metres long that provided additional space for the placing of funerary goods, from which descended a further chamber where the body and other objects were located (Williams 1986: 14–20). Tombs of this kind, for which a parallel exists at Hierakonpolis (Locality 6; Adams 2000: 22–3, 176, fig. 2, pl. 6: a), were distributed among smaller rectangular or oval burials at Qustul. A number of these smaller burials contained remains of sacrificed cattle, which appear to have been killed in a dramatic fashion by decapitation (Williams 1986: 16).

In Egypt itself, the use of mud-brick in constructing subterranean chambers, first practised at a handful of sites in late Naqada II times, was adopted as virtually a standard feature of high-status burials during the early Naqada III period. By the beginning of the First Dynasty (Naqada IIIC1) brick-built tombs are documented at numerous cemeteries from Minshat Abu Omar in the north (fig. 8.7) to Hierakonpolis in the south, with notable concentrations in the region of Memphis (for example at Tarkhan, Tura and Abu Rawash) and at Abydos in Upper Egypt.[16] At Abydos a series of brick-lined tombs,

---

[16] Kroeper 1992 (Minshat Abu Omar); Adams 1996a; 2000 (Hierakonpolis); Petrie 1914; Petrie *et al.* 1913 (Tarkhan); Junker 1912 (Tura); Klasens 1958b; 1959 (Abu Rawash); Amélineau 1899a: 106–16; 1904: 8–21; Petrie 1902: 3–8; Kaiser and Dreyer 1982: 212–41; Dreyer 1990: 54–62; Dreyer *et al.* 1993: 24–56; 1996: 22–30 (Abydos).

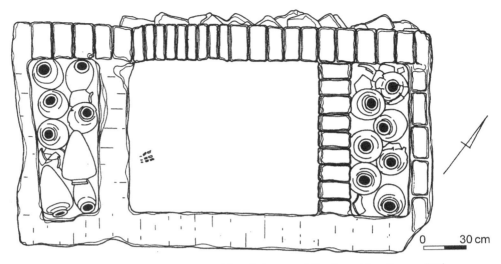

Figure 8.7 Tomb (1450) with mud-brick lining, Minshat Abu Omar, Nile delta, Naqada IIIA

some with multiple chambers, were built around the margins of an existing predynastic cemetery (Cemetery U) at the very beginning of Naqada III (fig. 9.11). Both in their mode of construction and location, they form direct precursors to the First and Second Dynasty royal tombs that extend away to the south (fig. 10.16). Within this single locale—comprising in chronological order Cemetery U, Cemetery B and the area known as Umm el-Qaab—a continuous record of burial rites now spans the entire fourth millennium, from Naqada I to the earliest monuments that commemorated kings whose power extended throughout Egypt. Owing to extensive plundering, little is known about treatments of the corpse in these early brick-lined tombs, or about the true nature and extent of their original furnishings. Some suggestion of the latter is provided by a tomb located along the Wadi Abu Suffian at Hierakonpolis (Locality 6). Dating to Naqada IIIA2, it contained traces of worked ivory, a wooden bed with legs terminating in carved bull's hooves, obsidian and crystal blades, and personal ornaments made in gold, silver, faience, turquoise, garnet, cornelian and lapis lazuli (Adams 2000: 26–7, 75–127, pls. 25–6, 34, fig. 12; cf. 1996b: 137–40). The preservation of such a range of materials is unusual, as is the detection of postholes around the perimeter of this tomb, which would imply that some form of perishable covering was erected over the rectangular burial chamber (Adams 2000, pl. 14: a). Such coverings, which may also have been present above other, less carefully excavated burials of the period, form a likely precursor to the mud-brick superstructures of First Dynasty mastaba tombs, the façades of which were ornamented to resemble prototypes in organic materials (fig. 10.9).

Lower Nubia: 'outside the bread-eating world'

At this point some important differences should be noted in the development of Egyptian and Lower Nubian societies: differences which had permutations beyond the realm of elite display. Mass-produced coarse wares, notably bread moulds and beer jars, which became increasingly dominant in Egyptian ceramic assemblages (both settlement and cemetery) from late Naqada II onwards, are notably absent from burials of the Late A-Group. This is the first indication of what would become an enduring disparity between ancient Egyptian culinary practices and those of centralised societies to the south, which lay, as David Edwards (2003) puts it, 'outside the bread-eating world'. As I have suggested, these new dietary practices underpinned new relations of dependency and an increasingly hierarchical structuring of Egypt's productive economy, notably in the sphere of agrarian labour. Similarities in scale and contents between elite burials in Lower Nubia and early Naqada III Egypt may therefore disguise an important set of regional differences in the articulation of ritual and economic power. Nubian elites, lacking access to capital-intensive modes of farming and large areas of arable land, remained dependent upon traditional sources of social power, such as imported prestige goods and mobile animal wealth. By contrast, aspiring elites in Egypt were able to convert their growing control over social networks and the flow of goods into a more pervasive domination of the land and its productive population.

8.8 The emergence of *Homo hierarchicus*

The archaeological record of the Naqada III period affords an opportunity for detailed comparison of parallel developments in the funerary and habitation spheres, which is not available for the later periods covered in this study. The emerging picture is, however, a prescient one. Archaeological evidence from the Nile delta demonstrates the broadly simultaneous establishment of new corporate foundations that prefigure the pattern of centrally governed estates familiar from dynastic sources. Their associated material culture is remarkably uniform across sites and indicates that each such unit possessed the capacity to provide for the everyday needs of its dependants. The widespread use of mud-brick and the adoption of common dietary practices at these sites further suggests that they constituted new forms of identity and new social worlds, demarcated from the surrounding landscape.

A parallel set of processes is documented in funerary practices, primarily by loss and absence. I have described the denuding of those mobile cultural landscapes that formerly enriched both the intimate space of social interaction and the ritual space of death. Grave goods for the majority of people no longer gave material expression to personal histories or individual relationships between

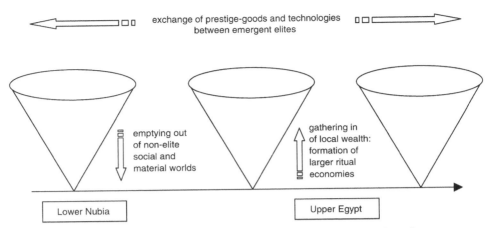

Figure 8.8 Towards state formation: model illustrating the cultural economy of power in early Naqada III Egypt and Lower Nubia as the interaction of multiple conical structures, such that the local development of hierarchies is at the same time their alliance on a supra-local level

the living and the dead, while the ability to attach further meaning to such objects through the addition of images was greatly reduced.

Linkages between these two trajectories of change may be discerned on a number of levels. In order to recruit a workforce for hierarchically organised estates, it would have been necessary to create a new class of individual, the elite perception of which is attested in private tombs of the later Old Kingdom (fig. 7.5). Labourers are depicted there as a broadly homogeneous group, whose simply clothed and unadorned bodies testify to the subordination of the in-dividual and the celebration of the collective. The burial record suggests that by early Naqada III similar values may have begun to permeate the sphere of funerary practices among the non-elite. Not only everyday needs of subsis-tence, but also the basic material constituents of important social rituals, were increasingly supplied from sources originating beyond the productive capacity of their individual participants and close kin (fig. 8.8).

At the upper end of this emerging field of power relations, elites also catered for the preservation of a traditional social order, direct access to which—other than as ancestral memory—was no longer possible for the majority of indivi-duals. Spectacular burials and associated objects, such as elaborately carved funerary furniture and golden weaponry embossed with animal images, belong to the realm of the 'circus', rather than that of the 'bread'. Moreover, the social values which they celebrated were not those of the new, domesticated world of agrarian estates, which formed the economic power base of emergent elites in Egypt. Rather the aesthetic labour they represent, including the mobilisation of exotic materials and sophisticated craft procedures, was invested in conventional sites of social reproduction: bodily performance, with its established repertoire of personal weaponry and cosmetic equipment; and the grave, which—through a process of competitive emulation—would become by degrees a technological marvel as well as an increasingly compelling magnet for the staging of ritual and acts of sacrifice. In the following chapter I explore how elite culture infused these traditional social worlds with a new set of images, centred upon the containment of violent and exotic forces, that projected hierarchy as a necessary, rather than arbitrary, feature of human existence.

EXTRAORDINARY BODIES AND BINDING TRUTHS: EARLY WRITING IN CONTEXT

What does one do with that human being who is charged with articulating the social order and the natural order? Does one place him at the centre of society or outside it? Or inside and outside at the same time?

De Heusch 1997: 219

9.1 Ceremonial objects: beyond the surface

The Brooklyn Knife (fig. 9.1) was discovered by H. de Morgan in the early years of the twentieth century in an early Naqada III burial at Abu Zaidan, in southern Upper Egypt (de Morgan 1909; Needler 1984: 46–72, 124–37). This paradoxical statement, which has more than a hint of the absurd about it, introduces a series of interrelated objects that have long presided over discussions of Egyptian state formation. All of them are small, portable, functional— or at least evoke certain traditional functions—and bear pictorial designs, often of great complexity, on their surfaces. They encompass the period between the end of Naqada II and the beginning of the First Dynasty, the transition from prehistory to 'proto-history', during which Egyptian society coalesced into a territorially bounded state under a single ruler. The Brooklyn Knife belongs to the earlier part of that time-span.[1] In the course of their life histories, many such objects—which also include stone cosmetic palettes and mace-heads, as well as bone and ivory combs—appear to have been installed within temples, where they may have remained accessible well into Old Kingdom times. In order to differentiate them from their less elaborate predynastic prototypes they are often described as 'ceremonial'. I retain that term here to signify their coherence as a cultural and chronological group.

The surface decoration of ceremonial objects has been extensively studied from perspectives drawing upon art history and linguistics, as well as more immediate Egyptological and archaeological sources.[2] In interpreting their imagery, many existing studies take later and more fully understood bodies of written and pictorial evidence as a point of departure. Ceremonial objects

---

[1] Needler 1984: 268–70; cf. Kantor 1944: 129; Ciałowicz 1992: 247.

[2] For a representative range of approaches, compare Groenewegen-Frankfort 1951: 15–27; Asselberghs 1961; Williams and Logan 1987; Millet 1990; Ciałowicz 2001: 166–207; Davis 1992; Baines 1995: 109–21; Goldwasser 1995: 4–19.

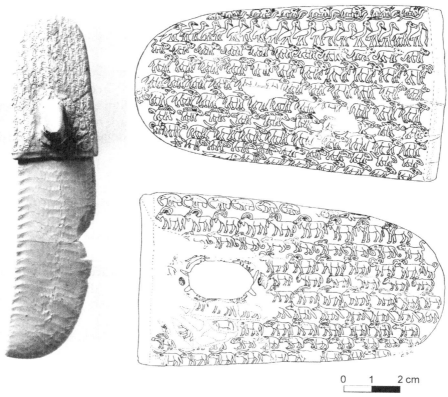

0 1 2 cm

Figure 9.1 The Brooklyn Knife, found at Abu Zaidan in Upper Egypt, Naqada III (excavations of H. de Morgan, 1907–8)

have thus been used to chart the development of religious concepts, political structures and modes of representation that constituted the building blocks of dynastic culture. Such approaches raise important but often unanswerable questions about the role of institutions (notably temples) that no doubt already existed during the Naqada III period, but for which very little direct archaeological evidence is currently available (cf. O'Connor 2002: 8–10; Baines 1997b: 219–21).[3] They are also oriented towards a strongly normative view of

[3] Widely divergent opinions can be found concerning the architectural form, scale and uniformity of early Egyptian temples. Related, and hence equally divergent, views have been formulated concerning the extent of courtly patronage exercised in their construction and functioning. Based upon fragmentary evidence from the Upper Egyptian sites of Elephantine, Medamud, Hierakonpolis, Abydos and Coptos, Kemp (1989: 65–83; 1995: 41–6) builds up a picture of diversity, reflecting a degree of local autonomy from state control that was only gradually lost during the course of the Old and Middle Kingdoms. O'Connor (1992) argues that many of the buildings discussed by Kemp were peripheral to larger, but as yet undiscovered, temples, which conformed more closely to later dynastic forms, and express extensive royal investment in, and centralised control over, centres of religious worship from early dynastic times onwards (a view reinforced by Baines 1997b: 221–6; but see Seidlmayer's reservations; 1996b: 115–19).

dynastic culture, which may disguise aspects of ceremonial objects—notably their distinctive characteristics *as objects*, rather than as carriers of imagery—which are particular to their period of manufacture and have no direct parallels from later times.

My aim here is to give a holistic account of ceremonial objects as social and technological products of emerging elites, based largely upon surviving archaeological evidence for their wider cultural milieu, including the earliest uses of writing in Egypt. Drawing upon the conclusions of earlier chapters, I consider aspects of continuity and change with earlier forms of display in greater detail than is usually attempted, providing what might be termed a prehistoric perspective on their development. Here I go beyond the interpretation of surface imagery in order to consider its articulation with the forms and functional attributes of particular artefacts.[4]

9.2 Reworking the ritual landscape: early relief carving

Like many ceremonial objects, the Brooklyn Knife has acquired an archaeological pseudonym that says more about its modern owner than about the object itself. Further examples purchased on the antiquities market that lack recorded provenance include the Pitt Rivers and Carnavon Knife-handles and the Davis Comb (fig. 9.2, bottom), all probably comparable in date.[5] Other elaborately decorated objects of this period, such as the Gebel el-Tarif and Gebel el-Araq Knife-handles (figs. 9.2, 2.4), were also purchased during the early twentieth century, but are named after their putative places of origin.[6] Still others—such as the Hunters' (fig. 9.6), Cities (fig. 9.14) and Bull Palettes—are named after the figures that appear on them.[7] The Narmer Palette alone is identified according to the hieroglyphic inscriptions it bears (figs. 2.1, 2.2), and marks the culmination, and end, of this series of objects at the beginning of the First Dynasty (c.3100 BC).

Seen against the backdrop of predynastic art, the decoration of the Brooklyn Knife-handle presents a number of strikingly novel features, the original impact of which is now difficult to appreciate. The object itself is carved from the tusk of an African elephant, an animal that also appears—standing atop

---

Reflecting on this debate, Kemp (1995: 42) observes: 'That there is scope at all for arguments over something as fundamental as what an Egyptian temple looked like prior to the New Kingdom is a sign of how limited our knowledge is of earlier periods.'

[4] I am in agreement with Davis's (1992: 14) view that ceremonial objects 'may have played a directly formative role in transforming the politico-cultural system', but seek to move beyond his treatment of them as 'stating symbolic propositions' towards a more integrated account of the interplay between decorative form and object function.

[5] Bénédite 1918; Dorman *et al*. 1987: 127; Ciałowicz 1992.

[6] Bénédite 1916; Asselberghs 1961, figs. 46–8, 55–8; Boehmer 1991.

[7] Asselberghs 1961, figs. 166–7; Spencer 1980: 79, cat. 575, pl. 63; Ciałowicz 1991: 55–6; Baines 2003: 29–34, 44–5, figs. 1, 2, 5.

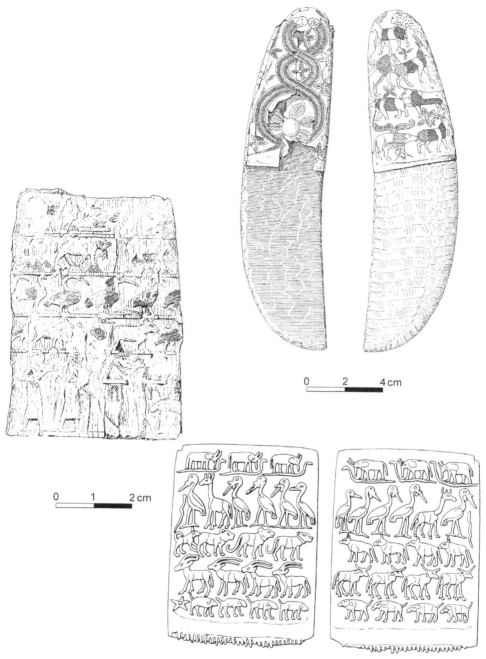

Figure 9.2 The Gebel el-Tarif Knife, carved ivory plaque from Hierakonpolis (Main Deposit) and the Davis Comb, Naqada III

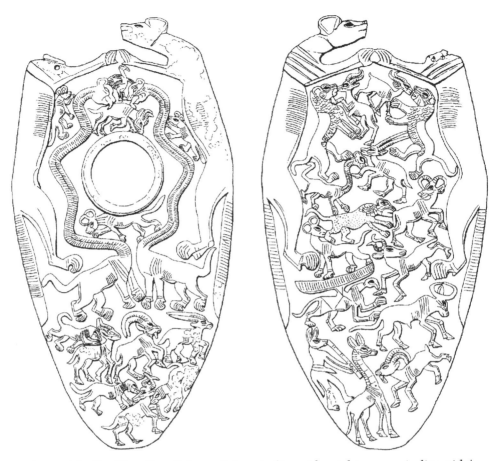

Figure 9.3 The Two Dog Palette (left: grinding side, right: non-grinding side), from the Main Deposit, Hierakonpolis, Naqada III

intertwined snakes—among the many figures that ornament its surface. All are carved in raised relief, a technique hardly attested in Egypt prior to the late Naqada II period, that was uniformly adopted for the decoration of ceremonial objects. Neither extending from their edges, nor adhering fully to their surfaces, figures of living beings appear instead to rise outlandishly from their very fabric. Relief carving is used to particular effect on the Two Dog Palette, which derives its name from the symmetrically opposed animals that frame its outer margins (fig. 9.3).[8] They are rendered in markedly higher relief than the figures they enclose, drawing the eye of the viewer in towards the centre of the palette. On one side this central area is occupied by the circular depression

---

[8] Asselberghs 1961, figs. 70–1; Ciałowicz 1991: 43–6; Baines 1993.

where cosmetic paste was contained. On the other we are plunged into the heart of a carefully orchestrated bedlam, in which various creatures play out a drama of confrontation to the tune of a pipe, played by a hybrid figure with a human body and the head and tail of an animal. As in earlier times this profusion of life appears to parade freely across the surface of the object, but the animals' movement is given new vitality by the depiction of joints, tendons, muscles and hooves, and by the play of light and shadow over their carved bodies.

Perhaps the most striking feature of the Brooklyn Knife-handle's decoration is the sheer diversity of animal species depicted there. Of those which can be identified (Churcher 1984), several—such as elephants, serpents, storks, lions, badgers, wild asses and cattle—are either rare or unknown in predynastic animal art. Others—including wild sheep, dogs, oryx and ibex—do find parallels on earlier painted pottery and related objects. The concentration of this range of subject matter within such a small space (the handle is 9.5 cm long and 5.6 cm wide), and the repetitious arrangement of animals according to type, suggest a systematic appropriation and reclassification of the moving landscape. The situation is not so simple, however. Around the margins of the rows of animals appear a number of anomalous images—including a catfish, a star, a dog with a curled tail, a heron and a serpent—and on close inspection the row of storks is interrupted by an intrusive giraffe, a detail found also on the Davis Comb (fig. 9.2; cf. Davis 1992: 48–55; Kemp 2000: 234). Furthermore, when we look to other objects such as the Two Dog Palette, we are confronted with living creatures that are pure products of the imagination. Among those on its non-cosmetic side are a winged griffin and a monster with the body and head of a lion that are separated by an elongated serpentine neck. Two more of these monsters surround and protect the cosmetic area from invading animals, which include a felled oryx, a bird, and three dogs of the same type that frame the outer margins of the palette. Hence there is continuity between the chaotic and orderly elements of the scene, suggesting a world of forces in turmoil, which threatens to break loose from the object that confines it. The cosmetic depression, after all, is the vulnerable point where representation meets reality, and where substances pass from the domain of images—which transform them—to the domain of the body, which is transformed by them.

As in earlier (and later) times, surface images could also 'emerge' into fully three-dimensional forms. An example is the ivory spoon from a grave at Ballas, now in the Ashmolean Museum, the handle of which extends into the carefully sculpted figures of a lion pursuing a dog (fig. 9.4). Their patterned bodies leave little doubt that they are solid renderings of the incised animal pairs on objects such as the Gebel el-Tarif handle (fig. 9.2). As Helen Whitehouse (2002: 428–9, 432–6, figs. 1, 6) has demonstrated, entire scenes of relief carving may have been recreated in small three-dimensional sculpture. The example she provides is that of bound captives and guards, which appear both as relief

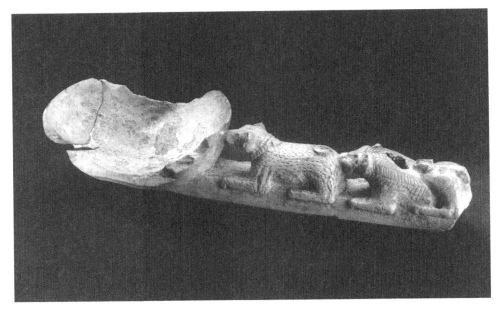

Figure 9.4 Ivory spoon with animal ornament, Ballas, Naqada III

carvings on a knife-handle of hippopotamus ivory and as small ivory sculptures (probably elements from pieces of furniture), all found within the same deposit at Hierakonpolis (fig. 9.5). Hence the fluid interplay between painted imagery and clay modelling, which are widely disseminated arts of addition, appears to have been replaced during Naqada III by that between relief carving and sculpture-in-the-round, which are restricted arts of subtraction. And for the first time, the capacity of pictorial signs for transformation was also expanded to take in elements of language. This latter development marks the invention of the hieroglyphic script, which Alan Gardiner (1957: 5) described, in a phrase redolent more of its earliest stages than of its later development, as 'a picture-writing eked out by phonetic elements'.

9.3 The 'Main Deposit' at Hierakonpolis

Many of the objects discussed so far, including the Two Dog and Narmer Palettes, derive from the so-called 'Main Deposit', a vast assemblage of objects discovered beneath the foundations of the Middle Kingdom temple of Horus at Hierakonpolis.[9] The deposit is one of two such concentrations excavated at the turn of the twentieth century, the other having been located beneath the Osiris Temple at Abydos.[10] Both contained large numbers of skilfully ornamented

[9] Quibell 1900; Quibell and Green 1902; Adams 1974a; 1974b; see also Whitehouse 1987; Dreyer 1986: 37–46.
[10] Petrie 1903: 23–9, pls. 2–10; see also Kemp 1968b; Dreyer 1986: 47–54.

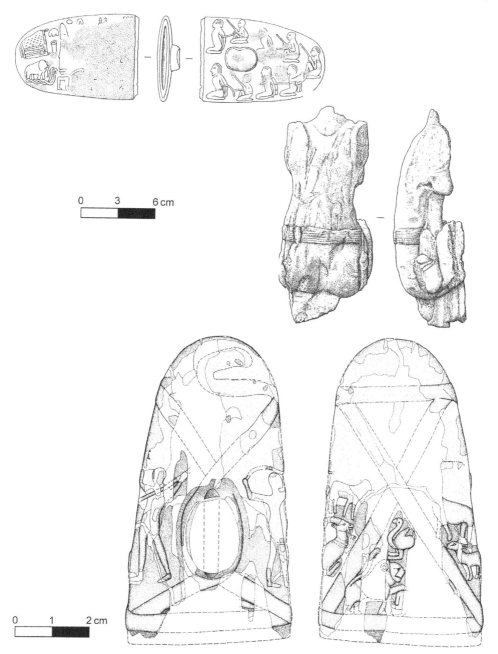

0   3   6 cm

0   1   2 cm

Figure 9.5 Ivory knife-handle and figurine of a bound captive from the Main Deposit, Hierakonpolis, late Naqada II–Naqada III; ivory knife-handle with relief carving from Abydos, Naqada IID

ivories, including decorated knife- and mace-handles, components of furniture and a wide range of anthropomorphic figures, as well as many miniature models of wild animals, humans and vessels in faience and other materials. On grounds of style and decorative content, as well as occasional inscriptions, the majority appear to have been produced between Naqada IID and the end of the First Dynasty (c.3300–2800 BC). Both earlier and later objects were also present, including a damaged limestone statue of Khasekhem, the last king of the Second Dynasty, enthroned and wearing ceremonial costume associated with the *sed*-festival (Quibell 1900, pls. 3–41; Smith 1998: 23–4). There has been much speculation as to when these objects were assembled and committed to the ground, and as to the reasons why this was done. The ambiguous nature of early site reports from Hierakonpolis and Abydos has only served to fuel controversy. The terms of the debate have since been altered by discoveries of comparable deposits beneath temples at Tell Ibrahim Awad, in the eastern Nile delta (van Haarlem 1995; 1996; 1998; 2001; 2002), and at Elephantine on Egypt's southern border (Dreyer 1986). In both cases the episode of deposition can be placed with some certainty towards the end of the Old Kingdom.

Petrie originally suggested that the Abydos deposit was composed of accumulated furnishings and other offerings to the Osiris Temple that had become damaged or redundant. This view has since been favoured by Barry Kemp (1968b: 153–5), among others. With reference to Hierakonpolis, Barbara Adams (cited in Whitehouse 2002: 426) considered whether the objects may have been deliberately assembled for use in a foundation ceremony that established the cultic significance of the site. Whitehouse (2002: 432) notes that many of the ivories in that deposit 'had been systematically deconstructed before deposition, either because there was some purposeful sorting of material beforehand, or because—in the case of weapons and symbols of power—they were being "decommissioned" and rendered actually and symbolically powerless'. The presence of many stone mace-heads within the Main Deposit seems particularly suggestive of some such process. They include the well-known ceremonial mace-heads of kings Narmer and Scorpion, discussed below, as well as many tens of undecorated examples (Adams 1974a: 5–13, pls. 5–6). A large assemblage of plain mace-heads was also found within the temple deposit at Tell Ibrahim Awad (van Haarlem 1995: 45; 1998: 12). We may then be faced with a countrywide phenomenon of some significance: an official break with the early dynastic past that took place around the Fifth Dynasty.

New discoveries

Since the 1990s a number of objects with relief carving have come to light through excavations, notably in Cemetery U at Abydos, and through conservation work on finds from the Main Deposit (Whitehouse 1987; 1992; 2002). The knife-handle decorated with guards and captives and the associated figurines discussed above (fig. 9.5) are among them. A ceremonial cosmetic palette has also come to light from a burial at Minshat Ezzat in the Nile delta (el-Baghdadi 1999). It had been placed within the burial chamber of a large, three-roomed tomb dating to the early First Dynasty (Naqada IIIC1). Both its decoration and poor condition suggest an earlier date of manufacture, implying that, like the material in later temple deposits, this object had a long history of use, exceeding the lifespan of any one individual.

The discoveries at Abydos comprise fragments from a number of ivory knife-handles.[11] One of the most fully reconstructed examples derives from the fill of a large Naqada IID grave (U-503), which contained some fifty ceramic vessels and is located close to the site of the earliest brick-lined burials in Cemetery U (fig. 9.5, lower; Dreyer *et al.* 1998: 98–100, fig. 7, pl. 5: a, b). The scene on the handle, insofar as it can be made out, is one of hunting, in which two human figures with ropes enclose an assortment of wild animals. The theme of binding is made central to the whole composition by a raised band—perhaps the body of a snake—that encircles both sides of the handle and wraps itself around the central boss (cf. Whitehouse 2002: 437). The rear part of a lion passes right over this raised outer band. This detail forges a link with the Two Dog Palette, and it is possible to see these scenes as evoking a liminal world of dangerous forces that are only partially controlled (cf. Baines 1993: 62–4; 1995: 114–15). Similar tensions are present in the decoration of an unprovenanced object known as the Hunters' Palette, purchased during the early twentieth century (fig. 9.6). Human figures brandishing various weapons partially encircle a prey of wild animals, some of which they bind with rope, but in the upper part of the scene one of the hunters is himself transformed into prey by a wounded lion that mauls him.

In the search for consistent meanings encapsulated within these scenes we should not lose sight of the diversity of the objects on which they appear, nor of their complex relationships to those objects and associated forms of practice, even if the latter are understood only in the most general terms. The outer layer of binding depicted on the Abydos knife-handle makes explicit what is only implied in other cases: a tension between image and object—a relation of containment that is not entirely secure. Knives penetrate the skin and may kill, while cosmetics decorate its surface. Combs give form to another vulnerable margin of the body, while maces extend the violent force of the arm in motion. In combination they formed a system of action which was familiar to their users and had an extensive prehistory reaching back to Neolithic times. By Naqada III these forms of action had become a restricted social currency. Ceremonial objects may therefore be understood as prestigious symbols of an

---

[11] An inventory of carved ivory knife-handles with and without provenance is provided by White-house 2002: 444–5, tables 1 and 2; and see Dreyer 1999.

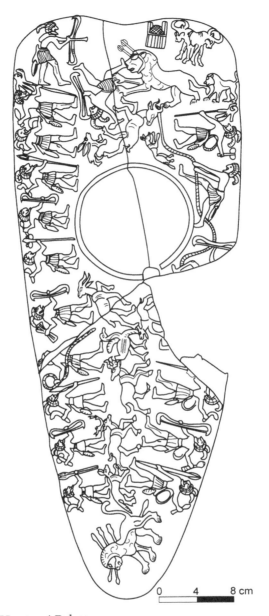

Figure 9.6 The Hunters' Palette

older mode of existence, imbued with the legitimising force of custom and ancestral memory. Emergent elites appropriated and transformed this archive of social knowledge, grafting their own ideological concerns—which empha-sise masculine activity in relation to non-human beings, omitting any direct visual reference to female creativity—on to time-honoured ways of living and dying. What we appear, then, to be witnessing is an invasion of the extraordinary into a particular space of social memory: the embodied memory of once widespread and habitual forms of interaction, now elevated to a restricted domain of ceremonial performance.

9.4 Cylinder seals: Egypt's reception of a Mesopotamian technique

On the positive side it is a matter of assessing the impact of certain Mesopotamian ideas . . . of Mesopotamian techniques . . . and of Mesopotamian images or visual formulae, whose precise original meanings may have been as obscure to the Predynastic Egyptians as they are to the modern commentator, but which clearly filled some gap in their own imagery at the time of initial transmission.

Moorey 1987: 44

As Roger Moorey (1987: 37) pointed out, engraved seals are 'the earliest objects of distinctively Mesopotamian type to appear in predynastic Egypt'. The oldest known examples, of which approximately twenty are documented, date to the middle and late Naqada II period, not long after the invention of the cylinder seal in Mesopotamia. They comprise mainly limestone cylinders engraved with combinations of fish motifs and various linear designs. Those with known archaeological provenance derive exclusively from burials in the Nile valley (Boehmer 1974a: 497–8, nos. 1–6). At Naga el-Deir, Naqada and Ballas they appear to have been integrated with local types of personal ornament (Podzorski 1988), and no doubt were valued in the manner of other exotic objects, such as lapis or obsidian beads, displayed on the person—that is, as bodily signs of extension in the social and material worlds.

The origins of sealing practices are to be found in northern Mesopotamian villages of the seventh millennium BC, the Late Neolithic period of that region (chapter 1.4). The earliest seals were not cylinders but stamps: flat stone objects, usually perforated for suspension, which bore incised designs on one of their surfaces. The designs were impressed on to a band of soft clay that covered the opening of a vessel or portal. Their efficacy in controlling access to goods was not simply physical, but also social and psychological. Petr Charvát (1994) has suggested (*à la* Mauss; 2002 [1925]) that this force initially derived from their parallel function as personal ornaments, projecting some part of the donor's social being on to inanimate things. Once broken and removed from their containers, clay sealings could be retained as records of transactions. Evidence from Tell Sabi Abyad in northern Syria suggests that, from the beginning, this was an important aspect of their use in Mesopotamia (Akkermans 1996; Akkermans and Duistermaat 1996). New possibilities of control were thereby generated over a vital social commodity: the memory of relationships formed through the exchange of goods. At such early fourth-millennium sites as Arslantepe and Tepe Gawra (chapter 1.8), extensive archives of this kind were formed through the physical ordering of sealings within particular buildings (Frangipane 1994).

During the mid-fourth millennium a new administrative technique was introduced in Mesopotamia, involving the enclosure of small tokens of exchange within hollow clay spheres known as bullae (singular, bulla). The outer surfaces of these clay envelopes bear the imprint of cylinder seals—another innovation of this period—and of tokens.[12] The linked use of bullae, cylinder seals and tokens was quite rapidly followed by the appearance of flat clay tablets bearing numerical signs and similarly overlain with seal impressions (Schmandt-Besserat 1992: 108–54; Nissen *et al.* 1993: 12–14). Numerical tablets and cylinder seals are attested throughout much of Mesopotamia during the late fourth millennium, including sites on the Middle and Upper Euphrates that had both close connections to the southern alluvium and access to the Levantine coastal region. By contrast, proto-cuneiform writing is documented largely from the vast urban site of Uruk, in southern Iraq. This limited distribution may owe much to factors of preservation and comparatively limited exploration of other early urban sites, but it also serves to highlight the relationship between the development of writing in Mesopotamia and the scale of the administrative functions that it was designed to perform (cf. Nissen *et al.* 1993: ix, 4–7, 19–24).

Prior to recent discoveries in Cemetery U at Abydos it was widely thought that the notational (as opposed to ornamental) properties of seals had not been exploited in Egypt before Naqada III. Impressions from locally made cylinder seals found within large Naqada IID burials now demonstrate otherwise (fig. 9.7: a, b; Hartung 1998). The sealings cover the surfaces of roughly shaped balls of clay that are perforated through the centre for attachment to goods and should not be confused with the hollow bullae found at contemporaneous sites in Mesopotamia. By Naqada III this method of attachment appears to have been largely abandoned in favour of the more economical technique of impressing cylinder seals directly on to clay stoppers applied over the rims of vessels (Williams 1977: 135).

Sealings, ceremonial objects and early writing

At Cemetery U, and no doubt at other sites, the capacity of seals to distribute signs in a novel way appears to have been quickly adapted to the marking of funerary goods, just as foreign motifs were either replaced or incorporated into a new repertoire of engraved signs. These signs were also rapidly extended on

---

[12] As Frankfort (1939: 3) observed, the 'form of the cylinder seal is adequately explained by the function which it was meant to fulfil, namely to impress a distinctive mark on a soft material of varying extent, the clay with which packages and store-jars were secured, and which, subsequently, became the vehicle of writing [in Mesopotamia]'.

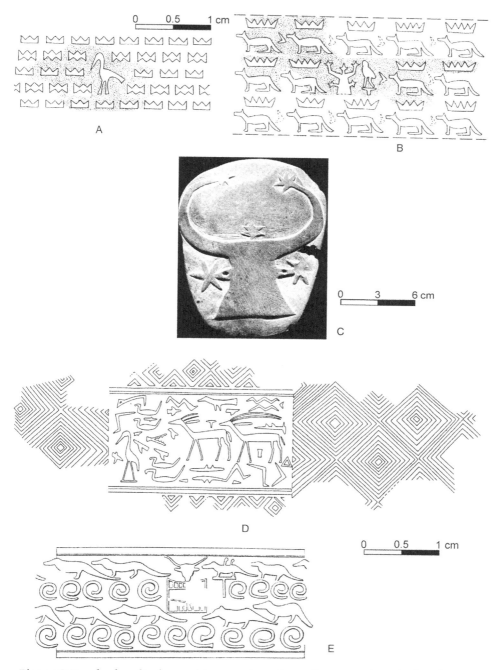

Figure 9.7 a, b, d: cylinder-seal impressions from Cemetery U, Abydos, late Naqada II–early Naqada III; c: stone palette with relief carving, el-Gerza; e: seal impression from Tarkhan, early Naqada III

to other media of personal display—knife-handles, cosmetic palettes and other ceremonial objects—in the form of relief carvings, reproducing on a larger scale the visual effect created by a cylinder seal on a piece of damp clay. One such palette, found in a late Naqada II burial at el-Gerza, bears a distinctive sign that has sometimes been thought to depict cattle horns, evoking the goddess Hathor or Bat (Petrie *et al.* 1912: 22, pl. 6: 7; Asselberghs 1961, fig. 118).[13] This motif reappears on a cylinder-seal impression found far to the south in burial U-210 at Abydos, adjacent to the image of a long-legged bird on some form of plinth (fig. 9.7: b, c). Alternating rows of recumbent canids and groups of triangles enclose this pair of images; groups of triangles are used in a similar fashion to frame the isolated image of a stork on another seal impression from the same burial (fig. 9.7: a; Hartung 1998: 200–2, fig. 8, nos. 22–3). Both the stork and the Hathor/Bat symbol recur as relief carvings on the rim of an enormous, black and white porphyry bowl from Hierakonpolis (Main Deposit), which has a superbly carved, fluted exterior (Adams 1974a: 50, no. 272, pl. 37).

Numerous other sealings were recovered from Naqada IID–IIIA burials at Cemetery U. They bear images of caprids, felids and boats, while a sign that closely resembles the later standard of the goddess Neith appears on a sealing from tomb U-j (Hartung 1998; Dreyer 1998: 109–10, fig. 72: e, type V). These designs, which have a bearing both on the development of ceremonial objects and on the origins of the Egyptian writing system (cf. Morenz 2004: 58–68), differentiate internally and systematically between two kinds of sign. The first—best described, in functional terms, as a motif—is used repeatedly to form an ornamental border around signs of the second kind, which are rendered individually or in pairs and seem to be intended to convey meaning in a distinct way. On a slightly later seal impression from a tomb at Tarkhan (fig. 9.7: e), the signs enclosed by ornamental motifs include one—damaged, perhaps deliberately, beyond recognition—that can be identified as writing a royal name due to its further enclosure within the rectangular motif known as a *serekh* (Petrie *et al.* 1913, pl. 2: 4; Dreyer 1992).[14] Whatever the precise nature of the *serekh*, further discussed below, the special status accorded to individual signs and sign-pairs on early seals appears to be given by context rather than content, being contingent upon their structural location within the design as a whole; the same signs may elsewhere serve as ornamental motifs.

[13] The identification of divine symbols among early Naqada III (or still earlier) imagery is a selective and speculative enterprise. In this particular instance the resemblance to later symbols of Hathor and Bat is not especially close. A more persuasive case can be made for another palette, found at el-Amra, which is similarly carved with a single, large emblem of a very distinct type, later associated with the ithyphallic god Min (Petrie 1953: 10, pl. A: 1; Asselberghs 1961, fig. 117). This emblem recurs in other contexts during Naqada III, some of which may be convincingly related to cultic activities, notably the Coptos Colossi.

[14] On the basis of this sealing Dreyer (1992) proposes the existence of a Dynasty 0 'counter-ruler' named 'Horus Crocodile'. Other interpretations remain possible. Tomb 414, in which it was found, dates to the time of Narmer, whose sealings were also present in considerable numbers; Petrie *et al.* 1913: 9, pl. 2: 1–3.

Given this, the best answer to the question 'is this particular sign evidence of early writing' may therefore be 'sometimes'.

9.5 Of knots and monsters: cognition and cultural borrowings on ceremonial objects

The appearance of Mesopotamian and Iranian motifs on many of the objects discussed in this chapter has been a topic of intense study since the early twentieth century.[15] The list of camouflaged borrowings is a long one. Much of it, purely zoomorphic images aside, may be summarised under the headings of 'knots' and 'monsters'. Lions with serpentine necks, winged griffins, snakes intertwined around rosettes, kneeling captives bound with rope, wild animals frozen in the moment of attack or maybe copulation, the 'master of animals' and perhaps also the *serekh* motif: all have close parallels on objects found far to the east of Egypt. The great majority are either cylinder seals or sealings from urban centres in south-west Iran and Mesopotamia, notably Susa and Uruk (fig. 9.8; Brandes 1979; Amiet 1972). In the absence of more direct evidence, it must be assumed that, towards the end of the fourth millennium, small numbers of such objects became entangled within larger exchange networks extending between South-West Asia and the Mediterranean coast, and that the images carried on them were absorbed into a creative process then underway among local elites within Egypt (chapters 1.9, 7.3). Ceremonial objects are, then, true exemplars of the process that Lévi-Strauss called *bricolage*: the building up of new cultural worlds from the scattered residues of earlier symbolic landscapes.[16]

In some well-known cases, such as the 'master of animals' design on the Gebel el-Araq Knife-handle (fig. 2.4), the decorative content of a foreign seal appears to have been transposed directly on to a locally crafted, Egyptian object. Such direct appropriations are no longer in evidence after the time of the Narmer Palette, and the long-term impact of Mesopotamian imagery upon the development of dynastic representation is generally considered to have been minimal.[17] Recent work in the field of cognitive studies suggests, however, that the relationship between what is retained and what is rejected in

---

[15] e.g. Frankfort 1924: 118–42; 1951: 100–11; Kantor 1942; 1944; 1992; Boehmer 1974b; Moorey 1987; Teissier 1987; H. S. Smith 1992; Pittman 1996. Unlike their anglophone counterparts, German scholars have long referred to this episode as the 'orientalising' of Egypt, a term more widely applied to the appearance of 'Eastern' (including Egyptian and Levantine) imagery and objects in the Aegean in the first half of the first millennium BC. The application of the term at this earlier date nicely exemplifies Whitley's (2001: 106) observation that there 'never was a stable or homogeneous "Oriental" culture, nor was there ever, except in Romantic retrospect, a stable Greek one'.

[16] Lévi-Strauss 1966: 21, citing Boas: 'it would seem that mythological worlds have been built up, only to be shattered again, and that new worlds were built from the fragments'.

[17] For an alternative view, see Pittman 1996.

Figure 9.8 Cylinder-seal impressions from Uruk, S. Iraq, late fourth millennium BC

such transfers should not be reduced to individual types of image (e.g. Sperber 1996). Monsters, for instance, fall into a recognised category of signs that violate normal cognitive expectations of what can be seen in the world, and as Holly Pittman (1996: 19–22) points out they are rare in the art of the Naqada I and II periods, which draws mainly upon 'phenomena that exist'. Pascal Boyer (1994; 1996) has discussed how such signs form a kind of 'intuitive ontology' for religious concepts, providing a particularly robust medium for their transmission across cultures.

At a slightly more impressionistic level, Susanne Küchler has explored how images of binding—which also travelled from Mesopotamia to Egypt—have a particular propensity to convey 'the fluid mechanics of persons and things' (2001: 64). Rooted in their everyday functions of linkage and containment, knots may be central to the development of complex designs, sinking into the background of a scene while at the same time constituting its elementary structure. They are constitutive of knowledge—knowledge of the forces which bind together things that may otherwise stay or drift apart. By implying its own reversal, the form of the knot also encapsulates a set of wider paradoxes at the heart of sacred power:

> formed and dissolved in the processes of tying and untying, knotted effigies recall the spatio-temporal conception of a body politic which mediates the contradictory nature of gods whose powers need to be arrested while being kept at a safe distance. Activated by binding, ancestral power appears in continuous motion—being conceived as a flow that is activated through periodic arrest and release from the space where the knot resides. (Küchler 2001: 73)

This is not the place to evaluate the long-term impact of such visual concepts upon Egyptian conventions of display, but some brief observations and qualifications are in order.

Composite images, fusing human and animal attributes, have long been central to the study and wider perception of ancient Egyptian religious practice. As Erik Hornung (1982: 109–19) observes, such images never 'superseded the representation of gods in purely human or purely animal form'. He further points out, following Henri Frankfort (1948b: 12), that many of the images in question should probably not be understood as depictions of beings that were imagined to exist, but rather as '"ideograms" or as pictorial signs that convey meaning in a metalanguage' (Hornung 1982: 117). Both reserve the term 'monster' for creatures associated with the margins of the ordered world and with transitional moments in the human lifecycle, such as Bes and Taweret (both associated with birth), the latter being made up of 'the head of a hippopotamus, the back and tail of a crocodile, the breasts of a woman, and the claws of a lion' (Frankfort 1948b: 12; cf. Hornung 1982: 118). Neither scholar, however, has proposed any absolute distinction between gods and monsters.

Many studies touch upon the significance of knots and bindings in ancient Egyptian religion and representation. They play a significant role in the carved decoration of ceremonial objects during the Naqada III period, as discussed earlier in this chapter and further below. In later times, both written and pictorial signs comprising images of binding were used to express pivotal relationships between kingship, the gods, the dead and the living elite. Many depict cult objects—which have rarely survived in the archaeological record—such as a sculpted stone dish of the First Dynasty (Fischer 1972), which takes

Figure 9.9 Silstone vessel forming the hieroglyphs 'ankh' and 'ka', probably First Dynasty

the form of a pair of arms (the hieroglyphic sign for *ka*)[18] grasping the *ankh* sign for 'life' in the shape of a knotted ribbon, the lower part of which acts as a spout (fig. 9.9). The flow of water from the dish would thus serve to release values of life bound up in the knotted *ankh*, transmitting them to a recipient, possibly via his mortuary images. *Ntr*, the word for 'god', is written with a sign which, in its most detailed rendering, depicts 'a pole wrapped round with a band of cloth, bound by a cord, the end projecting as a flap or streamer' (Hornung 1982: 35; cf. Baines 1991).[19] In titles which present the ruler in his conventional aspects as 'King of Upper and Lower Egypt' and 'Son of Re', the royal names are encircled by a cartouche, usually rendered in its abbreviated form as an oval or circular line with a flat base. This derives from a fuller depiction of 'a loop

---

[18] A complex term referring, among other things, to an aspect of the person that received nourishment after death via his statue forms (Bolshakov 1997).

[19] Hornung (1982: 37) goes on to note that strips of cloth 'are scarcely ever absent from the common depictions of wooden carrying poles with sacred objects that are charged with power ("standards"), which are found as early as predynastic times'. Other divine emblems that exhibit knots and binding include the *djed* pillar, associated with the cult of Osiris, and the related Isis-knot (Westendorf 1980: 203–4, with references). See, more generally, Staehelin (1980), and various entries for 'rope, fibre, baskets, bags etc.' in Gardiner's sign-list (1957: 521–7).

formed by a double thickness of rope, the ends tied together so as to offer to the spectator the appearance of a straight line' (Gardiner 1957: 74; Barta 1972).

These diverse uses of knots and bindings are consistent with the broader logic of Egyptian religious imagery, which sought to convey and protect royal and divine presence without implying its containment by any particular form (Hornung 1982: 117). A further characteristic of binding, which seems more central to its role in the objectification of hierarchy, is a dual capacity to express harmony (through linkage) and domination (through containment). Like the giving of gifts (Mauss 2002 [1925]), binding is at one and the same time an act of extension and restriction. In Egyptian royal iconography, this tension is exploited in the interplay of two motifs expressing central cosmological functions of kingship: the foreign captive bound with cord or grasped by a lock of hair (e.g. figs. 2.1, 9.5), and the knotted papyrus and reed plants (*zema-tawy*) which signify the union of the Two Lands of Upper and Lower Egypt (e.g. fig. 10.7: b). These motifs came into use during the First and Second Dynasties, when they are attested mainly on small ceremonial or cultic objects, and retained their importance throughout the dynastic period and into Graeco-Roman times, featuring among monumental relief carvings on temple exteriors. In some instances they are fully combined, the knotted plants extending to bind the arms of kneeling foes (Baines 1985: 226–76).

In following this detour into later dynastic imagery, my aim is not to imply an external source—Mesopotamian or otherwise—for these motifs. It is rather to suggest that the interplay of historically contingent and universal factors in the absorption of new knowledge and forms of representation may be more complex to unravel than hitherto supposed.

9.6 A mute *Ozymandias*?

The site of Coptos in Upper Egypt lies at the juncture of the Nile valley and the shortest passable route to the Red Sea coast across the Eastern Desert. It was there that Petrie, in the course of excavating a later temple site, discovered a series of damaged monumental statues in the winter of 1893–4. In his own words, the manner in which they were found shows nothing of their date 'except that they are earlier than the Ptolemaic times, as they lay beneath the thick sand bed of the Ptolemaic temple'.[20] The finds included three anthropomorphic statues and the sculpted figures of three lions and a bird rendered on a similarly gigantic scale (Petrie 1896: 7–9, pls. 3–4, 5: 4–6).[21] All appear to have been fashioned out of limestone blocks available from outcrops

---

[20] Petrie 1896: 7; see also Kemp 1989: 219–21; Adams 1997.
[21] Kemp and Boyce have produced the most complete study of these figures and their archaeological contexts to date (Kemp 2000). For further detail on the statue fragments in the Ashmolean Museum, see Payne 1993: 12–14, cat. 1–5, pls. 1–4. Adams and Jaeschke (1984) provided a thorough analysis of the Coptos lion statues, and assembled comparative material.

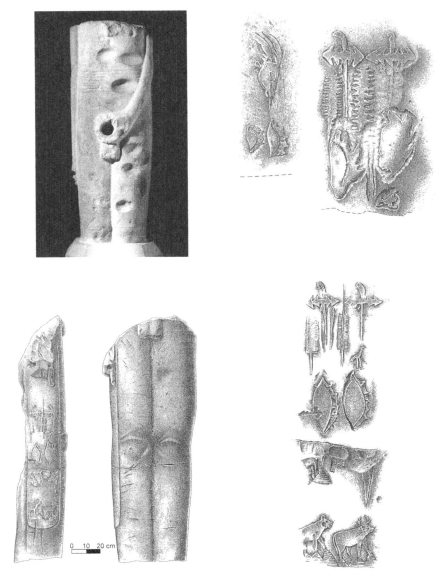

Figure 9.10 Colossal stone statues from Coptos, c.3300 BC, and detail of relief carving

in the escarpment bordering the Nile valley between Esna and Abydos. The surviving parts of the three anthropomorphic statues, known collectively as the Coptos Colossi, measure between 168 and 193 cm in height, and are today distributed between the Cairo Museum and the Ashmolean Museum in Oxford (fig. 9.10). The original statues would have stood to a height of around 4 m.

Their date of manufacture can be located with some confidence at the start of the Naqada III period.[22]

The Coptos Colossi are appropriately enigmatic symbols of an archaeological period in Egypt, the existence of which was still disputed into the 1980s (see Williams 1988a: 1–7). Their lower extremes, and the manner in which they were arranged, are largely a matter of conjecture, and a badly worn monumental head with a beard—also recovered by Petrie—offers the only direct indication of how their upper parts may have looked.[23] By contrast with later Egyptian sculpture, which took the squared block as its point of departure and orientation, the figures of the colossi are formed around roughly cylindrical cores. Aside from the detail of the incised lozenges that accentuate the knees, little in their shape or decoration anticipates later representations of the human form such as those on the Narmer Palette. The surviving torsos are naked except for a belt bound repeatedly around the waist, passing just above the buttocks. One arm is wrapped around the front of each statue, terminating in a hand that forms the opening of a socket into which a large stone penis would have been inserted. Such an object, made of a different material to the statues themselves, was discovered by Petrie nearby (Payne 1993: 13, cat. 4, pl. 5; cf. Kemp 2000: 212–13). The other arm follows the side of the body, overlying the continuation of the belt, which cascades into a raised sash passing down the thigh and lower leg. The hand resting upon the sash is perforated to hold an object that would have extended perpendicular to the body. By analogy with later images of the ithyphallic Min, the principal god of Coptos in dynastic times, this object may have been a flail.

On two of the statues the standard of Min features among a series of signs carved in low relief on to the surface of the sash. Only in one case, that of the Cairo statue, is the bottom of the sash visible, confirming that the signs did not continue beyond it and are to be considered part of the garment rather than of the body around which the garment is wrapped (fig. 9.10, lower). Barry Kemp (2000: 233) raises the possibility that they render into stone the painted signs on a length of textile, which would have constituted a 'prestige item like the combs, knife- and ceremonial mace-handles and even a ceremonial sickle on which a great many of the animal carvings appear'. Whether or not this was the case, their representation as both attached to and separate from the bodies of

---

[22] Dreyer 1995; cf. Williams 1988b: 36–7; Kemp 2000: 223–6.
[23] For a possible reconstruction of the statues' original appearance and setting, see Kemp 2000: 225. An anthropomorphic statue of similar scale and appearance to the Coptos Colossi, but clothed in a cloak that extends down to the knees and with the left arm passing over the upper body, was found in a secondary context at Hierakonpolis at the beginning of the twentieth century, and is now in the Ashmolean Museum (Quibell and Green 1902, pl. 57; Phillips 1995: 70). It was made in a similar limestone to the Coptos statues and must therefore have been transported some distance, presumably by river, because Hierakonpolis lies well south of the source area for this material (Kemp 2000: 236; Harrell 2000: 237).

the statues seems significant, alluding to the possibility of their having been distributed more widely.

The original meanings of these signs are far from clear. Some appear in pairs, including Min standards, Red Sea shells, an image variously identified as a swordfish spine or branched pole, and figures of a bull and what may be a lion standing atop rows of triangles. Single images distributed across the statues include a stork and a recumbent quadruped, perhaps a dog or lion, and the delicately formed head of an oryx from the mouth of which projects an elongated tongue or standard pole. The most extensively discussed sign to date is also among the most poorly preserved. Does it, as Bruce Williams (1988b: 37, 45) has suggested, represent part of a catfish above the image of a chisel, writing the hieroglyphic name of Narmer in the same manner as on his famous cosmetic palette? This might then imply, as Günter Dreyer (1998: 140–1, 173–80) has argued, that the other signs comprise a list of names belonging to otherwise forgotten kings, whose rule preceded the First Dynasty. Alternatively, as Kemp proposes, the surviving part of the sign may have extended into the figure of a bird perched above a triangle. This might also write a royal name or, alternatively, as he suggests, these signs may be better interpreted as 'emblems of spiritual forces which could also act as signifiers of groups of people' (Kemp 2000: 223–6, 236, fig. 10). Were they all executed at the same time, or—as Williams (1988b: 43) prefers—are we looking at a dynamic surface where signs were superimposed, one upon the other, to form a sequence of layers? The manner in which we approach these questions, and the wider implications of the answers we provide, were transformed by the discovery in 1989 of a tomb at Abydos, which also constitutes the main evidence for dating the colossi to the beginning of the Naqada III period.

9.7 Tomb U-j at Abydos and the origins of writing

Of the subterranean, brick-lined tombs established around the margins of Cemetery U during the early Naqada III period, tomb U-j (fig. 9.11) is by far the largest and most complex (Dreyer et al. 1993: 33–5; Dreyer 1998). Prior to its discovery the tomb had been extensively disturbed, and human remains were not preserved. Based upon radiocarbon determinations from some of the remaining objects found within its twelve chambers it has been securely dated to Naqada IIIA1 (c.3300 BC; Boehmer et al. 1993; Görsdorf et al. 1998). The chambers were linked by a series of narrow portals (c.1 m high and 20 cm wide), provided with sockets for the insertion of a crossing rail from which reed dividing mats would have been suspended. Dreyer, the excavator of the tomb, therefore suggests that it was laid out in imitation of an actual building, conceivably a palace (1998: 4–7). No such structures, however, are preserved from the period in question.

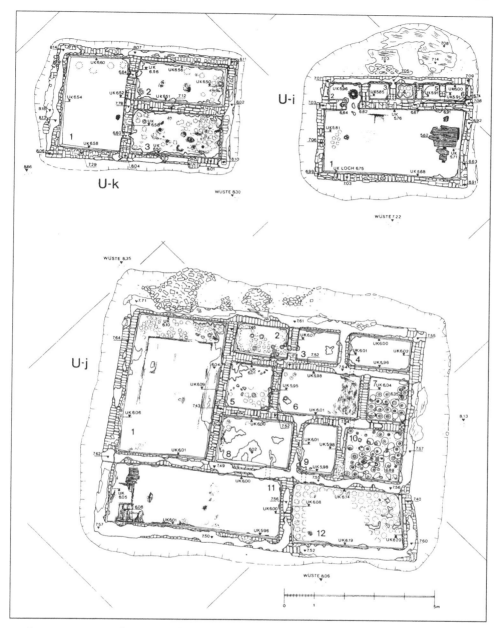

Figure 9.11 Tomb U-j at Abydos, with neighbouring mud-brick tombs for comparison, Naqada IIIA

The spatial location of tomb U-j, and that of neighbouring brick-lined burials, provides a long sought-after link between the last predynastic graves of Cemetery U and the earliest royal tombs to the south in Cemetery B, which contained objects marked with names of Sekhen/Ka, Narmer and Aha (fig. 10.16). No less than three distinct techniques, involving seals, paint and incised tags, were used to attach signs to the objects found within, each technique being reserved for a particular category of object (Kahl 2001a: 106). Attention has focused particularly upon a corpus of signs—painted on to ceramic vessels and incised on to the small, perforated tags—that represent a formative stage in the emergence of the hieroglyphic writing system (fig. 9.12). For reasons outlined above, the seal impressions found within the tomb (e.g. fig. 9.7: d) might also be considered in this context.

Signed, sealed and delivered: the contents of the tomb

Approximately 150 perforated tags were found within tomb U-j. They had probably been attached to grave goods (perhaps bolts of cloth) that had either decomposed or been looted prior to their discovery (Dreyer 1998: 113–45). Among the images inscribed on them are geometrical signs denoting a complex system of numeration, and approximately fifty distinct pictorial signs, most often executed in pairs, but also singly and occasionally in larger groups (fig. 9.12). They draw heavily from the animal world and exhibit a range of forms and subjects distinct, but not entirely divorced, from the animal art of the preceding Naqada II period. A new range of floral elements and topographical features is also present, in addition to images carried over from the earlier period. There appear to be specific continuities with signs appearing on the painted boats that ornamented Naqada II pottery (D-Ware), either atop the standards that adorn their central cabins (row of triangles, horned animal-head, elephant) or extending directly from the prow of the boat (palm frond). Other signs on the tags include human figures armed with bows, an early type of throne and schematic images of lattice structures, plausibly interpreted as shrines. The *serekh* motif, discussed below, appears as one of a series of signs upon which animal figures perch or stride. Another is the row of triangles, variously surmounted by elephants, birds or snakes in a manner that recalls various sign combinations on the Coptos Colossi (fig. 9.10) and on a number of carved ivory objects, such as a plaque from the Main Deposit at Hierakonpolis (fig. 9.2, middle). Further parallels for a number of images on tags are found on the Hunters' and Cities Palettes (figs. 9.6, 9.14).[24]

The inscriptional material from tomb U-j demonstrates the co-existence of at least two distinct, but compatible modes of writing during the early Naqada

---

[24] Dreyer 1995; 1998: 173–7; Williams 2003; Baines 2004.

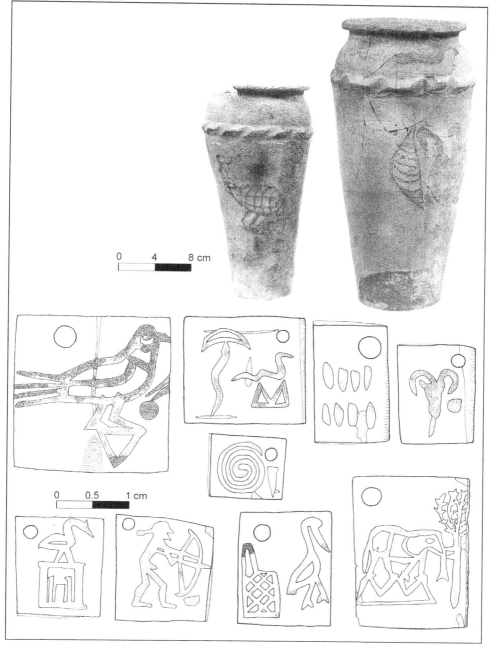

Figure 9.12 Vessels with painted signs and inscribed tags from tomb U-j, Abydos, c.3300 BC

III period. Of these the most closely related are the signs inscribed on tags, some of which were filled with paint, and much larger versions of comparable signs painted in ink on to the surface of ceramic vessels (fig. 9.12). The surviving range of ink signs is more limited than those on tags, the most numerous being images of scorpions, a distinct type of Red Sea shell which also appears on the Coptos Colossi, and a cattle-skull (bucranium) impaled or supported on a standard pole. They were executed in a cursive fashion on more than one hundred cylindrical jars with wavy handles (Dreyer 1998: 47–91). These had been stored in two adjacent chambers in the north-western part of the tomb, and were therefore kept spatially separate from the tags and their associated objects during the ritual process of deposition.

The tags themselves were concentrated within a long rectangular chamber to the south, the other surviving contents of which included parts of a cedar box and of a beautifully carved obsidian bowl, with a pair of hands rendered in relief on the base. Pieces from a very similar bowl in ivory were also recovered, as were the fragmentary remains of other ivory and bone objects including possible furniture elements, gaming pieces, a comb, spoon, pin and what may be a ceremonial adze (interpreted by Dreyer as a royal sceptre; 1998: 146–67). Two smaller chambers within the tomb appear to have been set aside for coarse wares and their contents, including bread moulds and beer jars, while three adjacent rooms held over two hundred ceramic bottles of an unusual kind, thought by the excavators to have originated in the Levant (Hartung 2001; 2002; but see below, chapter 9.8). On the assumption that each of the latter chambers had originally been filled to capacity, it has been estimated that tomb U-j contained around seven hundred of these bottles. Residue analysis demonstrates that their contents included wine infused with tere-binth resin and flavoured with sliced figs, and the total volume of imported wine consigned to the tomb may have been as much as 4,500 litres (McGovern et al. 1997).

Distributed among the ceramic bottles were the remains of mud sealings originally attached to their coverings, which were perhaps of leather or some similar material (Dreyer 1998: 108–12). Their upper sides bear cylinder-seal impressions that display a different repertoire of signs to the tags and painted jars, and were rendered on a far smaller scale than either of the latter. Some degree of overlap in content is, however, indicated by the presence on one type of sealing of a striding, long-beaked bird—probably a stork—also attested among the signs on tags (fig. 9.7: d). On the sealing in question the stork fea-tures within a larger animal frieze, hemmed in on all sides by a dense pattern of interlocked geometrical motifs, in the same manner as other seal designs from Cemetery U. The same figure also reappears—both individually and as an ornamental motif—on ceremonial objects discussed earlier in this chapter, including the Davis Comb (fig. 9.2, lower), the Carnavon, Brooklyn (fig. 9.1) and Pitt Rivers Knife-handles and the porphyry bowl from Hierakonpolis.

The numerical preponderance of scorpions among the ink signs on vessels leads Dreyer to identify it as the burial of an early ruler whose name was written with this sign, a view that has not been accepted by all. He further proposes that the corpus of written signs found within the tomb can be read in the manner of later hieroglyphs, and that they denote the names of no fewer than nine previously unknown rulers before the First Dynasty, and of estates from which funerary gifts were supplied (Dreyer 1998: 138–45, 173–80).[25] Various inconsistencies have since been identified in his suggested readings (e.g. Breyer 2002), and all that experts generally agree upon to date is that the signs notate prestigious names of some kind, perhaps including gods as well as persons and places; that they probably do not communicate more complex linguistic messages; and that the communicative system to which they belong was a direct precursor of the hieroglyphic writing system, and already made use of the rebus principle (for which, see chapter 9.9).[26]

9.8 An administrative origin for Egyptian writing?

While incorporating isolated elements of speech, the earliest Egyptian writing system—like that of Mesopotamia (Michalowski 1990; 1994; Damerow 1999)—was not initially designed or able to represent continuous spoken discourse. Natural language did not provide a primary model for its development. Rather, the representation of linguistic syntax was a later adaptation of its original structures and functions, which related more closely to other, non-linguistic modes of communication (Baines 2004). I now consider existing theories as to the nature of those functions, and suggest an alternative set of possibilities.

There has been wide, though by no means unanimous, acceptance of the notion that the inscriptions from tomb U-j demonstrate the development of formal administrative structures, used to command the flow of goods from one

---

[25] Comparisons between the inscriptions from tomb U-j, those on the Coptos Colossi and others on various ceremonial objects lead Dreyer to propose the existence of a further ten kings, making a total of nineteen before the First Dynasty. His view that complex estate holdings were established throughout much of Egypt during the early Naqada III period is broadly consistent with the account offered here in chapter 0, although this need not imply (as he suggests) that Egypt was already a unified polity at this time.

[26] Important commentaries to date include Kahl 2001a; 2003; Baines 2004; Morenz 2004. Kahl acknowledges the existence of at least ten rulers between the time of tomb U-j and the reign of Narmer, but sees them as contemporaries, whose power was restricted to particular locales, rather than as a single, unified dynasty controlling all of Egypt. He also casts doubt upon a number of Dreyer's readings of specific signs, and in his more recent study proposes an alternative set of readings, in which toponyms (including administrative districts and necropoleis) feature more commonly than royal names. Baines provides a broader examination of the relationship between early writing and language, based upon the data from tomb U-j and comparative material from other early states. He also finds fault with a number of Dreyer's proposed translations, but unlike Kahl (2001a: 118) is not convinced that determinatives were already used to ascribe words to particular semantic classes on the tags from tomb U-j.

part of the country to another and to control the conduct of foreign trade relations, notably with the Levant.[27] It seems also to be assumed that these structures transcended or replaced more localised mechanisms of exchange, through which goods had previously circulated over comparable distances. On closer inspection, however, the artefacts from tomb U-j provide little direct support for this view. Scientific provenance studies have shown not only that the sealings associated with wine bottles were composed of ordinary Nile mud, but that some (and perhaps many) of these unusual ceramic vessels were made in clays that were readily available in the Abydos region, so that they could not have originated in the Levant (McGovern et al. 1997: 12; Porat and Goren 2002). An unknown proportion would then fall into the established category of import substitutes, continuing a pattern that began with the imitation of Levantine wavy-handled jars in late Naqada II (chapter 4.5). This need not rule out the possibility that they were represented as exotic items in the context of burial rites.

Comparisons have often been drawn between the tags from tomb U-j and similar objects from high-status burials of the First and Second Dynasties. While usually larger, these later tags are made in similar materials (mainly wood, bone and ivory) and carry signs detailing quantities of precious oil and other highly valued products, accompanied by complex scenes of royal action (fig. 6.1). The scenes incorporate both written and pictorial elements, and often form year-names comparable to the entries on royal annals of the later Old Kingdom (chapter 6.1, 6.2). The earliest known example, from the reign of Narmer, has been recovered from a secondary context in Cemetery B at Abydos (Dreyer et al. 1998: 138–9, fig. 29; Dreyer 2000). Its inscription is divided into two registers (fig. 9.13). The surviving part of the lower register specifies a quantity of 'finest' oil, and by analogy with more fully preserved examples the missing section probably named its place of production. The upper register contains a scene commemorating the king's victory over a foreign enemy, which is generically related to that on the Narmer Palette, and more closely resembles the decoration of an ivory handle from the Main Deposit at Hier-akonpolis. Such scenes, however, relate to a cycle of ceremonial performances enacted and re-enacted by early rulers as part of their ascribed duties, and should not be treated as historical records in the usual sense.

Some have argued that the inscriptions on these later tags demonstrate an administrative (as opposed to ritual or ceremonial) function for the earlier writing found in tomb U-j (e.g. Postgate et al. 1995: 465–6). The assertion is

[27] Dreyer 1998: 89, 145; Postgate et al. 1995: 465–6; Wilkinson 1999: 41–4, 112. Related suggestions that 'the development of Egyptian and Mesopotamian bureaucracy seems much more similar than hitherto assumed' (Hartung 1998: 217) appear to be based upon an imprecise understanding of the functions of proto-cuneiform writing and contemporary sealing practices in Mesopotamia, which were concerned more with regulating the internal affairs of urban institutions than with controlling long-distance trade.

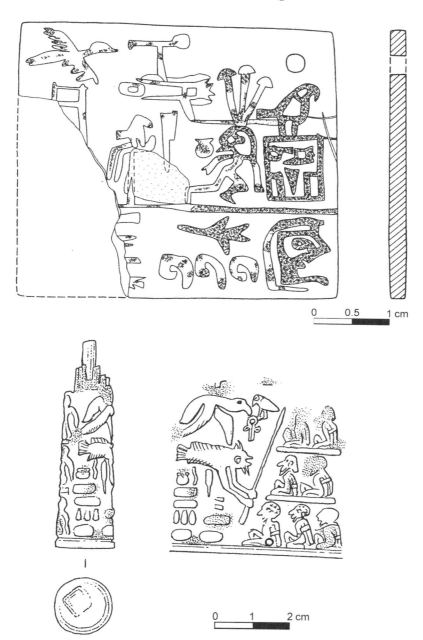

Figure 9.13 Ivory label of Narmer from Abydos and handle with relief carving from the Main Deposit, Hierakonpolis

that they served as little more than accounting devices, recording the provenance and year of manufacture of the goods to which they were attached. Such interpretations, however, take little account either of the scarcity of writing—and of visual signs in general—at this time, or of the density of high-status imagery on the tags themselves. Had the recording of a particular year for accounting purposes been the sole objective, more effective forms of notation would surely have been used—as they no doubt were in less prestigious contexts, which are barely attested in the archaeological record owing to the ephemeral nature of whatever writing medium was employed (such as papyrus). At the least, such tags create an official biography for the grave goods to which they were bound, locating their source in the productive domain of royal power, rather than in the mundane world of human labour and exchange. In the heightened context of a funerary ritual, the formation of linkages between the body of the deceased and the ceremonial lifecycle of the king—achieved through the grave goods to which inscriptions were attached—can hardly be explained adequately as an accounting device.

The least speculative method of establishing the nature of the wider system to which the images from tomb U-j belonged is to chart the occurrence of similar images elsewhere in the archaeological record. On current evidence they do not occur on other vessels of the Naqada IIIA period, while inscribed tags are not yet documented either from other tombs of this date or from Naqada IIIB contexts. Rather, as will by now be clear, those responsible for the creation of these signs drew from the same reservoir of knowledge as the makers and users of ceremonial cosmetic palettes, personal weaponry and monumental sculpture. Two further points seem important in this regard. The first is Dreyer's (1998: 137) observation that the signs on tags appear to have been inscribed first on larger plates of animal bone, which were then broken into segments to form tags.[28] Awkward truncations and the overlap of signs from one tag to another can be detected in certain cases where the break was not made in quite the right place, or the sign-maker exceeded the space available. Furthermore, as Jochem Kahl (2001a: 111, fig. 9) demonstrates, many different hands, of varying degrees of skill, were responsible for executing particular signs on tags and vessels. Given the number of inscribed objects found in the tomb, probably a fraction of the original quantity, this indicates the participation of a great many individuals in the funerary rite for which it was constructed. It also implies that their role as donors of gifts to the deceased was defined, not at the level of the individual agent, but as an enactment of group identity, expressed through focal symbols executed first on a shared surface and only then attached to individual objects. Lurking behind each sign-form in tomb U-j is a larger collectivity, and in their ritualised coming

---

[28] Unlike myself, Dreyer sees this as further evidence for the existence of an extensive administrative apparatus in early Naqada III Egypt.

together for an act of commemoration we can perceive a centralised society taking shape.

9.9 Narmer: towards the material biography of a name

No single object expresses the culmination of that process of centralisation more powerfully than the Narmer Palette (figs. 2.1, 2.2), and no other object disguises its true nature more eloquently. Much that would subsequently define dynastic culture—hieroglyphic writing, a particular manner of depicting the human form and organising images into registers, and a shared conception of the divine forces that animate the cosmos—is combined there into a single statement: the king has conquered his foreign enemies and unified the land on behalf of the gods. All memory of contingent events and all other genealogies of social power are effaced in favour of a series of artificial but compelling dualities: the Two Lands, the king and the gods, Egypt and its victory over the Other.[29]

Narmer's name occurs three times on his ceremonial palette. It occupies the centre of each top register, where it is enclosed by a *serekh* and framed by the mixed human and bovine heads of deities. It also goes before the smaller figure of the king on the obverse, where he strides towards the dismembered corpses of defeated foes. Here the king wears the Red Crown with its spiral-shaped extension, while in the smiting scene on the reverse he wears the White Crown. It is reasonably assumed that these emblems depict real items of costume (no actual crowns survive), which formed part of the regalia symbolising kingship over the Two Lands, the White Crown being associated with rulership of Upper Egypt, and the Red Crown with Lower Egypt (Goebs 2001: 323). 'Narmer' is written using a representational technique known as the rebus principle, which was an elementary foundation of the hieroglyphic writing system. In Gardiner's words (1957: 4–5), pictures of things are used 'not to denote those things themselves or any cognate notions, but to indicate certain other entirely different things not easily susceptible of pictorial representation, *the names of which chance to have a similar sound*'. Hence catfish (*n'r*) and chisel (*mr*) together write 'Narmer'.[30]

Earlier sign combinations, such as appear on seal impressions and the Hunters' Palette (figs. 9.6, 9.7), may already have used the rebus principle, but cannot be read by analogy with later hieroglyphs. The same is true of the captions that label a number of non-royal figures on the Narmer Palette. They include the kneeling foe whom Narmer is about to smite with his mace, the

---

[29] Frankfort's (1948a: 18–23) classic account of the role of dualism in ancient Egyptian thought, while based on an outmoded concept of 'cultural mentality', nevertheless captures well the ideological centrality of such oppositions in dynastic representation.

[30] An alternative reading as Nar(-meher) is proposed by Quack (2003); cf. Morenz (2004: 3).

two fleeing figures in the register below and the king's chief retainers—his sandal-bearer, who flanks him on both sides of the palette and occupies his own base-line on the reverse, and the figure with a wig and leopard skin who walks before him on the obverse. The equipment carried by these latter figures cannot always be identified with certainty. In addition to the royal footwear, the sandal-bearer carries what may be a cosmetic vessel and wears a seal (perhaps the royal seal) around his neck. The objects carried by the other chief retainer are usually identified as scribal equipment. As on later dynastic monuments, all of the written signs on the Narmer Palette are clearly distinguished from purely pictorial images by their small scale and/or by containment within a conventional motif that assigns them to a distinct semantic field (Fischer 1978; Baines 1989a: 474).

On early royal monuments these containing-motifs include the *serekh*, which frames the writing of royal names, and schematic representations of buttressed enclosure walls, which enclose the often indecipherable names of hostile peoples and places. The latter type of composite sign makes its first appearance on slightly earlier decorated palettes, such as the Bull and Cities Palettes (fig. 9.14). It also recurs in the lowest register of the Narmer Palette as a caption for defeated foes and as a larger pictorial element containing symbols that may indicate buildings. On each of these objects the buttressed enclosures, and by implication the subjects confined within them, are under attack from manifestations of royal agency. These take the forms of various dangerous animals—falcon, lion, scorpion, bull—all of which have the power, both in reality and in representation, to render opponents passive and helpless by sudden action (Wengrow 2001a: 94–5; Baines 2003: 29–30). The human embodiments of the king on the Narmer Palette also partake in the attributes of animals through the bull-tails and ornamented belts that they wear.[31]

Titles, dangerous animals and the contours of royal agency

The use of the *serekh* can be traced back to a time (Naqada IIIA–early IIIB) when it had independent meaning as a symbol deployed on funerary goods and ceremonial objects (Kaiser and Dreyer 1982: 260–9). On an early palette with relief carving, unprovenanced and now in the Metropolitan Museum of New York, the *serekh* (without royal name) is surmounted by a falcon and positioned above an image of a coiled snake that forms a raised, circular boundary around the cosmetic area (Fischer 1958; Ciałowicz 1991: 48–9). Around it a dense, swirling mass of real and mythical beasts radiates out towards the edges of the palette, which are worn away. On the Narmer Palette itself the cosmetic area is defined by the intertwined necks of two monsters in a more direct

---

[31] The same type of belt, from which are suspended rows of pendants shaped to represent the head and horns of cattle, reappears on a Third Dynasty statue fragment of Djoser from the Step Pyramid complex at Saqqara (Firth and Quibell 1935, pl. 59).

Figure 9.14 The Cities Palette, cities side

manner than on the Two Dog Palette. The spaces above their lower bodies are occupied by identical human figures, each wearing a knotted penis sheath and holding a rope that extends from the neck of a monster (see Baines 1975: 3).

By no later than Naqada IIIB (c.3200 BC) the use of the *serekh* as a conventional space for writing royal names is attested in the form of incised or painted signs on pottery and stone vessels, which were deposited in high-status and royal burials (fig. 9.15; Fischer 1963; van den Brink 1992c; 1996; 2001). Prior to the discovery of tomb U-j these signs on pottery constituted the earliest recognised corpus of writing in Egypt. The term 'corpus' seems highly appropriate here, since, as I go on to discuss, the names they distribute hark back to a shared point of origin in the bodies of particular rulers, whose social agency they extended in time and space. The incised marks are usually small and unassuming, and were typically executed on large liquid containers, plausibly termed 'wine jars' in the literature, near the shoulder and before firing. The painted signs are often larger and usually appear on the exteriors of cylindrical vessels (Kaplony 1963, pls. 1–2; Dreyer *et al.* 1998: 139–41, fig. 30). On both types of container royal names are sometimes accompanied by one or more other signs, which specify the provenance of the vessel and/or the nature of its contents (Kaplony 1963: 272–83; Kaiser and Dreyer 1982). The latter included

Figure 9.15 Wine jar with incised *serekh* of Narmer and cylindrical vessel inscribed with the name of Ka and contents, Dynasty 0

fine cosmetic oils and wines (Kahl 1994), the production of which was probably a monopoly of newly founded estates initially concentrated in and around the Nile delta, and subsequently distributed throughout much of the country (chapters 7.4, 8.4).

By far the largest concentrations of inscribed vessels have been found in burials at Abydos, with smaller groups at cemeteries in the region of Memphis, principally Saqqara, Tarkhan, Abu Rawash and Tura. As Edwin van den Brink notes (1992c: 270), this pattern—centred upon the locations of elite cemeteries in Upper and Lower Egypt—is strongly suggestive of royal involvement in the '(re)-distribution of certain commodities contained in the marked vessels'. In a funerary record increasingly denuded of other kinds of imagery, the distribution of these names also constitutes further evidence for the insertion of royal agency into a formerly widespread, but now highly restricted, area of social life: the attachment of visible marks of identity to objects placed with the dead. Significantly, the name of Narmer is the first to be widely attested in burials throughout Upper and Lower Egypt, also appearing on rock surfaces in the Eastern Desert and on pottery found in the southern Levant.[32] Inscriptions usually read as earlier royal names, such as those of Irihor (written without a *serekh*) and Sekhen/Ka, probably belong to regional rulers of Dynasty 0, and have a more limited distribution. Others, the readings of which remain still more obscure, are attested from just a handful of sites (Kaiser and Dreyer 1982: 232–5, 260–9; cf. Wilkinson 1993).

The vertical panels that usually appear in the lower part of the *serekh* indicate its function as a metonymic representation of the royal palace, identified by a panelled façade (Atzler 1974; Baines 1990; 1995: 121–2). The same design was also used to decorate the walls of early elite tombs and royal funerary enclosures (figs. 10.3, 10.13). From the First Dynasty onwards, *serekhs* were usually surmounted by an animal figure referring to that aspect of the royal person which embodies a deity. That deity was normally, but not exclusively, the god Horus, whose presence is indicated by a falcon, as exemplified in an early form on the carved palette in the Metropolitan Museum. The name enclosed by the *serekh*, which was not a birth name but one of a series of epithets acquired by the king upon accession, is accordingly known as his 'Horus name'. A full realisation of Narmer's Horus name appears on a decorated stone mace-head from the Main Deposit at Hierakonpolis, which presents a complex scene of tribute taking place within the context of a ceremony known as the *sed-festival*, familiar from later periods (fig. 2.3). Signs for cattle and human captives appear before the steps leading up to the king, and are labelled with numerals. A total of 1,822,000 animals and 120,000 captives is recorded—fictional quantities that demonstrate the subordination of an administrative idiom to the requirements of royal display (cf. Vernus 1993: 90–2). In the register above them, facing the king, is a figure seated beneath an arched canopy supported by a litter, which has papyrus-shaped finials and ornamented legs like those on the carrying beds that first appear in early Naqada III burials (fig. 8.5). The king's Horus name is located behind a vulture that protects the seated ruler on his raised canopy.

Vultures are closely related to royal power on a number of other early monuments. They join in the violent destruction of enemies on the Battlefield Palette, where royal agency takes the form of a feeding lion (Spencer 1980: 79–80, cat. 576, pl. 64). Evoking the goddess later called Nekhbet, the vulture was combined in the First Dynasty with the cobra, signifying the goddess Wadjet, to constitute a distinct royal title known as the 'Two Ladies' (*nebty*) name. The two goddesses were associated with locations in the southern and northern parts of the country,

[32] Kaiser and Dreyer 1982: 266; Kahl 2001a: 110, fig. 7; Levy *et al.* 2001.

respectively Hierakonpolis and Buto. This was one of two dualistic royal titles that appear alongside the Horus name by the early First Dynasty. The other, the *nswt-bity* name, comprises signs for 'king' that depict a plant (perhaps a sedge or reed) and bee, and were respectively associated with the White and Red Crowns of Egypt. The meanings of these titles are ultimately enigmatic. At a general level they appear to convey overlapping messages that recall the king's role as unifier of the Two Lands, emphasise his unique proximity to the gods and affirm his position as 'the unifying apex of a host of dualities that constituted society' (Baines 1995: 95, and 125–8 for early royal titulary). As material signs deployed on objects and surfaces where the royal name was exposed, they also served the more immediate function of enmeshing that name within a complex and extended web of symbols, discouraging any simple act of appropriation or nega-tion. Insofar as the purpose of titles was to create a mystique around the royal name, thereby protecting the identity behind it from harm or manipulation, any retrospective attempt to decode them may not be helpful.

On the Narmer Palette the Horus falcon appears, not above the *serekh*, but within the main scene.[33] It perches upon a composite hieroglyphic sign for 'land', which is personified by the head of a defeated foe. A human hand extending from the body of the falcon enables it to grasp a rope, with which it leads the personified land sign by the nose in a gesture of humiliation that echoes Narmer's grip on the forelock of his kneeling victim. John Baines (1985: 41–63, 277–305; 1989a: 473–4) has coined the term 'emblematic personification' to describe this convention, whereby signs that convey abstract concepts such as 'kingship' are equipped with human attributes in order to identify them as dynamic elements within a broader group of images. Emblematic personification also mediates between written and pictorial elements within a scene. This is clearly exemplified by the relief carving on an ivory handle, which shows the catfish element of Narmer's name, again shielded by a vulture, wielding a stave over three registers of bound captives (fig. 9.13, lower). An accompanying inscription identifies them as 'Libyans' (Whitehouse 2002: 433–4, 439, fig. 4). The design compares closely with that on the tag from Abydos, discussed earlier (fig. 9.13, upper). A falcon, hovering above the weapon, presents the royal name—the main agent of the scene—with the *ankh* sign for life, which has the form of a knotted cord. 'Life' itself is thereby brought into the realm of exchange as a finite quality extracted from conquered enemies and transformed, through an act of violence, into a gift of vitality from the gods to the king. The hierarchical nature of the transfer is clarified by the juxtaposition of the captives' bound hands—negating their capacity for giving or receiving—with the emblematic hand added to the Horus bird so that it may offer its own gift to the ruler.

---

[33] An alternative reading would see the decorative scheme of the palette as a hierarchically organised 'map' of the cosmos with the (absent) Horus bird located in the sky above the world as depicted; Baines 1989a: 475–6.

The king surrounded and protected

As Jochem Kahl (2001a: 114–15) has demonstrated, the name 'Narmer' appears in at least fifteen different versions on objects of the Naqada III period. The most abbreviated forms, comprising just the catfish element, are also the most widely distributed, taking the form of incised marks on pottery. As the medium of writing becomes more technologically complex and hence more restricted—from cylinder seals and stone vessels up to ceremonial objects such as decorated palettes and maces—so the core of the name expands and acquires further layers, leading back to its ultimate source in the royal body. We can gain some notion of how that body might itself have been circumscribed in life from its depiction in human form on the Narmer Palette and Mace-head, and on the ceremonial mace-head of another ruler whose name was written with a scorpion and rosette. Its treatment in death is considered in the next chapter.

The surviving portion (less than half) of the latter object, known as the Scorpion Mace-head, presents the king with a bull's tail and wearing the White Crown (fig. 9.16; Asselberghs 1961, figs. 172–6). His actions may be read as giving life and form to the land by opening a water channel, although other interpretations remain possible. Once again, however, royal power is shown to be an ambivalent and dangerous force by the images of standards in the upper register, from which lapwings and bows—respectively symbolising the subjects and external enemies of Egypt—are suspended. On these objects the body of the ruler, especially when not engaged in violent action, is never shown alone or isolated, but rather surrounded by figures that come between him and the bodies of ordinary beings. The protective functions of the sandal-bearer relate specifically to the margins of the royal body—the soles of the feet and perhaps also the skin—which mediate its contact with the surrounding world. Fan-bearers keep the air around the king in motion, performing an action that in later times—as Baines (1995: 120) observes—signifies that 'all protection and life' are around his person. Finally, standard-bearers tread the ground before him, bearing images—a jackal, two falcons and a cushion-like object—that invoke guardian deities and divine aspects of royal identity. Like vultures, the standards that surround the king may take on both protective and aggressive roles. On other ceremonial objects, such as the Bull and Battlefield Palettes, they are animated with human arms that extend to bind enemies with rope.

9.10 From ceremonial objects to elite culture

To be actualized, identity needs the Other, that is, it needs to circumscribe the Other as such. *Mestizo Logics*, J.-L. Amselle

How are we to relate the detailed content of individual ceremonial objects to the wider vistas of political and economic change described in earlier chapters?

Figure 9.16 The Scorpion Mace-head, from the Main Deposit, Hierakonpolis

What difference does the existence of these small but portentous artefacts make to the way we view those large-scale transformations? In part, I would suggest, the answer resides in the juxtapositions and paradoxes they embody, between the particular and the universal, and between the prehistoric past and the dynastic future. In order to expand upon this statement, I consider again the timing of their creation.

In chapter 8, I described how hierarchical relationships were constituted through the restriction of access to established forms of personal display during the Naqada III period. A further aspect of this process, perceptively discussed by Eric Kansa and Tom Levy (2002), was a reduction in the capacity to form and sustain new social alliances among non-elites. They point out that the expansion of social influence in predynastic times was an open-ended process, in which access to the material sources of power was achieved through the exchange, not just of goods, but of the cultural habits and forms of identity they embodied. Archaeologically this process is manifest in the northward spread of Upper Egyptian material culture and burial practices during Naqada II, and by the regular exchange of objects and techniques between Egypt and its neighbours to the north and south. In Lower Egypt this resulted in the almost total abandonment of an earlier cultural pattern and its associated forms of social practice. By contrast, the forging of alliances with Lower Nubia and the southern Levant remained, to a greater degree, a process of cross-cultural negotiation, with groups in each region selectively incorporating distinct foreign elements into the development of their own institutions. This process continued in the southern Levant for some time after close relationships with Lower Nubia were brought to an end, but during the First Dynasty the flow of interaction between Egypt and the former region was also curtailed (chapter 7.5). Kansa and Levy (2002: 205–6), following Stephan Seidlmayer (1996b: 113), relate these developments to the consolidation of royal power and to the 'codification' of a 'bounded national identity' by architects of the unified Egyptian state. The outcome of this process was not a diminished demand for exotic goods on the part of dynastic elites, but rather a fundamental redefinition of the terms of engagement between Egypt and the outside world, both in practice and as represented within Egypt itself.

Ceremonial objects, 'deeply concerned' as they are 'with transitions and boundaries', provide a unique perspective on this process of redefinition and its implications for the emerging self-image of Egyptian elites, which has been explored by Baines (1993: 62; 1995: 109–21; 2003). The following observations build upon some of his conclusions, notably those which relate to the formulation of an explicit ideology of closure during the late Naqada II and Naqada III periods. The earliest referents for this ideology on ceremonial palettes and knife-handles were drawn from the animal world. Lions, snakes, wild dogs, jackals and various other feral animals are beings of desert margins, which in early Egypt also demarcated the spatial boundary between the living and the dead. Objects such as the Two Dog Palette (fig. 9.3) locate these animals on a continuum with fantastic and monstrous creatures of external (and ultimately mysterious) origin, indicating that they occupy not just the boundaries of Egypt but those of the known and habitable world. Egypt, or more precisely the Nile alluvium, is thereby equated with the totality of that world. By the time of the Narmer Palette the world beyond the alluvium was personified by

human victims of royal power, which on later monuments came to be represented by a standardised repertoire of physical attributes comprising distinctive forms of dress, skin colour and hairstyles. Like the wild animals of the
desert margins these figures embody places—'Libya', 'Nubia', 'Syria', and so
on—that were both real entities and fictional 'outside' spaces (O'Connor 2003).
As such they are represented as the location of dangerous forces that threaten
society, but also as a repository of life that is violently appropriated by the ruler
for the gods.

Like all representations of social otherness, those on ceremonial objects and
later dynastic monuments were predicated upon the creation of absence:
absence, that is, of real and intimate human contact, of the kind that results
in the merging of identities and the fluid exchange of cultural practices. We
should not expect absolute correspondences between these representations
and patterns of economic or political interaction on the ground. The relationship was no doubt a complex and dialectical one, with ideology playing a
constructive role in bringing about and sustaining the boundaries of the early
Egyptian state. Questions then naturally arise about the audience for these
representations. Are we justified in ascribing strong ideological functions to
objects that are intimate in scale, and the full meanings of which were only
accessible to a highly restricted community of elites? One part of the answer to
this question no doubt lies in ceremonial performances that cannot be directly
traced in the archaeological record, but may be intimated from contemporary
depictions and later sources. Another resides in the fact that the signs and
values encapsulated on ceremonial objects, including royal names, constituted
the nexus of a wider economy of distribution, archaeologically attested by
their deployment—as 'emanations' from a hierarchically layered core—on
objects presented as gifts to the dead. As sophisticated craft products, ceremonial objects confined these values to restricted material forms that impeded
their flow back into the social fabric from which they emerged, a project that
was only ever partially realised, and which finds numerous echoes in later
(more or less successful) attempts by elites to monopolise access to ritual
knowledge.

Finally we should recall the appeal of these objects, and their associated
performances, to social memories of formerly widespread ways of living
and dying. Ceremonial objects are idealisations of social forms and aspirations
that had deep roots in the Nile valley. As much through their ascribed functions as weapons and cosmetic articles as through the images captured on their
surfaces, they establish a homology between the boundaries of individual
bodies and the margins of the social world. The fact that those margins are
populated by dangerous and unfathomable beings constitutes a subtle appropriation by the state of earlier modes of ritual knowledge in the formation of its
own spatial and conceptual boundaries. It also highlights an important legit-
imating function for royal power in its protective role as guardian of the social

order; a function which is widely paralleled in the symbolic mechanisms of other forms of sacred kingship in Africa and elsewhere.[34] At once restricted and all-inclusive, ceremonial objects equate the transformation of the self with the transformation of the cosmos, and in doing so they fashion the body of the ruler as a container for sacred power.

---

[34] The notion of the 'stranger-king', who comes from outside the normal bounds of society to impose his rule or usurp authority by an act of violence, was traced by Dumézil (1968–73) in the cosmologies of ancient Persia, India, Rome and Ireland. It has since been widely discussed in relation to more recent African and Polynesian societies, where the ruler 'consumes the land and appropriates its reproductive powers, only to suffer thereby his own appropriation' (Sahlins 1985: 75; cf. de Heusch 1982; Rowlands 1998). The main error of archaeologists such as Petrie and Capart, who proposed that dynastic civilisation was forcibly imposed on Egypt by conquering invaders from outside, may have been to take literally—that is, as historical events—what are in reality logical structures generated from within society, and in particular from within the ritual structures that underpin its political life (cf. Bloch 1992).

THEATRES OF SACRIFICE: DYNASTIC CONSTRUCTIONS OF DEATH

Claims to power can very commonly be recast into claims to the ultimate right to control life and death.

The Ceremonial Animal, W. James

10.1 A state in formation

It is tempting to take the Narmer Palette as evidence of a *fait accompli*—the formation of 'the state', or the emergence of 'complex society'. What, then, should be made of the fact that the centuries *following* Narmer's reign were a period of constant innovation in virtually all aspects of life affected by the state: cultural, economic, ritual, ceremonial and administrative? If we accept the ideological premise of the Narmer Palette at face value, then the analysis of all these developments is reduced to a study in political aesthetics, or a narrative about the material rewards of authority. It becomes little more than a story of how the dynastic state, once in existence, learned to represent its own identity and exploit the benefits of centralised power to the full: the birth and maturation of 'eternal Egypt', symbolised by the royal monuments of the Fourth Dynasty on the Giza plateau. In this final chapter I wish to argue that the archaeological record of early dynastic Egypt, despite its many lacunae and its bias towards the sphere of elite culture, suggests a different and more complex reality. That reality was one of new interest groups in search of ways to reproduce their own identities and expand their functions within society; of a state that remained constantly in formation.

Two features of that ongoing process, the parallel development of which may initially strike us as strange, may be identified at the outset. The first was the growth of a bureaucratic apparatus and formal administrative hierarchy, the theoretical implications of which I consider further in the conclusion to this study. The second was the practice of human sacrifice on a large scale in state-sponsored rituals, especially in the funerary ceremonies of First Dynasty kings and queens. The latter events also occasioned the sacrifice of unprecedented quantities of material wealth in the form of luxury comestibles, goods acquired from beyond Egypt through increasingly restricted trade networks, and other vital elements of an elite lifestyle. The ritual taking of human life had only limited precedents in the predynastic period (chapter 5.4), and was largely expunged from the royal mortuary cult during the Second Dynasty. It therefore serves to define a distinct phase in the early history of the Egyptian state.

My coverage of the archaeological record in this chapter is of necessity more selective than in previous ones. I offer no detailed analysis of developments in the written sources relating to titulary and administration (see Kaplony 1963; Wilkinson 1999: 109–49), and my analysis of funerary remains focuses strongly upon royal and elite monuments. My aim is to elucidate a number of key issues surrounding the character and purpose of early dynastic mortuary rites as a point of entry to broader social developments, and as a logical progression from the interpretations presented in earlier chapters. To that end, I draw selectively from the richer pictorial and textual record of later times, in order to highlight contrasts between predynastic society and the courtly society to which those early dynasties gave rise.

10.2 Constructing the elite body

In the Middle Kingdom *Tale of Sinuhe*, dating to the early second millennium BC, an Egyptian nobleman relates how he fled his homeland after hearing of the unexpected death of the king (Amenemhat I), and was accepted into the court of a Levantine prince called Ammunenshi.[1] Upon arrival he is given lands, wealth, authority and the hand of Ammunenshi's daughter in marriage. But in his old age, with death approaching, Sinuhe begins to yearn for the palace of the Egyptian king, for the life of a courtier, and for a place of burial in his homeland and among his peers. Word of his plight reaches the Egyptian king, Kheperkare (Senwosret I), who issues a decree inviting him to return to Egypt. Sinuhe describes his return to the royal court, where he is presented before the king:

> I found his Majesty on the great throne
> in the portal of electrum.
> Then I was stretched out prostrate,
> unconscious of myself in front of him,
> while this God was addressing me amicably.
> I was like a man seized in the dusk,
> my soul had perished, my limbs failed,
> my heart was not in my body.
> I did not know life from death.
>
> (Parkinson 1997: 40, B250–5)

His audience complete, Sinuhe is granted residence of a princely household:

---

[1] For critical literary analysis of the *Tale of Sinuhe*, see Baines 1982; Parkinson 1997 (translation and commentary); 2002.

> ... with costly things in it, with a bathroom in it
> and divine images of the horizon,
> with treasures from the Treasury in it,
> clothes of royal linen,
> myrrh and kingly fine oil
> . . .
> The years were made to pass from my limbs;
> I became clean-shaven, and my hair was combed.
> . . .
> I was clad in fine linen;
> I was anointed with fine oil.
> I slept in a bed.
> I returned the sand to those who are upon it
> and the tree oil to those smeared with it.
>   (Parkinson 1997: 42, B285–95)

He goes on to detail the provisions made for his death by the king:

> A pyramid of stone was built for me,
> in the midst of the pyramids.
> . . .
> All the equipment to be put in a tomb shaft—
> its share of these things was made.
> I was given funerary priests;
> a funerary demesne was made for me,
> with fields in it and a garden in its proper place,
> . . .
> My image was overlaid with gold,
> and its kilt with electrum.
> It is his Majesty who had caused this to be done.
>   (Parkinson 1997: 42–3, B300–5)

In spite—or perhaps by virtue—of its hyperbolical tone, Sinuhe's story reveals much about relationships between power and personhood; about the way in which the dynastic state created political subjects 'from the inside', and achieved an emotional purchase on their lives through the education of the body and senses, including norms of personal hygiene, sleeping practices, modes of comportment, and socially prescribed ways of experiencing and coping with death (cf. Meskell 2002: 45). In what follows I attempt to probe the early development of those patterns of activity and response via the objects that mediated them, and consider their involvement in the creation of new political identities.

The mortuary meal in early dynastic Egypt

On the east bank of the Nile at Helwan is a necropolis comprising tombs of the Egyptian elite dating to the First, Second and Third Dynasties (Saad 1947; 1951; Köhler 1998b; 2000). The largest have extensive substructures with rectilinear plans, built in mud-brick and the locally available limestone (see also Wood 1987). The burial chambers were entered via an imposing staircase, sealed, following the completion of funerary rites, with a large stone portcullis. In the course of those rites the tomb was endowed with large quantities of food, wine and luxury oils (presented in ceramic and stone containers, sometimes marked with a royal seal), as well as perfumes, finely crafted cosmetic implements, furniture, jewellery and sets for board-games played with small animal figurines (Saad 1969). It seems arbitrary to divide these objects into 'luxuries' and 'necessities'. All were necessary and interconnected parts of a total form of courtly behaviour; a concrete mode of social interaction and experience, created at the nexus of people and things.

A number of the Second and Third Dynasty tombs at Helwan also contained small stone slabs, carved in relief with offering scenes, which were installed within a specially constructed niche in the wall of the burial chamber (fig. 10.1, left).[2] These scenes cannot be treated as windows on to everyday experience, but neither was their chosen repertoire of imagery divorced from the social and material realities of courtly life. An image representing the tomb-owner is juxtaposed to depictions of material objects and substances, placed at his or her disposal. As depicted, however, the elite dead do not simply receive food, clothing, etc.; they receive it in a certain bodily manner, which is rigidly defined and cross-cuts differences of gender and official status that are apparent from the accompanying inscriptions. The body is seated upright on an ornate chair, the legs of which often terminate in bull-hooves. In some cases only the back legs of the chair are shown, such that person and chair seem almost to merge. Bodies are strikingly plain, with both sexes wearing a long robe to which a single belt or, more rarely, an amulet may be attached. Differences between women and men are most clearly expressed through their contrasting headgear, which is rendered in some detail. Faces are not highly individualised, with emphasis uniformly placed upon the largeness of the eyes, nose and lips. Individual identity is conferred upon the image, not primarily by the presentation of the body, but by hieroglyphic inscriptions placed above the head, which name the person and specify membership of the royal family or a prestigious function within the state.[3]

In each offering scene, the tomb-owner is shown in profile seated before a table on a high stand, which is laden with loaves of bread (see Emery 1962). One hand is open and reaches out towards the table while the other is often

---

[2] Saad 1957. Saad's report leaves some doubt as to where these slabs were actually located within the tomb structures (cf. Haeny 1971; Bolshakov 1997: 112–13; Kahl 1997). See also Der Manuelian 1998: 118; Kahl *et al.* 1995: 172–3 (D3/H1/1), 176–7 (D3/H1/2), 178–9 (D3/H1/13), and for comparable finds from Saqqara, 182–3 (D3/Sa/4), 200–1 (D3/Sa/18), 216–17 (D3/Sa/17).

[3] Fischer (1963: 34–9) discussed an exceptional case, in which body decoration may have been used to signify a distinct ethnicity, which he characterises as 'Nubian' (or perhaps 'Puntite') on the basis of comparisons with later pictorial sources.

Figure 10.1 Private funerary monuments from Helwan and Saqqara, First
Dynasty

closed and folded across the chest. The area to the right of the table is filled
with a tabular list of offerings, sometimes divided into formal registers. Its
standard components include bread, beer, wine, meat, oils, fruit and linen,
specified in quantities of tens, hundreds and thousands, and qualified as 'fine',
'sweet' or exotic in origin (e.g. 'best oil of Libya'). The various types of container depicted in these scenes have parallels among the objects placed within
high-status tombs at Helwan and elsewhere. Storage vessels include rows of
ovoid wine jars with conical stoppers and cylindrical vessels used for holding
oils and fats. Among the flat-based serving vessels are shallow stone plates,
bowls, concave cups, and metal pouring vessels with spouts. In a number of
scenes we can recognise imported Levantine flasks (or their local imitations),

small quantities of which are consistently found in royal and elite tombs (fig. 10.1; cf. fig. 7.7, lower). The ornamented furniture on which the tomb-owner sits closely renders actual objects, crafted in wood and ivory and fitted with metal finials (cf. fig. 10.6; Killen 1980). The world of actions and emotions mapped out by such equipment, and inhabited by the courtly body, is more tightly controlled than that of predynastic times—one of small, constrained movements played out on flat surfaces and best symbolised, perhaps, by the gaming boards and intricately carved playing pieces of this and later periods (Emery 1961: 248–51; Piccione 1990).

The surviving contents of high-status tombs at Helwan and elsewhere also include many types of prestigious object that do not feature in offering scenes. Ivory spoons, mirrors, decorated boxes, jewellery, combs, tweezers and other minute cosmetic implements, often exquisitely ornamented with precious metals and stones, are among them.[4] Where figural ornamentation is present on such objects, it often refers to the world of kingship and the gods, and in some cases to violent aspects of royal agency such as the conquering and humiliation of foreign enemies.[5] In conjunction with proliferating titles and ritual prerogatives, these objects represent a copious investment by the early Egyptian state in the production and dissemination of a courtly lifestyle. They also relate to a recurrent theme of this chapter: the neglected role of the miniature (alongside the monumental) in processes of state formation.

10.3 The extended death and the dependent body: an analytical framework

As demonstrated by the *Tale of Sinuhe*, and by the recovery of the items described from tomb deposits, participation in courtly society went hand in hand with a particular set of beliefs, desires and expectations regarding death. Here I introduce a broad, overtly idealised distinction between two cultural and emotional constructions of death, in order to provide a framework for understanding wider differences between predynastic and dynastic social development. The first, already discussed at length, is the expansive but ephemeral death of the predynastic body: a publicly orchestrated act of forgetting, in which the corpse—rendered as an extended image of its place in a social network— was removed permanently from the world, opening up new possibilities of extension among the living.

The second approach, which I associate broadly with dynastic society, was grounded in the notion that certain aspects of the deceased's being should remain in the world as parts of a ritually integrated network of objects,

---

[4] e.g. Saad 1969: 39–64, pls. 26–63, 71–83; Petrie 1900: 27–8, pls. 37–8; 1901a: 34–40, pls. 32–5; 1925: 4–6, pls. 2, 7–8; Emery 1958: 81–4, pls. 99, 103.
[5] e.g. Saad 1947, pl. 15; 1969, pl. 75; Petrie 1900: 23, pl. 17: 30; 1901a: 20–2, pls. 2–4; 1925, pl. 2: 6; Dreyer *et al.* 2003: 87–8, pl. 16c–h.

comprising tombs, coffins, stelae, statues, and the images and inscriptions they bore.[6] Some of these objects, including the modified corpse and its coffin, were consigned to invisible and inaccessible places during funerary rites, but others remained accessible. The survival of the network as a whole, and of the relations between the living and the dead that it encompassed, depended upon the actions of the living and the gods. The essential contrast with predynastic constructions of death is not in the realm of ideas about the needs of the dead and their power over the living. Such ideas existed in both predynastic and dynastic societies. Rather it resides in the way those ideas and emotional attachments were given new and restricted material forms, which redefined access to sacred power in relation to the state and its dependants. During the First Dynasty the primary foci around which this new approach to death developed were, I suggest, the bodies of kings. From the beginning, however, the royal mortuary cult also encompassed two other kinds of being: the gods, upon whom its successful conduct depended, and non-royal elites. A significant number of individuals, perhaps selected from the latter group, were initially incorporated as sacrificial victims, for whom the timing of bodily death was determined by the death and ceremonial rebirth of the king.

At the core of all these practices was the ritual production of a new kind of post-mortem existence, and interdependence, for the royal and elite dead, organised and expressed in terms of their differing relationships to the gods. Its development during the first two dynasties is difficult to reconstruct, owing to the extensive plundering of tombs, the limitations of written and pictorial sources, and a paucity of information regarding the status of temples (chapter 9.1). Central to any reconstruction is evidence for the creation and dedication of royal cult statues. The purpose of such statues in all periods was not to passively represent or commemorate the deceased, and they were frequently placed in hidden locations. Rather it was to occupy the ritually purified spaces of tomb and temple, and there to act as a channel for material offerings of sustenance passed from the living to the dead (Eaton-Krauss 1984: 70–6; Lorton 1999). Inscriptions in Old Kingdom tombs make it clear that the gods were the ultimate source of all sustenance. The king was required to make temple offerings to them so that they, in turn, might feed the dead within their tombs (chapter 6.2). Hence 'the dead participated both in the affairs of the living and in the regular cult of the gods' (Baines and Lacovara 2002: 12).

The ties of dependency that linked the king and the elite in life and death can be explored through the proliferation of official titles in mortuary contexts during the early dynastic period and Old Kingdom (Baer 1960; Strudwick 1985). The hierarchical listing of titles formed a crucial element in the self-presentation of the non-royal elite, constituting an official biography that expressed the

[6] For detailed surveys of ancient Egyptian mortuary culture and its temporal variations, see, e.g. Spencer 1982; Ikram and Dodson 1998; Taylor 2001.

development of a life towards an exalted conclusion. Such lists were usually inscribed on or close to the 'false door', an area of the tomb associated with the receipt of offerings. Among the most important titles were ones expressing the individual's proximity to and ritual care for the royal body and its appendages. Responsibility for the king's clothing, nails, hair, wigs, jewellery, and so on appears to have ranked alongside or, in some cases, above the possession of major administrative roles within the early Egyptian state (Helck 1954: 15–28; Baines 1995: 132).

For the First Dynasty, a key monument in this regard is a panel inscribed for the official Merika, recovered from the inner enclosure of a high-status tomb at Saqqara (fig. 10.1, right; Emery 1958: 30–1, pl. 39). It carries the longest known inscription of its time, comprising a vertical list of titles that culminate in the name and seated figure of the deceased courtier. Two titles are emphasised by their larger scale and placing at the end of the list. The first identifies Merika as a member of the *p't*—a highly restricted social group from which the king was probably drawn—while the second commemorates his role as a particular kind of priest, responsible for clothing the king's body. As Baines observes, Merika's 'chief executive activities in the state may have been covered by his other, less prominent titles, but the most important one for his self-presentation related him to the king and to ritual' (1995: 133; cf. 1999: 26–8).

In order to serve as a prototype for its cult images within the tomb, the 'dynastic body' was subject to extensive preservative treatment—including evisceration, desiccation, anointing with oils and wrapping in linen—each accompanied by appropriate rituals (Taylor 2001: 46–91). Evisceration transformed the natural body of the tomb-owner into an entity without a core; a register within an extended scale of relations and levels of containment projecting both inwards and outwards from its surface. In much later, New Kingdom times these relations were given form through the nesting of bodies like Russian dolls within a series of coffins, and through the production of *shabti* figurines and miniature coffins containing the viscera, each separately embalmed and bound with linen (Ikram and Dodson 1998: 207–28; cf. Roth 1998). In the early dynasties the 'palace façade' design may have played a similar mediating role, serving variously as a motif for enclosing the writing of the royal Horus name (distributed across a wide range of objects; e.g. figs. 9.13, 9.15, 10.7), as a decorative element on personal ornaments worn by the dead (fig. 10.17), and as a form of surface ornamentation for coffins, stelae and tombs (figs. 10.3, 10.9, 10.14). The image of a panelled façade was therefore rendered at a variety of scales, from the miniature to the monumental, and encompassed the static and mobile parts of the tomb, as well as its inner- and outermost surfaces.

Reciprocal relations between the transfigured corpse and its statue replicas were established through a ritual process called 'Opening the Mouth' (Otto

1960; Fischer-Elfert 1998). For statues, which texts refer to as being 'born' rather than 'made', this involved a mimesis of the final stages of manufacture, during which priests touched parts of the face with sculptors' tools. The same actions were performed upon mummified bodies at the entrance to the tomb. Many of these procedures are not clearly attested until Old Kingdom times, when they were depicted within elite tombs (Eaton-Krauss 1984). Their attestation in such contexts may, however, reflect the expanding functions of writing and depiction, rather than innovation in treatments of the corpse. Here I wish to emphasise that dynastic constructions of death were not simply a 'logical' extension or refinement of predynastic ones. In addition to their positive implications for the transfigured form and memory of the deceased, dynastic mortuary practices created new and more acute possibilities for its harm and neglect (Zandee 1960; Baines and Lacovara 2002). In becoming 'exalted', the ritually 'open' body and its ongoing ties to the living were also rendered fragmentary and reversible, literally bound into a hierarchical order of reality.

10.4 The king's two bodies?

In the archaeological record, striking evidence for a change in elite attitudes towards death comes at the very beginning of the First Dynasty, with the appearance of permanent and highly visible funerary monuments in the Egyptian landscape. Perishable materials had been used to mark the site of important graves in earlier periods, but traces are rarely preserved. Much early dynastic funerary architecture has, by contrast, survived above ground because it was built to last, mainly in mud-brick and plaster. For the internal lining and roofing of burial chambers, most high-status tombs also incorporated large quantities of wood, perhaps including coniferous timber imported from the Levant, as well as reed matting.[7] A variety of stones and metals were more sporadically employed for interior furnishings, and must have been transported to their final destinations over considerable distances. Boats and donkeys, which were primary means of transport, were sometimes accorded burials close to the site of the tomb (Jeffreys and Tavares 1994: 146).

It seems likely that these pronounced alterations in attitudes towards the tomb and its place in the world were accompanied by changes in the treatment of its material focus: the body of the deceased. A likely trajectory of change has been outlined above, and direct—if highly fragmentary—evidence may be cited

---

[7] Ben-Tor (1991: 4) cautions against assuming the use of imported timbers in the absence of direct evidence, which is still lacking for the First Dynasty; cf. Wilkinson 1999: 161, with references. However, Serpico and White (1996: 136) observe that small amounts of cedar and pine were already deposited in Egyptian burials in the predynastic period, and note the prevalence of cedar wood in the manufacture of Middle Kingdom coffins.

for the existence of cult statues during the First Dynasty: part of a wooden wig and a painted chest-piece from tombs at Abydos (Umm el-Qaab; Smith 1949: 9), and the bases of two wooden statues found *in situ* within an offering chamber attached to the tomb at North Saqqara from which Merika's inscribed panel derives (Emery 1958: 13, pl. 27; cf. Kemp 1967: 28–9, fig. 10.3).[8] These two necropoleis, Umm el-Qaab at Abydos and North Saqqara, stand at the centre of a debate, now some half a century old, concerning the location of dynastic Egypt's first royal cemetery. The roots of this controversy extend back further, to the very beginning of professional archaeology in Egypt at the close of the nineteenth century.[9]

Respectively situated in southern and northern Egypt, some 500 km apart, both Umm el-Qaab and North Saqqara have yielded unbroken records of high-status tombs containing inscriptions naming a succession of First Dynasty rulers (Edwards 1971: 17–22, 59–65; Wilkinson 1999: 230–60). These sequences cannot be paralleled at other cemeteries of the period. The argument that one site must be the true royal burial place—leaving the other as the location of 'dummy tombs', 'mere cenotaphs' or burials of the inner elite—is based on a questionable theoretical premise, shared (but rarely articulated) by many scholars on both sides of the debate.[10] The premise, that the person of the dead king was treated as spatially contiguous with his intact physical body, runs contrary to salient features of both earlier and later funerary practices. It also fails to address a paradox confronted by many, perhaps all, societies where power is not dispersed among 'a complex, anonymous collection of positions and institutions' but localised to the bodies of particular individuals (Turner 1992: 140). The enfeeblement and death of such individuals poses a problem of political representation, centred upon the protection of the body politic from the corruption and decay of its temporal container: the natural body of the ruler. In medieval Europe, for example, this paradox was resolved by distributing the corpse between distant locations (Brown 1981), while in early modern

---

[8] For Old Kingdom developments in wooden statuary, see Harvey 2001.
[9] In 1897, J. de Morgan published his description of a mastaba tomb at Naqada, identifying it as the burial place of Menes, the legendary founder of the First Dynasty. Petrie's (1901a: 4) subsequent excavations at Abydos led him to reject this identification, albeit in terms that express uncertainty—still ongoing—as to the criteria upon which such judgements should be made. Following Petrie, the Naqada mastaba is sometimes considered to have been constructed for a queen called Neith-hotep, perhaps the mother of Aha, whose name appears on a number of ivory tags found within, their reverse sides bearing numerals (Spencer 1980: 63, cat. 450, pls. 46, 51). For an alternative view, see Kahl 2001b; 2001c.
[10] The view that the royal cemetery of the First Dynasty lies at Saqqara rather than Abydos, with the monuments of the latter site recast as 'cenotaphs', was first proposed by Walter Emery (1954: 1–4; 1958: 3), who excavated at Saqqara. It has since been followed and expanded upon by writers including Brinks 1979; Stadelmann 1996; 1997; and Lehner 1998. Key studies presenting an opposing set of arguments in favour of Abydos as the site of the royal cemetery include Kemp 1966; 1967; Kaiser 1969; Kaiser and Dreyer 1982: 241–60; O'Connor 2001. See also Smith 1998: 17–18, 255, n.14.

times the king's official persona was separated from his physical body through the creation of an effigy, displayed and rendered services until kingship passed definitively into a new living form. While the natural body was subject to decay, the body politic thus remained a 'likeness of the "holy sprites and angels", because it represents, like the angels, the Immutable within Time' (Kantorowicz 1957: 8).

The notion of an exclusive site for royal burials also poses substantive and unresolved problems of archaeological interpretation. Since the late nineteenth century no fewer than three distinct tomb complexes have been identified as the burial place of Aha, the ruler often equated with Menes, to whom Herodotus attributed the founding of Egypt's first dynasty and royal capital at Memphis. Distributed throughout the country at Saqqara, Abydos and Naqada, all three tombs are comparable in scale, material investment and complexity, and each contained many objects marked with the names of Aha and the high elite of his court.[11] The problem is replicated for each successive ruler of the First Dynasty, all of whom, from Djer to Qa'a, had impressive monuments at both Abydos and Saqqara.[12] A number of rulers—notably Den—are also associated by inscriptions with large but relatively isolated mud-brick tombs at other cemeteries, principally Abu Rawash (Montet 1938; 1946; Klasens 1961), Giza (Petrie 1907: 2–8, pls. 3–6; Jeffreys and Tavares 1994: 145) and Tarkhan (Petrie et al. 1913: 13–20, pl. 18; Petrie 1914: 3–9, pl. 18). All lie near Memphis, at the juncture of the Nile valley and delta, which was by then the main centre of population in Egypt (Jeffreys and Tavares 1994; Jeffreys 1998).

In view of this evidence, it seems worth questioning some of the assumptions underlying long-running debates over the 'true' location of the royal cemetery. Is there a sense in which the dead king Aha was present at Saqqara, Abydos *and* Naqada, and his successors at both the former sites? Or, to state the problem in its broadest terms, can we envisage a situation more consistent with the evidence, whereby the distribution of impressive tombs and their inscribed contents between the northern and southern parts of the country could take on some positive significance? Given that the body of the living king claimed contiguity with the entire country and cosmos, we might consider whether elite funerary practices sought to resolve the paradox of his death by making the dead king present on a similar scale.[13]

---

[11] Saqqara: Emery 1939; Abydos: Petrie 1901a: 4–5; Kaiser and Dreyer 1982: 212–20; Dreyer 1990: 62–7 (tombs B10, B15 and B19, with adjacent subsidiary burials); Naqada: see above, and Kahl 2001b: 178–9.

[12] A possible exception is Semerkhet, whose sealings are associated with a large tomb at Abydos but appear only rarely at North Saqqara (Petrie 1900: 13; Dreyer et al. 2000: 119–22).

[13] This possibility was partially addressed by Jean Philippe Lauer (1955) in a neglected article, in which he interpreted the tombs of Saqqara and Abydos as complementary architectural manifestations of a pervasive dualism in Egyptian royal ideology, which found continued expression in Third Dynasty and Old Kingdom pyramid complexes (cf. Cervelló Autuori 2002).

10.5 'Mapping the royal cult': aspects of Third Dynasty mortuary ceremony

Support for such an approach derives from slightly later monuments, notably the Step Pyramid complex of Netjerikhet (Djoser), which stands in the western desert of North Saqqara behind the tombs of the First and Second Dynasties (Lauer 1936; 1939; 1962; Firth and Quibell 1935). Dating to the Third Dynasty, the complex was the first in a series of royal mortuary precincts built almost entirely in stone (Lehner 1997: 84–95). Its main enclosure wall, the exterior faces of which were ornamented with sunken niches and false (as well as one actual) gateways, circumscribed a vast area of 15 hectares, and encompassed not one but two burial places for the ruler. The North Tomb comprised a network of galleries hewn into the rock beneath the Step Pyramid, which occupied the heart of the precinct and stood to a height of approximately 60 m. The much smaller South Tomb abutted the southern enclosure wall of the precinct. Inscriptional and pictorial evidence from within the two structures leaves no doubt that both were constructed for Netjerikhet (Lauer 1936: 27–46, 94–112). Extending between the tombs was a ceremonial court, and below the western part of the enclosure ran a further network of passageways and chambers, which may originally have formed the substructure of an earlier royal tomb dating to the Second Dynasty (Stadelmann 1985, but see also Roth's reservations; 1993: 43, n.40). This would imply an appropriation of ancestral space and resources, which seems consistent with the known contents of galleries below the Step Pyramid. They included over forty thousand stone vessels, many inscribed with the names of earlier kings extending back to the beginning of the First Dynasty, and hence over a period of perhaps four centuries (e.g. fig. 10.7: a; Lacau and Lauer 1959; 1965; cf. Baines and Yoffee 1998: 242–3). It is likely that these vessels were assembled from existing royal tomb complexes. Similar acts of appropriation are attested in First Dynasty tombs such as that associated with the ruler Semerkhet at Umm el-Qaab (Abydos), which contained a preponderance of stone vessels inscribed for his predecessor Anejib (Petrie 1900: 20, pl. 6).

The themes of movement and the regeneration of life are central to the decorative programme of Netjerikhet's pyramid complex. Two closely interrelated groups of limestone panels, installed beneath the northern and southern tombs, bear relief carvings of the king performing part of the *sed*-festival (e.g. fig. 10.2; Friedman 1995).[14] The emphasis of these scenes, reinforced by their distribution in space, is upon the ability of the deceased king to move between ritually designated locations, including shrines and stone markers signifying the geographical extremities of the country. These locations were also incorporated into the architectural scheme of the precinct

---

[14] For a survey of earlier evidence relating to royal festivals, see Jiménez Serrano 2002.

Figure 10.2 Carved relief panel below the Step Pyramid of Djoser, Saqqara, Third Dynasty

above ground, which—although celebrated for its monumentality—seems best understood as a small-scale model of the entire country, and by extension of the cosmos (F. D. Friedman 1996). Accordingly, rites of encompassment enacted by the king or his statue images brought the spatial extent of his political domain within the scope of his bodily action and influence. The subterranean panels show Netjerikhet carrying two objects as he performs the circuit of the Two Lands. One is a ceremonial flail and the other is thought, on the basis of later sources, to contain a type of legal document called the *jmjt-pr*, meaning 'that which constitutes the house' (Gödecken 1980; Friedman 1995: 24).

The royal mortuary cult thus provided a ceremonial matrix through which the abstract linkage of royal body and land was reproduced and legitimised as a concrete reality. Other rulers of the Third Dynasty pursued distinct ceremonial strategies for securing similar ends. Huni, last in that line, is thought to have constructed an entire network of smaller step pyramids from the mouth of the Fayum to Egypt's southern border at Elephantine.[15] At the latter site a complex of mud-brick buildings, interpreted by the excavators as the remains of a royal estate—and replete with bread moulds, beer jars and royal sealings—has been identified adjacent to the pyramid (Seidlmayer 1996a). If correct, this interpretation highlights the direct implications of the royal mortuary cult for the organisation of productive life in its vicinity. As Stephan Seidlmayer observes, the cult of the king's body may have served 'to make explicit and intelligible the ideological background of the economic demands' placed by the state upon local communities. If the programme of Netjerikhet's pyramid complex was to circumscribe the country within its walls, then Huni's mortuary project seems to have been a contrasting, but similarly motivated, one of 'mapping the royal cult across the country' (Seidlmayer 1996b: 124). Although differently conceived, both strategies reasserted the claim already apparent on the Narmer Palette: that the spatial boundaries of land and cosmos are contiguous with the agency of the royal body. I now return to the discussion of First Dynasty funerary practices, considering in turn the high-status cemeteries of Saqqara and Abydos. I conclude this chapter with some observations on the relationship between them.

10.6 Saqqara: mastaba tombs of the First Dynasty

A high escarpment borders the west bank of the Nile at North Saqqara, on the opposite side of the river from Helwan. During the First Dynasty this prominent strip of land was occupied by a series of mastaba tombs, their façades aligned along the escarpment edge, overlooking the northernmost sector of the Nile valley, before it broadens into the very different landscape of the delta.[16] David Jeffreys (2004: 838) notes how the tombs 'capitalise on the natural topography by being ranged prominently along the highest part of the cliff top as a kind of parapet, or a conspicuous continuation of the coursed masonry-like

---

[15] Dreyer and Kaiser 1980; Dreyer and Swelim 1982; Lesko 1988; see also Seidlmayer 1996b: 122, fig. 10.3; Lehner 1997: 96; Wilkinson 1999: 278, pl. 8: 1.

[16] Primary publications are Emery 1938; 1939; 1949; 1954; 1958; and see also Jeffreys and Tavares 1994: 147–51. For analyses of the architectural evolution of mastaba tombs, heavily oriented towards the development of later pyramid complexes, see Lehner 1998; Stadelmann 1997. Three-dimensional colour reconstructions of First Dynasty mastabas can be found at: www. digitalegypt.ucl.ac.uk/tarkhan/tarkhangreattombs/index.html.

sedimentary geological strata, visible even from the immediately adjacent section of the valley below'. The Arabic word *mastaba* means simply 'bench', and describes—a little disparagingly—the niched and painted superstructures of these tombs. Leaving aside, for the moment, the vexed question of who was buried in them, I focus upon the tombs themselves and their role within a wider politics of inclusion and exclusion, centred upon relationships between the living and the dead.

All mastaba tombs, with a single exception built at Naqada during the reign of Aha, comprised two distinct structural elements: a series of subterranean chambers, housing the burial in a central pit, and the platform or 'superstructure' that remained visible, but impenetrable, above ground (fig. 10.3). The subterranean chambers were hewn deep into bedrock and lined with brick, plaster, timber and reeds. Traces of painted matting have sometimes been detected on the walls of the burial pit, and at least one such chamber at Saqqara was faced with gold foil, embossed to resemble similar reed-work (Emery 1954: 11). Bodies, removed or destroyed long ago by looters, were interred in large wooden coffins, of which only the base usually remained. Slightly later examples suggest that the coffins may have been decorated with external niches, replicating on a smaller scale the outer appearance of the tomb superstructure (Spencer 1982: 166; Ikram and Dodson 1998: 194–5). Some burial chambers were subject to intense burning, but whether this formed part of the original burial rites is not clear. Throughout the First Dynasty, new features were successively added to the substructure, heightening the theatrical qualities of the tomb as a setting for ritual action. They included the construction of imposing staircases, descending into the burial chamber along brick-lined ramparts, and thus enhancing movement into and out of the tomb as a choreographed social spectacle. The completion of depositional rites was marked by sealing this entranceway with a series of massive stone portcullises, lowered on ropes: a dramatic act of closure, fixing in collective memory the relationships enacted during the course of the ritual (fig. 10.4).

A further phase of construction involved the establishment of the massive mud-brick superstructure with its foundations at ground level, encompassing the chambers below. In the middle–later part of the First Dynasty (reigns of Den and Anejib) an intermediate phase of building was sometimes introduced into the ritual process, resulting in the creation of a low tumulus or stepped platform encased inside the superstructure (fig. 10.5; Emery 1949: 82–91, pls. 21–35; 1958: 75–80, pls. 92–3).[17] The form of the superstructure itself was always rectangular, with the largest examples extending over 50 m in length

---

[17] Roth (1998: 999–1,001) situates these tombs at the head of a long tradition, whereby older forms of funerary monument were incorporated into (or 'nested within') the fabric of later mortuary structures, and traces this practice through the pyramid complexes of the Old Kingdom and beyond.

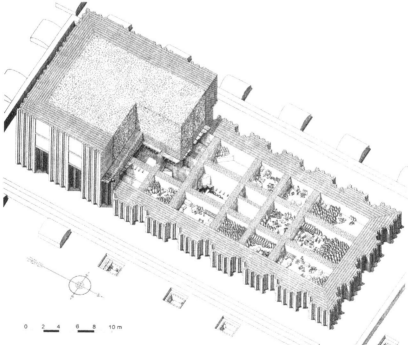

Figure 10.3 East façade of tomb 3357 at Saqqara with Step Pyramid of Djoser in background; idealised reconstruction of a First Dynasty mastaba tomb

Figure 10.4 Substructure of tomb 3500 at Saqqara, showing stepped entrance and portcullis

and standing more than 3 m high. Its hollow interior was divided into a series of regular compartments or 'magazines', the purpose of which was to be filled with objects, including vast quantities of food and luxury oils (presented in ceramic and stone containers), metal serving vessels, cosmetic implements and finely crafted furniture (figs. 7.7, 10.6).

In filling the tomb with objects, participants also filled it with the names attached to those objects, specifically those of kings, queens and high officials.

Figure 10.5 Stepped funerary structure within tomb 3038, Saqqara, reign of Anejib

Many scholars have attempted to distil the identities of particular tomb-owners or patrons from these names. Walter Emery (1939: 19) somewhat arbitrarily placed greater emphasis upon sealings than other types of inscribed material such as vessels and perforated tags. He later acknowledged the short-comings of this procedure, noting that sealings carrying the names of king Den and one or more high officials (Hemaka, Ankhka, Medjedka and Mesenka) were present in comparable numbers at Saqqara (tombs 3035, 3036, 3506) and at Abydos (tomb T; cf. Petrie 1900: 11, 22–5). 'There can be little doubt', he wrote, 'that the names of these officials appear on the jar sealings in their official capacity and certainly not as an indication of ownership of the object, much less of the tomb in which they are found' (Emery 1958: 3). Jochem Kahl (2001b: 184) suggests more explicitly that names inscribed or impressed on to grave goods may have served to identify the giver, rather than the recipient of the object. Noteworthy, in this context, is the presence of Netjerikhet's sealings in a tomb at Abydos dated to the reign of the last king of the Second Dynasty, Khasekhemui (Dreyer *et al.* 1998: 166, pl. 15: b).

In short, the names placed within a tomb cannot be used in any straight-forward way to identify its owner. Typically they refer, not to any one indivi-dual, but to a cluster of individuals—a collectivity, comprising a king, his successor, and between one and four high officials. In addition to hieroglyphic

Figure 10.6 Furniture fragments from tomb 3504, Saqqara

signs impressed with cylinder seals on to the clay stoppers of vessels, names were also painted and incised on to the surfaces of containers and implements, and carved on small tags that were bound to other objects (figs. 6.1, 10.7, 10.8). As in the earlier tomb U-j at Abydos, distinctions between these media correspond to differences in the type of information conveyed by inscriptions. In First Dynasty tombs—and by contrast with tomb U-j—these types of information are organised as complementary parts of a hierarchically ordered whole, unified by the distribution of royal Horus names, which were combined in each case with a different range of accompanying signs.

On cylindrical and small, baggy vessels, royal (and also some non-royal) names appear alongside the specification of a particular, prestigious type of oil or fat, accompanied by a group of signs meaning 'produce', 'delivery' or 'food' of 'Upper Egypt' or 'Lower Egypt' (fig. 9.15).[18] These inscriptions have sometimes been taken as evidence for the existence of an extensive system of taxation, based upon the regular levying of oil as a standard taxable resource, and the

[18] Saad 1939; Kaplony 1963: 292–7, 992–1,004; Kaiser and Dreyer 1982: 232–5; Kahl 1994: 99–104; 1995: 168, n.5, with references; Dreyer et al. 1998: 139–40, fig. 30.

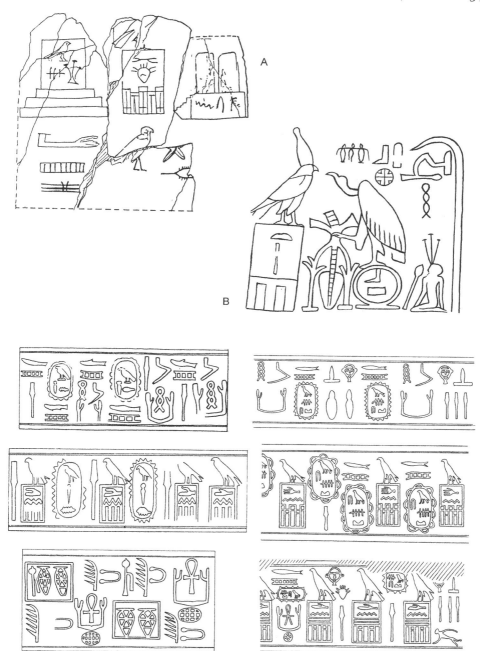

Figure 10.7 Vase inscriptions of (a) Anejib (from Saqqara, beneath the Step Pyramid) and (b) Khasekhem (from Hierakonpolis), and cylinder-seal impressions of the reign of Den from Abydos (left) and Saqqara (right)

Figure 10.8 Vessels with painted inscriptions giving the owner's name and indicating a commodity, from tomb 3507, Saqqara

division of the country into two units for administrative purposes (e.g. Kaplony 1963: 296, 1,001; Wilkinson 1999: 125–8). As Kahl (1995) has demonstrated, however, the terms 'produce' etc. of 'Upper' or 'Lower Egypt' were applied to a range of other commodities, and appear to be ceremonial, rather than narrowly administrative, in character. Sealings (fig. 10.7) did not generally carry information about particular products, which may have been obvious from the containers to which they were attached, notably wine jars. They were marked with royal names, sometimes accompanied by the name or title of an official.[19] On many seals these names were combined with enclosed signs designating royal foundations, including estates set up to provide for the mortuary cults of particular kings. Two different types of motif, one oval, the other rectangular,

[19] Williams (1977: 135, n.2) provides detailed references for the main corpus of First Dynasty sealings, which derives overwhelmingly from the tombs under discussion at Saqqara and Abydos, with relatively isolated examples from other high-status cemeteries in the Memphite region, and from a living complex discovered at Hierakonpolis and discussed below. See also Kaplony 1963: 49–153, pls. 9–84.

were used to contain place-names, which may also have served to indicate (by association) the quality of the commodity sealed. These motifs appear to correspond to distinct kinds of land-holding, and sometimes served to demarcate specialised functional units within a given estate, such as a vineyard or oil-press (Wilkinson 1999: 117–24; Moreno García 1999).

The most elaborate inscriptions appear on perforated tags (also referred to as 'year-labels') and encompass all the types of information present on sealings and inscribed vessels, adding two further elements: the quantity of the produce named, usually specified in hundreds or thousands, and a year-name, which refers to an event within the annual cycle of royal rituals that took place outside the tomb (fig. 6.1).[20] Kahl (1995: 171–2) interprets a particular type of tag, known both from the Naqada mastaba and a contemporaneous tomb at Umm el-Qaab, as showing the 'gathering in' of all kinds of produce—liquid commodities, livestock, bread—from 'Upper and Lower Egypt' (fig. 6.1, lower). The wider pictorial context is a royal ceremony forming part of a year-name. As he observes, the accumulation of produce to which it refers seems to have been a periodic occurrence, linked directly to the provision of the royal mortuary cult, and worthy of commemoration as a ceremonial occasion in its own right. The 'time' of administrative practice, insofar as it is represented in these sources, was not the mundane time of everyday production, but the ritual time of royal ceremony (cf. Endesfelder 1991; 1994).

Considerably more can be said about the external appearance of mastaba superstructures than about their internal decoration. Their outer surfaces conformed to an ornamental design known as the 'palace façade', comprising a continuous series of large and small niches sunk into the walls at close, regular intervals. The panelled façade of early mastaba tombs has long been thought by some scholars to derive from Mesopotamian architectural prototypes, also constructed in mud-brick, which were temples ('Houses of the Gods') rather than tombs, and therefore accessible to the living. The best exposition of this view remains that of Henri Frankfort (1941). As Roger Moorey (1987: 40) noted, however, this form of architectural ornament was common to elite funerary and living structures in Egypt, as demonstrated by the discovery of a niched gateway at the early dynastic town site of Hierakonpolis (Kom el-Gemuwiya; Weeks 1971–2; Fairservis 1986). The size of the gateway implies a building of much greater proportions than even the largest mastaba tomb. Its interior quarters, only a small portion of which are excavated, were distributed over two storeys, and included bread-baking facilities and evidence of administrative practices in the form of cylinder-seal impressions

[20] For further examples, see Petrie 1900: 21–4, pls. 10–17; 1901a: 19–29, pls. 2–3A, 8, 10–12; Emery 1938: 35–9, pls. 17–18; 1954: 102–7; Kaplony 1963: 284–92, pls. 143–5; Dreyer 1990: 80–1, pl. 26: a–d; Dreyer *et al.* 1993: 61, pl. 13: b; 1996: 73–5, pl. 14: d–e; 1998: 138–9, fig. 29, pl. 5: c; 12: a. For reasons that remain unclear, the production of royal year-labels appears to have ceased at the end of the First Dynasty.

(Brookner 1986). The excavators' identification of this complex as a palace appears to be based solely upon the appearance of its gateway, and remains otherwise unsubstantiated.

Niches on the exterior faces of mastaba tombs extended from the top of the superstructure down to the base or, in some cases, to a low mud-brick bench passing around its perimeter. The brick surfaces of the superstructure and bench were coated with a layer of wet mud, followed by a skin of white plaster. A low outer enclosure wall, or in some cases two, was usually constructed around the entire superstructure, forming a narrow corridor accessed through a doorway and concealing the lower part of the superstructure (and bench) from the outside. The superstructure itself was sealed shut following the completion of burial rites, and no point of access was provided to any part of the tomb's interior.

The 'palace façade' also provided the prototype for the *serekh* motif, first attested in the late fourth millennium BC (chapter 9.9). Accordingly the existence of similar structures, built in organic materials, may be assumed for earlier periods. It is noteworthy, in this context, that the superstructure of the earliest mastaba at North Saqqara (reign of Aha) was surrounded by two low enclosure walls and each of its niches was flanked by four postholes, some still containing wooden stumps, perhaps indicating that it replaced—or existed alongside—a perishable structure (Emery 1939: 13–14, fig. 10.7). Some such relationship is borne out by the painted decoration of mastaba tombs, which gave them a striking visual aspect. Traces of paint have been discovered on a number of superstructures, as well as on the mud-coated surfaces of the surrounding corridor. The original appearance of these surfaces is indicated by tomb 3505, dating to the end of the First Dynasty (reign of Qa'a), which exhibits a number of distinguishing features (Emery 1958: 5–13, pls. 6–8, 15–17).[21] These included a single, large subsidiary burial adjacent to the mastaba platform, where the inscribed panel of Merika (fig. 10.1, right) was found, and the extension of the tomb's outer enclosure walls to form an additional complex of small rooms, where the wooden statues mentioned above were installed (Kemp 1967: 26–9, figs. 2–3). Perhaps due to this exceptional configuration, the façade of the superstructure preserved on its outer surfaces an array of multi-coloured designs that would otherwise have weathered away (fig. 10.9). These replicate in precise detail the appearance of reed mats lashed to a framework of wooden poles, and have a kaleidoscopic quality that is at once mesmerising and disorientating. Positioned below them, riveted with wooden pegs to the usual type of low bench, were row upon row of

[21] Traces of paint were also present on the exteriors of tombs 3503, 3504 and 3507, and complex patterns were still visible on tomb 3121; Emery 1949: 116–17, pl. 50; 1954: 9, 130–1; 1958: 76, pl. 89.

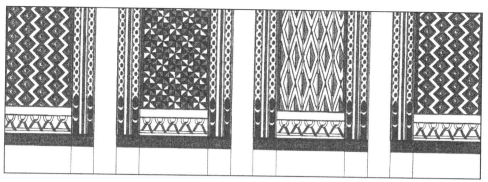

Figure 10.9 Reconstructed section of painted façade, tomb 3505, Saqqara

Figure 10.10 Clay heads with cattle-horns surrounding tomb 3504, Saqqara

large animal heads modelled in clay, into each of which was inserted a pair of cattle-horns (Emery 1958: 8).

Some hundreds of bucrania were discovered, still in place, around tomb 3504, dating to the reign of Djet (fig. 10.10; Emery 1954: 7, pls. 6–7).[22] A low enclosure wall surrounding the mastaba ensured that this ghostly herd could

---

[22] Bucrania were also distributed around tomb 3507 and horn fragments were found around the exterior of tomb 3506 (Emery 1958: 41, 76).

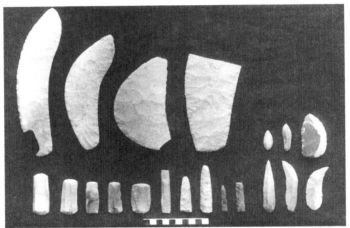

Figure 10.11 Granaries (above) and stone tools (below): tomb 3038, Saqqara

be encountered only at close quarters. Each bucranium was carefully located in front of a niche, emerging from the tomb to confront the viewer at waist height. The killing and consumption of these animals presumably formed part of the ceremonies surrounding the construction and endowment of the tomb, as further suggested by the frequent presence of cattle bones and elaborate flint butchering knives among the grave goods (fig. 10.11, lower). In tomb 385 at Helwan a pair of these knives, placed in a scissor-like formation, was found within an intact vessel containing remains of a number of cattle (Saad 1951: 10, pl. 7c; Hikade 1999).

Human, as well as animal, bodies were incorporated into the architectural scheme of mastaba tombs at Saqqara, forming a wall of subsidiary burials within or around the outer enclosure (fig. 10.3, lower). Over sixty individuals were interred around tomb 3504, their bodies aligned within long trenches divided into pits by cross-walls and sealed at the same time. Each of these smaller burials was roofed with timber and furnished with a small super-structure of its own (Emery 1954: 12–13, fig. 10.5).[23] Osteological remains from other funerary complexes of the First Dynasty, discussed below, confirm the practice of human sacrifice on a large scale in association with prestigious burials. A direct relationship between ritual killing and the establishment of the tomb is suggested by the contents of a subsidiary grave in which the individual was buried together with pots containing residues of green, red, black and yellow paint, traces of which were also noted on the mastaba façade (Emery 1954: 146–7). Other sacrificial victims were buried with copper tools, weapons and various types of storage and serving vessels.

The estate personified and immortalised

The niched gateway discovered at Hierakonpolis supports a long-held view that mastaba tombs were diminutive versions of living institutions, present and visible in the Egyptian landscape. Barry Kemp (1966: 17–18), for example, noted the small size of the door niches on mastaba façades at Saqqara, on average around 40 cm high, implying that they 'are only small-scale models of a much larger original'. The deposition within them of ornate furniture, lavish eating equipment and large quantities of luxury comestibles has often prompted the suggestion that their form replicates that of a domestic house or palace (e.g., recently, Lehner 1998: 191–7; Kahl 2001b: 183). Yet this falls short of a satisfactory explanation. It is striking, for instance, that alongside the trappings of courtly life, mastaba tombs often contained large numbers of craft instruments and agricultural tools. They included copper chisels, adzes and hoes, and varying quantities of prismatic end-scrapers and sickle-blades.[24] The presence within tombs of actual or model granaries also seems relevant here (fig. 10.11). Nine tubular grain-bins were installed within a brick platform located adjacent to the central burial pit of tomb 3038, their outlets sealed

---

[23] Twenty subsidiary graves were arranged around tomb 3503 (containing sealings of Merneith and Djer), ten around tomb 3506 (containing sealings of Den and various officials) and four (including one with a preserved, barrel-vaulted superstructure) along one side of tomb 3500 (dated to the reign of Qa'a; Emery 1954: 142–58; 1958: 46–9, 104). A further fifty-two subsidiary burials, all with 'knees sharply bent', were found around the First Dynasty mastaba at Giza (Petrie 1907: 4, pl. 6). At Abu Rawash, an unspecified number of subsidiary graves were marked with stone stelae bearing the name of the occupant (Montet 1938: 22–3), a practice more widely documented at Abydos.

[24] e.g. Emery 1938: 18–27, pls. 15–16; 1949: 24–48, 63–4, pls. 9A–10; 1954: 59–63, 66–8, pl. 34; 1958: 51, pl. 125.

with a layer of mud impressed with the seal of an official (Emery 1949: 85, fig. 50, pls. 29–30). Two rows of rectangular bins, still partly filled with emmer wheat, were built into the substructure of tomb 3500 (Emery 1958: 103, pl. 118). Both real and model granaries were also found within large tombs at Helwan (Saad 1947: 26, 109, pl. 11; 1969, pls. 86–7). In each case they were located within or next to the burial chamber, as also at Abu Rawash (Montet 1938, pl. 11: 2). Directly adjacent to the earliest mastaba at Saqqara, an entire miniature complex replete with terraces, store-houses and granaries was fashioned in mud over a rubble core. On the opposite side of this complex stood the remains of a wooden boat that had been encased in a low mud-brick tumulus, faced with plaster and gypsum (Emery 1939: 18, pl. 3; 1954: 170, pls. 57–9). Three more boats, including one that still contained storage vessels and a dismantled cabin, were interred to the north of other mastabas at Saqqara, and similar interments were made in association with large tombs at Helwan and Abu Rawash.[25]

The house that provided the prototype for the tomb was not the simple domestic unit. Rather, the mastaba complex constitutes a transformation of the extended household: a ritual space into which were crammed all the accoutrements and facilities of such an institution, from sumptuous living and entertainment quarters to granaries, boats, herds, store-houses, plantations[26] and also many of the people who belonged to it. The mastaba tomb complex was, in short, a model estate for the dead, encompassing (on a reduced scale) many of the functions of a living estate that was not simply a productive unit, but a source of life for its dependants. As on a living estate, those functions were divided between a human collective comprising the estate-owner, close kin, officials and various levels of subordinates whose survival—in death as in life—was contingent upon membership of this wider unit. The king, as owner of the entire country and all its wealth, must also be included in this group: all land-holdings were nominally his, and only delegated to others.[27] It is not surprising, therefore, to find royal and non-royal seals used in close conjunction on many of the objects found in mastaba tombs.

We are confronted here with a positive transformation, rather than a mere representation, of a living institution. Each tomb provided the focus for a ritual performance that reversed the normal flow of life and material goods through orchestrated acts of sacrifice and closure. Incorporation into the ancestral unit

---

[25] The Saqqara tombs in question are 3503, 3036 and 3506. In the last of these, the boat was provided with its own mud-brick enclosure, abutting that of the main mastaba (Emery 1949: 75; 1954: 138, pls. 44–5; 1958: 42, 49, pls. 44, 66–8). See also Saad 1947: 110–11; 1951: 41–2 (Helwan); Klasens 1961: 110–11, figs. 1–2 (Abu Rawash).

[26] Alignments of tree pits were detected adjacent to a number of mastaba tombs at Saqqara (Jeffreys and Tavares 1994: 148).

[27] The extent to which this was actually the case is far from clear, even for better documented periods (Eyre 1987; 1999; Baines 1997a).

objectified by the tomb was achieved through a contravention of the ordinary rhythms of living, ageing and dying. This was achieved through a controlled, collective procedure that superseded the timing of individual death and created a space that was sealed off from further intercourse. Boldly painted imitations of ornamental reed matting and vast rows of sunken recesses advertised the permeability and animacy of a structure that was in reality solid, static and protected. Reinforcement of the tomb's exterior with heads of cattle made explicit its aggressive aspect, and may have had specifically royal connotations, as on earlier ceremonial palettes (cf. Cervelló Autuori 2002: 45–6). Marking its outer boundaries, the orderly arrangement of sacrificed bodies identified the whole space of the tomb as a transformative one, where death was brought under human control and fashioned, through violence, into a generative force that emanated from its very surfaces.

The simultaneous capacity of mastaba tombs to captivate and repel, to generate life and to kill, would have ongoing implications for their role as containers, not only for human bodies, but also for objects consigned to them by the living. For the privileged few who participated in such transactions and survived, the world behind the sealed façade remained symbolically accessible as a layered structure, with internal parts as well as external surfaces, receding inwards from the tomb surface through a chain of replications towards the intimate confines of the burial chamber and body within. The same ritual artistry that protected the tomb from the harmful intentions of outsiders made possible its penetration, not as a physical movement, but as a movement of mind, anchored in the shared memory of past sacrifice.

10.7 Abydos: spaces of sacrifice

Close to the early dynastic town site of Abydos in southern Egypt, on the western side of the Nile, are the remains of a group of vast mud-brick enclosures, built adjacent to one another on the fringes of the alluvium (fig. 10.12).[28] Each is rectangular in plan and the majority measure approximately 90/50 m, with the largest reaching 130/70 m. Eight of these enigmatic structures—the interior spaces of which have yielded little clue as to their function—can be dated to the First Dynasty, and two to the Second. Their current assignment to particular reigns rests on minimal evidence and their relationship to the development of funerary architecture at Abydos and elsewhere has been a subject of ongoing debate.[29] Excavations under the supervision of David O'Connor (1989; and pers. com.) have clarified many architectural details for the known enclosures—first investigated in the early twentieth century—and

[28] Ayrton *et al.* 1904: 1–5; Peet 1914: 30–4; Petrie 1925; O'Connor 1989.
[29] e.g. Kemp 1966; Kaiser 1969; Kaiser and Dreyer 1982: 253–60; O'Connor 2001.

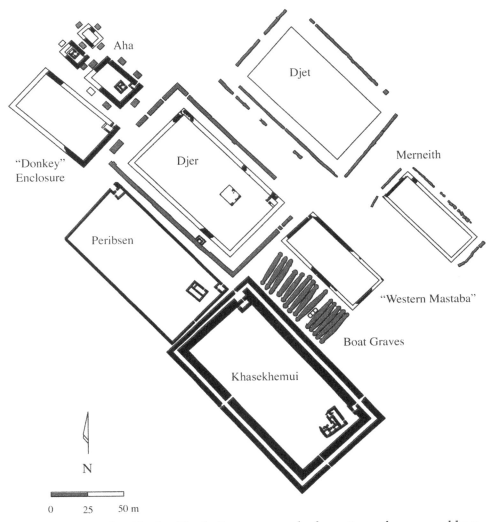

Figure 10.12 The Abydos North Cemetery: early dynastic enclosures and boat
graves

revealed the presence of three additional structures, probably dating to the
reign of Aha.

Two enclosures belonging to the earlier part of the First Dynasty were
surrounded by subsidiary burials, respectively 269 around an enclosure dated
to the reign of Djer, and 80 around another from the time of Merneith or Den;
154 burials dated to the reign of Djet demarcate a further rectangular area that
appears not to have been enclosed by a mud-brick wall. A possible parallel
exists at North Saqqara, where 231 small graves arranged in linear groups were
discovered in the Western Desert, a kilometre or so from the edge of the

Figure 10.13 Boat burials with enclosure of Khasekhemui (Shunet el-Zebib) in background

escarpment (Kaiser 1985b; cf. Wilkinson 1999: 239–40). Dating to the reign of Den, they were found to contain a preponderance of young and adult males, suggesting the intentional sacrifice of a particular social group. Petrie (1925: 8) favoured a similar explanation for the hasty construction of subsidiary graves around the Abydos enclosures, and suggested that the oddly expressive positions of some skeletons implied partial consciousness at the time of burial. These latter burial-groups may have circumscribed perishable structures or further mud-brick enclosures that remain to be discovered.[30]

The First Dynasty enclosures at Abydos are all severely eroded, a feature which is difficult to attribute to natural weathering processes, given their immense proportions (O'Connor 1995b: 328–9). Some indication of their original appearance is provided by the latest in the group, one of two dating to the reigns of Peribsen and Khasekhemui at the end of the Second Dynasty. Known colloquially as the Shunet el-Zebib, much of this latter structure still stands to over 10 m (fig. 10.13; Ayrton *et al.* 1904: 1–5, pl. 6; cf. O'Connor 1987: 36–9). Remnants of a niched façade that once covered its entire outer surface are clearly visible along its lower courses, as are traces of the plaster coating and wash that gave the walls their original, white colour. Periodic excavations

[30] Kaiser 1969; cf. O'Connor 1989: 62; Baines 1995: 139.

spanning the twentieth century have confirmed that the neighbouring enclosures of the First Dynasty also had niched façades and were similarly plastered
and painted. Like their later counterparts, they were provided with two buttressed gateways, one in the east and one in the north wall. On the eastern
façade, the niches followed the same intricate pattern used for contemporaneous mastaba tombs, but on the other three faces the smaller, internal
recesses were omitted (Kemp 1966; O'Connor 1989).

The Shunet el-Zebib dates to the reign of Khasekhem, who built another great
enclosure at Hierakonpolis. Traditionally referred to by archaeologists as 'the
Fort', the latter is the only such structure known from outside Abydos (Garstang
1907: 136–7, pls. 5–7; Kemp 1963; 1989: 53–6, fig. 18: a).[31] Like the Abydos
enclosures it was located to the west of a temple site, from which many portable
ceremonial objects of the early dynasties were recovered. Its construction is
usually attributed to a phase of dynastic rivalry that caused a temporary fragmentation of the state (see, e.g., O'Connor 1989: 84). During the period in which
his authority was restricted to Hierakonpolis, Khasekhemui (then called
Khasekhem) is thought to have constructed the Fort in anticipation of his burial
there, before going on to unify the country, at which time he built another
enclosure and tomb at the ancestral site of Abydos. This hypothesis is reinforced by peculiarities in the writing of Khasekhemui's name and that of his
predecessor Peribsen. The latter's *serekh* is surmounted by the god Seth rather
than Horus, while both gods are juxtaposed above the *serekh* of Khasekhemui,
who added the phrase 'The Two Lords are at Peace in Him' to his latter-day
name (Edwards 1971: 29; Baines 1995: 142–3).

The Fort at Hierakonpolis has immensely thick walls (c.5 m wide), which
still rise in places to their original height of 11 m. The single, imposing gateway is almost square (c.67/57 m), and its centre was occupied by a brick
building of unknown purpose.[32] Located somewhere within the enclosure
was a complex relief composition executed on slabs of pink granite, small
fragments of which were recovered from the area of the gateway (Lansing
1935; Alexanian 1998). The surviving pieces show the king wearing various
forms of ceremonial costume associated with his mortuary cult. On one fragment the upper part of a kiosk is depicted, and within it the *serekh* of Khasekhem and the tips of a flail and the White Crown are visible. The kiosk—first
attested on the Narmer Mace-head—formed part of the equipment used in the
sed-festival (see Alexanian 1998: 12–17, 21). Another related, early depiction
appears on an ebony tag from a First Dynasty tomb at Abydos, where it
constitutes the upper part of a year-name divided into a series of horizontal

---

[31] The identification of a brick-cased mound within the Shunet el-Zebib, which might have had
considerable implications for the evolution of royal funerary architecture (O'Connor 1991: 7–10;
Wilkinson 1999: 245–6), has proved erroneous: O'Connor 2001: 181–2 (postscript).

[32] Friedman 1999c; 1999d; Raue 1999; Herbich and Friedman 1999.

registers (fig. 6.1, upper). The remainder of the tag carries an inscription specifying a quantity of 'finest Libyan oil' and the names of two estates, adjacent to which is the Horus name of Den, flanked by the name and title of the high official Hemaka.

These vast, bounded spaces did not contain burials, but numerous features nevertheless invite comparison with the contemporaneous mastaba tombs of the Memphite region. Such features include the placing of subsidiary, and almost certainly sacrificial, bodies around a niched architectural surface, suggesting a common set of principles and procedures for demarcating ritually charged space. This comparison is drawn closer still by an enclosure at Abydos dating to the reign of Djer, which was surrounded by a low bench like those built around the superstructures of the Saqqara mastabas (O'Connor 1989: 65–9, 74–5, figs. 8–11). The subsidiary burials around these enclosures contained a range of objects broadly comparable to those found within mastaba tombs in the north, including ceramic storage vessels, cylindrical stone jars, flint butchering knives, copper tools and weapons, traces of gold foil, ivory gaming pieces and cosmetic implements. A number of graves dating to the reign of Djet contained model granaries—miniature versions of those installed within tombs at the Memphite cemeteries. Among the many inscribed objects were copper adzes and axes bearing the Horus name of Djet, which also appears on an ivory comb, below a boat—borne on wings—in which a falcon rides (fig. 2.5). Unlike the subsidiary burials at North Saqqara, at least some of those around the Abydos enclosures were marked by small stone stelae. Surviving examples are each inscribed with a name and title, one may write the name of a seal-bearer, and four wooden cylinder seals were recovered from graves around the enclosure dated to the time of Djer.[33]

Excavations at Abydos have uncovered fourteen boat burials occupying a space between the Shunet el-Zebib and the nearby enclosures of the First Dynasty (figs. 10.12, 10.13; O'Connor 1991; 1995a; Ward 2003). Each boat had a long, slender hull (on average 18–21 m long), assembled from wooden planks lashed together along a network of transverse channels. The hulls had been lowered into shallow trenches and then filled with mud-bricks. A low brick platform, echoing in relief the shape of the vessel below, was then constructed over the trench. Like the surrounding enclosures, each raised boat platform was coated in mud-plaster and whitewashed. It is not yet known whether the boat burials were created simultaneously or accumulated over time in relation to the building of successive enclosures. Whichever may be the case, these burials serve as a reminder that the static monuments today lining the edge of the alluvium once formed part of a

---

[33] Evidence cited here is briskly described and selectively illustrated in Petrie 1925: 3–7, pls. 1–14.

dynamic ritual landscape, in which motion—potentially over considerable distances—was both actually and symbolically important.

Umm el-Qaab: the dialectic of forms, names and substances

The ritual landscape of Abydos extended well beyond the fringes of the alluvium into the adjoining desert, which is bordered by an imposing arc of limestone cliffs (Petrie 1900: 2, pl. 3; Kemp 1975). Each of the enclosures described above forms one-half of a total mortuary complex, the second part of which—comprising a large burial pit, subterranean storage chambers and further subsidiary graves—lay approximately 2 km to the south-west at the necropolis called Umm el-Qaab ('Mother of Pots').[34]

The existence of a functional relationship between the Abydos enclosures and tombs is now almost universally accepted, and may be linked—by analogy with the decoration of the Hierakonpolis 'Fort'—to the establishment and performance of successive royal mortuary cults (cf. Alexanian 1998). O'Connor (1995b: 328) considers whether each enclosure 'might have been deliberately razed after the burial ritual was concluded or when the next great enclosure was ready'. This would account for their eroded state, and—as he further suggests—may have provided a mechanism for the transfer of mortuary endowments and personnel between successive rulers. Walter Fairservis (1989) floated the alternative idea that the enclosures, by analogy with widely documented structures in sub-Saharan Africa, served as animal pens, 'built to demonstrate in some regular fashion the cattle wealth of a given . . . monarch'. No evidence, however, has been produced to support this hypothesis.

The chronological sequence of tombs at Umm el-Qaab echoes that of the datable funerary enclosures, spanning the First Dynasty and the last two reigns of the Second, with a lacuna during the reigns of Hetepsekhemui, Raneb and Ninetjer. The substructures of Second Dynasty tombs associated through inscriptional evidence with these latter rulers have been identified at North Saqqara, and comprise vast networks of chambers hewn into bedrock.[35] Others may be obscured by the construction of later pyramid complexes (Giddy 1997), and one has been excavated beneath a private tomb of the New Kingdom (van Walsem 2003). It has been suggested that the Second Dynasty tombs at North Saqqara were also associated with separate enclosures, built in stone on an even larger scale than the mud-brick enclosures at Abydos. The groundwork of

---

[34] Amélineau 1899a; 1899b; 1902; 1904; Petrie 1900; 1901a; 1902: 3–8, pls. 1–15; Naville 1914: 35–9. Renewed excavations by the German Institute of Archaeology have refined and in some cases corrected many details of the tombs' construction, described by Petrie and Amélineau. The current work also includes conservation and reconstruction of some tombs, and the sifting of old spoil heaps, yielding many small finds; Dreyer 1990: 71–81; Dreyer et al. 1993: 57–61; 1998: 141–66; 2000: 97–128; 2003: 88–124.

[35] Barsanti 1901: 250–2; 1902: 183–4; Munro 1993; see also Fischer 1961; Dodson 1996.

dating and surveying the features in question—including the so-called Gisr el-Mudir, lying west of the Step Pyramid—is still at a preliminary stage, as is the exploration of the tombs themselves.[36]

The tombs of the First Dynasty at Umm el-Qaab represent the continuation of a cemetery lying near the escarpment, which was used without any major interruption since Naqada I times (fig. 10.16). The large, multi-chambered tomb U-j, dating to the late fourth millennium, forms part of it. Separating the latter tomb from those of Umm el-Qaab is a series of small, quickly constructed brick-lined pits, arranged in pairs and ascribed to the reigns of Ka (tombs B7/9) and Narmer (tombs B17/18) by associated sealings (Petrie 1901a: 7, pl. 59; Kaiser and Dreyer 1982: 212–13, 220–2). A second concentration of Narmer's sealings is known from a brick-lined tomb at Tarkhan, far to the north on the outskirts of the Memphite region (chapter 9.4). The construction of large-scale tombs at Umm el-Qaab was taken up again during the reign of Narmer's successor, Aha, which also witnessed the establishment of the first mastabas at Naqada, to the south, and at Saqqara, in the north. His reign established a trend towards ever larger and more elaborate tomb structures, which continued throughout the First Dynasty at Umm el-Qaab and was briefly resumed there under Peribsen and Khasekhemui at the close of the Second Dynasty.

The tombs of the first two dynasties at Umm el-Qaab have produced vast quantities of inscriptional data in the form of incised and painted pottery, seal impressions and inscribed tags (chapter 10.6; for pot-marks, van den Brink 1992c; 1996; 2001). Comparably large corpora are known only from the mastaba tombs at North Saqqara, and comprise essentially the same types of objects and information, relating to the distribution of centrally controlled resources such as wine and oil between members of the royal court. As at Saqqara, the content and distribution of these inscriptions, which were similarly attached to mobile grave goods, does not correlate in any simple fashion with tomb-ownership. Rather, it implicates a small group of principal actors in the endowment of each tomb. Furthermore, the same clusters of names, both royal and non-royal, recur frequently and on similar types of object at Umm el-Qaab and North Saqqara (cf. Kahl 2001b: 178–9). Since the circulation of these inscriptions cannot be separated from that of the commodities to which they were attached, this pattern of distribution constitutes evidence for a centrally organised flow of state resources—on a conspicuous, ceremonial scale—to burial sites far apart in the two halves of the country.

The tomb complex of Aha's reign at Umm el-Qaab differed markedly in plan from contemporaneous mastaba tombs (fig. 10.16, and above). It comprised three separate rectangular pits, lined with mud-brick and timber, and

---

[36] Swelim 1991; Mathieson and Tavares 1993; Bettles *et al.* 1995; Mathieson *et al.* 1995.

thirty-four smaller graves arranged in orderly rows to the east. The majority of these subsidiary graves belonged to young men, aged twenty to thirty, and at least seven lions were interred alongside them (Dreyer 1990: 62–7, 81–9).[37] The practice of human sacrifice, the ultimate demonstration of the 'right to control life and death', was taken to new lengths during the time of Aha's successor Djer. The tomb dating to his reign at Umm el-Qaab was surrounded by 318 subsidiary graves and a further 269 burials were distributed around its mortuary enclosure to the north (Petrie 1901a: 8–9; 1925: 3; Dreyer 1990: 71–2). Among the subsidiary burials around Djer's tomb, Emile Amélineau (1904: 227–33) discovered a number of corpses wrapped in multiple layers of natron-soaked linen, associated with the remains of wooden coffins (cf. Kemp 1967: 25).

Unlike mastaba tombs, those at Umm el-Qaab did not have storage chambers above ground. Their superstructures, if any such existed, may have comprised a simple tumulus of sand and rubble framed by a mud-brick border (Dreyer 1991; cf. O'Connor 2001: 174). There is uncertainty as to whether these mounds could have been seen above ground, and their remote location—set back some 1.7 km into the desert—means that, by contrast with their associated enclosures, the tombs themselves were never intended to be highly visible features of the landscape (cf. Roth 1993: 47). This may have been offset, in terms of prestige, by their spatial separation from non-royal burials and by the antiquity of the site itself (Baines 1995: 137). The panelled façade was present as an image forming part of the Horus names carved in relief on to limestone stelae, two of which marked the location of each tomb (fig. 10.14; Fischer 1961; 1963: 41–3). Subsidiary graves were also marked above ground with inscribed stelae, much smaller and more rapidly executed than their royal counterparts (fig. 10.15).[38] Many bore only personal names, perhaps implying that status was conveyed primarily in spatial terms, through their patterned distribution around a central tomb (Baud and Etienne 2000: 65). On the basis of their inscriptions, a full study of which is forthcoming (G. T. Martin, pers. com.; Martin 2003), Kemp (1967: 25–6) suggested that a majority of private stelae at Abydos were associated with graves of women (see also Kaplony 1963: 222–6, 886–942).

Like their associated mortuary enclosures, the tombs at Umm el-Qaab developed in a tight spatial cluster, forming a contrast with the linear arrangement of mastabas along the escarpment at North Saqqara. Their substructures varied widely in plan from one reign to the next, but all express the underlying notion of a central body as the focus of a larger, post-mortem social unit

---

[37] Baines (1995: 135–7) observes, following Dreyer, that the uniform ages of burials in this group imply something other than a natural cause of death, and provides a valuable general discussion of human sacrifice around First Dynasty tombs.

[38] Amélineau 1899a, pls. 34–7; 1904, pl. 18; Petrie 1900: 26–7, pls. 30–6; 1901a: 32–3, pls. 26–30A; Spencer 1980: 15–16, cat. 7–14, pls. 4–7.

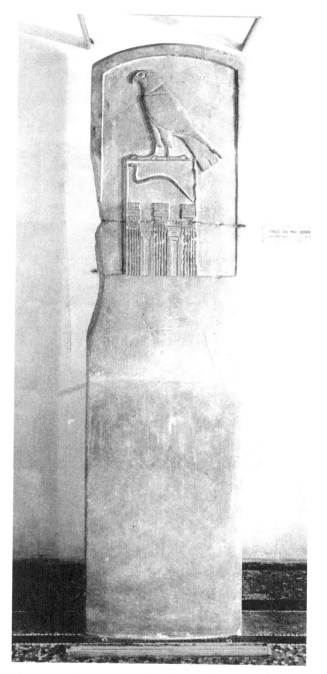

Figure 10.14 Limestone funerary stela of Djet, from Abydos, Umm el-Qaab

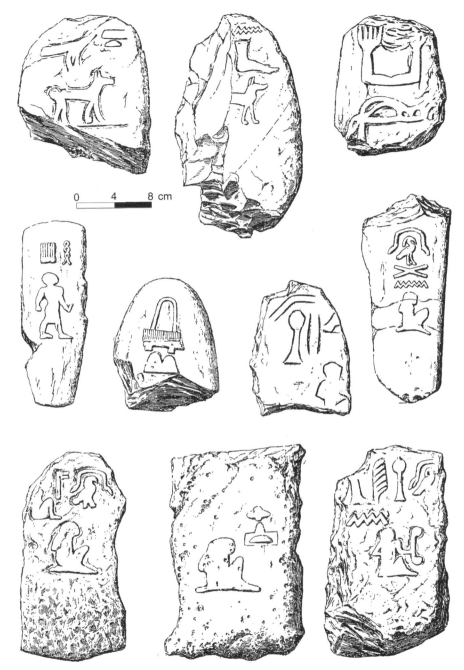

Figure 10.15 Private stelae from subsidiary burials, Abydos, Umm el-Qaab

(cf. Baud and Etienne 2000). In almost every case but that of Aha, an inward spatial progression can be traced from the protective wall of subsidiary burials to an inner circuit of storage chambers circumscribing the central burial pit. From the reigns of Aha to Anejib, subsidiary graves were arranged in separate groups at a remove from the main burial chamber, while during those of Semerkhet and Qa'a they were built directly on to it.

As at Saqqara, tomb chambers were formed through the accretion of reeds, timber and plaster over a mud-brick core. Paint was used in various ways to further enhance their internal appearance, including the rendering of 'false doors' and the daubing of courtiers' names on the walls of subsidiary burials (Petrie 1900: 8, pl. 63; 1901a: 8). Red granite, probably brought by boat from Aswan, was used to pave a large tomb dating to the reign of Den, which was also the first at Umm el-Qaab to incorporate a staircase and ramp leading down to the burial chamber (fig. 10.16, lower; Petrie 1901a: 9–11; Dreyer *et al.* 1993: 57–60; 1998: 141–7; 2000: 97–9; 2003: 88–9).

As noted, the surviving portable contents of the tombs at Umm el-Qaab are broadly comparable to those deposited at North Saqqara and in prestigious tombs elsewhere, providing further testimony to state control over skilled craft production, long-distance trade and the resources of Egypt's desert margins. Stone vessels, deposited in their thousands, were made from a wide variety of materials, including—in addition to the ubiquitous travertine or 'Egyptian alabaster'—many procured from the Eastern Desert, such as porphyry, serpentine, greywacke and dolomite. Copper was present in abundance in the form of serving vessels, tools and weapons, as were copious amounts of furniture and miniatures in ebony and ivory. Levantine imports included 'cedar oil', which is mentioned in a number of inscriptions, and may be counted among the unknown contents of elegant loop-handled flasks and 'metallic ware' storage jars.[39] Chance discovery of an assemblage of personal ornaments within the burial complex of Djer provides a valuable indication of one type of grave good that has not generally survived, as well as a rare insight into the treatment of the corpse. Still enclosed within the linen wrappings of a human arm, it included a bracelet composed of gold and turquoise plaques, each in the form of a *serekh* surmounted by a Horus bird (fig. 10.17). The same design was used for a faience bracelet recovered from a mastaba tomb at Giza, dating to the reign of Djet (Petrie 1901a: 16–17, pl. 1; 1907, pl. 3), and a further plaque, made of lapis lazuli, was found in more recent excavations at Abydos (Dreyer *et al.* 2003, pl. 16: b).

---

[39] When clearing the entrance to the tomb of Semerkhet's reign, Petrie (1900: 14) exposed an area filled 'to three feet deep with sand saturated with ointment'. He observed that 'hundredweights of it must have been poured out here, and the scent was so strong when cutting away this sand that it could be smelt over the whole tomb'.

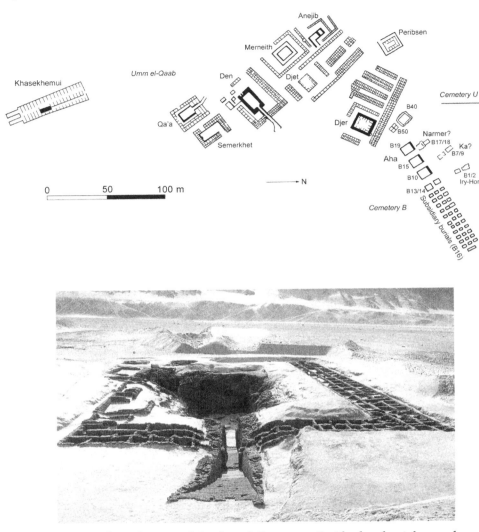

Figure 10.16 Plan of Umm el-Qaab and Cemetery B, Abydos; burial complex of Den

The scale of movement implied by the flow of goods to the tombs at Abydos and Saqqara seems pertinent in understanding certain marked consistencies in their architectural development, which have long been noted. In both cemeteries, the first tombs to incorporate monumental staircases and ramps date to the reign of Den (cf. Emery 1949: 7, 71–5; 1958: 37–49). Their substructures were built to similar scale and dimensions, and the further addition of a smaller flight of steps descending from the opposite side of the burial chamber is also common to tombs at both sites. At Umm el-Qaab this smaller stairway

Figure 10.17 Bracelet comprising gold and turquoise *serekh* plaques, Abydos, reign of Djer

led down to a sealed annexe, paved with granite and containing a limestone plinth, which Dreyer (1990: 76–8, fig. 10.8) has reconstructed as the base of a statue placed there to serve the royal mortuary cult. A further parallel transformation in the layout of tomb substructures took place at these sites during the reign of Qa'a, with magazines added at the base of the stairway leading to the burial chamber,[40] while vessels from the tomb associated with Anejib at Umm el-Qaab were inscribed with the image of a stepped platform, apparently echoing the design of a contemporaneous tomb (3038) at North Saqqara, and surmounted by the place-name 'Protection around the Lord/Horus' (fig. 10.7: a; Petrie 1900, pls. 8: 11; 46: 111–57; 1901a, pl. 55: 16–26). Rainer Stadelmann (1997: 23–4) considers the name to be that of tomb 3038 at Saqqara, which had a stepped interior (fig. 10.5). Ann Macy Roth (1991: 167–8; 1998: 998), following a hypothetical suggestion by Kemp (1966: 18–19), prefers to see this as evidence for the contemporaneous development of stepped tombs at Abydos, of which there is, however, no other indication. Given the abundant evidence for wider relationships between the Saqqara and Abydos cemeteries and their mobile contents, no such recourse to absent evidence seems necessary. Similarly inscribed vessels were also found beneath the Step Pyramid of Netjerikhet at Saqqara (Lacau and Lauer 1959: 16, pl. 3: 6, 7).

The overall impression is not of two separate necropoleis, defined in opposition to one another as royal versus non-royal. Rather, it is one of a single community of ritual actors, exercising extensive control over the land, its

---

[40] Emery 1958: 5–36, pls. 2–4 (tomb 3505); cf. Petrie 1900: 14–16, pls. 60, 66–7; Dreyer *et al.* 1996: 57–81 (tomb Q).

labour and its resources, drawing upon and enriching a common fund of material goods, knowledge, dramaturgical techniques, images, memories and presumably specific forms of ritual practice.

By establishing a tension between presence and absence—the invisible and visible aspects of the deceased's persona—the mortuary complexes at Abydos and Saqqara conform, in their essentials, to the dynastic construction of death, defined earlier in this chapter. Both expressed the idea that death and sacrifice give rise to a new physical structure that dominates the world of the living. In this sense, and also in aspects of its visual appearance, the mortuary enclosure was analogous to the mastaba superstructure, just as correspondences existed between their associated subterranean parts. Such relationships should not blind us, however, to the contrasting features of these monuments and their complementary roles within an evolving ritual landscape that encompassed much of the state. Unlike mastaba platforms, mortuary enclosures were hollow spaces, physically separated from the site of burial and provided with real entrances and exits. Their role within the royal mortuary cult went beyond the visual domination of space to encompass embodied performances—movements in time that extended the generative power of death into the rhythms of ongoing life, and constituted the body politic as a container of potentially limitless capacity.

CONCLUSION: SUBTERRANEAN HISTORIES OF POWER

Power is established on death's borders . . . All the agencies of repression and control are installed in this divided space, in the suspense between a life and its proper end, that is, in the production of a literally fantastic and artificial temporality.

Symbolic Exchange and Death, J. Baudrillard

In this book I have explored social transformations in Egypt from the end of the last Ice Age to the emergence of the dynastic state, a period of approximately seven millennia. By way of conclusion, I wish to situate my characterisation of Egyptian state formation within a set of broader observations on the distinction between ancient and modern forms of political authority. I will return to some of the wider questions with which I began, in order to consider constructions of political experience supplied by disciplines ranging from anthropology and sociology to modern history, as well as some of the challenges posed to them by long-term histories of the kind that archaeology provides. My focus is upon the central theme of the role of the 'body politic' as an image and framework of social power.

The origins of state power: disciplinary constructions

Writing in a less introspective age, the archaeologist and art historian Henri Frankfort (1948a: x) argued that 'the achievements of the Greeks and the teachings of the Old and New Testaments' are the basis of modern Europe's alienation from the ancient Near East. Today this seems a partial, perhaps even naïve, view. The political revolutions of the past three centuries, republican idealism and the experience of empire have all played their roles in making the history of *Homo hierarchicus* incomprehensible to *Homo aequalis*, to use the terms of Louis Dumont (1980). As William Arens (1979; 1984) discovered, in comparing forms of sacred kingship in early twentieth-century Southern Sudan and Renaissance Europe, the idea of the 'body politic' straddles a conceptual fault-line in understandings of the past: a fault-line which the study of ancient polities has often sought to bridge.

In European history, change is often understood in relation to the personal agency and fortunes of particular rulers. In the early stages of our education we are allowed to feel that we can know the minds of medieval kings and queens in a way that would have been impossible for most of their subjects. We have come to accept the idea that recent history was given meaningful shape by their successes and failures in battle, and by their ability to form alliances, make strategic decisions and control the dynastic court. From this vantage point, modern nation-states—whether they followed the path of republicanism or constitutional monarchy—may be seen as arising from the redistribution of rational control-structures. Once embodied in ruling individuals and their courtly advisors, such structures now appear to be generalised to the government of society as a whole through the expansion of bureaucracy and the 'secularisation of sovereign bodies' (Turner 1992: 139–59).

By contrast, anthropological studies of kingship in recent, but more remote, societies rarely tell us the names of those sacred rulers whose strange lives and still stranger deaths they describe. Political experience in the historical kingdoms of sub-Saharan Africa, Oceania and India is more often portrayed as if seen through a veil of ceremonial practices. Such practices are held to embody timeless notions—deeply held and experienced by political subjects—concerning the structure of the cosmos and the efficacy of ritual. The traditional focus of ethnography upon collective responses to moments of political crisis and transition amplifies this difference of perception.

There are, however, important exceptions on both fronts, inspired notably by the *Annales* school of European history[1] and in anthropology by various strands of Marxian thought.[2] It remains to be seen whether, in combination, these studies will lead to a new configuration of global political history. Marshall Sahlins (1985: 77) seems to imply as much in his observation that 'the conception of divine kings we find in Hawaii or Fiji also happens to preside over the subterranean histories of our own democracies'.

Established accounts of human political development trace present forms of democratic and republican government to ancient (Greek and Roman) precedents, or characterise them as the result of a long evolutionary process extending back into prehistory. A linear view of political evolution is supported by the use of terms such as 'archaic state', 'early civilisation' and 'early complex societies'. They define an ancient set of political values, held to be ancestral to—and yet categorically different from—those of medieval and early modern Europe, which in turn provided the foundations (and battle-grounds) upon which modern nation-states emerged. Sahlins's observation evokes an alternative, perhaps less reassuring, perspective on political history. It draws attention to the preponderance of extreme forms of hierarchy in recent times, much as Dumont (1980) perceived a continuum from the values of Europe's *ancien régime* to phenomena such as secular totalitarianism and forms of biological

---

[1] e.g. Bloch 1973 [1924]; Giesey 1960; Cannadine and Price 1987; Boureau and Ingerflom 1992; Monod 1999; Klaniczay 2002.

[2] e.g. Eckholm Friedman 1991; Meillassoux 1991; Simonse 1992; Gell 1997; Rowlands 1998.

discrimination—a relationship epitomised in the nineteenth-century writings of Arthur de Gobineau (see Smith 1984). In this context we might also consider the cultural strategies through which, in our own societies, emotional ties between subject and ruler have been overturned or redirected to distant spaces of the imagination. A pertinent example is the transformation of the Louvre from palace into modern museum around the time of the French Revolution (McClellan 1994). In an architectural space where crowds had once gathered to receive the miraculous healing power of the royal touch, citizens could now come to measure their own being against the exposed husk of a divine Egyptian king, at the same time measuring the body of the latter against his boastful monuments (Wengrow 2003c; 2005). Such processes of memory-displacement, in which the remains of 'exotic' civilisations play a variety of roles, have contributed to the formation of modern political identities in ways that remain largely unexplored (cf. Ozouf 1988; Hughes 1995).

It was the desire to reawaken a sense of the uniqueness and fragility of modern democracy that led the nineteenth-century scholar Fustel de Coulanges to go in search of the religious institutions at the heart of the ancient Mediterranean *polis*. He sought to demonstrate to his contemporaries that they had 'deceived themselves about the liberty of the ancients, and on this very account liberty among the moderns has been put in peril' (1901 [1864]: 10). Social scientists still recognise the result of his labours, *The Ancient City*, as a foundational work. In it we find the argument that the binding principles of political life in ancient Greece and Rome derived, not from democratic or republican values, but from much older institutions, specifically the sacred rites and customs that defined relationships between the living and the dead in the domestic household. In this underground world of ancestors, and their capacity to lay hold upon the resources of the living, Fustel identified the social foundations of the ancient city-state; and it was his pupil, Emile Durkheim, who later 'envisaged a sociology which (unlike purely historical work) would place the institutions of ancient literate societies studied by historians and classical scholars in a wider context of living primitive custom and belief' (Lienhardt 1966: 29).

The accompanying shift of perspective from past to present, which fuelled the practice of ethnographic fieldwork, has had both positive and negative consequences. While social anthropologists continue to trace their intellectual roots back to *The Ancient City* and James Frazer's *The Golden Bough* (1911–15), they have largely abandoned any serious interest in the long-term evolution of institutions. The interface between political and religious experience remains a vital topic of study (e.g. Bloch 1992). Anthropological perspectives on such matters tend, however, to shift with dizzying speed between local and universal scales of analysis, leaving untouched the historical formation of large political entities. From the viewpoint of the immediate present or short-term past, rites of passage often appear caged within particular social forms. It is society, conceived as a set of identities existing beyond the ritual, which seems stable, and to which initiates return upon completion of a rite of passage, their bodies inscribed with its marks of membership. Hence Victor Turner (1967: 110) urged anthropologists to focus on phenomena of 'mid-transition', which 'paradoxically expose the basic building blocks of culture just when we pass out of and before we re-enter the structural realm'.

Short-term perspectives on the role of ritual in social reproduction have provided the basis for general models of egalitarian behaviour, applied to a wide range of societies, both recent and prehistoric. The image thereby produced of 'tribal society' is commensurate with Durkheim's (1984 [1893]) notion of 'mechanical solidarity', in which collective ritual practices ensure that each member of the clan occupies the same social space as any other.[3] Pierre Clastres (1989 [1974]: 188) goes so far as to define the authority of the state, encoded in what he views as its most important invention—writing—as power that has somehow escaped the confines of embodied ritual:

Archaic societies, societies of the mark, are societies without a State, *societies against the State*. The mark on the body, on all bodies alike, declares: *You will not have the desire for power; you will not have the desire for submission*. And that non-separate law can only have for its inscription a space that is not separate: that space is the body itself. [original emphasis]

The predicament then arises: where does institutionalised political power come from? How does the rupture that leads from societies of the latter kind to hierarchical states occur? Clastres's enigmatic response to this self-imposed dilemma is that the sources of state authority, while rooted in human behaviour rather than environmental change, are nevertheless external to society itself. Their arrival on the historical stage took the form of a violent imposition upon communities that did not contain the germ of coercive authority. He draws no firm distinction between ancient and modern states in this regard. Both lie on the same side of a fundamental break with the long, egalitarian past; and the causes of that break remain, for the time being, mysterious. In Clastres's view, their analysis should proceed from the conditions that kept coercive power at bay for much of human history. Those conditions, he suggests, are most clearly visible among living 'tribal' societies, although he is aware of that category's many shortcomings as an object of analysis.

In formulating this argument, Clastres goes as far as any late twentieth-century scholar in making a case for the primacy of comparative ethnography over archaeology in the study of political evolution. His central hypothesis

---

[3] By way of contrast, Simon Harrison (1992) provides a lucid account of how the symbolic representations and knowledge condensed within ritual performances may themselves be subject to competing ownership claims, an observation borne out by the present study, among others.

exposes a conceptual void left by archaeological explanations of state formation, which for too long accepted the terms of an evolutionary debate that
originated through the study of living societies (see Yoffee 2005). As Clastres
himself acknowledges, the issues he raises are concerned most directly, not
with the present or recent past, but with the more distant transformations that
bridge—and are so often eclipsed by—Gordon Childe's two great revolutions:
Neolithic and Urban. No adequate term exists to describe this intermediate
phase; 'late prehistory' and 'proto-history' may continue to suffice.

When confronted with this crucial transition, anthropologists have often
abandoned the archaeological record, turning instead to models of political
change based upon the study of recent societies. By the nineteenth century,
however, many of the supposedly 'pristine' polities studied by ethnographers
had, as a result of dominant European interests, undergone what Kasja
Eckholm Friedman calls an 'involution of sacred power'. As she points out
(1991: 167), the 'powerless royal marionettes' described by western observers
were often 'recent phenomena': products of an imperial policy which sought,
in the interests of expedience, to reduce indigenous political institutions to so
many forms of 'ornamentalism' (Cannadine 2001). In some cases, societies
facing crisis and collapse imposed rigid sanctions upon rulers—ranging from
confinement to ritual killing—in an attempt to control and revitalise higher
forces that had abandoned them (Simonse 1992; Eckholm Friedman 1991) or
as a demonstration of intransigence to their colonial governers (Gell 1997;
cf. Rowlands 2004).

The 'state' against which Clastres's tribal societies struggled is not an
evolutionary phantasm, but the real forces of global capitalism and imperialism, radiating outwards from their heartlands in western Europe. Accordingly
there remains much to learn about sacred kingship: an institutional form
common at one time or another to much of the Old World, originating millennia ago at the heart of the ancient world system, and imploding on the margins
of its modern successor.

The early Egyptian state in context

A central aim of this study has been to reassert the primacy of the past, and of
archaeological interpretation, in telling the earlier part of that story, two
centres of which lay in the river valleys of Egypt and Mesopotamia. It is only
through close analysis of the actual remains of later prehistory that we are able
to demystify the process of state formation at its point of departure, by expos-
ing the multiple (pre)histories of the body that lie behind the creation of any
particular 'body politic'. In doing so, it may be possible to restore to the study
of early states something of its original character as a critique of the present,
such as we find in the writings of Fustel de Coulanges or the Comte de Volney,
with which this book began.

By rewriting the history of the body politic, we also redefine the scope of its theoretical antithesis: the magical hand of bureaucracy and its postulated role in the transformation of human societies. I have argued that the development of bureaucracy was largely a result, rather than a cause, of state formation in early Egypt. The centralisation of power, elucidated in the course of this study, took place much as Fustel de Coulanges envisaged it (rightly or wrongly) for ancient Greece; that is, through the incremental control exercised by particular groups over relations between the living and the dead. In Egypt, changes in the form of those relations were mediated, not through the social idiom of the domestic household, but principally through the extension of the human body itself as a framework of signification: a trajectory of development symbolised by the material signatures of later Egyptian prehistory—cosmetic palettes, combs, maces, knives, and a multitude of vessels and personal ornaments— the evolution of which has formed a guiding thread in this study. In tracing that thread, and by situating Egypt within a wider world of change and interaction, I have also tried to discern some of the hidden borrowings, social ruptures and ideological strategies that lie behind continuities in cultural form.

In the opening chapters I presented arguments against the notion that early states in the Middle East and North Africa arose from what Trigger (2003: 37) terms a common 'Neolithic *oecumene*'. Within a relatively small area of the western Old World—on the cusp of Africa, Asia and Europe—it has been possible to identify three clearly distinct trajectories of Neolithic social development, while more fine-grained approaches reveal a plethora of small-scale variations within their respective ambits. The initial domestication of plants and animals in South-West Asia occurred in a context of settled village life. In the Nile valley—from central Egypt at least as far south as the confluence of the Blue and White Niles—the reception of these new techniques was characterised by a contrasting shift to increased mobility, with greater cultural emphasis upon the circulation of animal wealth, and upon personal display for both the living and the dead. I introduced the term 'primary pastoral community' to summarise the core features of this cultural pattern during the fifth millennium BC.

Why, then, have earlier studies clung so tenaciously—and in the face of much countervailing evidence—to the view that social development in late prehistoric Egypt was rooted in the material and social possibilities of permanent village life? Part of the explanation, I have suggested, may reside in the avoidance of a problematic legacy of colonial scholarship, which sought to identify living prehistory among the cattle-keepers of the Upper Nile region, in Southern Sudan (see also Wengrow 2003b). More influential, perhaps, are romantic notions of pastoralism as an inherently marginal pursuit, bolstered by 'ethno-archaeological' studies of nomadic (and often impoverished) communities in modern, agro-industrial states. No less relevant is the pervasive emphasis upon urbanisation in late twentieth-century theories of social evolution, which has only rarely been combined with sensitivity to regional variations in the character of urban life. Here I have attempted to provide a modified account of developments towards urbanism in Egypt during the fourth millennium BC, based upon the patterning of the archaeological record rather than abstract models. I emphasised the social and strategic importance of ritual centres—especially cemeteries—as foci for the growth of settlement along key trade routes, as frameworks for the expansion of craft production, and as filters for the dissemination of new sumptuary values and codes of behaviour.

In the second part of the study I traced the appropriation of material and symbolic resources by local elites, culminating—at the end of the fourth millennium—in the political unification of Egypt, from the Mediterranean coast to the First Cataract of the Nile. I sought to show how large-scale political and economic transformations had their roots in small-scale alterations of the social environment, an evolutionary trajectory that can also be identified in Mesopotamia, albeit through a quite different set of archaeological traces and cultural contexts (Wengrow 1998). In both regions, the process of state formation may be elucidated via long-term patterns of continuity and change in the intimate material practices through which social identities were constituted.

In the case of Egypt, my analysis centred upon transformations within a relatively stable set of artefacts and implements relating to the care and presentation of the body, as detailed above. From Neolithic times onwards, this suite of portable implements, ornaments and substances was used habitually to define the boundaries of the person in life and death: its vulnerable margins and its possibilities of extension within the social landscape. During Naqada I–II (c.4000–3300 BC) pictorial images were widely employed to enhance the roles of objects such as cosmetic palettes, combs and ceramic containers as carriers of social knowledge. In funerary rites such images were used alongside a variety of new ritual techniques—including the dismemberment and distribution of body-parts—to form a composite representation of the deceased as a relational being, which was committed to the ground and transmitted to the living as an intangible memory-trace; a void in need of substance.

Towards the end of the fourth millennium, these same 'technologies of the self' provided the raw material from which emergent elites crafted an image of the royal body as contiguous with the margins of the habitable world. At much the same time, many of the object-types concerned ceased to be available in everyday life, and were replaced—for the majority of people—by a less elaborate set of bodily practices that affirmed the subordinate role of the individual within a hierarchical order. A similar, long-term process of cultural elaboration followed by widespread divestment and the confinement of display media to a small minority ('the evolution of simplicity') characterises the transition from Neolithic societies to early states in some other parts of the world (Wengrow 2001b; Yoffee 2005).

Royal ideology was formulated at a time (c.3300–2900 BC) when fluid social relations between Egypt and her territorial neighbours were replaced by new modes of interaction, ranging from the military domination of Lower Nubia to the use of prestigious—and hence restricted—forms of transport and communication in the Eastern Mediterranean. The common aim of these strategies was to redefine long-distance trade in terms of a moral economy of movement, conceived in cosmological terms and centred upon the person of the king. The absence created by this breakdown of regular contacts was filled by an ideology of the 'other', which can be seen taking shape in the decoration of traditional, but now highly restricted, artefact types, such as ceremonial cosmetic palettes, maces and knives. The legitimation of central power progressed in step with a monopoly over inter-regional exchange, which furnished elites with techniques of domination ranging from new methods of farming to new modes of consumption and signification, including the use of seals to redefine patterns of exchange.

A related feature of Egyptian state formation was the translation of ritual authority into durable forms of institutional and economic power, centred upon the establishment of landed estates—a process from which certain groups were excluded, most visibly in Nubia. Dynastic estates were internally complex and hierarchically organised social units, the integrity of which was celebrated and reinforced in spectacular funerary rituals. However, the bulk of their agricultural products—the plain, mass-produced containers of which loom large in the archaeological record—bore the external hallmarks of simplicity and anonymity. Furthermore, many of the technologies upon which new modes of agrarian production were based—such as plough agriculture and viticulture—were of exotic origin, and imposed a complex division of labour upon the workforce. An unprecedented social and cognitive distance was thereby established between the production of commodities and their deployment in socially meaningful transactions, including the presentation of gifts to the dead. It was within this 'divided space' that many restricted forms of communication, including the earliest writing practices, were developed. I have argued, accordingly, that the origin and early role of writing in Egypt cannot be adequately characterised as either 'administrative' or 'ceremonial'. By distributing signs of royal agency within the world of objects, writing—from its first stages of use—fulfilled both kinds of role, ordering and directing the flow of material goods, while at the same time redefining the social histories of the commodities to which it was attached.

In chapter 10 I focused upon the interpretation of royal and elite burial practices during the opening centuries of the third millennium BC. Here my primary aim was to elucidate a structural shift in ritual behaviour that accompanied the early development of the Egyptian state. This change centred upon the adoption, by the inner elite, of a new system of mortuary practices, which extended the physical needs of the dead into the time and space of the living. The new system was grafted on to—and emerged out of—an existing tradition of competitive funerary display, formerly based upon the orchestrated removal of the corpse and its accoutrements from the visible world. The alternative practice, of keeping the dead in the world as recipients of offerings and care from the living, incurred the negative possibility that they might suffer on-going harm and neglect. The emotional force of this relationship, which was subsequently extended to larger parts of society, remained a cornerstone of dynastic power in Egypt down to Graeco-Roman times and beyond, and it was subject to continuous cultural elaboration and negotiation among elites.

From its initial stages of development, during the early dynastic period (c.3100–2580 BC), this new construction of death had both private and public aspects, involving ritual techniques such as mummification and the dedication of cult statues—to which few had access—as well as the construction of functioning and highly visible mortuary complexes at various points within the Egyptian landscape. The resulting, open-ended relationship between the living and the royal dead provided the early Egyptian state with an ideological framework for extracting labour and local resources on an unprecedented scale.

An anthropological study of the 'symbolic roots of western bureaucracy' by Michael Herzfeld suggests that this seamless development from ritual-cum-charismatic to bureaucratic forms of control may not be particular to ancient or otherwise remote societies. Focusing upon European nation-states, he argues that modern forms of bureaucratic behaviour are directly analogous to the ritual systems of religions:

Both are founded on the principle of identity: the elect as an exclusive community, whose members' individual sins cannot undermine the ultimate perfection of the ideal they all share. Both posit a direct identification between the community of believers and the unity of that ideal . . . We may view the continual reaffirmation of transcendent identity as an effect of some bureaucratic labour. The labour itself is highly ritualistic: forms, symbols, texts, sanctions, obeisance.
. . . in a world where human beings make history, as Vico and Marx both argued, one need only ask what a disembodied bureaucracy could actually be to make the absurdity of such a notion fully apparent. (Herzfeld 1992: 20, 47)

The opposition of bureaucracy and charisma as distinct 'types' of authority and modes of rationality is enshrined in the sociology of Max Weber (1978 [1921]). It has hitherto been instrumental in defining the relationship between ancient and modern, as well as European and non-European, forms of social power as one of radical difference (cf. Peters 1989). In conclusion I offer some critical observations on these dichotomies, arising from the study of early Egyptian state formation. I argue that a long-term perspective allows us to take Herzfeld's observations a stage further, by exploring how, in a particular historical case, bureaucratic procedures arose through the extension of ritual control over the dead into the world of the living.

Bureaucracy and charisma: an archaeological perspective

It is a working tenet of much social theory that bureaucracy solidifies social arrangements, moulding effervescent political change into workaday routines and enduring institutions, and creating impersonal roles and functions for successive generations of individuals to inhabit. For this reason, sociology has tended to cast bureaucracy and charisma as historically opposed, though sometimes interpenetrating, forces. For Weber, the result of encounters between the two has generally been the same: in the long run of history, secular rationality and calculated material interests win out over the ecstatic fervour of the prophet and the revolutionary acts of the military hero. The 'monumentalised individual' may be the 'sovereign of history', but his reign is destined to be short, leaving little in its wake but stories and memories. The explanation for this trend is that charismatic power is opposed to rational or systematic forms of management; it is defined, as a historical phenomenon, by the transcendence or breakdown of institutional routines that follows in its wake (Weber 1978 [1921]: 956–1,005, 1,111–57; Gerth and Mills 1946: 51–5).

The logic of this formulation seems inescapable, but flowing beneath its surface are assumptions about the human body, and its potential as a symbolic framework for long-term political organisation, that rest, I suggest, upon shakier foundations. For Weber, the genuine charismatic encounter is always an embodied encounter, just as charismatic power is diminished by the death of its unique human carrier. Bureaucracy brings into play a contrasting process, which he called (after Schiller) the 'disenchantment of the world'. This amounts to the divestment of personal forces from the worlds of nature, objects and human relations, and is therefore also conceived as a process of disembodiment: the replacement of unique individuals and personalities by anonymous, time-transcendent roles and categories; of the body politic by the administrative machine (see Kamenka 1989).

The dialectic between bureaucracy and charisma undoubtedly captures the spirit of real historical transformations, and was intended first and foremost as a response to the ascendance of capitalist values and cultures of officialdom in western societies (Mommsen 1974). Implied within it, however, is there not the possibility of an alternative formulation, a 'routinisation of charisma' based not upon the disembodiment of social roles, but upon the manufacture of a charismatic body that is co-extensive with the socially habitable world and can be possessed by a succession of individuals? All successful systems of bureaucracy must look to some such stable reference point, a centre of moral or coercive force that allows them to exist as fluid social fictions and to insinuate themselves into the conduct of life and exchange through a latent promise that—should the need arise—fiction will be translated into fact, sign into object, obligation into action. I propose that, in the early Egyptian state, that stable centre took the form of a culturally constructed and reproduced body capable of transcending the vicissitudes of life and death, the boundaries of which were presented as coterminous with those of the habitable world. That body, the body of the ruler, provided a material core from which emanated further mechanisms and structures of control over people, households, land, goods and the dead.

This alternative formulation allows us to address a central problem that has arisen in the archaeology of early Egypt. As will by now be apparent, the raw materials for a study of administration and bureaucracy during the early dynasties derive overwhelmingly from highly ritualised settings, whose *raison d'être* was the chain of ceremonial activities set in motion by the death of rulers. This pattern of preservation does not exclude the use of similar materials and techniques in other, largely unrecoverable contexts, but it nevertheless requires elucidation as a phenomenon in its own right. Royal tomb complexes were places where wealth and—for a short period—life were sacrificed on a spectacular scale. Such activities, reminiscent of the North American potlatch, run counter to basic expectations of what constitutes bureaucratic rationality, such as the maximisation of material interests and investments, including those vested in functioning human bodies and minds. The many objects on which administrative inscriptions appear in early dynastic Egypt formed part of this 'economy of sacrifice', a phrase coined by Susanne Küchler (1997) to describe systems of economic action in which political value is generated through the orchestrated riddance or destruction of material goods, not to be confused with 'waste'. Such systems have most often been recognised in their twilight, on the fringes of colonial expansion and the modern world system. The archaeology of early Egypt stands as testimony to an alternative set of possibilities, whereby bureaucracy emerged in the service of a flourishing and expanding ritual economy, and developed in the context of a society where the orchestrated taking of human life lay close to the centre of political culture. On first appearance the juxtaposition of these two phenomena, bureaucracy and sacrifice, appears paradoxical. On reflection, however, do they not express, albeit in a different configuration, the same forms of control and extremes of authority to which modern states lay claim?

APPENDIX: CHRONOLOGICAL NOTE
AND TABLES

As discussed in chapter 6, the chronology of early Egypt is a *mélange*. There is at best only limited correspondence between the historical writings of later antiquity, pharaonic king-lists and annals, and the earliest preserved groups of royal names in the archaeological record. The latter must in turn be reconciled with a prehistoric time sequence, itself measured according to various relative criteria, including ceramic typology, spatial distribution of burial assemblages and an increasing number of stratified cultural sequences from Lower Egypt. These sequences are underpinned by a growing suite of radiocarbon determinations (Hassan 1985; 1986; 2000b; Hassan and Robinson 1987; Boehmer *et al.* 1993; Görsdorf *et al.* 1998), and by increasingly rigorous comparison with others in neighbouring regions, notably the southern Levant (Kantor 1992; van den Brink and Levy 2002). The formulation of an increasingly precise chronology from these overlapping sets of information is a work in progress, and a source of ongoing methodological and substantive debate, as reviewed in a number of recent works (von Beckerath 1997; Wilkinson 1999; Midant-Reynes 2000; Ciałowicz 2001).

The chronological framework for Egyptian prehistory followed in this book is the now generally preferred one of S. Hendrickx (1996; 1999), which builds upon and refines W. Kaiser's (1957; 1990) *Stufen* chronology, itself constructed upon the foundations of Petrie's (1901b) 'sequence dating' system. Since many existing publications use Kaiser's chronology, I include a table for cross-reference (Table 1, kindly provided by Stan Hendrickx), taking the morphological development of wavy-handled and cylindrical jars as a visual index of difference, both across time and between the two systems (vessel types are labelled after Petrie 1921; 1953). Three further tables (2–4) illustrate the chronology of early Egypt and neighbouring regions, tied in each case to calibrated radiocarbon determinations. Much recent debate centres upon the number of Dynasty 0 kings that can be identified in the inscriptional record, following G. Dreyer's remarkable discovery of an assemblage of inscribed labels at tomb U-j, Abydos. These debates, which expand upon issues raised by Kaiser (1964), are still some way from being resolved, and their chronological implications remain unclear. Table 5 favours a minimalist reading of the evidence for royal names, and tends towards a view that the earliest names written with (and in some cases without) the *serekh* may refer to the heads of regional economic and/or political units smaller than the later, unified Egyptian state, into which these same social entities had coalesced by no later than the time of Narmer (cf. Kaiser and Dreyer 1982; Baines 1995; Kahl 2001a; also chapters 8 and 9, above). For an alternative view, stipulating as many as nineteen kings of Egypt before Dynasty 1, see Dreyer 1998; cf. Williams 2003.

Table 1. *Relative chronologies compared*

	Kaiser 1957, 1990		Hendrickx 1996, 1999	
	–	–	Naqada IIID	no cylindrical jars
	50 t	Stufe IIIc3	Naqada IIIC2	50 b-c, h-t
	50 d	Stufe IIIc2	Naqada IIIC1	50 d-g
	48 s, t / 49 d,l 50 d	Stufe IIIc1	–	–
	48 s, t / 49 d,l	Stufe IIIb2	–	–
	47	Stufe IIIb1	Naqada IIIB	47 r-t / 48 s 49 d,g
	W 50 / W 51 a W 55 / W 56 g W 61 / W 62	Stufe IIIa2	Naqada IIIA2	W 55 / W 58 W 60 / W 61 W 62
	–	–	Naqada IIIA1	W 49 / W 50 W 51 / W 56 a,g
	W 41 / W 43 b W 47 g	Stufe IIIa1	–	–
	W 41 / W 43 b W 47 g	Stufe IId2	Naqada IID2	W 41 / W 42 W 43 b / W 47 a,g W 47 m
	W 24 / W 25	Stufe IId1	Naqada IID1	W 24 / W 25 W 27
	W 3 / W 19	Stufe IIc	Naqada IIC	W 3 / W 19

Table 2. *Major cultural sequences of the fourth–early third millennium BC:
Nubia, Egypt and the Levant*

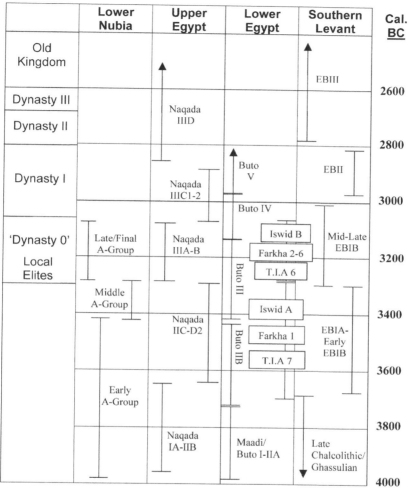

Table 3. *Regional chronology of Egypt and Sudan, c.10,000–2000 BC*

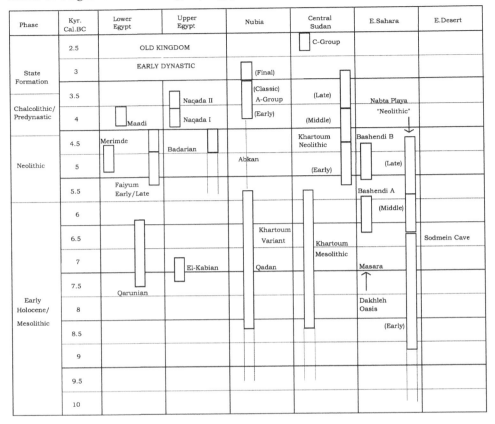

Phase	Kyr. Cal.BC	Lower Egypt	Upper Egypt	Nubia	Central Sudan	E.Sahara	E.Desert
State Formation	2.5	OLD KINGDOM			C-Group		
	3	EARLY DYNASTIC		(Final)			
Chalcolithic/ Predynastic	3.5		Naqada II	(Classic) A-Group	(Late)	Nabta Playa "Neolithic"	
	4	Maadi	Naqada I	(Early)	(Middle)		
Neolithic	4.5	Merimde	Badarian		Khartoum Neolithic	Bashendi B	
	5			Abkan	(Early)	(Late)	
	5.5	Faiyum Early/Late				Bashendi A	
Early Holocene/ Mesolithic	6					(Middle)	
	6.5			Khartoum Variant	Khartoum Mesolithic		Sodmein Cave
	7		El-Kabian	Qadan		Masara	
	7.5	Qarunian					
	8					Dakhleh Oasis	
	8.5					(Early)	
	9						
	9.5						
	10						

Table 4. *Chronology of Mesopotamia and neighbouring regions, c.11,000–3000 BC*

Phase	Kyr. Cal.BC	Levant	Middle-Upper Euphrates	Northern Mesopotamia	Central Mesopotamia	Zagros/ Khuzistan	Southern Mesopotamia
State Formation	3.5	Early Bronze I	URUK EXPANSION				LATE URUK
	4		LATE CHALCOLITHIC I-III				EARLY-MIDDLE URUK
	4.5	Ghassulian (Late)	LATE UBAID			Susa A	UBAID III-IV
	5	Chalcolithic	(Chalcolithic)				
Late Neolithic	5.5	(Middle)	Tell Sabi Abyad 4	HALAF			UBAID II Hajji Muhammad
	6	(Early)	BALIKH II-III			Sabz	UBAID I (Eridu)
	6.5	Pottery Neolithic	Tell Sabi Abyad 6	Yarim Tepe I Tell Es-Sawwan HASSUNA - SAMARRA		Surkh	UBAID 0 (Tell El-Awayli)
Transition	7	PPNC		Proto-Hassuna		Mohammed Jaffar	
Early (Pre-Pottery) Neolithic	7.5	(Late)	Abu Hureyra IIB	Tell Maghzaliya		Jarmo Ganj Dareh D	
	8	PPNB (Middle)	PPNB			Bus Mordeh-Ali-Kosh	
	8.5	(Early)	Mureybet IV	Nemrik			
	9						
	9.5	PPNA				Aceramic Neolithic	
	10		Mureybet IB-IIIB	Qermez Dere			
Epi-Palaeolithic (Mesolithic)	10.5	Natufian				Zawi Chemi Shanidar	
	11	↓	Abu Hureyra I			↓	

Table 5. *Rulers of the earliest dynasties*

Dynasty 0 (c.3300–3100 BC)
Owner of tomb U-j at Abydos (?); heads of other regional polities within Egypt
   (names mostly unclear; possible readings include Ny-Hor and Hat-Hor)
'Irihor'
Sekhen/Ka
Scorpion
Narmer
Dynasty 1 (c.3100–2800 BC)
Aha (= 'Menes'?)
Djer
Djet
Merneith
Den
Anejib
Semerkhet
Qa'a
(Sneferka: absent from later king-lists)
Dynasty 2 (c.2800–2650 BC)
Hetepsekhemui
Raneb
Ninetjer
(dynastic fragmentation: Weneg, Sened, Nubnefer)
Horus Sekhemib Perenmaat = Seth Peribsen
Horus Khasekhem = Horus-and-Seth Khasekhemui
Dynasty 3 (c.2650–2580 BC)
Netjerikhet (Djoser)
Sekhemkhet
Sanakht
Khaba
'Huni' (Horus name unknown)

REFERENCES

Abbreviations

AAR	African Archaeological Review
AN	Archéo-Nil
ASAE	Annales du service des antiquités de l'Egypte
BASOR	Bulletin of the American Schools of Oriental Research
BIFAO	Bulletin de l'Institut Français d'Archéologie Orientale
BSFE	Bulletin de la Société Française d'Egyptologie
CCdE	Cahiers Caribéens d'Egyptologie
CdE	Chronique d'Egypte
GM	Göttinger Miszellen
JAA	Journal of Anthropological Archaeology
JARCE	Journal of the American Research Center in Egypt
JEA	Journal of Egyptian Archaeology
JNES	Journal of Near Eastern Studies
LÄ	*Lexikon der Ägyptologie* (1972–92). Edited by W. Helck and E. Otto (Vol. I); W. Helck and W. Westendorf (Vols. II–VII). Wiesbaden: Harrassowitz.
MDAIK	Mitteilungen des Deutschen Archäologischen Instituts, Abteilung Kairo
NN	Nekhen News
OJA	Oxford Journal of Archaeology
PPS	Proceedings of the Prehistoric Society
WA	World Archaeology
ZÄS	Zeitschrift für Ägyptische Sprache und Altertumskunde

Abdel Tawab, M., Castel, G. and Pouit, G. 1990. Archéo-géologie des anciennes mines de cuivre et d'or des régions el-Urf/Mongul-Sud et Dara-Ouest. *BIFAO* 90: 359–64, figs. 1–18.

Adams, B. 1974a. *Ancient Hierakonpolis*. Warminster: Aris and Phillips.

1974b. *Ancient Hierakonpolis, Supplement*. Warminster: Aris and Phillips.

1987. *The Fort Cemetery at Hierakonpolis: Excavated by John Garstang*. London, New York: Kegan Paul International.

1988. *Predynastic Egypt*. Princes Risborough: Shire.

1995. *Ancient Nekhen: Garstang in the City of Hierakonpolis*. New Malden: SIA.

1996a. Elite graves at Hierakonpolis. In Spencer 1996: 1–15.

1996b. Imports and imitations in predynastic funerary contexts at Hierakonpolis. In Krzyżaniak *et al.* 1996: 133–43.

1997. Petrie at the cult centre of Min at Koptos. In J. Phillips (ed.), *Ancient Egypt, the Aegean, and the Near East: Studies in Honour of Martha Rhoads Bell,* 1–16. San Antonio: Van Siclen Books.

1998. Something very special down in the elite cemetery. *NN* 10: 3–4.

2000. *Excavations in the Locality 6 Cemetery at Hierakonpolis.* Oxford: BAR.

2001. Locality 6 in 2000: amazing revelations. *NN* 13: 4–7.

2002. Decorated sherds from renewed excavations at Locality 6, Hierakonpolis. *CCdE* 3–4: 5–27.

Adams, B. and Ciałowicz, K. M. 1997. *Protodynastic Egypt.* Princes Risborough: Shire.

Adams, B. and Friedman, R. F. 1992. Imports and influences in the predynastic and protodynastic settlement and funerary assemblages at Hierakonpolis. In van den Brink 1992b: 317–38.

Adams, B. and Hoffman, M. A. 1987. Analysis and regional perspective. In Adams 1987: 176–202.

Adams, B. and Jaeschke, R. 1984. *The Koptos Lions.* Milwaukee: The Milwaukee Public Museum.

Adams, B. and Porat, N. 1996. Imported pottery with potmarks from Abydos. In Spencer 1996: 98–107.

Adler, J. and Fardon, R. (eds.) 1999. *Orientpolitik, Value, and Civilization: Franz Baermann Steiner, Selected Writings* II. New York, Oxford: Berghahn.

Akkermans, P. M. M. G. 1993. *Villages in the Steppe: Late Neolithic Settlement and Subsistence in the Balikh Valley, Northern Syria.* Ann Arbor: International Monographs in Prehistory.

1996. *Tell Sabi Abyad, the Late Neolithic Settlement: Report on the Excavations of the University of Amsterdam (1988) and the National Museum of Antiquities, Leiden (1991–1993) in Syria.* Istanbul: Nederlands Historisch-Archaeologisch Instituut te Istanbul.

Akkermans, P. M. M. G. and Duistermaat, K. 1996. Of storage and nomads: the sealings from Late Neolithic Sabi Abyad. *Paléorient* 22(2): 17–44.

Akkermans, P. M. M. G. and Schwartz, G. 2003. *The Archaeology of Syria: From Complex Hunter-Gatherers to Early Urban Societies (c. 16,000–300 BC).* Cambridge: Cambridge University Press.

Alexanian, N. 1998. Die Reliefdekoration des Chasechemui, aus dem sogenannten *Fort* in Hierakonpolis. In N. Grimal (ed.), *Les critères de datation stylistiques à l'Ancien Empire,* 1–21, pls.1–8. Cairo: Institut Français d'Archéologie Orientale.

Alfano, C. 1992. Rock pictures of the Eastern Desert of Egypt (1989 Campaign). In C. Bonnet (ed.), *Etudes Nubiennes* II: *Conférence de Genève: Actes du VIIe Congrès International d'Etudes Nubiennes, 3–8 Septembre 1990,* 117–24. Geneva: Bonnet.

Algaze, G. 1993. *The Uruk World System: The Dynamics of Expansion of Early Mesopotamian Civilization.* Chicago: Chicago University Press.

Allchin, F. R. 1963. *Neolithic Cattle-Keepers of South India: A Study of the Deccan Ashmounds.* Cambridge: Cambridge University Press.

Allen, J. P. 1988. *Genesis in Egypt: The Philosophy of Ancient Egyptian Creation Accounts.* New Haven: Yale Egyptological Seminar.

1992. Menes the Memphite. *GM* 126: 19–22.

Almagro Basch, M. and Almagro Gorbea, M. A. 1968. *Estudios de arte rupestre nubio* I. Madrid: Ministerio de la Misión Arqueológica Española en Egipto.

Amélineau, E. 1899a. *Les nouvelles fouilles d'Abydos* I *(1895–1896)*. Paris: Ernest Leroux.

1899b. *Le tombeau d'Osiris.* Paris: Ernest Leroux.

1902. *Les nouvelles fouilles d'Abydos* II *(1896–1897)*. Paris: Ernest Leroux.

1904. *Les nouvelles fouilles d'Abydos* III *(1897–1898)*. Paris: Ernest Leroux.

Amiet, P. 1972. *Glyptique susienne: des origines à l'époque des Perses Achéménides.* Paris: Geuthner.

Amiran, R. 1970. *Ancient Pottery of the Holy Land.* Jerusalem: Massada Press.

Amselle, J.-L. 1998. *Mestizo Logics: Anthropology of Identity in Africa and Elsewhere.* (Translated by C. Royal.) Stanford: Stanford University Press.

Anderson, P. C. 1999. Experimental cultivation, harvest, and threshing of wild cereals: their relevance for interpreting the use of Epipalaeolithic and Neolithic artefacts. In P. C. Anderson (ed.), *Prehistory of Agriculture: New Experimental and Ethnographic Approaches*, 118–44. Los Angeles: Institute of Archaeology, University of California.

Anderson, P. C. and Inizan, M. L. 1994. Utilisation du tribulum au début de IIIe millénaire: des lames 'canaanéenes' lustrées à Kutan (Ninivé V) dans la region de Mosul, Iraq. *Paléorient* 20(2): 85–103.

Anderson, W. 1992. Badarian burials: evidence of social inequality in the Middle East during the early predynastic era. *JARCE* 29: 51–66.

Arens, W. 1979. The divine kingship of the Shilluk: a contemporary re-evaluation. *Ethnos* 3–4: 167–81.

1984. The demise of kings and the meaning of kingship: royal funerary ceremony in the contemporary Southern Sudan and Renaissance France. *Anthropos* 79: 355–67.

Arkell, A. J. 1949. *Early Khartoum: An Account of the Excavation of an Early Occupation Site Carried out by the Sudan Government Antiquities Service in 1944–45.* London: Oxford University Press.

1953. *Shaheinab: An Account of the Excavation of a Neolithic Occupation Site Carried out for the Sudan Antiquities Service in 1949–50.* London: Oxford University Press.

Arkell, A. J. and Ucko, P. J. 1965. Review of predynastic development in the Nile valley. *Current Anthropology* 6: 145–66.

Aron, R. 1967. *Main Currents in Sociological Thought* II: *Durkheim, Pareto, Weber.* Harmondsworth: Penguin.

Artzy, M. 1994. Incense, camels and collared rim jars: desert trade routes and maritime outlets in the second millennium. *OJA* 13: 121–47.

Asad, T. (ed.) 1973. *Anthropology and the Colonial Encounter.* London: Ithaca.

1979. Equality in nomadic systems? Notes towards the dissolution of an anthropological category. In L'Equipe écologie et anthropologie des sociétés pastorales (ed.), *Pastoral Production and Society*, 419–28. Cambridge: Cambridge University Press.

Asselberghs, H. 1961. *Chaos en Beheersing: documenten uit aeneolithisch Egypte.* Leiden: E. J. Brill.

Assmann, J. 2001. *The Search for God in Ancient Egypt.* (Translated by D. Lorton.) Ithaca and London: Cornell University Press.

2002. *The Mind of Egypt: History and Meaning in the Time of the Pharaohs.* (Translated by A. Jenkins.) New York: Metropolitan Books, Henry Holt.

Aston, B. G. 1994. *Ancient Egyptian Stone Vessels: Materials and Forms.* Heidelberg: Heidelberger Orientverlag.

Aston, B. G., Harrell, J. A. and Shaw, I. 2000. Stone. In Nicholson and Shaw 2000: 5–77.

Atzler, M. 1974. Einige Erwägungen zum *srḫ*. *Oriens* 23–4: 406–34.

Avner, U. 1990. Ancient agricultural settlement and religion in the Uvda valley, southern Israel. *Biblical Archaeologist* 53: 125–41.

Ayrton, E. R., Currelly, C. T. and Weigall, A. E. P. 1904. *Abydos* III. London: Egypt Exploration Fund.

Ayrton, E. R. and Loat, W. L. S. 1911. *Pre-Dynastic Cemetery at El Mahasna*. London: Egypt Exploration Fund.

Badawi, F. A. 2003. A preliminary report on 1984–86 excavations at Maadi-West. *MDAIK* 59: 1–10.

Baer, K. 1960. *Rank and Title in the Old Kingdom: The Structure of the Egyptian Administration in the Fifth and Sixth Dynasties*. Chicago: University of Chicago Press.

el-Baghdadi, S. G. 1999. La palette décorée de Minshat Ezzat (delta). *AN* 9: 9–11.

Baines, J. 1975. 'Ankh-sign, belt and penis sheath. *Studien zur altägyptischen Kultur* 3: 1–24.

  1982. Interpreting *Sinuhe*. *JEA* 68: 31–44.

  1985. *Fecundity Figures: Egyptian Personification and the Iconology of a Genre*. Warminster: Aris and Phillips.

  1989a. Communication and display: the integration of early Egyptian art and writing. *Antiquity* 63: 471–82.

  1989b. Ancient Egyptian concepts and uses of the past: 3rd to 2nd millennium BC evidence. In R. Layton (ed.), *Who Needs the Past? Indigenous Values and Archaeology*, 131–49. London: Unwin Hyman.

  1990. Trône et dieu: aspects du symbolisme royal et divin des temps archaïques. *BSFE* 118: 5–37.

  1991. On the symbolic context of the principal hieroglyph for 'god'. In U. Verhoeven and E. Graefe (eds.), *Religion und Philosophie im alten Ägypten: Festgabe für Philippe Derchain zu seinem 65. Geburtstag*, 29–46. Leuven: Peeters.

  1993. Symbolic aspects of canine figures on early monuments. *AN* 3: 57–74.

  1994. On the status and purposes of Egyptian art. *Cambridge Archaeological Journal* 4(1): 67–94.

  1995. Origins of Egyptian kingship. In D. O'Connor and D. P. Silverman (eds.), *Ancient Egyptian Kingship*, 95–156. Leiden, New York, Cologne: E. J. Brill.

  1997a. Kingship before literature: the world of the king in the Old Kingdom. In R. Gundlach and C. Raedler (eds.), *Selbstverständnis und Realität: Akten des Symposiums zur ägyptischen Königsideologie Mainz 15–17.6.1995*, 125–86. Wiesbaden: Harrassowitz.

  1997b. Temples as symbols, guarantors, and participants in Egyptian civilization. In S. Quirke (ed.), *The Temple in Ancient Egypt: New Discoveries and Recent Research*, 216–41. London: British Museum Press.

  1999. Forerunners of narrative biographies. In A. Leahy and J. Tait (eds.), *Studies on Ancient Egypt in Honour of H. S. Smith*, 23–37. London: Egypt Exploration Society.

  2003. Early definitions of the Egyptian world and its surroundings. In Potts *et al.* 2003: 27–57.

2004. The earliest Egyptian writing: development, context, purpose. In
S. D. Houston (ed.), *The First Writing: Script Invention as History and Process*, 150–89. Cambridge: Cambridge University Press.

Baines, J. and Lacovara, P. 2002. Burial and the dead in ancient Egyptian society: respect, formalism, neglect. *Journal of Social Archaeology* 2: 5–36.

Baines, J. and Yoffee, N. 1998. Order, legitimacy and wealth in ancient Egypt and Mesopotamia. In G. M. Feinman and J. Marcus (eds.), *Archaic States*, 199–260. Santa Fe: School of American Research Press.

Bakr, M. I. 1988. The new excavations at Ezbet el-Tell, Kufur Nigm: the first season (1984). In van den Brink 1988b: 49–62.

1994. Excavations at Kufur Nigm. In C. Berger *et al.* 1994: 9–17.

2000. Recent excavations at Ezbet et-Tell. In Z. Hawass and A. Milward Jones (eds.), *Eighth International Congress of Egyptologists: Cairo, 28 March–3 April, 2000 (publication of abstracts)*, 25–6. Cairo: Supreme Council for Antiquities.

Bakr, M. I, Abd el-Moneim, M. A. M. and Selim, M. O. M. 1996. Protodynastic excavations at Tell Hassan Dawud (eastern delta). In Krzyżaniak *et al.* 1996: 277–8.

Bar-Adon, P. 1980. *The Cave of Treasure: The Finds from the Caves in Nahal Mishmar*. Jerusalem: Israel Exploration Society.

Bar-Yosef, D. E. 1991. Changes in the selection of marine shells from the Natufian to the Neolithic. In Bar-Yosef and Valla 1991: 629–36.

Bar-Yosef, O. and Belfer-Cohen, A. 1989. The origins of sedentism and farming communities in the Levant. *Journal of World Prehistory* 3: 447–98.

Bar-Yosef, O. and Khazanov, A. (eds.) 1992. *Pastoralism in the Levant: Archaeological Materials in Anthropological Perspective*. Madison: Prehistory Press.

Bar-Yosef, O. and Meadow, R. H. 1995. The origins of agriculture in the Near East. In T. D. Price and A. B. Gebauer (eds.), *Last Hunters, First Farmers: New Perspectives on the Prehistoric Transition to Agriculture*, 39–94. Sante Fe: School of American Research Press.

Bar-Yosef, O. and Tchernov, E. 1970. The Natufian bone industry of Hayonim Cave. *Israel Exploration Journal* 20: 141–50.

Bar-Yosef, O. and Valla, F. R. (eds.) 1991. *The Natufian Culture in the Levant*. Ann Arbor: International Monographs in Prehistory.

Barakat, H. 1990. Plant remains from el-Omari. In Debono and Mortensen 1990: 109–14.

Bard, K. 1987. The geography of excavated predynastic sites and the rise of complex society. *JARCE* 24: 81–93.

1989. Predynastic settlement patterns in the Hu-Semaineh region, Egypt. *Journal of Field Archaeology* 16: 475–8.

1994a. The Egyptian predynastic: a review of the evidence. *Journal of Field Archaeology* 21: 265–88.

1994b. *From Farmers to Pharaohs: Mortuary Evidence for the Rise of Complex Society in Egypt*. Sheffield: Sheffield Academic Press.

Barocas, C., Fattovitch, R. and Tosi, M. 1989. The Oriental Institute of Naples expedition to Petrie's South Town (Upper Egypt), 1977–83: an interim report. In Krzyżaniak and Kobusiewicz 1989: 295–301.

Barsanti, A. 1901. Rapports sur les déblaiements opérés autour de la pyramide d'Ounas, pendant les années 1899–1901. *ASAE* 2: 244–57.

1902. Fouilles autour de la pyramide d'Ounas (1901–1902). *ASAE* 3: 182–4.

Barta, W. 1972. Der Königsring als Symbol zyklischer Wiederkehr. *ZÄS* 98: 5–16.

Battaglia, D. 1990. *On the Bones of the Serpent: Person, Memory and Mortality in Sabarl Island Society.* Chicago: University of Chicago Press.

Baud, M. 1999. Ménès, la mémoire monarchique et la chronologie du IIIe millénaire. *AN* 9: 109–21.

2003. Review of T. A. H. Wilkinson, *Royal Annals of Ancient Egypt: The Palermo Stone and its Associated Fragments. CdE* 78: 145–8.

Baud, M. and Dobrev, V. 1995. De nouvelles annales de l'Ancien Empire égyptien: une 'Pierre de Palerme' pour la VIe dynastie. *BIFAO* 95: 23–92.

1997. Le verso des annales de la VIe dynastie: Pierre de Saqqara-Sud. *BIFAO* 97: 35–42.

Baud, M. and Etienne, M. 2000. Le vanneau et le couteau: un rituel monarchique sacrificiel dans l'Egypte de la Ie dynastie. *AN* 10: 55–78.

Baudrillard, J. 1993. *Symbolic Exchange and Death.* (Translated by I. H. Grant.) London: Sage.

Baumgartel, E. J. 1955. *The Cultures of Prehistoric Egypt.* London: Oxford University Press for Griffith Institute.

1960. *The Cultures of Prehistoric Egypt* II. London: Oxford University Press for Griffith Institute.

1970. *Petrie's Naqada Excavation: A Supplement.* London: Bernard Quaritch.

Belfer-Cohen, A. 1988. The Natufian graveyard in Hayonim Cave. *Paléorient* 14: 297–308.

Ben-Tor, A. 1971. The date of the Kfar Monash hoard. *Israel Exploration Journal* 21: 201–6.

1973. Plans of dwellings and temples in Early Bronze Age Palestine. *Eretz Israel* 11: 91–7 (with English summary).

1975. Two burial caves of the proto-urban period at Azor, 1971. *Qedem* 1: 1–53.

1991. New light on the relations between Egypt and southern Palestine during the Early Bronze Age. *BASOR* 281: 3–10.

1992. The Early Bronze Age. In A. Ben-Tor (ed.), *The Archaeology of Ancient Israel*, 81–125. New Haven: Yale University Press.

Bender, B. 1989. The roots of inequality. In Miller *et al.* 1989: 83–95.

Bénédite, G. 1916. Le couteau de Gebel el Arak: étude sur un nouvel objet préhistorique acquis par le musée du Louvre. *Fondation Eugène Piot, Monuments et Mémoires* 22: 1–34.

1918. The Carnavon ivory. *JEA* 5: 1–15, 225–41.

Berger, C., Clerc, G. and Grimal, N.-C. (eds.) 1994. *Hommages à Jean Leclant* IV. Cairo: Institut Français d'Archéologie Orientale du Caire.

Berger, M. A. 1982. The petroglyphs of Locality 61. In Hoffman *et al.* 1982: 61–5.

1992. Predynastic animal-headed boats from Hierakonpolis and southern Egypt. In Friedman and Adams 1992: 107–20.

Bettles, E., Clarke, J., Dittmer, J., Duhig, C., Ikram, S., Mathieson, I., Smith, H. and Tavares, A. 1995. *National Museums of Scotland Saqqara Project Report 1995.* Edinburgh: National Museums of Scotland.

Bevan, A. 2003. Reconstructing the role of Egyptian culture in the value regimes of the Bronze Age Aegean: stone vessels and their social contexts. In Matthews and Roemer 2003: 57–75.

Bietak, M. (ed.) 1996. *Haus und Palast im alten Ägypten/ House and Palace in Ancient Egypt.* Vienna: Österreichische Akademie der Wissenschaften.

Bietak, M. and Engelmayer, R. 1963. *Eine früdynastische Abri-Siedlung mit Felsbilden aus Sayala-Nubien.* Vienna: Hermann Böhlau.

Blench, R. M. and MacDonald, K. C. 2000. *The Origins and Development of African Livestock: Archaeology, Genetics, Linguistics and Ethnography.* London: University College London Press.

Bloch, M. 1973 [1924]. *The Royal Touch: Sacred Monarchy and Scrofula in England and France.* (Translated by J. E. Anderson.) London: Routledge and Kegan Paul.

Bloch, M. 1986. *From Blessing to Violence: History and Ideology in the Circumcision Ritual of the Merina of Madagascar.* Cambridge: Cambridge University Press.

1987. The ritual of the royal bath in Madagascar: the dissolution of death, birth and fertility into authority. In Cannadine and Price 1987: 271–97.

1992. *Prey into Hunter: The Politics of Religious Experience.* Cambridge: Cambridge University Press.

1998. *How We Think They Think: Anthropological Approaches to Cognition, Memory, and Literacy.* Boulder: Westview.

Bloch, M. and Parry, J. P. (eds.) 1982. *Death and the Regeneration of Life.* Cambridge: Cambridge University Press.

Boas, F. 1955 [1927]. *Primitive Art.* New York: Dover.

Boehmer, R. M. 1974a. Das Rollsiegel im prädynastischen Ägypten. *Archäologischer Anzeiger* 4: 495–514.

1974b. Orientalische Einflüsse auf verzierten Messergriffen aus dem prädynastichen Ägypten. *Archäologischen Mitteilungen aus Iran* 7: 15–40.

1991. Gebel-el-Arak-und Gebel-el-Tarif-Griff: keine Fälschungen. *MDAIK* 47: 51–60.

1999. *Uruk: früheste Siegelabrollungen.* Mainz am Rhein: Philipp von Zabern. 47: 51–60.

Boehmer, R. M., Dreyer, G. and Kromer, B. 1993. Einige frühzeitliche 14C-Datierungen aus Abydos and Uruk. *MDAIK* 49: 63–8.

Boessneck, J., von den Driesch, A. and Ziegler, R. 1989. Die Tierreste von Maadi und dem Friedhof am Wadi Digla. In Rizkana and Seeher 1989: 87–128.

Bolshakov, A. 1997. *Man and his Double in Egyptian Ideology of the Old Kingdom.* Wiesbaden: Harrassowitz.

Bourdieu, P. 1977. *Outline of a Theory of Practice.* (Translated by R. Nice.) Cambridge: Cambridge University Press.

Boureau, A. and Ingerflom, C. S. 1992. *La royauté sacrée dans le monde chrétien.* Paris: Ecole des Hautes Etudes en Sciences Sociales.

Bourriau, J. 1981. *Umm El-Gaab: Pottery from the Nile Valley before the Arab Conquest.* Exhibition catalogue. Cambridge: Cambridge University Press.

Bourriau, J., Nicholson, P. and Rose, P. 2000. Pottery. In Nicholson and Shaw 2000: 121–47.

Bowman, A. K. and Rogan, E. L. (eds.) 1999. *Agriculture in Egypt, from Pharaonic to Modern Times.* Oxford: Oxford University Press for the British Academy.

Boyd, B. 1995. Houses and hearths, pits and burials: Natufian mortuary practices at Mallaha (Eynan), Upper Jordan valley. In Campbell and Green 1995: 17–23.

Boyer, P. 1994. *The Naturalness of Religious Ideas: A Cognitive Theory of Religion.* Berkeley: University of California Press.

1996. What makes anthropomorphism natural: intuitive ontology and cultural representations. *Journal of the Royal Anthropological Institute* (N. S.) 2: 83–97.

Bradley, D. G. and Loftus, R. 2000. Two Eves for *taurus*? Bovine mitochondrial DNA and African cattle domestication. In Blench and MacDonald 2000: 244–51.

Braidwood, R. J. and Howe, B. 1960. *Prehistoric Investigations in Iraqi Kurdistan.* Chicago: University of Chicago Press.

Brandes, M. 1979. *Siegelabrollungen aus den archäischen Bauschichten in Uruk-Warka.* Wiesbaden: Franz Steiner.

Braudel, F. 1985. *Civilization and Capitalism, 15ᵗʰ–18ᵗʰ Century* I: *The Structures of Everyday Life: The Limits to the Possible.* London: Collins.

Braun, E. 1985. *En Shadud: Salvage Excavations at a Farming Community in the Jezreel Valley, Israel.* Oxford: BAR.

1989. The problem of the apsidal house: new aspects of Early Bronze I domestic architecture in Israel, Jordan, and Lebanon. *Palestine Exploration Quarterly* 121: 1–43.

Braun, E. and van den Brink, E. C. M. 1998. Some comments on the Late EBI sequence of Canaan and the relative dating of tomb U-j at Umm el-Ga'ab and Graves 313 and 787 from Minshat Abu Omar with imported ware: views from Egypt and Canaan. *Ägypten und Levante* 7: 71–94.

Bret, P. 1999. *L'Expédition d'Egypte, une entreprise des Lumières, 1798–1801: actes du colloque international.* Paris: Technique et Documentation.

Brewer, D. J. 1989a. A model for resource exploitation in the prehistoric Fayum. In Krzyżaniak and Kobusiewicz 1989: 127–38.

1989b. *Fishermen, Hunters, Herders: Zooarchaeology in the Fayum, Egypt (c.8200–5000 bp).* Oxford: BAR.

Breyer, F. A. K. 2002. Die Schriftzeugnisse des prädynastichen Königsgrabes U-j in Umm el-Qaab: Versuch einer Neuinterpretation. *JEA* 88: 53–65.

Brinks, J. 1979. *Die Entwicklung der königlichen Grabanlagen des Alten Reiches.* Hildesheim: Gerstenberg.

Brookner, J. 1986. The Archaic period sealings. In Fairservis 1986: 24–6.

Brown, E. A. R. 1981. Death and the human body in the later Middle Ages: the legislation of Boniface VIII on the division of the corpse. *Viator* 12: 221–70.

Brunton, G. 1934. Modern painting on predynastic pots. *ASAE* 34: 149–56.

1937. *Mostagedda and the Tasian Culture: British Museum Expeditions to Middle Egypt 1928, 1929.* London: Bernard Quaritch.

1948. *Matmar: British Museum Expeditions to Middle Egypt, 1929–1931.* London: Bernard Quaritch.

Brunton, G. and Caton-Thompson, G. 1928. *The Badarian Civilization and Prehistoric Remains near Badari.* London: Bernard Quaritch.

Buchez, N. 1998. Le mobilier céramique et les offrandes à caractère alimentaire au sein des dépôts funéraires prédynastiques: éléments de réflexion à partir de l'example d'Adaïma. *AN* 8: 83–104.

Burton, J. W. 1980. The village and the cattle camp: aspects of Atuot religion. In I. Karp and C. Bird (eds.), *Explorations in African Systems of Thought*, 268–97. Bloomington: Indiana University Press.

Butzer, K. W. 1976. *Early Hydraulic Civilization in Egypt: A Study in Cultural Ecology.* Chicago: University of Chicago Press.

1980. Pleistocene history of the Nile valley in Egypt and Lower Nubia. In M. A. J. Williams and H. Faure (eds.), *The Sahara and the Nile: Quaternary Environments and Prehistoric Occupation in Northern Africa*, 253–80. Rotterdam: Balkema.

1995. Environmental change in the Near East and human impact on the land. In Sasson et al. (eds.) 1995: 123–51.

2000. Late Quaternary problems of the Egyptian Nile: stratigraphy, environments, prehistory. *Paléorient* 23(2): 151–73.

2002. Geoarchaeological implications of recent research in the Nile delta. In van den Brink and Levy 2002: 83–97.

Byrd, B. F. and Monahan, C. M. 1995. Death, mortuary ritual, and Natufian social structure. *JAA* 14: 251–87.

Campana, D. 1989. *Natufian Protoneolithic Bone Tools: The Manufacture and Use of Bone Implements in the Zagros and the Levant*. Oxford: BAR.

Campbell, S. 2000. The burnt house at Arpachiyah: a re-examination. *BASOR* 318: 1–40.

Campbell, S. and Green, A. (eds.) 1995. *The Archaeology of Death in the Ancient Near East*. Oxford: Oxbow.

Caneva, I. 1988. *El Geili: The History of a Middle Nile Environment 7000 BC–AD 1500*. Oxford: BAR.

1991. Prehistoric hunters, herders and tradesmen in central Sudan: data from the Geili region. In Davies 1991: 6–15.

1992. Predynastic cultures of Lower Egypt: the desert and the Nile. In van den Brink 1992b: 217–24.

Cannadine, D. 2001. *Ornamentalism: How the British Saw Their Empire*. London: Allen Lane.

Cannadine, D. and Price, S. R. F. (eds.) 1987. *Rituals of Royalty: Power and Ceremonial in Traditional Societies*. Cambridge: Cambridge University Press.

Capart, J. 1904. *Les débuts de l'art en Egypte*. Brussels: Vromant.

1905. *Primitive Art in Egypt*. (Translated by A. S. Griffith.) London: Grevel.

Carr, C. J. 1977. *Pastoralism in Crisis: The Dasanetch and their Ethiopian Lands*. Chicago: University of Chicago Press.

Carsten, J. and Hugh-Jones, S. (eds.) 1995. *About the House: Lévi-Strauss and Beyond*. Cambridge: Cambridge University Press.

Case, H. and Payne, J. C. 1962. Tomb 100: the Decorated Tomb at Hierakonpolis. *JEA* 48: 5–18.

Castel, G., Mathieu, B., Hélal, H., Abdallah, T. and el-Hawary, M. 1992. Les mines de cuivre du Ouadi Dara: rapport préliminaire sur les travaux de la saison 1991. *BIFAO* 92: 51–65.

Castillos, J. J. 1982. *A Reappraisal of the Published Evidence on Egyptian Predynastic and Early Dynastic Cemeteries*. Toronto: Benben.

Caton-Thompson, G. and Gardner, E. W. 1934. *The Desert Fayum*. 2 volumes. London: Royal Anthropological Institute of Great Britain and Ireland.

Cauvin, J. 1972. *Religions neolithiques de Syro-Palestine: documents*. Paris: Librairie d'Amerique et d'Orient.

1994. *Naissance des divinités, naissance de l'agriculture: la révolution des symboles au néolithique*. Paris: CNRS.

2000. *The Birth of the Gods and the Origins of Agriculture*. Cambridge: Cambridge University Press.

Cauvin, M.-C. and Chataigner, C. 1998. Distribution de l'obsidienne dans les sites archéologiques du Proche et Moyen Orient. In Cauvin et al. 1998: 325–50.

Cauvin, M.-C., Gourgaud, A., Gratuze, B., Arnaud, N., Poupeau, G., Poidevin, J.-L. and Chataigner, C. 1998. *L'obsidienne au Proche et Moyen Orient: du volcan à l'outil*. Oxford: BAR.

Cervelló Autuori, J. 2002. Back to the mastaba tombs of the First Dynasty at Saqqara: officials or kings? In R. Pirelli (ed.), *Egyptological Essays on State and Society*, 27–61. Naples: Università degli Studi di Napoli 'L'Orientale'.

Červíček, P. 1974. *Felsbilder des Nord-Etbai, Oberägyptens und Unternubiens.* Wiesbaden: Franz Steiner.

  1986. *Rock Pictures of Upper Egypt and Nubia.* Herder-Roma: Instituto Universitario Orientale di Napoli.

  1994. Archaische Orantendarstellungen auf ägyptischen und nubischen Felsbildern. In C. Berger *et al.* 1994: 97–103.

Chakrabarty, D. 2000. *Provincializing Europe: Postcolonial Thought and Historical Difference.* Princeton: Princeton University Press.

Chang, C. and Koster, H. A. 1986. Beyond bones: towards an archaeology of pastoralism. *Advances in Archaeological Method and Theory* 9: 97–148.

Charvát, P. 1994. The seals and their functions in the Halaf- and Ubaid-cultures (a case study of materials from Tell Arpachiyah and Nineveh 2–3). In R. B. Wartke (ed.), *Handwerk und Technologie im Alten Orient: ein Beitrag zur Geschichte der Technik im Altertum*, 9–16. Mainz am Rhein: Philipp von Zabern.

Chazan, M. and Lehner, M. 1990. An ancient analogy: pot baked bread in ancient Egypt and Mesopotamia. *Paléorient* 16(2): 21–35.

Chenal-Velardé, I. 1997. Le boeuf domestique en Afrique du Nord. In A. Gautier (ed.), *Animals and People in the Holocene of North Africa*, 11–40. Grenoble: La pensée sauvage.

Childe, V. G. 1936. *Man Makes Himself.* London: Watts.

Chłodnicki, M. 1984. Pottery from the Neolithic settlement at Kadero (central Sudan). In Krzyżaniak and Kobusiewicz 1984: 337–43.

Chłodnicki, M. and Ciałowicz, K. M. 2002. Tell el-Farkha seasons 1998–1999: preliminary report. *MDAIK* 58: 88–117.

Chłodnicki, M., Fattovitch, R. and Salvatori, S. 1992. The Nile delta in transition: a view from Tell el-Farkha. In van den Brink 1992b: 171–90.

Churcher, C. S. 1984. Zoological study of the ivory knife handle from Abu Zaidan. In Needler 1984: 152–69.

Ciałowicz, K. M. 1991. *Les palettes égyptiennes aux motifs zoomorphes et sans décoration.* Krakow: Uniwersytet Jagielloński.

  1992. *La composition, le sens et la symbolique des scènes zoomorphes prédynastiques en relief: les manches de couteau.* In Friedman and Adams 1992: 247–58.

  2001. *La naissance d'un royaume: l'Egypte dès la période prédynastique à la fin de la Ière dynastie.* Krakow: Uniwersytet Jagielloński Instytut Archeologii.

  2003. Tell el-Farkha 2000: excavations at the Western Kom. In Krzyżaniak *et al.* 2003: 163–76.

Clark, J. D. 1984. Prehistoric cultural continuity and economic change in the central Sudan in the Early Holocene. In J. D. Clark and S. A. Brandt (eds.), *From Hunters to Farmers: The Causes and Consequences of Food Production in Africa*, 113–26. Berkeley: University of California Press.

Clastres, P. 1989 [1974]. *Society against the State.* (Translated by R. Hurley and A. Stein.) New York: Zone.

Close, A. E. 1984. Early Holocene raw material economies in the Western Desert of Egypt. In Krzyżaniak and Kobusiewicz 1984: 163–70.

(ed.) 1987. *Prehistory of Arid North Africa: Essays in Honor of Fred Wendorf*. Dallas: Southern Methodist University Press.

1995. Few and far between: early ceramics in North Africa. In W. K. Barnett and J. W. Hoopes (eds.), *The Emergence of Pottery: Technology and Innovation in Ancient Societies*, 23–37. Washington: Smithsonian Press.

1996. Plus ça change: the Pleistocene-Holocene transition in Northeast Africa. In L. G. Straus *et al.* (eds.), *Humans at the End of the Ice Age: The Archaeology of the Pleistocene-Holocene Transition*, 43–57. New York and London: Plenum Press.

2001. Site E-75–8: additional excavation of the seventh millennium site at Nabta Playa. In Wendorf and Schild 2001: 352–85.

Clutton-Brock, J. and Grigson, C. (eds.) 1984. *Animals and Archaeology* III: *Early Herders and their Flocks*. Oxford: BAR.

Cohen, A. 1974. *Two-Dimensional Man: An Essay on the Anthropology of Power and Symbolism in Complex Society*. Berkeley and Los Angeles: University of California Press.

Cohen, R. and Westbrook, R. (eds.) 2000. *Amarna Diplomacy: The Beginnings of International Relations*. Baltimore: Johns Hopkins University Press.

Collingwood, R. G. 1946. *The Idea of History*. Oxford: Clarendon Press.

Comaroff, J. and Comaroff, J. 1992. *Ethnography and the Historical Imagination*. San Francisco: Westview.

Connor, R. D. and Marks, A. 1986. The Terminal Pleistocene on the Nile: the final Nilotic adjustment. In L. G. Straus (ed.), *The End of the Palaeolithic in the Old World*, 171–99. Oxford: BAR.

Crawford, H. 1998. *Dilmun and its Gulf Neighbours*. Cambridge: Cambridge University Press.

Cribb, R. 1991. *Nomads in Archaeology*. Cambridge: Cambridge University Press.

Crubézy, E. 1998. La nécropole d'Adaïma: une première synthèse. *AN* 8: 33–66.

Crubézy, E., Janin, T. and Midant-Reynes, B. 2002. *Adaïma* II: *la nécropole prédynastique*. Cairo: IFAO.

Crubézy, E. and Midant-Reynes, B. 2000. Les sacrifices humains à l'époque prédynastique: l'apport de la nécropole d'Adaïma. *AN* 10: 21–40.

Cunliffe, B. (ed.) 1994. *Prehistoric Europe: An Illustrated History*. Oxford: Oxford University Press.

Damerow, P. 1999. The origins of writing as a problem of historical epistemology. Max Planck Institute for the History of Science, Pre-Print 114. (www.mpiwg-berlin.mpg.de/Preprints/P114.PDF)

Daniel, G. 1950. *A Hundred Years of Archaeology*. London: Duckworth.

1962. *The Idea of Prehistory*. Harmondsworth: Penguin.

Davies, W. V. (ed.) 1991. *Egypt and Africa: Nubia from Prehistory to Islam*. London: British Museum Press.

Davis, S. J. 1984. The advent of milk and wool production in western Iran: some speculations. In J. Clutton-Brock and C. Grigson (eds.), *Animals and Archaeology* III: *Early Herders and their Flocks*, 265–78. Oxford: BAR.

Davis, W. 1983. Cemetery T and Naqada. *MDAIK* 39: 17–28.

1992. *Masking the Blow: The Scene of Representation in Late Prehistoric Egyptian Art*. Berkeley: University of California Press.

Dayan, T. and Simberloff, D. 1995. Natufian gazelles: proto-domestication revisited. *Journal of Archaeological Science* 22: 671–5.

Debono, F. 1948. El-Omari (près d'Hélouan). *ASAE* 48: 561–8.

1950. Désert oriental: mission archéologique royale 1949. *CdE* 25: 237–40.

1951. Expedition archéologique royale au Desert oriental (Keft-Kosseir): rapport préliminaire sur la campagne 1949. *ASAE* 51: 59–110.

Debono, F. and Mortensen, B. 1988. *The Predynastic Cemetery of Heliopolis.* Mainz am Rhein: Philipp von Zabern.

1990. *El Omari: A Neolithic Settlement and Other Sites in the Vicinity of Wadi Hof, Helwan.* Mainz am Rhein: Philipp von Zabern.

DeMarrais, E., Gosden, C. and Renfrew, C. (eds.) 2004. *Rethinking Materiality: The Engagement of Mind with the Material World.* Cambridge: McDonald Institute.

Dodson, A. 1996. The mysterious 2nd Dynasty. *KMT* 7(2): 19–31.

Donadoni Roveri, A. M. 1990. Gebelein. In G. Robins (ed.), *Beyond the Pyramids: Egyptian Regional Art from the Museo Egizio*, 23–9. Exhibition catalogue. Atlanta: Emery Museum of Art and Archaeology and Museo Egizio di Torino.

Dorman, P. F., Harper, P. O. and Pittman, H. 1987. *The Metropolitan Museum of Art: Egypt and the Ancient Near East.* New York: The Metropolitan Museum of Art.

Dreyer, G. 1986. *Elephantine* VIII: *der Tempel der Satet: die Funde der Frühzeit und des Alten Reiches.* Mainz am Rhein: Philipp von Zabern.

1987. Ein Siegel der frühzeitlichen Königsnekropole von Abydos. *MDAIK* 43: 33–43.

1990. Umm el-Qaab: Nachuntersuchungen im frühzeitlichen Königsfriedhof. 3./4. Vorbericht. *MDAIK* 46: 53–90.

1991. Zur Rekonstruktion der Oberbauten der Königsgräber der 1. Dynastie in Abydos. *MDAIK* 47: 93–104.

1992. Horus Krokodil, ein Gegenkönig der Dynastie 0. In Friedman and Adams 1992: 259–63.

1995. Die Datierung der Min-Statuen aus Koptos. In R. Stadelmann and H. Sourouzian (eds.), *Kunst des Alten Reiches: Symposium im DAIK am 29. und 30. Oktober 1991*, 49–56. Mainz am Rhein: Philipp von Zabern.

1998. *Umm el-Qaab I: das Prädynastische Königsgrab U-j und seine frühen Schriftzeugnisse.* (With contributions by U. Hartung and F. Pumpenmeier.) Mainz am Rhein: Philipp von Zabern.

1999. Motive und Datierung der dekorierten prädynastischen Messergriffe. In C. Ziegler (ed.), *L'art de l'Ancien Empire égyptien*, 195–226. Paris: Documentation française.

2000. Egypt's earliest historical event. *Egyptian Archaeology* 16: 6–7.

Dreyer, G., Engel, E-M., Hartung, U., Hikade, T., Köhler, E. C., Pumpenmeier, F., von den Driesch, A. and Peters, J. 1996. Umm el-Qaab: Nachuntersuchungen im frühzeitlichen Königsfriedhof. 7./8. Vorbericht. *MDAIK* 52: 11–81.

Dreyer, G., Hartmann, R., Hartung, U., Hikade, T., Köpp, H., Lacher, C., Müller, V., Nerlich, A. and Zink, A. 2003. Umm el-Qaab: Nachuntersuchungen im frühzeitlichen Königsfriedhof. 13./14./15. Vorbericht. *MDAIK* 59: 67–138.

Dreyer, G., Hartung, U., Hikade, T., Köhler, E. C., Müller, V. and Pumpenmeier, F. 1998. Umm el-Qaab: Nachuntersuchungen im frühzeitlichen Königsfriedhof. 9./10. Vorbericht. *MDAIK* 54: 77–167.

Dreyer, G., Hartung, U. and Pumpenmeier, F. 1993. Umm el-Qaab: Nachuntersuchungen im frühzeitlichen Königsfriedhof. 5./6. Vorbericht. *MDAIK* 49: 23–62.

Dreyer, G. and Kaiser, W. 1980. Zu den kleinen Stufenpyramiden Ober-und Mittelägyptens. *MDAIK* 36: 43–59.

Dreyer, G. and Swelim, N. 1982. Die kleine Stufenpyramide von Abydos-Süd (Sinki), Grabungsbericht. *MDAIK* 38: 83–93.

Dreyer, G., von den Driesch, A., Engel, E.-M., Hartmann, R., Hartung, U., Hikade, T., Müller, V. and Peters, J. 2000. Umm el-Qaab: Nachuntersuchungen im frühzeitlichen Königsfriedhof. 11./12. Vorbericht. *MDAIK* 56: 43–129.

Drower, M. 1985. *Flinders Petrie: A Life in Archaeology*. London: Victor Gollancz.

Dumézil, G. 1968–73. *Mythe et épopée*. Paris: Gallimard.

Dumont, L. 1980. *Homo Hierarchicus: The Caste System and its Implications.* (Translated by M. Sainsbury, L. Dumont and B. Gulati.) Chicago: University of Chicago Press.

Dunbar, J. H. 1941. *The Rock-Pictures of Lower Nubia*. Cairo: Government Press.

Durkheim, E. 1984 [1893]. *The Division of Labour in Society*. (Translated by W. D. Halls; introduction by L. Coser.) London: Macmillan.

Eaton-Krauss, M. 1984. *The Representations of Statuary in Private Tombs of the Old Kingdom*. Wiesbaden: Harrassowitz.

Eckholm Friedman, K. 1991. *Catastrophe and Creation: The Transformation of an African Culture*. Chur, Reading: Harwood.

Edens, P. 1999. The chipped stone industry at Hacinebi: technological styles and social identity. *Paléorient* 25: 23–33.

Edwards, D. 2003. Ancient Egypt in the Sudanese Middle Nile: a case of mistaken identity? In O'Connor and Reid 2003a: 137–50.

Edwards, I. E. S. 1971. The Early Dynastic period in Egypt. In I. E. S. Edwards, C. J. Gadd and N. G. L. Hammond (eds.), *The Cambridge Ancient History* I:2: *Early History of the Middle East*, 1–70. 3rd ed. Cambridge: Cambridge University Press.

Edzard, D. 1997. *Gudea and his Dynasty*. Toronto: University of Toronto Press.

Ehrich, R. W. (ed.) 1992. *Chronologies in Old World Archaeology*. 3rd ed., 2 volumes. Chicago and London: University of Chicago Press.

Eiwanger, J. 1982. Die neolithische Siedlung von Merimde-Benisalame. *MDAIK* 38: 67–82.

    1984. *Merimde-Benisalâme* I: *Die Funde der Urschicht*. Archäologische Veröffentlichungen, Deutsches Archäologisches Institut, Abteilung Kairo, 47. Mainz am Rhein: Philipp von Zabern.

    1988. *Merimde-Benisalâme* II: *Die Funde der mittleren Merimdekultur*. Archäologische Veröffentlichungen, Deutsches Archäologisches Institut, Abteilung Kairo, 51. Mainz am Rhein: Philipp von Zabern.

    1992. *Merimde-Benisalâme* III: *Die Funde der jüngeren Merimdekultur*. Archäologische Veröffentlichungen, Deutsches Archäologisches Institut, Abteilung Kairo, 59. Mainz am Rhein: Philipp von Zabern.

Eliade, M. 1978. *A History of Religious Ideas* I: *From the Stone Age to the Eleusian Mysteries*. Chicago: University of Chicago Press.

Elias, N. 1994 [1939]. *The Civilizing Process: The History of Manners and State Formation and Civilization*. Oxford: Blackwell.

Emery, W. B. 1938. *Excavations at Saqqara: The Tomb of Hemaka.* Cairo: Government Press.

1939. *Excavations at Saqqara 1937–1938: Hor-Aha.* Cairo: Government Press.

1949. *Great Tombs of the First Dynasty*, I. Cairo: Government Press.

1954. *Great Tombs of the First Dynasty*, II. London: Egypt Exploration Society.

1958. *Great Tombs of the First Dynasty*, III. London: Egypt Exploration Society.

1961. *Archaic Egypt.* Harmondsworth: Penguin.

1962. *A Funerary Repast in an Egyptian Tomb of the Archaic Period.* Leiden: Nederlands Instituut voor het Nabije Oosten.

1963. Egypt Exploration Society: preliminary report on the excavations at Buhen, 1962. *Kush* 11: 116–20.

Endesfelder, E. 1991. Die Formierung der altägyptischen Klassengesellschaft: Probleme und Beobachtungen. In E. Endesfelder (ed.), *Probleme der frühen Gesellschaftsentwicklung im Alten Ägypten*, 5–62. Berlin: Humboldt-Universität zu Berlin.

1994. Königliches Boden-Eigentum in der ägyptischen Früh-Zeit. In S. Allam (ed.), *Grund und Boden in Altägypten*, 261–74. Tübingen: published by edition.

Engelbach, R. 1923. *Harageh.* London: British School of Archaeology in Egypt.

Engelmayer, 1965. *Die Felsgravierung im Distrikt Sayala-Nubien* I: *Die Schiffsdarstellungen.* Vienna: Hermann Böhlaus.

Englund, R. K. and Grégoire, J.-P., with a contribution by R. J. Matthews. 1991. *The Proto-Cuneiform Texts from Jemdet Nasr.* Berlin: Gebrüder Mann.

Epron, L., Daumas, F. and Goyon, G. 1939. *Le tombeau de Ti* I: *les approches de la chapelle.* Cairo: Institut français d'archéologie orientale.

Esse, D. L. 1991. *Subsistence, Trade and Social Change in Early Bronze Age Palestine.* Chicago: Oriental Institute of the University of Chicago.

Eyre, C. 1987. Work and the organization of work in the Old Kingdom. In M. A. Powell (ed.), *Labor in the Ancient Near East*, 5–47. New Haven: American Oriental Society.

1994. The water regime for orchards and plantations in Pharaonic Egypt. *JEA* 80: 57–80.

1999. The village economy in Pharaonic Egypt. In Bowman and Rogan 1999: 33–60.

Fairservis, W. A. 1983. *Hierakonpolis: The Graffiti and the Origins of Egyptian Hieroglyphic Writing.* Poughkeepsie: Vassar College.

1986. *Excavation of the Archaic Remains East of the Niched Gate, Season of 1981: The Hierakonpolis Project, Occasional Papers in Anthropology 3.* Poughkeepsie: Vassar College.

1989. Cattle and archaic Egypt. *The Review of Archaeology* 10: 5–9.

Fairservis, W. A., Weeks, K. R. and Hoffman, M. A. 1971–2. Preliminary report on the first two seasons at Hierakonpolis. *JARCE* 9: 7–68.

Faltings, D. 1998a. Canaanites at Buto in the early fourth millennium BC. *Egyptian Archaeology* 13: 29–32.

1998b. *Die Keramik der Lebensmittelproduktion im Alten Reich: Ikonographie und Archäologie eines Gebrauchsartikels.* Heidelberg: Heidelberger Orientverlag.

2002. The chronological frame and social structure of Buto in the fourth millennium BCE. In van den Brink and Levy 2002: 165–70.

Faltings, D., Ballet, P., Förster, F., French, P., Ihde, C., Sahlmann, H., Thomalsky, J., Thumshirn, C. and Wodzinska, A. 2000. Zweiter Vorbericht über die Arbeiten in Buto von 1996 bis 1999. *MDAIK* 56: 131–80.

Faltings, D. and Köhler, E. C. 1996. Vorbericht über die Ausgrabungen des DAI in Tell el-Fara'in/Buto, 1993 bis 1995. *MDAIK* 52: 87–114.

Faulkner, R. O. (trans.) 1985. *The Ancient Egyptian Book of the Dead*. Revised edition, Carol Andrews ed. Austin: University of Texas Press; London: British Museum Press.

Ferioli, P., Fiandra, E., Giacomo Fissore, G. and Frangipane, M. (eds.) 1994. *Archives Before Writing: Proceedings of the International Colloquium, Oriolo Romano, October 23–25, 1991*. Turin: Scriptorium.

Finkelstein, I. 1995. *Living on the Fringe: The Archaeology and History of the Negev, Sinai and Neighbouring Regions in the Bronze and Iron Ages*. Sheffield: Sheffield University Press.

Finkenstaedt, E. 1981. The location of styles of painting: White Cross-Lined Ware at Naqada. *JARCE* 18: 7–10.

1985. Cognitive vs. ecological niches in prehistoric Egypt. *JARCE* 22: 143–8.

Firth, C. M. 1912. *The Archaeological Survey of Nubia: Report for 1907–1908*. 2 volumes. Cairo: National Printing Department.

1915. *The Archaeological Survey of Nubia: Report for 1909–1910*. 2 volumes. Cairo: Government Press.

1927. *The Archaeological Survey of Nubia: Report for 1910–1911*. Cairo: National Printing Department.

Firth, C. M. and Quibell, J. E. 1935. *The Step Pyramid*. 2 volumes. Cairo: Institut français d'archéologie orientale.

Fischer, H. G. 1958. A fragment of a late predynastic Egyptian relief from the eastern delta. *Artibus Asiae* 21: 64–88.

1961. An Egyptian royal stela of the Second Dynasty. *Artibus Asiae* 24: 45–56.

1963. Varia Aegyptiaca. *JARCE* 2: 17–52.

1972. Some emblematic uses of hieroglyphs, with particular reference to an archaic ritual vessel. *Metropolitan Museum Journal* 5: 5–23.

1978. The evolution of composite hieroglyphs in ancient Egypt. *Metropolitan Museum Journal* 12: 5–19.

Fischer-Elfert, H.-W. 1998. *Die Vision von der Statue im Stein: Studien zum altägyptischen Mundöffnungsritual*. Heidelberg: Universitätsverlag: C. Winter.

Flores, D. V. 2003. *Funerary Sacrifice of Animals in the Egyptian Predynastic Period*. Oxford: BAR.

Foucault, M. 1979. *Discipline and Punish*. (Translated by A. Sheridan.) Harmondsworth: Penguin.

Francaviglia, V. and Palmieri, A. M. 1983. Petrochemical analysis of 'Early Khartoum' pottery: a preliminary report. *Origini* 12: 191–205.

Frangipane, M. 1994. The record function of clay sealings in early administrative systems as seen from Arslantepe-Malatya. In Ferioli *et al*. 1994: 125–36.

1997. A 4th-millennium temple/palace complex at Arslantepe-Malatya: north–south relations and the formation of early state societies in the northern regions of Greater Mesopotamia. *Paléorient* 23: 45–73.

2001. Centralization in Greater Mesopotamia: Uruk 'Expansion' as the climax of systemic interactions among areas of the Greater Mesopotamian region. In Rothman 2001a: 307–47.

Frangipane, M., Hauptmann, H., Liverani, M., Matthiae, P. and Mellink, M. (eds.) 1993. *Between the Rivers and Over the Mountains: Archaeologica Anatolica et Mesopotamica Alba Palmieri Dedicata*. Rome: Università di Roma 'La Sapienza'.

Frankfort, H. 1924. *Studies in Early Pottery of the Near East* I: *Mesopotamia, Syria and Egypt, and their Earliest Interrelations*. London: Royal Anthropological Institute of Great Britain and Ireland.

1939. *Cylinder Seals: A Documentary Essay on the Art and Religion of the Ancient Near East*. London: Macmillan.

1941. The origin of monumental architecture in Egypt. *American Journal of Semitic Languages and Literatures* 58: 329–58.

1948a. *Kingship and the Gods: A Study of Ancient Near Eastern Religion as the Integration of Society and Nature*. Chicago: University of Chicago Press.

1948b. *Ancient Egyptian Religion: An Interpretation*. New York: Columbia University Press.

1951. *The Birth of Civilization in the Near East*. Bloomington: Indiana University Press.

1996. *The Art and Architecture of the Ancient Orient*. 5th ed. New Haven and London: Yale University Press.

Frazer, J. G. 1887. *Totemism*. Edinburgh: A. and C. Black.

1910. *Totemism and Exogamy: A Treatise on Certain Early Forms of Superstition and Society*. London: Macmillan.

1911–15. *The Golden Bough: A Study in Magic and Religion*. 3rd edition. London: Macmillan.

Friedman, F. D. 1995. The underground relief panels of King Djoser at the Step Pyramid complex. *JARCE* 32: 1–42.

1996. Notions of cosmos in the Step Pyramid complex. In Der Manuelian and Freed 1996: 337–51.

Friedman, J. and Rowlands, M. J. 1977. Notes towards an epigenetic model of the evolution of 'civilisation'. In J. Friedman and M. J. Rowlands (eds.), *The Evolution of Social Systems*, 201–76. London: Duckworth.

Friedman, R. F. 1994. Predynastic settlement ceramics of Upper Egypt: a comparative study of the ceramics of Hemamieh, Nagada, and Hierakonpolis. PhD dissertation. Ann Arbor: University Microfilms International.

1996. The ceremonial centre at Hierakonpolis Locality HK29A. In A. J. Spencer 1996: 16–35.

1998. More mummies: the 1998 season at HK43. *NN* 10: 4–6.

1999a. Badari Grave Group 569. In W. V. Davies (ed.), *Studies in Egyptian Antiquities: A Tribute to T. G. H. James*, 1–11. London: British Museum.

1999b. Pots, pebbles and petroglyphs part II: 1996 excavations at Hierakonpolis Locality HK64. In Leahy and Tait 1999: 101–8.

1999c. Investigations in the Fort of Khasekhemwy. *NN* 11: 9–12.

1999d. The magnetic anomalies near the Fort. *NN* 11: 15–16.

2000. Ceramic nails. *NN* 12: 13.

(ed.) 2002a. *Egypt and Nubia: Gifts of the Desert*. London: British Museum Press.

2002b. The predynastic cemetery at HK43: excavations in 2002. *NN* 14: 9–10.

2003. Return to the temple: excavations at HK29A. *NN* 15: 4–5.

Friedman, R. F. and Adams, B. (eds.) 1992. *The Followers of Horus: Studies Dedicated to Michael Allen Hoffman*. Oxford: Oxbow.

Friedman, R. F. and Hobbs, J. J. 2002. A 'Tasian' tomb in Egypt's Eastern Desert. In Friedman 2002a: 178–91.

Friedman, R. F., Maish, A., Fahmy, A. G., Darnell, J. C. and Johnson, E. D. 1999. Preliminary report on field work at Hierakonpolis: 1996–1998. *JARCE* 36: 1–35.

Fuchs, G. 1989. Rock engravings in the Wadi el-Barramiya, Eastern Desert of Egypt. *AAR* 7: 127–53.

Fuller, D. 1998. Palaeoecology of the Wadi Muqaddam: a preliminary report on the significance of the plant and animal remains. *Sudan and Nubia* 2: 52–60.
2004. The central Amri to Kirbekan survey: a preliminary report on excavations and survey, 2003–2004. *Sudan and Nubia* 8: 4–10.

Fustel de Coulanges, N. D. 1901 [1864]. *The Ancient City: A Study on the Religions, Laws, and Institutions of Greece and Rome.* (Translated by W. Small.) Boston: Lothrop, Lee & Shepard.

Galaty, J. G. and Salzman, P. C. (eds.) 1981. *Change and Development in Nomadic and Pastoral Societies.* Leiden: E. J. Brill.

Galili, E., Rosen, B., Gopher, A. and Kolska-Horwitz, L. 2002. The emergence and dispersion of the eastern Mediterranean fishing village: evidence from submerged Neolithic settlements off the Carmel coast, Israel. *Journal of Mediterranean Archaeology* 15: 167–98.

Gardiner, A. H. 1957. *Egyptian Grammar: Being an Introduction to the Study of Hieroglyphs.* 3rd ed., revised. Oxford: Griffith Institute, Ashmolean Museum.
1959. *The Royal Canon of Turin.* Oxford: Oxford University Press for Griffith Institute.

Gardiner, A. H. and Peet, T. E. 1952. *The Inscriptions of Sinai,* I. 2nd ed., revised and augmented by J. Černy. London: Egypt Exploration Society.

Gardiner, A. H., Peet, T. E. and Černy, J. 1955. *The Inscriptions of Sinai,* II (by J. Černy). London: Egypt Exploration Society.

Garfinkel, Y. 2001. Dancing or fighting? A recently discovered predynastic scene from Abydos, Egypt. *Cambridge Archaeological Journal* 11: 241–54.

Garrard, A. N. 1999. Charting the emergence of cereal and pulse domestication in south-west Asia. *Environmental Archaeology* 4: 67–86.

Garrard, A. N., Colledge, S. and Martin, L. 1996. The emergence of crop cultivation and caprine herding in the 'Marginal Zone' of the southern Levant. In Harris 1996: 204–26.

Garrod, D. A. E. and Bate, D. M. A. 1937. *The Stone Age of Mount Carmel* I. Oxford: Clarendon Press.

Garstang, J. 1907. Excavations at Hierakonpolis, at Esna, and in Nubia. *ASAE* 8: 132–48.

Gatto, M. C. 2002. Early Neolithic pottery of the Nabta-Kiseiba area: stylistic attributes and regional relationships. In Nelson 2002: 65–78.

Gauthier, H. 1914. Quatre fragments nouveaux de la Pierre de Palerme au musée du Caire. *Comptes Rendus à l'Academie des Inscriptions et Belles-Lettres* 1914: 489–96.

Gautier, A. 1980. Contributions to the archaeozoology of Egypt. In Wendorf and Schild 1980: 317–42.
1984. The fauna of the Neolithic site of Kadero (central Sudan). In Krzyżaniak and Kobusiewicz 1984: 317–20.
1987. Prehistoric men and cattle in North Africa: a dearth of data and a surfeit of models. In Close 1987: 163–87.

1990. *La domestication: et l'homme créa l'animal*. . . Paris: Errance.

2001. The Early to Late Neolithic archeofaunas from Nabta and Bir Kiseiba. In Wendorf and Schild 2001: 609–35.

Gebel, H. G., Kafafi, Z. and Rollefson, G. O. (eds.) 1997. *The Prehistory of Jordan* II: *Perspectives from 1997*. Berlin: Ex Oriente.

Gell, A. 1993. *Wrapping in Images: Tattooing in Polynesia*. Oxford: Clarendon Press.

1997. Exalting the king and obstructing the state: a political interpretation of royal ritual in Bastar District, central India. *Journal of the Royal Anthropological Institute* 3: 433–50.

Geller, J. R. 1984. The predynastic ceramics industry at Hierakonpolis, Egypt. PhD dissertation. Ann Arbor: University Microfilms International.

1989. Recent excavations at Hierakonpolis and their relevance to predynastic production and settlement. *Cahiers de Recherches de l'Institut de Papyrologie et d'Egyptologie de Lille* 11: 41–52, pls. 4–6.

1992. From prehistory to history: beer in Egypt. In Friedman and Adams 1992: 19–26.

Gerth, H. H. and Mills, C. W. 1946. *From Max Weber: Essays in Sociology*. New York: Oxford University Press.

Geus, F. 1984a. Excavations at El Kadada and the Neolithic of the central Sudan. In Krzyżaniak and Kobusiewicz 1984: 361–72.

1984b. *Rescuing Sudan Ancient Cultures*. Khartoum: French Unit of the Directorate General of Antiquities and National Museums of the Sudan.

1986. Des tombes contemporaines du Néolithique de Khartoum à el Ghaba (Taragma). In M. Krause (ed.), *Nubische Studien*, 67–70. Mainz am Rhein: Philipp von Zabern.

1991. Burial customs in the Upper Main Nile: an overview. In Davies 1991: 57–73.

Giddy, L. L. 1997. Digging diary 1996. *Egyptian Archaeology* 10: 27–30.

Giesey, R. E. 1960. *The Royal Funeral Ceremony in Renaissance France*. Geneva: Droz.

Gifford, D. 1978. Ethnoarchaeological observations of natural processes affecting cultural materials. In Gould 1978: 77–102.

Ginter, B. and Koslowski, J. K. 1994. *Predynastic Settlement near Armant*. Heidelberg: Heidelberger Orientverlag.

Giveon, R. 1974. A second relief of Sekhemkhet in Sinai. *BASOR* 216: 17–20.

Gödecken, K. B. 1980. Imet-per. In *LÄ* III: 142–7.

Goebs, K. 2001. Crowns. In Redford 2001: 321–6.

Goff, B. 1963. *Symbols of Prehistoric Mesopotamia*. New Haven and London: Yale University Press.

Golden, J. 2002. The origins of the metals trade in the Eastern Mediterranean: social organization of production in the early copper industries. In van den Brink and Levy 2002: 225–38.

Goldwasser, O. 1995. *From Icon to Metaphor: Studies in the Semiotics of the Hieroglyphs*. Fribourg and Göttingen: University Press; Vandenhoeck & Ruprecht.

Gophna, R. and Gazit, D. 1985. The First Dynasty Egyptian residency at 'En Besor. *Tel Aviv* 12: 9–16.

Gophna, R. and van den Brink, E. C. M. 2002. Core-periphery interaction between the pristine Egyptian Nagada IIIb state, late Early Bronze Age l Canaan, and Terminal A-Group Lower Nubia: more data. In van den Brink and Levy 2002: 280–5.

Goring-Morris, A. N. 1993. From foraging to herding in the Negev and Sinai: the Early to Late Neolithic transition. *Paléorient* 19: 65–89.

Görsdorf, J., Dreyer, G. and Hartung, U. 1998. 14C dating results of the archaic royal necropolis Umm el-Qaab at Abydos. *MDAIK* 54: 169–75.

Gould, R. A. (ed.) 1978. *Explorations in Ethnoarchaeology.* Albuquerque: University of Mexico Press.

Graff, G. 2002. Approche de l'iconographie prédynastique: Les peintures sur vases Nagada I–Nagada II: problèmes de lecture et essais d'interpretation. PhD dissertation, Université de Paris IV-Sorbonne.

Graham, A. 2005. Plying the Nile: not all plain sailing. In K. Piquette and S. Love (eds.), *Current Research in Egyptology 2003*, 41–56. Oxford: Oxbow.

Grayson, A. K. 1972. *Assyrian Royal Inscriptions* I: *From the Beginning to Ashur-resha-ishi I.* Wiesbaden: Harrassowitz.

Greenberg, R. and Porat, N. 1996. A third millennium Levantine pottery production center: typology, petrography, and provenance of the Metallic Ware of northern Israel and adjacent regions. *BASOR* 301: 5–24.

Grigson, C. 1995. Plough and pasture in the early economy of the southern Levant. In Levy 1995a: 245–68.

  2000. *Bos Africanus* (Brehm)? Notes on the archaeozoology of the native cattle of Africa. In Blench and MacDonald 2000: 38–60.

Griswold, W. A. 1992. Measuring social inequality at Armant. In Friedman and Adams 1992: 193–8.

Groenewegen-Frankfort, H. A. 1951. *Arrest and Movement: An Essay on Space and Time in the Representational Art of the Ancient Near East.* London: Faber and Faber.

Guksch, H. and Polz, D. (eds.) 1998. *Stationen: Beiträge zur Kulturgeschichte Ägyptens: Rainer Stadelmann Gewidmet.* Mainz am Rhein: Philipp von Zabern.

Haaland, R. 1987. *Socio-Economic Differentiation in the Neolithic Sudan.* Oxford: BAR.

  1992. Fish, pots and grain: Early and Mid-Holocene adaptations in the central Sudan. *AAR* 10: 43–64.

  1993. Aqualithic sites of the Middle Nile. *Azania* 28: 47–86.

el-Hadidi, M. N. 1982. The predynastic flora of the Hierakonpolis region. In Hoffman *et al.* 1982: 102–22.

Haeny, G. 1971. Zu den Platten mit Opfertischszene aus Heluan und Giseh. In G. Haeny (ed.), *Aufsätze zum 70. Geburtstag von Herbert Ricke*, 143–64. Wiesbaden: Steiner.

Hahn, E. 1896. *Die Haustiere und ihre Beziehungen zur Wirtschaft des Menschen.* Berlin: Duncker & Humblot.

Hall, E. S. 1986. *The Pharaoh Smites his Enemies: A Comparative Study.* Munich: Deutscher Kunstverlag.

el-Hangary, S. M. 1992. The excavations of the Egyptian Antiquities Organization at Ezbet Hassan Dawud (Wadi Tumilat), season 1990. In van den Brink 1992b: 215–16.

Hansen, M. H. (ed.) 2000. *A Comparative Study of Thirty City-State Cultures: An Investigation Published by the Copenhagen Polis Centre.* Copenhagen: Kongelige dansk videnskabernes selskab.

Harpur, Y. 1987. *Decoration in Egyptian Tombs of the Old Kingdom: Studies in Orientation and Scene Content.* London: KPI.

Harrell, J. A. 2000. Appendix: petrology and provenance of limestone used for the Coptos-Hierakonpolis sculptures. In Kemp 2000: 237–9.

Harris, D. R. (ed.) 1996. *The Origins and Spread of Agriculture and Pastoralism in Eurasia.* London: UCL Press.

Harrison, S. 1992. Ritual as intellectual property. *Man* (N. S.) 27: 225–45.

Hartog, F. 1988. *The Mirror of Herodotus: The Representation of the Other in the Writing of History.* (Translated by J. Lloyd.) Berkeley: University of California Press.

Hartung, U. 1998. Prädynastische Siegelabrollungen aus dem Friedhof U in Abydos (Umm el-Qaab). *MDAIK* 54: 187–217.

2001. *Umm el-Qaab* II: *Importkeramik aus dem Friedhof U in Abydos (Umm el-Qaab) und die Beziehungen Ägyptens zu Vorderasien im 4. Jahrtausend v. Chr.* (with a contribution by L. J. Exner). Mainz am Rhein: Philipp von Zabern.

2002. Imported jars from Cemetery U at Abydos and the relations between Egypt and Canaan in predynastic times. In van den Brink and Levy 2002: 437–49.

Hartung, U., Abd el-Gelil, M., von den Driesch, A., Fares, G., Hartmann, R., Hikade, T. and Ihde, C. 2003. Vorbericht über neue Untersuchungen in der prädynastischen Siedlung von Maadi. *MDAIK* 59: 149–98.

Harvey, J. C. 2001. *Wooden Statues of the Old Kingdom: A Typological Study.* Leiden: Brill.

Hassan, F. A. 1984. Radiocarbon chronology of Neolithic and predynastic sites in Upper Egypt and the delta. *AAR* 3: 95–116.

1985. Radiocarbon chronology of Neolithic and predynastic sites in Upper Egypt and the delta. *AAR* 3: 95–116.

1986. Chronology of the Khartoum 'Mesolithic' and 'Neolithic' and related sites in the Sudan: statistical analysis and comparisons with Egypt. *AAR* 4: 83–102.

1988. The predynastic of Egypt. *Journal of World Prehistory* 2: 136–85.

2000a. Kafr Hassan Dawood. *Egyptian Archaeology* 16: 37–9.

2000b. Holocene environmental change and the origins and spread of food production in the Middle East. *Adumatu* 1: 7–28.

Hassan, F. A. and Gross, G. T. 1987. Resources and subsistence during the Early Holocene at Siwa Oasis. In Close 1987: 85–104.

Hassan, F. A. and Matson, R. G. 1989. Seriation of predynastic potsherds from the Naqada region (Upper Egypt). In Krzyżaniak and Kobusiewicz 1989: 303–15.

Hassan, F. A. and Robinson, S. W. 1987. High-precision radiocarbon chronometry of ancient Egypt, and comparison with Nubia, Palestine and Mesopotamia. *Antiquity* 61: 119–35.

Hauptmann, A. 1991. From the use of ore to the production of metal: the discovery of copper metallurgy at Feinan/Wadi Arabah/Jordan. In J.-P. Mohen and C. Eluère (eds.), *Découverte du metal*, 397–412. Paris: A. & J. Picard.

Hayes, W. C. 1953. *The Sceptre of Egypt*, I: *From the Earliest Times to the End of the Middle Kingdom.* Cambridge: Harvard University Press.

1965. *Most Ancient Egypt.* Chicago: Chicago University Press.

Haynes, C. V., Eyles, C. H., Pavlish, L. A., Ritchie, J. C. and Rybak, M. 1989. Holocene palaeoecology of the eastern Sahara: Selima Oasis. *Quaternary Science Reviews* 8: 109–36.

Hays, T. R. 1976. Predynastic Egypt: recent field research. *Current Anthropology* 17: 552–3.

Hays, T. R. and Hassan, F. A. 1974. Mineralogical analysis of 'Sudanese Neolithic' ceramics. *Archaeometry* 16: 71–9.

Helck, W. 1954. *Untersuchungen zu den Beamtentiteln des ägyptischen Alten Reiches.* Glückstadt and New York: J. J. Augustin.

Hellström, P. 1970. *The Rock Drawings: Scandinavian Joint Expedition to Sudanese Nubia* 1. 2 volumes. Stockholm: Lärondedelsfölagen-Svenska Bokförlaget.

Hendrickx, S. 1994. *Elkab* V: *The Naqada III Cemetery.* Brussels: Musées royaux d'art et d'histoire, Comité des fouilles belges en Egypte.

1996. The relative chronology of the Naqada culture: problems and possibilities. In Spencer 1996: 36–69.

1998. Peaux d'animaux comme symboles prédynastiques: à propos de quelques representations sur les vases *White Cross-Lined. CdE* 73: 203–30.

1999. La chronologie de la préhistoire tardive et des débuts de l'histoire de l'Egypte. *AN* 9: 13–81, 99–107.

2000. Autruches et flamants: les oiseaux représentés sur la céramique prédynastique de la catégorie *Decorated. CCdE* 1: 21–52.

2002a. Checklist of predynastic 'Decorated' pottery with human figures. *CCdE* 3–4: 29–50.

2002b. Bovines in Egyptian predynastic and Early Dynastic iconography. In F. A. Hassan (ed.), *Drought, Food and Culture: Ecological Change and Food Security in Africa's Late Prehistory*, 275–318. New York and London: Kluwer Academic/Plenum.

Hendrickx, S. and Bavay, L. 2002. The relative chronological position of Egyptian predynastic and Early Dynastic tombs with objects imported from the Near East and the nature of interregional contacts. In van den Brink and Levy 2002: 58–80.

Hendrickx, S., Friedman, R., Ciałowicz, K. M. and Chłodnicki, M. (eds.) 2004. *Egypt at its Origins: Studies in Memory of Barbara Adams.* Leuven: Peeters.

Hendrickx, S., Friedman, R. and Loyens, F. 2000. Experimental archaeology concerning black-topped pottery from ancient Egypt and the Sudan. *Cahiers de la Céramique Egyptienne* 6: 171–87.

Hendrickx, S., Midant-Reynes, B. and van Neer, W. 2001. *Mahgar Dendera 2 (Haute Egypte): un site d'occupation Badarian.* Leuven: Leuven University Press.

Hendrickx, S. and Vermeersch, P. 2000. Prehistory: from the Palaeolithic to the Badarian culture. In Shaw 2000a: 17–44.

Hennessey, J. B. 1967. *The Foreign Relations of Palestine during the Early Bronze Age.* London: Bernard Quaritch.

Hennessey, J. B. and Millett, A. 1963. Spectrographic analysis of the foreign pottery from the royal tombs of Abydos and Early Bronze Age pottery of Palestine. *Archaeometry* 6: 10–17.

Henrickson, E. F. and Thuesen, I. 1989. *Upon this Foundation: The 'Ubaid Reconsidered.* Copenhagen: Museum Tusculanum Press.

Herbich, T. and Friedman, R. 1999. The geophysical survey. *NN* 11: 17.

Hertz, R. 1960 [1909]. *Death and the Right Hand.* (Translated by R. and C. Needham.) London: Cohen and West.

Herzfeld, M. 1992. *The Social Production of Indifference: Exploring the Symbolic Roots of Western Bureaucracy*. Chicago: University of Chicago Press.

Hestrin, R. and Tadmor, M. 1963. A hoard of tools and weapons from Kfar Monash. *Israel Exploration Journal* 13: 265–88.

de Heusch, L. 1982. *The Drunken King, or, the Origins of the State*. (Translated and annotated by Roy Willis.) Bloomington: Indiana University Press.

1997. The symbolic mechanisms of sacred kingship: rediscovering Frazer. *Journal of the Royal Anthropological Institute* (N. S.) 3: 213–32.

Higgs, E. S. (ed.) 1972. *Papers in Economic Prehistory*. Cambridge: Cambridge University Press.

Higgs, E. S. and Jarman, M. R. 1972. The origins of animal and plant husbandry. In Higgs 1972: 3–14.

Hikade, T. 1999. An Early Dynastic flint workshop at Helwan, Egypt. *Bulletin of the Australian Center of Egyptology* 10: 47–57.

Hillman, G. C. 1996. Late Pleistocene changes in wild plant-foods available to hunter-gatherers of the northern Fertile Crescent: possible preludes to cereal cultivation. In Harris 1996: 159–203.

Hocart, A. M. 1927. *Kingship*. London: Oxford University Press.

Hodder, I. 1990. *The Domestication of Europe: Structure and Contingency in Neolithic Societies*. Oxford: Blackwell.

1992. The domestication of Europe. In I. Hodder, *Theory and Practice in Archaeology*, 241–53. London and New York: Routledge.

Hoffman, M. A. 1980. A rectangular Amratian house from Hierakonpolis and its significance for predynastic research. *JNES* 39: 119–37.

1991 [1980]. *Egypt before the Pharaohs: The Prehistoric Foundations of Egyptian Civilization*. 1st University of Texas Press ed., revised and updated. Austin: University of Texas Press.

Hoffman, M. A., Adams, B., Berger, M., el-Hadidi, M. N., Harlan, J. F., Hamroush, H. A., Lupton, C., McArdle, J., McHugh, W., Allen, R. O. and Rogers, M. 1982. *The Predynastic of Hierakonpolis: An Interim Report*. Giza: Cairo University Herbarium; Department of Sociology and Anthropology, Western Illinois University.

Hoffman, M. A., Hamroush, H. and Allen, R. O. 1986. A model of urban development for the Hierakonpolis region from predynastic through Old Kingdom times. *JARCE* 23: 175–87.

Hole, F. 1978. Pastoral nomadism in western Iran. In Gould 1978: 127–68.

Holmes, D. 1989. *The Predynastic Lithic Industries of Upper Egypt*. 2 volumes. Oxford: BAR.

1992. Chipped stone-working craftsmen, Hierakonpolis and the rise of civilization in Egypt. In Friedman and Adams 1992: 37–44.

Holmes, D. and Friedman, R. 1994. Survey and test excavations in the Badari region, Egypt. *PPS* 60: 105–42.

Hornung, E. 1982. *Conceptions of God in Ancient Egypt: The One and the Many*. (Translated by J. Baines.) Ithaca, NY: Cornell University Press.

Hughes, P. 1995. Ruins of time: estranging history and ethnology in the Enlightenment and after. In D. O. Hughes and T. R. Trautmann (eds.), *Time: Histories and Ethnologies*, 269–90. Michigan: University of Michigan Press.

Huyge, D. 1998a. Hilltops, silts, and petroglyphs: the fish hunters of El-Hosh (Upper Egypt). *Bulletin des Musées royaux d'Art et d'Histoire* 69: 97–113.

1998b. Battered bulls: rock art destruction in Egypt. *AAR* 15: 3–11.

2002. Cosmology, ideology and personal religious practice in ancient Egyptian rock art. In Friedman 2002a: 192–206.

Ikram, S. and Dodson, A. 1998. *The Mummy in Ancient Egypt: Equipping the Dead for Eternity*. London: Thames and Hudson.

Ilan, O. 2002. Egyptian pottery from Small Tel Malhata and the interrelations between the Egyptian 'colony' in southwest Palestine and the 'Canaanite' Arad Basin and Central Highlands. In van den Brink and Levy 2002: 306–22.

Ingold, T. 2000. *The Perception of the Environment: Essays on Livelihood, Dwelling and Skill*. London and New York: Routledge.

Isaac, E. 1971. On the domestication of cattle. In S. Struever (ed.), *Prehistoric Agriculture*, 451–70. New York: Natural History Press.

Jacobsen, T. 1939. *The Sumerian King List*. Chicago: University of Chicago Press.

Jacquet-Gordon, H. 1962. *Les noms des domaines funéraires sous l'ancien empire égyptien*. Cairo: IFAO.

1981. A tentative typology of Egyptian bread moulds. In Dorothea Arnold (ed.), *Studien zur Altägyptischen Keramik*, 11–24. Mainz am Rhein: Philipp von Zabern.

James, T. G. H. 1995. The earliest history of wine and its importance in ancient Egypt. In P. E. McGovern, S. J. Fleming and S. H. Katz (eds.), *The Origins and Ancient History of Wine*, 197–213. Luxembourg: Gordon & Breach.

James, W. 2003. *The Ceremonial Animal: A New Portrait of Anthropology*. Oxford: Oxford University Press.

James, W. and Allen, N. J. (eds.) 1998. *Marcel Mauss: A Centenary Tribute*. New York: Berghahn.

Janin, T. 1992. Archéologie funéraire et anthropologie: l'exemple du cimetière prédynastique d'Adaïma (Haute-Egypte). *AN* 2: 31–6.

Jeffreys, D. 1998. The topography of Heliopolis and Memphis: some cognitive aspects. In Guksch and Poltz 1998: 63–71.

2004. Hierakonpolis and Memphis in predynastic tradition. In Hendrickx *et al.* 2004: 837–45.

Jeffreys, D. and Tavares, A. 1994. The historic landscape of Early Dynastic Memphis. *MDAIK* 50: 143–73.

Jesse, F. 2002. Wavy line ceramics: evidence from northeastern Africa. In Nelson 2002: 79–96.

Jiménez Serrano, A. 2002. *Royal Festivals in the Late Predynastic Period and the First Dynasty*. Oxford: BAR.

Joffe, A. H. 1993. *Settlement and Society in the Early Bronze I and II Southern Levant: Complementarity and Contradiction in Small-Scale Complex Society*. Sheffield: Sheffield Academic Press.

1998. Alcohol and social complexity in ancient western Asia. *Current Anthropology* 39: 297–310.

2000. Egypt and Syro-Mesopotamia in the 4th millennium: implications of the New Chronology. *Current Anthropology* 41: 113–23.

2001. Early Bronze Age seal impressions from the Jezreel valley and the problem of sealing in the southern Levant. In Wolff 2001: 355–75.

Jones, A. 1998. Where eagles dare: landscape, animals and the Neolithic of Orkney. *Journal of Material Culture* 3: 301–24.

Jones, J. 2002a. Towards mummification: new evidence for early developments. *Egyptian Archaeology* 21: 5–7.

2002b. Funerary textiles of the rich and poor. *NN* 14: 13.

Jucha, M. 2003. Tell el-Farkha 2001: the settlement pottery of phases 5 and 4a: a preliminary report. In Krzyżaniak *et al.* 2003: 185–99.

Junker, H. 1912. *Bericht über die Grabungen der Kaiserl. Akademie der Wissenschaften in Wien auf dem Friedhof in Turah: Winter 1909–1910.* Vienna: Alfred Hölder.

1919. *Bericht über die Grabungen der Akademie der Wissenschaften in Wien auf den Friedhöfen von El-Kubanieh Süd, Winter 1910–11.* Vienna: Alfred Hölder.

1929–40. Vorläufiger Bericht über die Grabung der Akademie der Wissenschaften in Wien auf der neolithischen Siedlung von Merimde Benisalame (Westdelta). *Anzeiger der Akademie der Wissenschaften in Wien, Philosophisch-historische Klasse* 1929/XVI–XVIII: 156–250; 1930/V–XIII: 21–83; 1932/I–IV: 36–97; 1933/XVI–XXVII: 54–97; 1934/X: 118–32; 1940/I–IV: 3–25.

Kabacinski, J. 2003. Lithic industry at Tell el-Farkha (eastern delta). In Krzyżaniak *et al.* 2003: 201–12.

Kahl, J. 1994. *Das System der ägyptischen Hieroglyphenschrift in der 0.–3. Dynastie.* Wiesbaden: Harrassowitz.

1995. Zur Problematik der sogenannten Steuervermerke im Ägypten der 0.–1. Dynastie. In C. Fluck, L. Langener, S. Richter, S. Schaten and G. Wurst (eds.), *Divitiae Aegypti: Koptologische und verwandte Studien zu Ehren von Martin Krause*, 168–76.

1997. Zur Datierung der frühen Grabplatten mit Opfertischszene. *Studien zur Altägyptischen Kultur* 24: 137–45.

2001a. Hieroglyphic writing during the fourth millennium BC: an analysis of systems. *AN* 11: 103–25.

2001b. Die Funde aus dem 'Menesgrab' in Naqada: ein Zwischenbericht. *MDAIK* 57: 171–85.

2001c. *Vergraben, verbrannt, verkannt und vergessen: Funde aus dem 'Menesgrab'.* Münster: Linden.

2003. Die frühen Schriftzeugnisse aus dem Grab U-j in Umm el-Qaab. *CdE* 78: 112–35.

Kahl, J., Kloth, N. and Zimmermann, U. 1995. *Die Inschriften der 3. Dynastie: eine Bestandsaufnahme.* Wiesbaden: Harrassowitz.

Kaiser, W. 1956. Stand und Probleme der ägyptischen Vorgeschichtsforschung. *ZÄS* 81: 87–109.

1957. Zur inneren Chronologie der Naqadakultur. *Archaeologia Geographica* 6: 69–77.

1958. Zur vorgeschichtlichen Bedeutung von Hierakonpolis. *MDAIK* 16: 183–92.

1959. Einige Bemerkungen zur ägyptischen Frühzeit, I. *ZÄS* 84: 119–32.

1960. Einige Bemerkungen zur ägyptischen Frühzeit, I. (Forts.). *ZÄS* 85: 118–37.

1961. Einige Bemerkungen zur ägyptischen Frühzeit, II. *ZÄS* 86: 39–61.

1964. Einige Bemerkungen zur ägyptischen Frühzeit, III. Die Reichseinigung. *ZÄS* 91: 86–125.

1969. Zu den königlichen Talbezirken der 1. und 2. Dynastie in Abydos und zur Baugeschichte des Djosergrabmals. *MDAIK* 25: 1–21.

1985a. Zur Südausdehnung der vorgeschichtlichen Deltakulturen und zur frühen Entwicklung Oberägyptens. *MDAIK* 41: 47–60.

1985b. Ein Kultbezirk des Königs Den in Sakkara. *MDAIK* 41: 46–60.

1986. Zum Siegel mit frühen Königsnamen von Umm el-Qaab. *MDAIK* 43: 115–19.

1990. Zur Entstehung des gesamtägyptischen Staates. *MDAIK* 46: 287–99.

1995. Trial and error. *GM* 149: 5–14.

Kaiser, W. and Dreyer, G. 1982. Umm el-Qaab: Nachuntersuchungen im frühzeitlichen Königsfriedhof. 2. Vorbericht. *MDAIK* 38: 211–70.

Kamenka, E. 1989. *Bureaucracy: New Perspectives on the Past.* Oxford: Blackwell.

Kanawati, N. 1981. The living and the dead in Old Kingdom tomb scenes. *Studien zur altägyptischen Kultur* 9: 213–25.

Kansa, E. and Levy, T. E. 2002. Ceramics, identity and the role of the state: the view from Nahal Tillah. In van den Brink and Levy 2002: 190–212.

Kantor, H. J. 1942. The early relations of Egypt with Asia. *JNES* 1: 174–213.

1944. The final phase of predynastic culture, Gerzean or Semainean? *JNES* 3: 110–36.

1953. Prehistoric Egyptian pottery in the Art Museum. *Princeton University, Record of the Art Museum* 12: 67–83.

1992. The relative chronology of Egypt and its foreign correlations before the First Intermediate Period. In Ehrich 1992: 3–21.

Kantorowicz, E. H. 1957. *The King's Two Bodies: A Study in Mediaeval Political Theology.* Princeton: Princeton University Press.

Kaplony, P. 1963. *Die Inschriften der ägyptischen Frühzeit.* 3 volumes. Wiesbaden: Harrassowitz.

Karageorghis, V. 1991. *The Coroplastic Art of Ancient Cyprus* I: *Chalcolithic – Late Cypriote I.* Nicosia: A. G. Leventis Foundation.

Keding, B. 1998. The Yellow Nile: new data on settlement and the environment in the Sudanese eastern Sahara. *Sudan and Nubia* 2: 2–12.

Kees, H. 1961. *Ancient Egypt: A Cultural Topography.* (Edited by T. G. H. James; translated by I. F. D Morrow.) London: Faber and Faber.

Kemp, B. J. 1963. Excavations at Hierakonpolis Fort, 1905: a preliminary note. *JEA* 49: 24–8.

1966. Abydos and the royal tombs of the First Dynasty. *JEA* 52: 13–22.

1967. The Egyptian 1st Dynasty royal cemetery. *Antiquity* 41: 22–32.

1968a. Merimda and the theory of house burial in prehistoric Egypt. *CdE* 43: 22–33.

1968b. The Osiris temple at Abydos. *MDAIK* 23: 138–55.

1973. Photographs of the Decorated Tomb at Hierakonpolis. *JEA* 59: 36–43.

1975. Abydos. In *LÄ* I: 28–42.

1977. The early development of towns in Egypt. *Antiquity* 51: 185–200.

1989. *Ancient Egypt: Anatomy of a Civilization.* London and New York: Routledge.

1995. How religious were the ancient Egyptians? *Cambridge Archaeological Journal* 5: 25–54.

2000. The Colossi from the early shrine at Coptos in Egypt. *Cambridge Archaeological Journal* 10: 211–42 (with illustrations by A. D. Boyce).

Kempinski, A. 1992. Reflections on the role of the Egyptians in the Shefelah of Palestine in the light of recent soundings at Tel Erani. In van den Brink 1992b: 419–25.

Khazanov, A. 1984. *Nomads and the Outside World*. Cambridge: Cambridge University Press.

el-Khouli, A. 1978. *Egyptian Stone Vessels: Predynastic Period to Dynasty III: Typology and Analysis*. 3 volumes. Mainz am Rhein: Philipp von Zabern.

Killen, G. 1980. *Ancient Egyptian Furniture* I: *4000–1300 BC*. Warminster: Aris & Phillips.

Klaniczay, G. 2002. *Holy Rulers and Blessed Princesses: Dynastic Cults in Medieval Central Europe*. (Translated by Eva Pálmai.) Cambridge: Cambridge University Press.

Klasens, A. 1957. The excavations of the Leiden Museum of Antiquities at Abu-Roash: report of the first season: 1957. Part I. *Oudheidkundige Mededelingen uit het Rijksmuseum van Oudheden te Leiden* 38: 58–68.

1958a. The excavations of the Leiden Museum of Antiquities at Abu-Roash: report of the second season: 1957. Part II. *Oudheidkundige Mededelingen uit het Rijksmuseum van Oudheden te Leiden* 39: 20–31.

1958b. The excavations of the Leiden Museum of Antiquities at Abu-Roash: report of the second season: 1958. Part I. *Oudheidkundige Mededelingen uit het Rijksmuseum van Oudheden te Leiden* 39: 32–55.

1959. The excavations of the Leiden Museum of Antiquities at Abu-Roash: report of the second season: 1958. Part II: Cemetery 400. *Oudheidkundige Mededelingen uit het Rijksmuseum van Oudheden te Leiden* 40: 41–61.

1960. The excavations of the Leiden Museum of Antiquities at Abu-Roash: report of the third season: 1959. Part I. *Oudheidkundige Mededelingen uit het Rijksmuseum van Oudheden te Leiden* 41: 69–94.

1961. The excavations of the Leiden Museum of Antiquities at Abu-Roash: report of the third season: 1959. Part II. *Oudheidkundige Mededelingen uit het Rijksmuseum van Oudheden te Leiden* 42: 108–28.

Klees, F. 1989. Lobo: a contribution to the prehistory of the eastern Sand Sea and the Egyptian oases. In Krzyżaniak and Kobusiewicz 1989: 223–32.

Köhler, E. C. 1992. The pre- and Early Dynastic pottery of Tell el-Fara'in-Buto. In van den Brink 1992b: 11–22.

1995. The state of research on late predynastic Egypt: new evidence for the development of the Pharaonic state. *GM* 147: 79–92.

1998a. *Tell el-Fara'in-Buto* III: *die Keramik von der späten Naqada-Kultur bis zum frühen Alten Reich: Schichten III–VI*. Mainz am Rhein: Philipp von Zabern.

1998b. Excavations at Helwan: new insights into Early Dynastic stone masonry. *Bulletin of the Australian Center of Egyptology* 9: 65–72.

2000. Excavations in the Early Dynastic cemetery at Helwan: a preliminary report of the 1998/9 and 1999/2000 seasons. *Bulletin of the Australian Center of Egyptology* 11: 83–92.

2002. History or ideology? New reflections on the Narmer Palette and the nature of foreign relations in pre- and Early Dynastic Egypt. In van den Brink and Levy 2002: 499–513.

Kramer, C. 1982. *Village Ethnoarchaeology: Rural Iran in Archaeological Perspective*. New York: Columbia University Press.

Kristiansen, K. 1998. Chiefdoms, states and systems of social evolution. In Kristiansen and Rowlands 1998: 243–67.

Kristiansen, K. and Rowlands, M. 1998. *Social Transformations in Archaeology: Global and Local Perspectives.* London and New York: Routledge.

Kroeper, K. 1988. The excavations of the Munich East-Delta Expedition in Minshat Abu Omar. In van den Brink 1988b: 11–46.

  1992. Tombs of the elite in Minshat Abu Omar. In van den Brink 1992b: 127–50.

  1996. Minshat Abu Omar—burials with palettes. In Spencer 1996: 70–92.

Kroeper, K. and Wildung, D. 1985. *Minshat Abu Omar: Münchner Ostdelta-Expedition: Vorbericht 1978–1984.* Munich: Staatliche Sammlung Ägyptischer Kunst.

  1994. *Minshat Abu Omar: ein vor- und frühgeschichtlicher Friedhof im Nildelta* I: *Gräber 1–114.* Mainz am Rhein: Philipp von Zabern.

  2000. *Minshat Abu Omar: ein vor- und frühgeschichtlicher Friedhof im Nildelta* II: *Gräber 115–204.* Mainz am Rhein: Philipp von Zabern.

Kroll, H. 1989. Die Planzenfunde von Maadi. In Rizkana and Seeher 1989: 129–35.

Krzyżaniak, L. 1977. *Early Farming Cultures on the Lower Nile: The Predynastic Period in Egypt.* Warsaw: Centre d'Archéologie Méditerranéenne de l'Académie polonaise des sciences.

  1984. The Neolithic habitation at Kadero (central Sudan). In Krzyżaniak and Kobusiewicz 1984: 309–16.

  1989. Recent archaeological evidence on the earliest settlement in the eastern Nile delta. In Krzyżaniak and Kobusiewicz 1989: 267–85.

  1991. Early farming in the Middle Nile Basin: recent discoveries at Kadero (central Sudan). *Antiquity* 65: 515–32.

Krzyżaniak, L. and Kobusiewicz, M. (eds.) 1984. *Origin and Early Development of Food-Producing Cultures in North-Eastern Africa.* Poznan: Archaeological Museum.

  1989. *Late Prehistory of the Nile Basin and the Sahara.* Poznan: Archaeological Museum.

Krzyżaniak, L., Kobusiewicz, M. and Alexander, J. (eds.) 1993. *Environmental Change and Human Culture in the Nile Basin and Northern Africa until the Second Millennium BC.* Poznan: Archaeological Museum.

Krzyżaniak, L., Kroeper, K. and Kobusiewicz, M. (eds.) 1996. *Interregional Contacts in the Later Prehistory of Northeastern Africa.* Poznan: Archaeological Museum.

  2003. *Cultural Markers in the Later Prehistory of Northeastern Africa and Recent Research.* Poznan: Archaeological Museum.

Küchler, S. 1993. Landscape as memory: the mapping of process and its representation in a Melanesian society. In B. Bender (ed.), *Landscapes: Politics and Perspective*, 85–106. Oxford and Washington DC: Berg.

  1997. Sacrificial economy and its objects: rethinking colonial collecting in Oceania. *Journal of Material Culture* 2: 39–60.

  2001. Why knot? Towards a theory of art and mathematics. In C. Pinney and N. Thomas (eds.), *Beyond Aesthetics: Art and the Technologies of Enchantment*, 57–77. Oxford: Berg.

Kuijt, I. 1996. Negotiating equality through ritual: a consideration of Late
    Natufian and Pre-pottery Neolithic A period mortuary practices. *JAA* 15:
    313–36.

    2000. Keeping the peace: ritual, skull caching, and community integration in the
    Levantine Neolithic. In I. Kuijt (ed.), *Life in Neolithic Farming Communities:
    Social Organization, Identity and Differentiation*, 137–64. New York: Kluwer
    Academic/Plenum.

Kuper, A. 1988. *The Invention of Primitive Society: Transformations of an
    Illusion.* London: Routledge.

Kuper, R. 1993. Sahel in Egypt: environmental change and cultural
    development in the Abu Ballas area, Libyan Desert. In Krzyżaniak *et al.*
    1993: 213–24.

    2002. Routes and roots in Egypt's Western Desert: the Early Holocene
    resettlement of the eastern Sahara. In Friedman 2002a: 1–12.

Kus, S. 1989. Sensuous human activity and the state: towards an archaeology of
    bread and circuses. In Miller *et al.* 1989: 140–54.

Lacau, P. and Lauer, J. P. 1959. *La Pyramide à Degrees* IV: *Inscriptions graveés sur
    les vases.* Cairo: IFAO.

    1965. *La Pyramide à Degrees* V: *Inscriptions à l'encre sur les vases.* Cairo: IFAO.

Landström, B. 1970. *Ships of the Pharaohs: 4000 Years of Egyptian Shipbuilding.*
    London: Allen and Unwin.

Lansing, A. 1935. The Museum's excavation at Hierakonpolis. *Bulletin of the
    Metropolitan Museum of Art, Supplement* 30(11): 37–45.

Larsen, M. T. 1996. *The Conquest of Assyria. Excavations in an Antique Land,
    1840–1860.* London: Routledge.

Lauer, J.-P. 1936. *La Pyramide à Degrés* I–II: *L'architecture.* 2 volumes.
    Cairo: IFAO.

    1939. *La Pyramide à Degrés* III: *Compléments.* Cairo: IFAO.

    1955. Sur le dualisme de la monarchie égyptienne et son expression
    architecturale sous les premières dynasties. *BIFAO* 55: 153–71.

    1962. *Histoire monumentale des pyramides d'Egypte, I: Les pyramides à degrés
    (IIIe Dynastie).* Cairo: IFAO.

Layton, R. 1992. *Australian Rock Art: A New Synthesis.* Cambridge: Cambridge
    University Press.

Leahy, A. and Tait, J. (eds.) 1999. *Studies on Ancient Egypt in Honour of H. S.
    Smith.* London: Egypt Exploration Society.

Lecointe, Y. 1987. Le site néolithique d'El Ghaba: deux années d'activité (1985–6).
    Archéologie du Nil Moyen 2: 69–87.

Legge, A. J. 1972. Prehistoric exploitation of the gazelle in Palestine. In Higgs 1972:
    119–24.

    1996. The beginning of caprine domestication in southwest Asia. In Harris 1996:
    238–62.

Legrain, G. 1903. Notes d'inspection. *ASAE* 4: 193–226.

Lehner, E. 1998. *Wege der architektonischen Evolution: die Polygenese von
    Pyramiden und Stufenbauten, Aspekte zu einer vergleichenden
    Architekturgeschichte.* Vienna: Phoibos.

Lehner, M. 1997. *The Complete Pyramids.* London: Thames and Hudson.

Lepsius, C. R. 1849–56. *Denkmaeler aus Aegypten und Aethiopien.* 12 volumes.
    Berlin: Nicolai.

Lesko, L. H. 1988. Seila 1981. *JARCE* 25: 215–35.

Lévi-Strauss, C. 1963. *Structural Anthropology.* (Translated by C. Jacobson and B. G. Schoepf.) Harmondsworth: Penguin.

—— 1966. *The Savage Mind (La pensée sauvage).* (Translation anon.) London: Weidenfield & Nicolson.

Levy, T. E. (ed.) 1995a. *The Archaeology of Society in the Holy Land.* New York: Facts on File.

—— 1995b. Cult, metallurgy and rank societies—Chalcolithic period (ca. 4500 – 3500 BCE). In Levy 1995a: 226–44.

Levy, T. E., Alon, D., van den Brink, E. C. M., Kansa, E. and Yekutieli, Y. 2001. The protodynastic/Dynasty I Egyptian presence in southern Canaan: a preliminary report of the 1994 excavations at Nahal Tillah, Israel. In Wolff 2001: 407–38.

Levy, T. E. and van den Brink, E. C. M. 2002. Interaction models, Egypt and the Levantine periphery. In van den Brink and Levy 2002: 3–38.

Lewis-Williams, J. D. 1983. *The Rock Art of Southern Africa.* Cambridge: Cambridge University Press.

Lichtheim, M. 1973. *Ancient Egyptian Literature* I: *The Old and Middle Kingdoms.* Berkeley and London: University of California Press.

Lieberman, D. E. 1993. The rise and fall of seasonal mobility among hunter-gatherers. *Current Anthropology* 34: 599–631.

Lienhardt, G. 1966. *Social Anthropology.* London: Oxford University Press.

Linseele, V. and van Neer, W. 2003. Gourmets or priests? Fauna from the predynastic temple. *NN* 15: 6–7.

Lipschitz, N., Gophna, R., Hartman, M. and Biger, G. 1991. The beginning of olive (*Olea europaea*) cultivation in the Old World: a reassessment. *Journal of Archaeological Science* 18: 441–53.

Littauer, M. A. and Crouwel, J. H. 1990. Ceremonial threshing in the ancient Near East. *Iraq* 52: 15–19.

Litynska, M. 1994. Remains of plants. In Ginter and Koslowski 1994: 103–7.

Loos, A. 1998 [1908]. *Ornament and Crime: Selected Essays.* (Translated by M. Mitchell.) Riverside, CA: Ariadne Press.

Lorton, D. 1999. The theology of cult statues in ancient Egypt. In M. Dick (ed.), *Born in Heaven, Made on Earth: The Making of the Cult Image in the Ancient Near East,* 123–210. Winona Lake, Indiana: Eisenbraun.

Lucas, A. 1932. Black and black-topped pottery. *ASAE* 32: 93–6.

—— 1962. *Ancient Egyptian Materials and Industries.* 4th ed., revised and enlarged by J. R. Harris. London: Edward Arnold.

Lupton, C. 1992. Another predynastic pot with forged decoration. In Friedman and Adams 1992: 203–6.

Lythgoe, A. M. and Dunham, D. 1965. *The Predynastic Cemetery N7000: Naga-ed-Dêr.* Part IV. Berkeley and Los Angeles: University of California Press.

McClellan, A. 1994. *Inventing the Louvre: Art, Politics, and the Origins of the Modern Museum in Eighteenth-century Paris.* Cambridge: Cambridge University Press.

McCormick, F. 1992. Early faunal evidence for dairying. *OJA* 11: 201–10.

McCorriston, J. 1997. The fiber revolution: textile extensification, alienation, and social stratification in ancient Mesopotamia. *Current Anthropology* 38(4): 519–49.

MacDonald, K. C. 2000. The origins of African livestock: indigenous or imported? In Blench and MacDonald 2000: 2–17.

McDonald, M. M. A. 1998. Early African pastoralism: view from Dakhleh Oasis (south central Egypt). *JAA* 17: 124–42.

1999. Neolithic cultural units and adaptations in the Dakhleh Oasis. In C. S. Churcher and A. J. Mills (eds.), *Reports from the Survey of Dakhleh Oasis, 1977–1987*, 117–32. Oxford: Oxbow.

MacGaffey, W. 1966. Concepts of race in the historiography of Northeast Africa. *Journal of African History* 7: 1–17.

McGovern, P. E., Hartung, U., Badler, V. R., Glusker, D. L. and Exner, L. J. 1997. The beginnings of winemaking and viniculture in the ancient Near East and Egypt. *Expedition* 39(1): 3–21.

Machiavelli, N. 1993 [1513]. *The Prince.* (Translated by C. E. Detmold.) Ware: Wordsworth Editions.

McIntosh, R. J. 1999. Western representations of urbanism and invisible African towns. In S. K. McIntosh (ed.), *Beyond Chiefdoms: Pathways to Complexity in Africa*, 1–30. Cambridge: Cambridge University Press.

Maish, A. and Friedman, R. 1999. Pondering Paddy: unwrapping the mysteries of HK43. *NN* 11: 6–7.

Majer, J. 1992. The Eastern Desert and Egyptian prehistory. In Friedman and Adams 1992: 227–34.

Majidzadeh, Y. 1979. An early prehistoric coppersmith workshop at Tepe Ghabristan. In *Akten des VII: Internationalen Kongresses für iranische Kunst und Archäologie, München 7.–10. September 1976*, 82–92. Berlin: Dietrich Reimer.

Malek, J. 1982. The original version of the Royal Canon of Turin. *JEA* 68: 93–106.

2003. *Egypt: 4000 Years of Art.* London: Phaidon.

Mann, G. E. 1989. On the accuracy of sexing of skeletons in archaeological reports. *JEA* 75: 246–9.

Manuelian, P. der 1998. The problem of the Giza slab stelae. In Guksch and Polz 1998: 115–34.

Manuelian, P. der and Freed, R. (eds.) 1996. *Studies in Honor of William Kelly Simpson.* 2 volumes. Boston: Museum of Fine Arts.

Marcus, E. 2002. Early seafaring and maritime activity in the southern Levant from prehistory through the third millennium BC. In van den Brink and Levy 2002: 403–17.

Marfoe, L. 1987. Cedar forest to silver mountain: social change and the development of long-distance trade in early Near Eastern societies. In Rowlands *et al.* 1987: 25–35.

Martin, G. T. 2003. An Early Dynastic stela from Abydos: private or royal? In S. Quirke (ed.), *Discovering Egypt from the Neva: The Egyptological Legacy of Oleg D. Berlev*, 79–84. Berlin: Achet.

Martin, L. 2000. Mammalian remains from the eastern Jordanian Neolithic, and the nature of caprine herding in the steppe. *Paléorient* 25: 87–104.

Mathieson, I. J. and Tavares, A. 1993. Preliminary report on the National Museums of Scotland Saqqara Survey Project, 1990–91. *JEA* 79: 17–31.

Mathieson, I. J., Tavares, A. and Jeffreys, D. 1995. Sensing the past. *Egyptian Archaeology* 16: 26–7.

Matthews, R. J. 2000. *The Early Prehistory of Mesopotamia, 500,000 – 4,500 BC.* Turnhout: Brepols.

2002. *Secrets of the Dark Mound: Jemdet Nasr, 1926–1928.* Warminster: Aris & Phillips for British School of Archaeology in Iraq.

Matthews, R. J. and Fazeli, H. 2004. Copper and complexity: Iran and Mesopotamia in the fourth millennium BC. *Iran* 42: 61–75.

Matthews, R. J. and Roemer, C. (eds.) 2003. *Ancient Perspectives on Egypt*. London: UCL Press.

Mauss, M. 1979 [1935]. The notion of body techniques. In M. Mauss, *Sociology and Psychology: Essays*, 97–123. (Translated by B. Brewster.) London: Routledge and Kegan Paul.

2002 [1925]. *The Gift: The Form and Reason for Exchange in Archaic Societies*. (Translated by W. D. Halls.) London: Routledge.

Mauss, M. and Beuchat, H. 1979 [1906]. *Seasonal Variations of the Eskimo: A Study in Social Morphology*. (Translated by J. J. Fox.) London: Routledge and Kegan Paul.

Meeks, D. 2003. Locating Punt. In O'Connor and Quirke 2003a: 53–80.

Meillassoux, C. 1991. *The Anthropology of Slavery: The Womb of Iron and Gold*. London: Athlone.

Mellaart, J. 1967. *Çatal Hüyük: A Neolithic Town in Anatolia*. London: Thames and Hudson.

Mellink, M. J. and Filip, J. 1974. *Frühe Stufen der Kunst*. Berlin: Propyläen.

Meskell, L. 2002. *Private Life in New Kingdom Egypt*. Princeton: Princeton University Press.

Michalowski, P. 1983. History as charter: some observations on the Sumerian king list. *Journal of the American Oriental Society* 103: 237–48.

1990. Early Mesopotamian communicative systems: art, literature, and writing. In A. C. Gunter (ed.), *Investigating Artistic Environments in the Ancient Near East*, 53–69. Washington: Smithsonian Institution.

1994. Writing and literacy in early states: a Mesopotamianist perspective. In D. Keller-Cohen (ed.), *Literacy: Interdisciplinary Conversations*, 49–70. Cresstaill NJ: Hampton Press.

Midant-Reynes, B. 1992. *Préhistoire de l'Egypte: des premiers hommes aux premiers pharaons*. Paris: Armand Colin.

1994. Egypte prédynastique et art rupestre. In Berger *et al.* 1994: 229–35.

2000. *The Prehistory of Egypt: From the First Egyptians to the First Pharaohs*. (Translated by I. Shaw.) Oxford: Blackwell.

2003. *Aux Origines de l'Egypte: du Néolithique à l'émergence de l'État*. Paris: Fayard.

Midant-Reynes, B. and Buchez, N. 2002. *Adaïma* I: *Economie et habitat*. Cairo: IFAO.

Midant-Reynes, B., Buchez, N., Crubézy, E. and Janin, T. 1996. The predynastic site of Adaima: settlement and cemetery. In Spencer 1996: 93–7.

Mienis, H. K. 1987. Molluscs from the excavation of Mallaha (Eynan). *Mémoires et Travaux du Centre de Recherche Français de Jérusalem* 6: 157–78.

Millard, A. R. 1988. The bevel rim bowls: their purpose and significance. *Iraq* 50: 49–57.

Miller, D., Rowlands, M. and Tilley, C. (eds.) 1989. *Domination and Resistance*. London: Unwin Hyman.

Millet, N. B. 1990. The Narmer Macehead and related objects. *JARCE* 27: 53–9.

de Miroschedji, P. 2002. The socio-political dynamics of Egyptian–Canaanite interaction in the Early Bronze Age. In van den Brink and Levy 2002: 39–57.

Mohamed, A. A. B. 2001. Site E-94-2: a Late Neolithic occupation at Nabta. In Wendorf and Schild 2001: 412–26.

Mohammed-Ali, A. S. A. 1982. *The Neolithic Period in Sudan, c.6000 – 2500 BC*. Oxford: BAR.

Mommsen, W. J. 1974. *The Age of Bureaucracy: Perspectives on the Political Sociology of Max Weber*. Oxford: Blackwell.

Mond, R. L. and Myers, O. H. 1937. *Cemeteries of Armant* I. London: Egypt Exploration Society.

Monod, P. K. 1999. *The Power of Kings: Monarchy and Religion in Europe, 1589–1715*. New Haven and London: Yale University Press.

Montet, P. 1938. Tombeaux de la Ière et de la IVe dynasties à Abou-Roach. *Kêmi* 7: 11–69.

    1946. Tombeaux de la Ière et de la IVe dynasties à Abou-Roach. Deuxième partie: inventaire des objects. *Kêmi* 8: 157–223.

Moore, A. M. T., Hillman, G. C. and Legge, A. J. (eds.) 2000. *Village on the Euphrates: From Foraging to Farming at Abu Hureyra*. Oxford: Oxford University Press.

Moorey, P. R. S. 1987. On tracking cultural transfers in prehistory: the case of Egypt and Lower Mesopotamia in the fourth millennium BC. In Rowlands et al. 1987: 36–46.

    1990. From Gulf to delta in the fourth millennium BC: the Syrian connection. *Eretz-Israel* 21: 62–9.

    1994. *Ancient Mesopotamian Materials and Industries: The Archaeological Evidence*. Oxford: Clarendon Press.

    2001. The mobility of artisans and opportunities for technology transfer between western Asia and Egypt in the Late Bronze Age. In A. Shortland (ed.), *The Social Context of Technological Change in Egypt and the Near East, 1650–1550 BC*, 1–14. Oxford: Oxbow.

Moreno García, J. C. 1999. *Ḥwt et le milieu égyptien du IIIe millénaire: économie, administration et organisation territoriale*. Paris: Champion.

Morenz, L. D. 2004. *Bild-Buchstaben und symbolische Zeichen: die Herausbildung der Schrift in der hohen Kultur Altägyptens*. Fribourg, Göttingen: Academic Press, Vandenhoeck and Ruprecht.

de Morgan, H. 1909. L'Egypte primitive (suite). *Revue de l'Ecole d'Anthropologie de Paris* 19: 263–81.

de Morgan, J. 1896. *Recherches sur les origines de l'Egypte*, I: *L'Age de la pierre et les métaux*. Paris: Ernest Leroux.

    1897. *Recherches sur les origines de l'Egypte*, II: *Ethnographie préhistorique, et, Tombeau royal de Négadah*. Paris: Ernest Leroux.

Morgan, L. H. 1877. *Ancient Society*. New York: Holt.

Morphy, H. 1989. On representing ancestral beings. In H. Morphy (ed.), *Animals into Art*, 144–59. London: Unwin Hyman.

    1991. *Ancestral Connections: Art and an Aboriginal System of Knowledge*. Chicago and London: University of Chicago Press.

Munn, N. 1973. *Walbiri Iconography*. Ithaca NY: Cornell University Press.

Munro, P. 1993. Report on the work of the Joint Archaeological Mission, Free University Berlin/University of Hannover during their 12th campaign (15th March until 14th May, 1992) at Saqqâra. *Discussions in Egyptology* 26: 47–58.

Murnane, W. J. 1987. The Gebel Sheikh Suleiman monument: epigraphic remarks. *JNES* 46: 282–5.

Murray, G. and Derry, D. 1923. A pre-dynastic burial on the Red Sea coast of Egypt. *Man* 23: 129–31.

Murray, M. A., Boulton, N. and Heron, C. 2000. Viticulture and wine production. In Nicholson and Shaw 2000: 577–608.

Muzzolini, A. 1989. Les débuts de la domestication des animaux en Afrique: faits et problèmes. *Ethnozootechnie* 42: 7–22.

1993. The emergence of a food-producing economy in the Sahara. In Shaw *et al.* 1993: 227–39.

Myers, O. H. 1949. Rock-drawings found by the Gordon College Expedition in the Second Cataract region of the Nile. *Actes du XXIe Congrès International des Orientalistes, Paris, 23–31 Juillet 1948*, 375–6. Paris: Société Asiatique.

1958. Abka re-excavated. *Kush* 6: 131–41.

1960. Abka again. *Kush* 8: 174–81.

Naville, E. 1914. *The Cemeteries of Abydos* I: *The Mixed Cemetery and Umm El-Ga'ab*. London: Egypt Exploration Fund.

Needler, W. 1984. *Predynastic and Archaic Egypt in the Brooklyn Museum*. Brooklyn NY: The Brooklyn Museum.

Nelson, K. (ed.) 2002. *Holocene Settlement of the Egyptian Sahara* II: *The Pottery of Nabta Playa*. New York: Kluwer Academic and Plenum Publishers.

Nicholson, P. and Shaw, I. (eds.) 2000. *Ancient Egyptian Materials and Technology*. Cambridge: Cambridge University Press.

Nissen, H. J. 1988. *The Early History of the Ancient Near East, 9000 – 2000 BC*. (Translated by E. Lutzeier and K. J. Northcott.) Chicago, London: University of Chicago Press.

2001. Cultural and political networks in the ancient Near East during the fourth and third millennia BC. In Rothman 2001a: 149–80.

2002. Uruk: key site of the period and key site of the problem. In Postgate 2002: 1–16.

Nissen, H. J., Damerow, P. and Englund, R. K. 1993. *Archaic Bookkeeping: Early Writing and Techniques of Economic Administration in the Ancient Near East*. Chicago: University of Chicago Press.

Nordström, H. A. 1972. *Neolithic and A-Group Sites: Scandinavian Joint Expedition to Sudanese Nubia* 3. Stockholm: Läronmedelsförlagen-Svenska Bokförlaget.

Nordström, H. A. and Bourriau, J. 1993. Ceramic technology: clays and fabrics. In Dorothea Arnold and J. Bourriau (eds.), *An Introduction to Ancient Egyptian Pottery*, 143–90. Mainz am Rhein: Philipp von Zabern.

Noy, T. 1991. Art and decoration of the Natufian at Nahal Oren. In Bar-Yosef and Valla 1991: 557–68.

Oates, J. 1973. The background and development of early farming communities in Mesopotamia and the Zagros. *PPS* 39: 147–81.

1993. Trade and power in the fifth and fourth millennia BC: new evidence from northern Mesopotamia. *WA* 24: 403–22.

2002. Tell Brak: the 4th millennium sequence and its implications. In Postgate 2002: 111–22.

O'Connor, D. 1987. The earliest pharaohs and the University Museum: old and new excavations: 1900–1987. *Expedition* 29(1): 27–39.

1989. New funerary enclosures (*Talbezirke*) of the Early Dynastic period at Abydos. *JARCE* 26: 51–86.

1990. Egyptology and archaeology: an African perspective. In P. Robertshaw (ed.), *A History of African Archaeology*, 236–51. London: Currey.

1991. Boat graves and pyramid origins: new discoveries at Abydos, Egypt. *Expedition* 33(3): 5–17.

1992. The status of early Egyptian temples: an alternative theory. In Friedman and Adams 1992: 83–98.

1993. *Ancient Nubia: Egypt's Rival in Africa*. Philadelphia: University Museum, University of Pennsylvania.

1995a. The earliest royal boat graves. *Egyptian Archaeology* 6: 3–7.

1995b. The social and economic organization of ancient Egyptian temples. In Sasson *et al.* 1995: 319–29.

2001. Pyramid origins: a new theory. In E. Ehrenberg (ed.), *Leaving No Stones Unturned: Essays on the Ancient Near East and Egypt in Honour of Donald P. Hansen*, 169–82. Winona Lake IN: Eisenbrauns.

2002. Context, function and program: understanding ceremonial slate palettes. *JARCE* 39: 5–25.

2003. Egypt's views of 'others'. In J. Tait (ed.), *Never Had the Like Occurred: Egypt's View of its Past*, 155–86. London: UCL Press.

O'Connor, D. and Quirke, S. (eds.) 2003a. *Mysterious Lands*. London: UCL Press.

2003b. Introduction: mapping the unknown in ancient Egypt. In O'Connor and Quirke 2003a: 1–22.

O'Connor, D. and Reid, A. (eds.) 2003a. *Ancient Egypt in Africa*. London: UCL Press.

2003b. Introduction – locating ancient Egypt in Africa: modern theories, past realities. In O'Connor and Reid 2003a: 1–23.

Ogden, J. 2000. Metals. In Nicholson and Shaw 2000: 148–76.

Oren, E. D. 1989. Early Bronze Age settlement in north Sinai: a model for Egypto-Canaanite interconnections. In P. de Miroschedji (ed.), *L'urbanisation de la Palestine à l'âge du bronze ancien: bilan et perspectives des recherches actuelles*, 389–405. Oxford: BAR.

Oren, E. D. and Yekutieli, Y. 1992. Taur Ikhbeineh: earliest evidence for Egyptian interconnections. In van den Brink 1992b: 361–84.

Otto, E. 1960. *Das Ägyptische Mundöffnungsritual*. 2 volumes. Wiesbaden: Harrassowitz.

Otto, K.-H. and Buschendorf-Otto, G. 1993. *Felsbilder aus dem sudanesischen Nubien*. Berlin: Akademie Verlag.

Ovadia, E. 1992. The domestication of the ass and pack animals: a case of technological change. In Bar-Yosef and Khazanov 1992: 19–28.

Ozouf, M. 1988. *Festivals and the French Revolution*. Cambridge, MA and London: Harvard University Press.

Paddaya, K. 1973. *Investigations into the Neolithic Culture of Shorapur Doab, South India*. Leiden: E. J. Brill.

Page-Gasser, M. and Wiese, A. B. (eds.) 1997. *Ägypten: Augenblicke der Ewigkeit: Unbekannte Schätze aus Schweizer Privatbesitz*. Exhibition catalogue. Mainz am Rhein: Philipp von Zabern.

Parkinson, R. B. 1997. *The Tale of Sinuhe and Other Ancient Egyptian Poems, 1940 – 1640 BC*. Oxford: Clarendon Press.

2002. *Poetry and Culture in Middle Kingdom Egypt: A Dark Side to Perfection*. London: Continuum.

Patch, D. C. 1991. *The origin and early development of urbanism in ancient Egypt: a regional study*. PhD dissertation. Ann Arbor: University Microfilms International.

Payne, J. C. 1993. *Catalogue of the Predynastic Egyptian Collection in the Ashmolean Museum*. Oxford: Clarendon Press.

Peet, E. 1914. *The Cemeteries of Abydos* II: *1911–1912*. London: Egypt Exploration Society.

Peltenburg, E. J., Colledge, S., Croft, P., Jackson, A., McCartney, C. and Murray, M. A. 2001. Neolithic dispersals from the Levantine Corridor: a Mediterranean perspective. *Levant* 33: 35–64.

Perrot, J. 1984. Structures d'habitat, mode de vie et environnement: les villages souterrains des pasteurs de Beershéva dans le sud d'Israël, au IVe millénaire avant l'ère chrétienne. *Paléorient* 10: 75–96.

Peters, B. G. 1989. *The Politics of Bureaucracy*. 3rd edition. New York: Longman.

Peters, J. 1986. A revision of the faunal remains from two central Sudanese sites: Khartoum Hospital and Esh Shaheinab. *Archeozoologia* 5: 11–35.

Peters, J., Helmer, D., von den Driesch, A. and Saña Segui, M. 2000. Early animal husbandry in the northern Levant. *Paléorient* 25(2): 27–48.

Petrie, W. M. F. 1896. *Koptos*. London: Bernard Quaritch.

    1900. *The Royal Tombs of the First Dynasty*, I. London: Egypt Exploration Fund.

    1901a. *The Royal Tombs of the Earliest Dynasties*, II. London: Egypt Exploration Fund.

    1901b. *Diospolis Parva: The Cemeteries of Abadiyeh and Hu: 1898–1899*. London: Egypt Exploration Fund.

    1902. *Abydos* I. London: Egypt Exploration Fund.

    1903. *Abydos* II. London: Egypt Exploration Fund.

    1907. *Gizeh and Rifeh*. London: School of Archaeology in Egypt and Bernard Quaritch.

    1914. *Tarkhan* II. London: School of Archaeology in Egypt.

    1920. *Prehistoric Egypt*. London: British School of Archaeology in Egypt.

    1921. *Corpus of Prehistoric Pottery and Palettes*. London: British School of Archaeology in Egypt.

    1925. *Tombs of the Courtiers and Oxyrhynkhos*. London: British School of Archaeology in Egypt.

    1931. *Seventy Years in Archaeology*. London: Sampson Low, Marston.

    1953. *Ceremonial Slate Palettes: Corpus of Protodynastic Pottery*. London: British School of Egyptian Archaeology.

Petrie, W. M. F. and Quibell, J. E. 1896. *Naqada and Ballas*. London: British School of Archaeology in Egypt and Bernard Quaritch.

Petrie, W. M. F, Wainwright, G. A. and Gardiner, A. H. 1913. *Tarkhan* I *and Memphis* V. London: School of Archaeology in Egypt.

Petrie, W. M. F., Wainwright, G. A. and MacKay, E. 1912. *The Labyrinth, Gerzeh and Mazghunah*. London: British School of Archaeology in Egypt and Bernard Quaritch.

Pettinato, G. 1981. *The Archives of Ebla: An Empire Inscribed in Clay*. New York: Doubleday.

Pfaffenberger, B. 1988. Fetishized objects and humanized nature: towards a social anthropology of technology. *Man* (N. S.) 23: 236–52.

Philip, G. 2001. The Early Bronze I–III Ages. In B. MacDonald, R. Adams and P. Bienkowski (eds.), *The Archaeology of Jordan*, 163–232. Sheffield: Sheffield Academic Press.

    2002. Contacts between the 'Uruk' world and the Levant during the fourth millennium BC: evidence and interpretation. In Postgate 2002: 207–35.

Philip, G. and Rehren, T. 1996. Fourth millennium BC silver from Tell esh-Shuna, Jordan: archaeometallurgical investigation and some thoughts on ceramic skeuomorphs. *OJA* 15: 129–50.

Philip, G. and Williams-Thorpe, O. 1993. A provenance study of Jordanian basalt vessels of the Chalcolithic and Early Bronze Age I periods. *Paléorient* 19(2): 51–63.

Phillips, T. (ed.) 1995. *Africa: The Art of a Continent*. Exhibition catalogue. Munich and New York: Prestel.

Piccione, P. A. 1990. The historical development of the game of senet and its significance for Egyptian religion. PhD dissertation, University of Chicago.

Pittman, H. 1996. Constructing context: the Gebel el-Arak Knife: Greater Mesopotamian and Egyptian interaction in the late fourth millennium BC. In J. S. Cooper and G. M. Schwartz (eds.), *The Study of the Ancient Near East in the Twenty-first Century: The William Foxwell Albright Centennial Conference*, 9–32. Winona Lake IN: Eisenbrauns.

2001. Mesopotamian intraregional relations reflected through glyptic evidence in the Late Chalcolithic 1–5 periods. In Rothman 2001a: 403–43.

Pocock, J. G. A. 1957. *The Ancient Constitution and the Feudal Law: A Study of English Historical Thought in the Seventeenth Century*. Cambridge: Cambridge University Press.

Podzorski, P. V. 1988. Predynastic Egyptian seals of known provenience in the R. H. Lowie Museum of Anthropology. *JNES* 47: 259–68.

Pope, M. 1975. *The Story of Decipherment, from Egyptian Hieroglyphic to Linear B*. London: Thames and Hudson.

Porat, N. 1992. An Egyptian colony in southern Palestine during the late predynastic–Early Dynastic period. In van den Brink 1992b: 433–40.

Porat, N. and Goren, Y. 2002. Petrography of the Naqada IIIa Canaanite pottery from tomb U-j in Abydos. In van den Brink and Levy 2002: 252–70.

Porat, N. and Seeher, J. 1988. Petrographic analysis of pottery and basalt from predynastic Maadi. *MDAIK* 44: 215–28.

Porter, B. and Moss, R. L. B. 1937. *Topographical Bibliography of Ancient Egyptian Hieroglyphic Texts, Reliefs, and Paintings, V: Upper Egypt: Sites*. Oxford: Oxford University Press at the Clarendon Press.

Postgate, J. N. (ed.) 2002. *Artefacts of Complexity: Tracking the Uruk in the Near East*. London: British School of Archaeology in Iraq.

Postgate, N., Tao, W. and Wilkinson, T. A. H. 1995. The evidence for early writing: utilitarian or ceremonial? *Antiquity* 69: 459–80.

Potts, D. T. 1999. *The Archaeology of Elam: Formation and Transformation of an Ancient Iranian State*. Cambridge: Cambridge University Press.

Potts, T. F. 1993. Patterns of trade in third-millennium BC Mesopotamia and Iran. *WA* 24: 379–402.

Potts, T. F., Roaf, M. and Stein, D. (eds.) 2003. *Culture through Objects: Ancient Near Eastern Studies in Honour of P. R. S. Moorey*. Oxford: Griffith Institute.

Quack, J. F. 2003. Zum Lautwert von Gardiner Sign-List U 23. *Lingua Aegyptiaca* 11: 113–16.

Quibell, J. E. 1898. Slate palette from Hieraconpolis. *ZÄS* 36: 81–6.

1900. *Hierakonpolis* I. London: Bernard Quaritch.

1905. *Catalogue général des antiquités égyptiennes du Musée du Caire: nos. 11.001 – 12.000 et 14.001 – 14.754: Archaic Objects*. 2 volumes. Cairo: IFAO.

1923. *Excavations at Saqqara (1912–1914): Archaic Mastabas*. Cairo: IFAO.

Quibell, J. E. and Green, F. W. 1902. *Hierakonpolis* II. London: Bernard Quaritch.

Randall-MacIver, D. and Mace, A. C. 1902. *El Amrah and Abydos 1899–1901*. London: Egypt Exploration Society.

Raue, D. 1999. Pottery from the Hierakonpolis Fort. *NN* 11: 13.

Redford, D. B. 1986. *Pharaonic King-lists, Annals, and Day-books: A Contribution to the Study of the Egyptian Sense of History*. Mississauga Ont.: Benben.

2001. *The Oxford Encyclopedia of Ancient Egypt*. 3 volumes. New York: Oxford University Press.

Redford, S. and Redford, D. B. 1989. Graffiti and petroglyphs old and new from the Eastern Desert. *JARCE* 26: 3–49.

Reed, C. A. 1960. A review of the archaeological evidence on animal domestication in the prehistoric Near East. In Braidwood and Howe 1960: 119–45.

Rehren, T., Hess, K. and Philip, G. 1997. Fourth millennium BC copper metallurgy in northern Jordan: the evidence from Tell es-Shuna. In Gebel *et al.* 1997: 625–40.

Reinold, J. 1987. Les fouilles pré- et proto-historiques de la Section Française de la Direction des Antiquités du Soudan: les campagnes 1984–85 et 1985–86. *Archéologie du Nil Moyen* 2: 17–67.

1991. Néolithique soudanais: les coutumes funéraires. In Davies 1991: 16–29

1994. Le cimetière néolithique KDK 1 de Kadruka (Nubie soudanaise): premiers résultats et essai de correlation avec les sites du Soudan central. In C. Bonnet (ed.), *Etudes nubiennes*, 93–100. Geneva: Bonnet.

2000. *Archéologie au Soudan: les civilisations de Nubie*. Paris: Errance.

2001. Kadruka and the Neolithic in the northern Dongola Reach. *Sudan and Nubia* 5: 2–10.

Reisner, G. A. 1910. *Archaeological Survey of Nubia: Report for 1907–1908*. 2 volumes. Cairo: Ministry of Finance, Survey Department.

1955. *A History of the Giza Necropolis II: The Tomb of Hetep-heres, the Mother of Cheops*. (Completed and revised by W. Stevenson Smith.) Cambridge: Harvard University Press.

Resch, W. F. E. 1963a. Neue Felsbilderfunde in der ägyptischen Ostwüste. *Zeitschrift für Ethnologie* 8: 86–97.

1963b. Eine vorgeschichtliche Grabstätte auf dem Ras Samadi. *Mitteilungen der Anthropologischen Gesellschaft in Wien* 93–4: 119–21.

1967. *Die Felsbilder Nubiens: Eine Dokumentation der ostägyptischen und nubischen Petroglyphen*. Graz: Akademische Druck-u. Verlagsanstalt.

Rizkana, I. and Seeher, J. 1985. The chipped stones at Maadi: preliminary reassessment of a predynastic industry and its long-distance relations. *MDAIK* 41: 235–55.

1987. *Maadi* I: *The Pottery of the Predynastic Settlement*. Mainz am Rhein: Philipp von Zabern.

1988. *Maadi* II: *The Lithic Industries of the Predynastic Settlement*. Mainz am Rhein: Philipp von Zabern.

1989. *Maadi* III: *The Non-Lithic Small Finds and the Structural Remains of the Predynastic Settlement*. Mainz am Rhein: Philipp von Zabern.

1990. *Maadi* IV: *The predynastic cemeteries of Maadi and Wadi Digla*. Mainz am Rhein: Philipp von Zabern.

Roaf, M. D. 1984. 'Ubaid houses and temples. *Sumer* 43: 80–90.

1989. 'Ubaid social organization and social activities as seen from Tell Madhhur. In Henrickson and Thuesen 1989: 91–148.

1990. *Cultural Atlas of Mesopotamia and the Ancient Near East*. Oxford: Equinox.

Robertson Smith, W. 1889. *Lectures on the Religion of the Semites*. Edinburgh: A. and C. Black.

Rollefson, G. O. and Köhler-Rollefson, I. 1989. The collapse of Early Neolithic settlements in the southern Levant. In I. Hershkovitz (ed.), *People and Culture in Change: Proceedings of the Second Symposium on Upper Palaeolithic, Mesolithic, and Neolithic Populations of Europe and the Mediterranean Basin*, 73–90. Oxford: BAR.

Rosen, A. M. 1996. Phytoliths in the predynastic: a microbotanical analysis of plant use at HG, in the Hu-Semaineh region, Egypt. *AN* 6: 77–80.

Rosen, S. A. 1983. The Canaanean blade and the Early Bronze Age. *Israel Exploration Journal* 33: 15–29.

1988. A preliminary note on the Egyptian component of the chipped stone assemblage from Tel 'Erani. *Israel Exploration Journal* 38: 105–16.

1997. *Lithics After the Stone Age: A Handbook of Stone Tools from the Levant*. Walnut Creek, California: Altamira Press.

Roth, A. M. 1991. *Egyptian Phyles in the Old Kingdom: The Evolution of a System of Social Organization*. Chicago: The Oriental Institute of the University of Chicago.

1993. Social change in the Fourth Dynasty: the spatial organization of pyramids, tombs, and cemeteries. *JARCE* 30: 33–55.

1998. Buried pyramids and layered thoughts: the organisation of multiple approaches in Egyptian religion. In C. J. Eyre (ed.), *Proceedings of the Seventh International Congress of Egyptologists, Cambridge 3–9 September 1995*, 991–1,003. Leuven: Peeters.

Rothman, M. S. 1994. Seal and sealing findspot, design, audience, and function: monitoring changes in administrative oversight and structure at Tepe Gawra during the fourth millennium BC. In Ferioli *et al.* 1994: 97–119.

(ed.) 2001a. *Uruk Mesopotamia and its Neighbours: Cross-Cultural Interactions in the Era of State Formation*. Oxford and Santa Fe: James Currey, School of American Research Press.

2001b. The Tigris piedmont, eastern Jazira, and highland western Iran in the fourth millennium BC. In Rothman 2001a: 349–401.

2002. *Tepe Gawra: The Evolution of a Small, Prehistoric Center in Northern Iraq*. Philadelphia: University of Pennsylvania, Museum of Archaeology and Anthropology.

Rowlands, M. J. 1998. Ritual killing and historical transformation in a West African kingdom. In Kristiansen and Rowlands 1998: 397–409.

2003. The unity of Africa. In O'Connor and Reid 2003a: 39–54.

2004. The materiality of sacred power. In DeMarrais *et al.* 2004: 197–203.

Rowlands, M. J. and Frankenstein, S. 1998. The internal structure and regional context of Early Iron Age society in south-west Germany. In Kristiansen and Rowlands 1998: 334–74.

Rowlands, M. J., Kristiansen, K. and Larsen, M. T. (eds.) 1987. *Centre and Periphery in the Ancient World*. Cambridge: Cambridge University Press.

Runnels, C. and van Andel, Tj. H. 1988. Trade and the origins of agriculture in the Eastern Mediterranean. *Journal of Mediterranean Archaeology* 1: 83–109.

Saad, Z. Y. 1939. Pottery inscriptions. In Emery 1939: 74–6.

    1947. *Royal Excavations at Saqqara and Helwan (1941 – 1945)*. Cairo: Government Press.

    1951. *Royal Excavations at Helwan (1945 – 1947)*. Cairo: Government Press.

    1957. *Ceiling Stelae in the Second Dynasty Tombs from the Excavations at Helwan*. Cairo: Government Press.

    1969. *The Excavations at Helwan: Art and Civilization in the First and Second Egyptian Dynasties*. Norman: University of Oklahoma Press.

Sadr, K. 1991. *The Development of Nomadism in Ancient Northeast Africa*. Philadelphia: University of Pennsylvania Press.

    1997. The Wadi Elei finds: Nubian desert gold mining in the 5th and 4th millennia BC? *Cahiers de Recherches de l'Institut de Papyrologie et d'Egyptologie de Lille* 17: 67–76.

Safar, F., Mustafa, M. A. and Lloyd, S. 1981. *Eridu*. Baghdad: Republic of Iraq, Ministry of Culture and Information, State Organisation of Antiquities and Heritage.

Sahlins, M. 1976. *Culture and Practical Reason*. Chicago and London: University of Chicago Press.

    1985. *Islands of History*. Chicago: University of Chicago Press.

Said, E. 1995. *Orientalism: Western Conceptions of the Orient*. 4th edition. London: Penguin.

Salvatori, S. and Usai, D. 2001. First season of excavations at R12, a Late Neolithic cemetery in the northern Dongola Reach. *Sudan and Nubia* 5: 11–20.

    2002. The second excavation season at R12, a Late Neolithic cemetery in the northern Dongola Reach. *Sudan and Nubia* 6: 2–7.

Samuel, D. 2000. Brewing and baking. In Nicholson and Shaw 2000: 537–76.

Sanders, E. R. 1969. The Hamitic hypothesis: its origin and functions in time perspective. *Journal of African History* 10: 521–32.

Sasson, J. M., Baines, J., Beckman, G. and Rubinson, K. S. (eds.) 1995. *Civilizations of the Ancient Near East*. New York: Scribner.

Savage, S. H. 1997. Descent group competition and economic strategies in predynastic Egypt. *JAA* 16: 226–8.

    2000. The status of women in predynastic Egypt as revealed through mortuary analysis. In A. Rothman (ed.), *Reading the Body: Representations and Remains in the Archaeological Record*, 77–92. Philadelphia: University of Pennsylvania Press.

Scamuzzi, E. 1965. *Egyptian Art in the Egyptian Museum of Turin*. New York: Harry N. Abrams.

Schäfer, H. 1902. *Ein Bruchstück altägyptischer Annalen*. Berlin: Königliche Akademie der Wissenschaften.

Scharff, A. 1926. *Die archäologischen Ergebnisse des vorgeschichtlichen Gräberfeldes von Abusir el-Meleq: nach den Aufzeichnungen Georg Möllers*. Leipzig: J. C. Hinrichs.

    1928. Some prehistoric vases in the British Museum and remarks on Egyptian prehistory. *JEA* 14: 261–76.

    1929–31. *Die Altertümer der Vor- und Frühzeit*. 2 volumes. Berlin: Karl Curtis.

Schild, R., Chmielewska, M. and Wieckowska, H. 1968. The Arkinian and Shamarkian industries. In Wendorf 1968: 651–767.

Schild, R., Kobusiewicz, M., Wendorf, F., Irish, J. D., Kabacinski, J. and Królik, H. 2002. Gebel Ramlah Playa. In T. Lenssen-Erz (ed.), *Tides of the Desert:*

Contributions to the Archaeology and Environmental History of Africa in Honour of Rudolph Kuper, 117–24. Cologne: Heinrich-Barth-Institut.

Schmandt-Besserat, D. 1992. *Before Writing.* 2 volumes. Austin: University of Texas Press.

1993. Images of Enship. In Frangipane *et al.* 1993: 201–20.

Schmidt, K. 1982. Zur Verwendung der Mesopotamischen 'Glockentöpfe'. *Archäologisches Korrespondenzblatt* 12: 317–19.

1992. Tell el-Fara'in/Buto and el-Tell el-Iswid (South): the lithic industries from the Chalcolithic to the early Old Kingdom. In van den Brink 1992b: 31–41.

Schnapp, A. 1996. *The Discovery of the Past: The Origins of Archaeology.* London: British Museum Press.

Seeher, J. 1990. Maadi: eine prädynastische Kulturgruppe zwischen Oberägypten und Palästina. *Prähistorische Zeitschrift* 65: 123–56.

Segal, D. 2000. 'Western Civ' and the staging of history in American higher education. *American Historical Review* 105: 770–805.

Seidlmayer, S. J. 1996a. Die staatliche Anlage der 3. Dyn. in der Nordweststadt von Elephantine: archäologische und historische Probleme. In Bietak 1996: 195–214.

1996b. Town and state in the early Old Kingdom: a view from Elephantine. In Spencer 1996: 108–27.

Seligman, C. G. 1913. Some aspects of the Hamitic problem in the Anglo-Egyptian Sudan. *Journal of the Royal Anthropological Institute* 43: 593–705.

1934. *Egypt and Negro Africa: A Study of Divine Kingship.* London: Routledge.

Serpico, M. and White, R. 1996. A report on the analysis of the contents of a cache of jars from the tomb of Djer. In Spencer 1996: 128–39.

Shalev, S. 1994. The change in metal production from the Chalcolithic period to the Early Bronze Age in Israel and Jordan. *Antiquity* 68: 630–7.

Sharvit, J., Galili, E., Rosen, B. and van den Brink, E. C. M. 2002. Predynastic maritime traffic along the Carmel coast of Israel: a submerged find from North Atlit Bay. In van den Brink and Yannai 2002: 159–66.

Shaw, I. (ed.) 2000a. *The Oxford History of Ancient Egypt.* Oxford: Oxford University Press.

2000b. Egypt and the outside world. In Shaw 2000a: 314–29.

Shaw, T., Andah, B., Sinclair, P. and Okpoko, A. (eds.) 1993. *The Archaeology of Africa: Food, Metals, and Towns.* London: Routledge.

Sherratt, A. G. 1980. Water, soil and seasonality in early cereal cultivation. *WA* 11: 313–30.

1981. Plough and pastoralism: aspects of the Secondary Products Revolution. In I. Hodder, G. Isaac and N. Hammond (eds.), *Pattern of the Past: Studies in Honour of David Clark*, 261–305. Cambridge: Cambridge University Press.

1982. Mobile resources: settlement and exchange in early agricultural Europe. In A. C. Renfrew and S. J. Shennan (eds.), *Ranking, Resources and Exchange*, 13–26. Cambridge: Cambridge University Press.

1989. V. Gordon Childe: archaeology and intellectual history. *Past and Present* 125: 151–85.

1994. The transformation of early agrarian Europe: the later Neolithic and Copper Ages, 4500 – 2500 BC. In Cunliffe 1994: 167–201.

1995. Reviving the grand narrative: archaeology and long-term change. *Journal of European Archaeology* 3: 1–32.

1997a. *Economy and Society in Prehistoric Europe: Changing Perspectives.* Edinburgh: Edinburgh University Press.

1997b. Climatic cycles and behavioural revolutions: the emergence of modern humans and the beginning of farming. *Antiquity* 71: 271–87.

1999. Cash-crops before cash: organic consumables and trade. In C. Gosden and J. G. Hather (eds.), *The Prehistory of Food: Appetites for Change,* 13–34. London: Routledge.

2002. Diet and cuisine: farming and its transformations as reflected in pottery. *Documenta Praehistorica* 29: 61–71.

Sherratt, A. G. and Sherratt, E. S. 1991. From luxuries to commodities: the nature of Mediterranean Bronze Age trading systems. In N. Gale (ed.), *Bronze Age Trade in the Mediterranean,* 351–86. Jonsered: Paul Åström.

Shiner, J. L. 1968a. The cataract tradition. In Wendorf 1968: 535–629.

1968b. The Khartoum Variant industry. In Wendorf 1968: 768–90.

Shinnie, P. L. 1996. *Ancient Nubia.* London: Kegan Paul International.

Sievertsen, U. 1992. Das Messer vom Gebel el-Arak. *Baghdader Mitteilungen* 23: 1–75.

Simonse, S. 1992. *Kings of Disaster: Dualism, Centralism and the Scapegoat King in Southeastern Sudan.* Leiden: E. J. Brill.

Singer, C., Holmyard, E. J., Hall, A. R. and Williams, T. I. 1954. *A History of Technology.* Oxford: Oxford University Press.

Smith, A. 1984. *Gobineau et l'histoire naturelle.* Geneva: Droz.

Smith, A. B. 1986. Cattle domestication in North Africa. *AAR* 4: 197–203.

1992. *Pastoralism in Africa: Origins and Development Ecology.* London: Hurst.

Smith, A. L. 1993. Identification d'un potier prédynastique. *AN* 3: 23–33.

Smith, A. T. 2003. *The Political Landscape: Constellations of Authority in Early Complex Polities.* Berkeley: University of California Press.

Smith, H. S. 1991. The development of the 'A-Group' culture in northern Lower Nubia. In Davies 1991: 92–111.

1992. The making of Egypt: a review of the influence of Susa and Sumer on Upper Egypt and Lower Nubia in the 4th millennium BC. In Friedman and Adams 1992: 235–46.

Smith, W. S. 1949. *A History of Egyptian Sculpture and Painting in the Old Kingdom.* 2nd ed. London: Oxford University Press for Museum of Fine Arts Boston.

1965. *Interconnections in the Ancient Near East: A Study of the Relationships Between the Arts of Egypt, the Aegean, and Western Asia.* New Haven: Yale University Press.

1998. *The Art and Architecture of Ancient Egypt.* 3rd ed., revised with additions by W. K. Simpson. New Haven and London: Yale University Press.

Sparks, R. T. 2003. Egyptian stone vessels and the politics of exchange (2617 – 1070 BC). In Matthews and Roemer 2003: 39–56.

Spencer, A. J. 1980. *Catalogue of Egyptian Antiquities in the British Museum, V: Early Dynastic Objects.* London: British Museum.

1982. *Death in Ancient Egypt.* Harmondsworth: Penguin.

1993. *Early Egypt: The Rise of Civilisation in the Nile Valley.* London: British Museum Press.

(ed.) 1996. *Aspects of Early Egypt.* London: British Museum Press.

Spencer, P. 1998. *The Pastoral Continuum. The Marginalization of Tradition in East Africa.* Oxford: Clarendon Press.

Sperber, D. 1996. *Explaining Culture: a Naturalistic Approach.* Oxford: Blackwell.

Stadelmann, R. 1985. Die Oberbauten der Königsgräber der 2. Dynastie in Sakkara. In P. Posener-Kriéger (ed.), *Mélanges Gamal Eddin Mokhtar* II, 295–307. Cairo: IFAO.

1996. Origins and development of the funerary complex of Djoser. In Der Manuelian and Freed 1996: 787–800.

1997. *Die ägyptischen Pyramiden: vom Ziegelbau zum Weltwunder.* 3rd ed. Mainz am Rhein: Philipp von Zabern.

Staehelin, E. 1980. Knoten. In *LÄ* III: 459–60.

Stager, L. E. 1985. The first fruits of civilization. In J. N. Tubb (ed.), *Palestine in the Bronze and Iron Ages: Papers in Honour of Olga Tufnell*, 172–88. London: Institute of Archaeology.

1992. The periodization of Palestine from Neolithic through Early Bronze times. In Ehrich 1992: 22–41.

Stein, G. 1999. *Rethinking World-Systems: Diasporas, Colonies and Interaction in Uruk Mesopotamia.* Tucson: University of Arizona Press.

2002. The Uruk expansion in Anatolia: a Mesopotamian colony and its indigenous host community at Hacinebi, Turkey. In Postgate 2002: 149–71.

Stemler, A. 1990. A scanning electron microscope analysis of plant impressions in pottery from the sites of Kadero, El Zakiab, Um Direiwa and El-Kadada. *Archéologie du Nil Moyen* 4: 87–106.

Stordeur, D. 1988. *Outils et armes en os du gisement natoufien de Mallaha (Eynan).* Paris: Association Paléorient.

Strudwick, N. 1985. *The Administration of Egypt in the Old Kingdom: The Highest Titles and their Holders.* London: KPI.

Suter, C. 2000. *Gudea's Temple Building: The Representation of an Early Mesopotamian Ruler in Text and Image.* Groningen: Styx.

Sutton, J. E. G. 1977. The African Aqualithic. *Antiquity* 51: 25–34.

Swelim, N. 1991. Some remarks on the great rectangular monuments of Middle Saqqara. *MDAIK* 47: 389–402.

Tadmor, M. 2002. The Kfar Monash hoard again: a view from Egypt and Nubia. In van den Brink and Levy 2002: 239–51.

Tangri, D. 1992. A reassessment of the origins of the predynastic in Upper Egypt. *PPS* 58: 112–25.

Taylor, J. H. 2001. *Death and the Afterlife in Ancient Egypt.* London: British Museum Press.

Tchernov, E. 1984. Commensal animals and human sedentism in the Middle East. In Clutton-Brock and Grigson 1984: 91–105.

Tefnin, R. 1993. L'image et son cadre: réflexions sur la structure du champ figurative en Egypte prédynastique. *AN* 3: 7–22.

Teissier, B. 1987. Glyptic evidence for a connection between Iran, Syro-Palestine and Egypt in the fourth and third millennia. *Iran* 25: 27–53.

Thanheiser, U. 1990. Untersuchungen zur Landwirtschaft der vor- und frühdynastischen Zeit in Tell el-Fara'in-Buto: vorbericht. *Ägypten und Levante* 2: 39–45.

1992. Plant-food remains at Tell Ibrahim Awad: preliminary report. In van den Brink 1992b: 117–21.

1996. Local crop production *versus* import of cereals during the predynastic period in the Nile delta. In Krzyżaniak *et al.* 1996: 291–302.

Tigani el-Mahi, A. 1988. *Zooarchaeology in the Middle Nile Valley: A Study of Four Neolithic Sites near Khartoum.* Oxford: BAR.

Trigger, B. G. 1976. *Nubia Under the Pharaohs.* London: Thames and Hudson.

1979. Egypt and the comparative study of early civilizations. In K. Weeks (ed.), *Egypt and the Social Sciences: Five Studies*, 23–56. Cairo: American University in Cairo Press.

1983. The rise of Egyptian civilization. In Trigger *et al.* 1983: 1–70.

1985. The evolution of pre-industrial cities: a multilinear perspective. In F. Geus and F. Thill (eds.), *Mélanges offerts à Jean Vercoutter*, 343–53. Paris: Editions Recherche sur les Civilisations.

1989. *A History of Archaeological Thought.* Cambridge: Cambridge University Press.

2003. *Understanding Early Civilizations: A Comparative Study.* Cambridge: Cambridge University Press.

Trigger, B. G., Kemp, B. J., O'Connor, D. and Lloyd, A. B. 1983. *Ancient Egypt: A Social History.* Cambridge: Cambridge University Press.

Turner, B. S. 1992. *Max Weber: From History to Modernity.* London and New York: Routledge.

Turner, V. 1967. *The Forest of Symbols: Aspects of Ndembu Ritual.* Ithaca and London: Cornell University Press.

Tutundzic, S. P. 1989. The problem of foreign north-eastern relations of Upper Egypt, particularly in the Badarian period: an aspect. In Krzyżaniak and Kobusiewicz 1989: 255–60.

Ucko, P. J. 1967. The predynastic cemetery N 7000 at Naga-ed-Dêr. *CdE* 84: 345–53.

1968. *Anthropomorphic Figurines of Predynastic Egypt and Neolithic Crete with Comparative Material from the Prehistoric Near East and Mainland Greece.* London: Andrew Szmidla.

Ucko, P. J. and Hodges, H. W. M. 1963. Some pre-dynastic Egyptian figurines: problems of authenticity. *Journal of the Warburg and Courtauld Institutes* 26: 205–22.

Ucko, P. J. and Rosenfeld, A. 1967. *Palaeolithic Cave Art.* London: Weidenfeld and Nicolson.

Ucko, P. J., Tringham, R. and Dimbleby, G. W. (eds.) 1972. *Man, Settlement and Urbanism: Proceedings of a Meeting of the Research Seminar in Archaeology and Related Subjects Held at the Institute of Archaeology, London University.* London: Duckworth.

Uerpmann, H.-P. 1979. *Probleme der Neolithisierung des Mittelmeerraums.* Wiesbaden: Ludwig Reichert.

Valla, F. R. 1995. The first settled societies—Natufian (12,500–10,200 BP). In Levy 1995a: 169–89.

Valla, F. R., Le Mort, F. and Plisson, H. 1991. Les fouilles en cours sur la terrasse d'Hayonim. In Bar-Yosef and Valla 1991: 95–110.

van de Mieroop. M. 1997. *The Ancient Mesopotamian City.* Oxford: Clarendon Press.

van den Brink, E. C. M. 1988a. The Amsterdam University Survey Expedition to the northeastern delta (1984–1986). In van den Brink 1988b: 65–114.

1988b. *The Archaeology of the Nile Delta, Egypt: Problems and Priorities.* Amsterdam: Netherlands Foundation for Archaeological Research in Egypt.

1989. A transitional late predynastic–Early Dynastic settlement site in the northeastern Nile delta, Egypt. *MDAIK* 45: 55–108.

1992a. Preliminary report on the excavations at Tell Ibrahim Awad, seasons 1988–1990. In van den Brink 1992b: 43–68.

(ed.) 1992b. *The Nile Delta in Transition: 4th–3rd Millennium BC: Proceedings of the Seminar Held in Cairo, 21–24 October 1990, at the Netherlands Institute of Archaeology and Arabic Studies.* Tel Aviv: Edwin C. M. van den Brink.

1992c. Corpus and numerical evaluation of the 'Thinite' potmarks. In Friedman and Adams 1992: 265–92.

1996. The incised *serekh*-signs of Dynasties 0–1. Part 1: Complete vessels. In Spencer 1996: 140–58.

2001. The pottery-incised *serekh*-signs of Dynasties 0–1. Part II: Fragments and additional complete vessels. *AN* 11: 24–99.

van den Brink, E. C. M. and Braun, E. 2002. Wine jars with *serekhs* from Early Bronze Lod: appellation vallée du Nil contrôlée, but for whom? In van den Brink and Yannai 2002: 167–87.

van den Brink, E. C. M. and Levy, T. E. (eds.) 2002. *Egypt and the Levant: Interrelations from the 4th through the early 3rd Millennium BC.* London, New York: Leicester University Press.

van den Brink, E. C. M., Schmidt, K., Boessneck, J., von den Driesch, A. and de Roller, G. J. 1989. A late predynastic–Early Dynastic settlement site in the northeastern Nile delta, Egypt. *MDAIK* 45: 55–108.

van den Brink, E. C. M. and Yannai, E. 2002. *In Quest of Ancient Settlements and Landscapes: Archaeological Studies in Honour of Ram Gophna.* Tel Aviv: Ramot Publishing House, Tel Aviv University.

van Driel-Murray, C. 2000. Leatherwork and skin products. In Nicholson and Shaw 2000: 299–319.

van Haarlem, W. M. 1995. Temple deposit at Tell Ibrahim Awad: a preliminary report. *GM* 148: 45–52.

1996. Temple deposits at Tell Ibrahim Awad: an update. *GM* 154: 31–4.

1998. Les fouilles à Tell Ibrahim Awad (delta oriental du Nil): résultats récents. *BSFE* 141: 8–19.

2001. Tell Ibrahim Awad. *Egyptian Archaeology* 18: 33–5.

2002. The ivory objects from Tell Ibrahim Awad. *Egyptian Archaeology* 20: 16–17.

van Lepp, J. 1999. The misidentification of the predynastic Egyptian bull's head amulet. *GM* 168: 101–11.

van Neer, W. 1989. Fishing along the prehistoric Nile. In Krzyżaniak and Kobusiewicz 1989: 49–56.

van Rossum, V. 1994. Human remains from the predynastic cemetery at Elkab. In Hendrickx 1994: 225–37.

van Walsem, R. 2003. Une tombe royale de la deuxième dynastie à Saqqara sous la tombe Nouvel Empire de Meryneith, Campagne de fouille 2001–2002. *AN* 13: 6–13.

van Wetering, J. and Tassie, G. J. 2003. Socio-political hierarchy of First Dynasty sites: a ranking of east delta cemeteries based on grave architecture. In A. K. Eyma and C. J. Bennett (eds.), *A Delta-Man in Yebu*, 123–46. (Occasional Volume of the Egyptologists' Electronic Forum, 1.) USA: Universal Publishers. (www.uPUBLISH.com/books/eyma_bennett.htm)

Vandier, J. 1952. *Manuel d'archéologie égyptienne* I: *Les époques de formation: la préhistoire.* Paris: A. & J. Picard.

Verbrugghe, G. P. and Wickersham, J. M. 1996. *Berossos and Manetho, Introduced and Translated: Native Traditions in Ancient Mesopotamia and Egypt.* Ann Arbor: University of Michigan Press.

Verhoeven, M. 1999. *An Archaeological Ethnography of a Neolithic Community: Space, Place and Social Relations in the Burnt Village at Tell Sabi Abyad, Syria.* Leiden: Nederlands Historisch-Archaeologisch Instituut te Istanbul.

Vermeersch, P. M. 1978. *El-Kab* II: *L'Elkabien, épipaléolithique de la vallée du Nil égyptien.* Leuven: University Press.

1984. Subsistence activities on the Late Palaeolithic site of el-Kab (Upper Egypt). In Krzyżaniak and Kobusiewicz 1984: 87–114.

Vermeersch, P. M., Paulissen, E. and van Neer, W. 1989. The Late Palaeolithic Makhadma sites (Egypt): environment and subsistence. In Krzyżaniak and Kobusiewicz 1989: 87–114.

Vermeersch, P. M., van Peer, P., Moeyersons, J. and van Neer, W. 1994. Sodmein Cave Site, Red Sea Mountains (Egypt). *Sahara* 6: 31–40.

Vernant, J. P. 1991. India, Mesopotamia, Greece: three ideologies of death. In F. I. Zeitlin (ed.), *Mortals and Immortals: Collected Essays, Jean Pierre Vernant,* 75–83. Princeton: Princeton University Press.

Vernus, P. 1993. La naissance de l'écriture dans l'Egypte ancienne. *AN* 3: 75–108.

Vinnicombe, P. 1976. *People of the Eland: Rock Paintings of the Drakensberg Bushmen as a Reflection of their Life and Thought.* Pietermaritzburg: Natal University Press.

Volney, C.-F. 1791. *Les ruines, ou Méditation sur les révolutions des empires.* Paris: Desenne, Volland, Plassan.

1991 [reproduced from 1890 ed.]. *The Ruins, or, Meditation on the Revolutions of Empires.* (Translation anon.) Baltimore: Black Classic Press.

von Beckerath, J. 1984. Bemerkungen zum Turiner Königspapyrus und zu den Dynastien der ägyptischen Geschichte. *Studien zur altägyptischen Kultur* 11: 49–57.

1997. *Chronologie des pharaonischen Ägypten: die Zeitbestimmung der ägyptischen Geschichte von der Vorzeit bis 332 v. Chr.* Mainz am Rhein: Philipp von Zabern.

von Bissing, F. W. 1913. *Tongefässe: erster Teil, bis zum Beginn des Alten Reiches.* Catalogue Général des Antiquités Egyptiennes du Musée du Caire. Vienna: Adolf Holzhausen.

von den Driesch, A. 1986. Tierknochenfunde aus Qasr el-Sagha/Fayum (Neolithicum-Mittleres Reich). *MDAIK* 42: 1–8.

von der Way, T. 1987. Tell Fara'in-Buto 2. Bericht. *MDAIK* 43: 241–57.

1992. Excavations at Tell el-Fara'in-Buto in 1987–1989. In van den Brink 1992b: 1–10.

1997. *Tell el-Fara'in-Buto* I: *Ergebnisse zum frühen Kontext Kampagnen der Jahre 1983–1989.* Mainz am Rhein: Philipp von Zabern.

Wachsmann, S. 1998. *Seagoing ships and Seamanship in the Bronze Age Levant.* College Station: Texas A & M University Press.

Waddell, W. G. 1940. *Manetho.* Loeb Classical Library. Cambridge MA and London: Harvard University Press; Heinemann.

Wallerstein, I. 1974. *The Modern World-System: Capitalist Agriculture and the Origins of the European World-Economy in the Sixteenth Century*. New York: Academic Press.

Ward, C. A. 2000. *Sacred and Secular: Ancient Egyptian Ships and Boats*. Philadelphia: University Museum, University of Pennsylvania.

2003. Sewn plank boats from Early Dynastic Abydos, Egypt. In C. Beltrame (ed.), *Boats, Ships and Shipyards: Proceedings of the Ninth International Symposium on Boat and Ship Archaeology, Venice 2000*, 19–23. Oxford: Oxbow.

Ward, W. 1991. Early contacts between Egypt, Canaan, and Sinai: remarks on the paper by Amnon Ben-Tor. *BASOR* 281: 11–26.

Warman, S. 2000. How now, large cow? *NN* 12: 8–9.

Wasylikowa, K. 2001. Site E-75-6: vegetation and subsistence of the Early Neolithic at Nabta Playa, Egypt, reconstructed from charred plant remains. In Wendorf and Schild 2001: 544–91.

Wasylikowa, K., Harlan, J. R., Evans, J., Wendorf, F., Schild, R., Close, A. E., Krolik, H. and Housley, R. A. 1993. Examination of botanical remains from Early Neolithic houses at Nabta Playa, Western Desert, Egypt, with special reference to sorghum grains. In Shaw *et al.* 1993: 154–64.

Watrall, E. C. 2001a. Excavations at Locality HK11. *NN* 12: 11–12.

2001b. Tales of trash: excavations at HK11. *NN* 13: 8–9.

Weber, M. 1978 [1921]. *Economy and Society: An Outline of Interpretive Sociology*. 2 volumes; edited by G. Roth and C. Wittich. Berkeley: University of California Press.

Weeks, K. 1971–2. The Early Dynastic palace. In Fairservis *et al.* 1971–2: 29–33.

Weigall, A. E. P. 1909. *Travels in the Upper Egyptian Deserts*. Edinburgh and London: W. Blackwood.

Weinstein, J. M. 1984. The significance of Tell Areini for Egyptian–Palestinian relations at the beginning of the Bronze Age. *BASOR* 256–63.

Weiss, H. and Young, T. C. 1975. The merchants of Susa: Godin V and plateau–lowland relations in the late fourth millennium BC. *Iran* 13: 1–17.

Welsby, D. 2003. *Survey above the Fourth Nile Cataract*. Oxford: BAR.

Wendorf, F. 1968. *The Prehistory of Nubia*. 2 volumes and atlas. Dallas: Fort Burgwin Research Center and Southern Methodist University Press.

Wendorf, F. and Schild, R. 1976. *Prehistory of the Nile Valley*. New York: Academic Press.

1980. *The Prehistory of the Eastern Sahara*. New York: Academic Press.

1989. Summary and synthesis. In Wendorf *et al.* 1989: 768–824.

1998. Nabta Playa and its role in northeastern African prehistory. *JAA* 17: 97–123.

2001. *Holocene Settlement of the Egyptian Sahara* I: *The Archaeology of Nabta Playa*. New York: Kluwer Academic/Plenum.

2002. Implications of incipient social complexity in the Late Neolithic in the Egyptian Sahara. In Friedman 2002a: 13–20.

Wendorf, F., Schild, R. and Close, A. 1989. *The Prehistory of Wadi Kubbaniya* III: *Late Palaeolithic Archaeology*. Dallas: Southern Methodist University Press.

Wengrow, D. 1998. The changing face of clay: continuity and change in the transition from village to urban life in the Near East. *Antiquity* 72: 783–95.

1999. The intellectual adventure of Henri Frankfort: a missing chapter in the history of archaeological thought. *American Journal of Archaeology* 103: 597–613.

2001a. Rethinking 'cattle cults' in early Egypt: towards a prehistoric perspective on the Narmer Palette. *Cambridge Archaeological Journal* 11: 91–104.

2001b. The evolution of simplicity: aesthetic labour and social change in the Neolithic Near East. *WA* 33: 168–88.

2003a. Interpreting animal art in the prehistoric Near East. In Potts *et al.* 2003: 139–60.

2003b. Landscapes of knowledge, idioms of power: the African foundations of ancient Egyptian civilization reconsidered. In O'Connor and Reid 2003a: 121–35.

2003c. Forgetting the *ancien régime*: republican values and the study of the ancient Orient. In D. Jeffreys (ed.), *Views of Ancient Egypt since Napoleon Bonaparte: Imperialism, Colonialism and Modern Appropriations*, 179–93. London: UCL Press.

2004. Violence into order: materiality and sacred power in ancient Iraq. In DeMarrais *et al.* 2004: 261–70.

2005. Kingship, revolution and time: perspectives on materiality and modernity. In W. James and D. Mills (eds.), *The Qualities of Time: Anthropological Approaches*, 137–51. Oxford and New York: Berg.

Wengrow, D. and Baines, J. 2004. Images, human bodies, and the ritual construction of memory in late predynastic Egypt. In Hendrickx *et al.* 2004: 1,081–114.

Westendorf, W. 1980. Isisknoten. In *LÄ* III: 205.

Wetterstrom, W. 1993. Foraging and farming in Egypt: the transition from hunting and gathering to horticulture in the Nile valley. In Shaw *et al.* 1993: 165–226.

Wheatley, P. 1972. The concept of urbanism. In Ucko *et al.* 1972: 601–37.

Whitehouse, H. 1987. King Den in Oxford. *OJA* 6: 257–67.

1992. The Hierakonpolis ivories in Oxford: a progress report. In Friedman and Adams 1992: 77–82.

2002. A decorated knife handle from the 'Main Deposit' at Hierakonpolis. *MDAIK* 58: 425–46.

Whitley, J. 2001. *The Archaeology of Ancient Greece*. Cambridge: Cambridge University Press.

Whittle, A. 1994. The first farmers. In Cunliffe 1994: 136–66.

Wickede, A. von. 1990. *Prähistorische Stempelglyptik in Vorderasien*. Munich: Profil Verlag.

Wilde, H. and Behnert, K. 2002. Salzherstellung im vor- und frühdynastischen Ägypten? Überlegungen zur Funktion der sogenannten Grubenkopfnägel in Buto. *MDAIK* 58: 447–60.

Wildung, D. 1969a. *Die Rolle ägyptischer Könige im Bewusstsein ihrer Nachwelt* I: *Posthume Quellen über die Könige der ersten vier Dynasten*. Berlin: Bruno Hessling.

1969b. Zur Frühgeschichte des Amun-Temples von Karnak. *MDAIK* 25: 212–19.

1984. Terminal prehistory of the Nile delta: theses. In Krzyżaniak and Kobusiewicz 1984: 265–9.

Wilkinson, T. A. H. 1993. The identification of tomb B1 at Abydos: refuting the existence of a king *Ro/*Iry-Hor. *JEA* 79: 241–3.

1996. *State Formation in Egypt: Chronology and Society*. Oxford: BAR.

1999. *Early Dynastic Egypt.* London: Routledge.

2000a. Rock drawings of the Eastern Desert. In D. M. Rohl (ed.), *The Followers of Horus: Eastern Desert Survey Report*, 158–65. Basingstoke: Institute for the Study of Interdisciplinary Sciences.

2000b. *Royal Annals of Ancient Egypt: The Palermo Stone and its Associated Fragments.* London: Kegan Paul International.

2002. Reality versus ideology: the evidence for 'Asiatics' in predynastic and Early Dynastic Egypt. In van den Brink and Levy 2002: 514–22.

Wilkinson, T. A. H., Butzer, K. W., Huyge, D., Hendrickx, S., Kendall, T. and Shaw, I. 2004. A review of *Genesis of the Pharaohs: Dramatic New Discoveries that Rewrite the Origins of Ancient Egypt. Cambridge Archaeological Journal* 14: 113–35.

Williams, B. B. 1977. Aspects of sealing and glyptic in Egypt before the New Kingdom. In M. Gibson and R. Biggs, *Seals and Sealing in the Ancient Near East*, 135–40. Malibu: Undena.

1980. The lost pharaohs of Nubia. *Archaeology* 33: 14–21.

1986. *The A-Group Royal Cemetery at Qustul, Cemetery L.* Chicago: The Oriental Institute of the University of Chicago.

1988a. *Decorated Pottery and the Art of Naqada III.* Berlin: Deutscher Kunstverlag.

1988b. Narmer and the Coptos Colossi. *JARCE* 25: 35–59.

1989. *Neolithic, A-Group and Post-A-Group remains from cemeteries W, V, S, Q, T, and a Cave East of Cemetery K.* Chicago: The Oriental Institute of the University of Chicago.

1994. Security and the problem of the city in the Naqada period. In D. P. Silverman (ed.), *For His Ka: Studies Offered in Memory of Klaus Baer*, 271–83. Chicago: The Oriental Institute of the University of Chicago.

2003. Review of 'Umm el-Qaab I', by G. Dreyer. *JNES* 62: 142–7.

Williams, B. B. and Logan, T. J. 1987. The Metropolitan Museum knife handle and aspects of pharaonic imagery before Narmer. *JNES* 46: 245–85.

Winkler, H. A. 1937. *Völker und Völkerbewegungen im vorgeschichtlichen Oberägypten im Lichte neuer Felsbilderfunde.* Stuttgart: W. Kohlhammer.

1938. *Rock-Drawings of Southern Upper Egypt* I. London: Egypt Exploration Society.

1939. *Rock-Drawings of Southern Upper Egypt* II. London: Egypt Exploration Society.

Winter, I. J. 1996. 'Agency': an alternative to subjectivity. In M. Garber, P. B. Franklin and R. L. Walkowitz (eds.), *Field Work: Sites in Literary and Cultural Studies*, 196–203. New York, London: Routledge.

2000. 'Le Palais imaginaire': scale and meaning in the iconography of Neo-Assyrian cylinder seals. In C. Uehlinger (ed.), *Images as Media: Sources for the Cultural History of the Near East and the Eastern Mediterranean (1st Millennium BC)* 51–87. Fribourg: University Press; Göttingen: Vandenhoeck & Ruprecht.

Wolf, E. R. 1982. *Europe and the People without History.* Berkeley: University of California Press.

Wolff, R. (ed.) 1998. *Possible Urban Worlds: Urban Strategies at the End of the 20th Century.* Basel: Birkhäuser.

Wolff, S. R. (ed.) 2001. *Studies in the Archaeology of Israel and Neighbouring Lands in Memory of Douglas L. Esse*. Chicago: The Oriental Institute of the University of Chicago.

Wood, W. 1987. The Archaic stone tombs at Helwan. *JEA* 73: 59–70.

Woolley, L. 1934. *Ur Excavations: Publications of the Joint Expedition of the British Museum and of the Museum of the University of Pennsylvania to Mesopotamia II: The Royal Cemetery: A Report on the Predynastic and Sargonid Graves Excavated between 1926 and 1931*. London and Philadelphia: British Museum, University Museum.

Wright, H. T. and Johnson, G. A. 1975. Population, exchange and early state formation in southwestern Iran. *American Anthropologist* 77: 267–89.

Wright, K. I. 1994. Ground-stone tools and hunter-gatherer subsistence in southwest Asia: implications for the transition to farming. *American Antiquity* 59: 238–63.

Wright, K. I. and Garrard, A. N. 2003. Social identities and the expansion of stone bead-making in Neolithic western Asia: new evidence from Jordan. *Antiquity* 77: 267–84.

Yates, F. A. 1966. *The Art of Memory*. London: Routledge and Kegan Paul.

Yener, K. A. 2000. *The Domestication of Metals: The Rise of Complex Metal Industries in Anatolia*. Leiden: Brill.

Yoffee, N. 1993. Too many chiefs? (or, safe texts for the '90s). In N. Yoffee and A. Sherratt (eds.), *Archaeological Theory: Who Sets the Agenda?*, 60–78. Cambridge: Cambridge University Press.

2002. The evolution of simplicity: review of *Seeing Like a State*, by J. C. Scott. *Current Anthropology* 42: 767–9.

2005. *Myths of the Archaic State: Evolution of the Earliest Cities, States, and Civilizations*. Cambridge: Cambridge University Press.

Zandee, J. 1960. *Death as an Enemy: According to Ancient Egyptian Conceptions*. (Translated by W. F. Klasens.) Leiden: Brill.

Zarins, J. 1989. Ancient Egypt and the Red Sea trade: the case for obsidian in the predynastic and Archaic periods. In A. Leonard and B. B. Williams (eds.), *Essays in Ancient Civilization Presented to Helene J. Kantor*, 339–68. Chicago: The Oriental Institute of the University of Chicago.

Zeuner, F. E. 1954. Domestication of animals; cultivation of plants. In Singer *et al.* 1954: 327–75.

Ziermann, M. 1993. *Elephantine XVI: Befestigungsanlagen und Stadtentwicklung in der Frühzeit und im frühen Alten Reich*. Mainz am Rhein: Philipp von Zabern.

Zohary, D. 1995. The domestication of the grapevine *Vitis vinifera* L. in the Near East. In P. E. McGovern, S. J. Fleming and S. H. Katz (eds.), *The Origins and Ancient History of Wine*, 23–30. Luxemburg: Gordon & Breach.

INDEX

Lightning Source UK Ltd.
Milton Keynes UK
UKOW07f1041090615

253140UK00007B/398/P

9 780521 543743